The Human Tradition in America

CHARLES W. CALHOUN
Series Editor
Department of History, East Carolina University

The nineteenth-century English author Thomas Carlyle once remarked that "the history of the world is but the biography of great men." This approach to the study of the human past had existed for centuries before Carlyle wrote, and it continued to hold sway among many scholars well into the twentieth century. In more recent times, however, historians have recognized and examined the impact of large, seemingly impersonal forces in the evolution of human history—social and economic developments such as industrialization and urbanization as well as political movements such as nationalism, militarism, and socialism. Yet even as modern scholars seek to explain these wider currents, they have come more and more to realize that such phenomena represent the composite result of countless actions and decisions by untold numbers of individual actors. On another occasion, Carlyle said that "history is the essence of innumerable biographies." In this conception of the past, Carlyle came closer to modern notions that see the lives of all kinds of people, high and low, powerful and weak, known and unknown, as part of the mosaic of human history, each contributing in a large or small way to the unfolding of the human tradition.

This latter idea forms the foundation for this series of books on the human tradition in America. Each volume is devoted to a particular period or topic in American history and each consists of mini-biographies of persons whose lives shed light on that period or topic. Well-known figures are not altogether absent, but more often the chapters explore a variety of individuals who may be less conspicuous but whose stories, nonetheless, offer us a window on some aspect of the nation's past.

By bringing the study of history down to the level of the individual, these sketches reveal not only the diversity of the American people and the complexity of their interaction but also some of the commonalities of sentiment and experience that Americans have shared in the evolution of their culture. Our hope is that these explorations of the lives of "real people" will give readers a deeper understanding of the human tradition in America.

Volumes in the Human Tradition in America series:

Ian K. Steele and Nancy L. Rhoden, eds., *The Human Tradition in Colonial America* (1999). Cloth ISBN 0-8420-2697-5
Paper ISBN 0-8420-2700-9

Nancy L. Rhoden and Ian K. Steele, eds., *The Human Tradition in the American Revolution* (2000). Cloth ISBN 0-8420-2747-5
Paper ISBN 0-8420-2748-3

Ballard C. Campbell, ed., *The Human Tradition in the Gilded Age and Progressive Era* (2000). Cloth ISBN 0-8420-2734-3
Paper ISBN 0-8420-2735-1

Steven E. Woodworth, ed., *The Human Tradition in the Civil War and Reconstruction* (2000). Cloth ISBN 0-8420-2726-2
Paper ISBN 0-8420-2727-0

David L. Anderson, ed., *The Human Tradition in the Vietnam Era* (2000). Cloth ISBN 0-8420-2762-9   Paper ISBN 0-8420-2763-7

Kriste Lindenmeyer, ed., *Ordinary Women, Extraordinary Lives: Women in American History* (2000). Cloth ISBN 0-8420-2752-1
Paper ISBN 0-8420-2754-8

Michael A. Morrison, ed., *The Human Tradition in Antebellum America* (2000). Cloth ISBN 0-8420-2834-X
Paper ISBN 0-8420-2835-8

Malcolm Muir Jr., ed., *The Human Tradition in the World War II Era* (2001). Cloth ISBN 0-8420-2785-8
Paper ISBN 0-8420-2786-6

ORDINARY WOMEN, EXTRAORDINARY LIVES

ORDINARY WOMEN, EXTRAORDINARY LIVES

WOMEN IN AMERICAN HISTORY

No. 6
The Human Tradition in America

Edited by
Kriste Lindenmeyer

A Scholarly Resources Inc. Imprint
Wilmington, Delaware

Chapter 2, "Susanna Haswell Rowson: America's First Best-Selling Author," © 2000 by Patricia L. Parker

© 2000 by Scholarly Resources Inc.
First published 2000
Printed and bound in the United States of America

Scholarly Resources Inc.
104 Greenhill Avenue
Wilmington, DE 19805-1897
www.scholarly.com

Library of Congress Cataloging-in-Publication Data

Ordinary women, extraordinary lives : women in American history /
edited by Kriste Lindenmeyer.
    p. cm. — (The human tradition in America ; no. 6)
    Includes bibliographical references and index.
    ISBN 0-8420-2752-1 (alk. paper) — ISBN 0-8420-2754-8 (pbk. :
alk. paper)
    1. Women—United States—Biography. 2. Women—United
States—History. I. Lindenmeyer, Kriste, 1955– . II. Series.

CT3260.O67 2000
920.72'0973—dc21

                                                00-025659

∞ The paper used in this publication meets the minimum requirements of the American National Standard for permanence of
paper for printed library materials, Z39.48, 1984.

About the Editor

KRISTE LINDENMEYER is associate professor of U.S. history at Tennessee Technological University in Cookeville. She teaches classes in U.S. social history, women and gender in American history, immigration and ethnicity in U.S. history, and historical methods. Her other publications include *A Right to Childhood: The U.S. Children's Bureau and Child Welfare, 1912–1946* (1997), and numerous articles. Her current research examines public policy and the defining of adolescence in the twentieth-century United States. Lindenmeyer is also an active editor with H-Net, Humanities and Social Sciences On-Line, <http://www.h-net.msu.edu/>.

I believe in aristocracy, though—if that is the right word, and if a democrat may use it. Not an aristocracy of power, based upon rank and influence, but an aristocracy of the sensitive, the considerate, and the plucky. Its members are to be found in all nations and classes, and all through the ages, and there is a secret understanding between them when they meet. They represent the true human tradition, the one permanent victory of our queer race over cruelty and chaos. Thousands of them perish in obscurity, a few are great names. They are sensitive for others as well as for themselves, they are considerate without being fussy, their pluck is not swankiness but the power to endure, and they can take a joke.

—E. M. Forster, *Two Cheers for Democracy* (1951)

Contents

Acknowledgments

I would like to thank the authors who contributed to this volume for their scholarship, professionalism, and patience. I would also like to thank the series editor, Charles Calhoun, for offering me the opportunity to coordinate this project. So many friends and colleagues have influenced and helped me with this work. I am especially grateful to the coeditors of H-Women (<http://www.h-net.msu.edu/~women/>) and H-SAWH (<http://www.h-net.msu.edu/~sawh>) and to Margaret Breashears, Stacy Cordery, Kathleen Hilton, Jennifer McDaid, Heather Munro Prescott, Maria Elena Raymond, Steve Reschly, Nancy Marie Robertson, Melanie Shell-Weiss, Jean Stuntz, and Kathy Walbert, who continue to unselfishly expand and develop my interpretation of U.S. women's history. As always, my husband, Michael, has willingly listened to my frustrations and boasts. I am forever grateful.

Introduction
The Importance of
"Ordinary" Women's Lives

Kriste Lindenmeyer

This collection of seventeen minibiographies sheds light on the often neglected "herstory" of U.S. history from the revolutionary era through the late twentieth century. In addition this volume suggests the complexity of studying the past when gender, race, class, region, age, and ethnicity are included in the analysis. This book is unique in that it focuses on the lives of ordinary women. The names of the vast majority of those whose stories are included here will likely be unfamiliar even to serious students of American women's history. The varied experiences of such women help to create a more complete picture of the past by revealing the influence general historical trends have had on the lives of "ordinary" individuals.

But "ordinary" does not mean lesser; nor does it denote class, race, ethnicity, or age. The individual women's stories that are told in the following pages show that even people who are not featured in mainstream history texts led lives that deserve the attention of those interested in understanding the past. The authors of these chapters have found support for generalizations commonly held by American women's historians. Nonetheless, their research has also led to unexpected findings that ask students of women's history to examine assumptions about the past more closely.

The study of American women's history began by mirroring traditional historical frameworks that generally focus on the famous and/or infamous. For example, as early as the 1830s, the popular periodical *Godey's Lady's Book* included brief historical portraits of women's "firsts," "biggests," and "bests" linked to events identified as significant by scholarship centered primarily on the study of "great white men." In 1848, Elizabeth Fries Lummis Ellet published her two-volume *The Women of the American Revolution*. Ellet hoped to uncover the contributions of white women in that seminal event. Other nineteenth-century authors, especially women's rights activists, wrote similarly styled works. During the first half of the twentieth century, pioneering women's historians such as Julia

Cherry Spruill (*Women's Life and Work in the Southern Colonies*, 1938) and Mary Ritter Beard (*Women as a Force in History*, 1946) added to this small but growing field. In the early 1970s, colleges established the first women's studies courses, and scholars influenced by the women's liberation movement looked to the past for feminist models. These histories tended to celebrate the lives and accomplishments of reformers, suffragists, and women who made significant contributions in the public realm. Research into the lives and the stories of female leaders such as Elizabeth Cady Stanton, Susan B. Anthony, Sojourner Truth, Catharine Beecher, Eleanor Roosevelt, and others helped to legitimize the study of women's history in only three short decades.[1]

Nevertheless, building women's history on a traditionally based model of scholarship centered much of the story on white female reformers or women linked to powerful men.[2] As the field of women's history has matured, there is increasing attention to the situations of more politically conservative females and the nonfamous or the ordinary. But who is ordinary? And what do the lives of ordinary individuals reveal about the general experiences of women in the United States? For the purposes of this volume the women's stories told here reflect general trends affecting the lives of many American women, although experiences of the individuals included in this volume were not universal. Each dealt with the choices she faced in a way distinct to her own life. Interestingly, the majority of authors writing for this volume did not start their quest intending to write a biography. Instead, while researching other topics, they became intrigued with the life of an ordinary woman who seemed both to mirror and to challenge the norm. In other words, they selected women whose individuality made them extraordinary.

The book is organized into four chronological sections: early Republic; early and mid–nineteenth century; late nineteenth and early twentieth century; and second half of the twentieth century. Each section is prefaced with a brief introduction outlining the major trends of the period and fitting the women featured in that section into the historical and social background.

Obviously, it is impossible to cover all the factors that differentiated the lives of individual American women. It is also unrealistic to write an inclusive history that fully balances the impact of race, class, ethnicity, region, age, and religion on American women's history. More work needs to be done on women of color, immigrants, and the nonliterate. Indeed, the very premise of this volume presents a challenge. Ordinary individuals seldom leave the kinds of written records commonly used by historians. Some of the chapter authors utilized diaries, letters, newspaper accounts, and autobiographical materials. But often they had to look for the story by integrating a variety of less conventional sources: oral history, court and church records, last wills and testaments, the descriptions of contemporaries, census materials, and government reports. Consequently, some questions are left unanswered simply because the historical record is shallow or unavailable. Despite these gaps, the following chapters suggest the importance of ordinary women's experiences to understanding the past and in shaping our contemporary lives.

It was not easy to choose the selections for this book. The original call for contributors was distributed on the H-Women and H-SAWH electronic discussion networks of the H-Net (www.h-net.msu.edu). I received more than fifty wonderful proposals. I believe that those chosen for this volume complement one another and best support the volume's primary purpose: to show how ordinary women's lives reflect and challenge general assumptions about the past. Each chapter was specifically written for this book, although the individual authors may have published other works that include information about the women described here.

Notes

1. Mary Hartman and Lois Banner, eds., *Clio's Consciousness Raised: New Perspectives on the History of Women* (New York: Harper and Row, 1974); Gerda Lerner, *The Majority Finds Its Past* (New York: Oxford University Press, 1979); Glenda Riley, *Inventing the American Woman: A Perspective of Women's History, 1607 to the Present* (New York: Harlan Davidson, 1986); and G. J. Barker-Benfield and Catherine Clinton, *Portraits of American Women: From Settlement to the Present* (New York: Oxford University Press, 1991), rev. ed., 1998.

2. Elizabeth Jameson and Susan Armitage, introduction to *Writing the Range: Race, Class, and Culture in the Women's West* (Norman: University of Oklahoma Press, 1997), 3–16.

I

The Revolutionary Era and the Early Republic

Defining the American Woman

Although Christopher Columbus arrived in the "New" World in 1492, Britain did not have a permanent settlement in North America until 1607, with the establishment of Jamestown, Virginia. Two earlier attempts in the Southern colonies, one in 1585 and another in 1587, had failed. Although often overlooked, gender played an important part in shaping early Euro-America. All 144 individuals who left England for the London Company of Virginia's Jamestown colony in 1607 were male. The 104 who survived the trip were unable to find the gold or silver they sought and under martial law organized settlements based on cash-crop agriculture. But it soon became obvious that an agricultural colony needed the labor and reproductive capacity of English women as well as men. Moreover, British males would not voluntarily remain in the colony for long without women. The 1614 marriage of Pocahontas (the daughter of Native American leader Powhatan) and Englishman John Rolfe has become an American legend. But this interracial marriage was more the exception than the rule. In general, British male colonists did not establish permanent families with Indian female partners. From 1619 on, the colonies included Africans, and by the 1660s slavery had become well entrenched as a part of American society. But until natural increase eventually erased the gender imbalance in the late eighteenth century, black males far outnumbered black females. Interracial marriage was prohibited by law in most places.

The first two white women from Great Britain arrived in Jamestown in 1608. But the dangerous ocean voyage, deadly environmental conditions in the colony, and its remote location meant that few other English females followed. Beginning in 1619, working-class women with little opportunity to better their status in England agreed to come to Jamestown to be "sold" as wives to the colony's bachelor landowners. Therefore, during the seventeenth century the majority of white women arriving in the Southern colonies came as indentured servants, some of their own free will, and some with little other choice. But throughout the 1600s, white men continued to outnumber by far white women in the South. Under British law, free single women had an independent legal status known as "femme sole." Married women's status, "femme covert," however, meant that they could not own property, sign contracts, sue, vote, or (in most cases) receive custody of their children upon divorce. The scarcity of white women in the Southern colonies opened some opportunities by stretching the boundaries of gender-based English Common Law. White women were a valued commodity, but still hampered by gender-based stereotypes and legal obstacles. In addition, life in the Southern colonies was difficult, and the gender ratio remained unbalanced during the seventeenth century.

In New England, first settled in 1620 by British Separatist Pilgrims at Plymouth, Massachusetts, white women lived under the same British laws as those in the Southern colonies. But owing to religious theology and distinct settlement patterns, white women in New England lived in a society with more rigidly defined gender roles than their Southern sisters did. Pilgrims at Plymouth Plantation and Puritan Congregationalists who settled Massachusetts Bay came as families. Therefore, gender ratios were much more balanced than in the South, although women died at younger ages than men because of mortality in childbirth. Slavery was not as common as in the South, and Northern white men had even less incentive than Southerners to intermarry with Native American females. Puritan society valued families highly, and it was not unusual for a New England woman to have twelve to fifteen pregnancies during her lifetime. Premarital pregnancy was common, but births to unmarried women were not. As Marla Miller shows in Chapter 1, conformity was the rule and there were few opportunities for women outside of marriage. Nonetheless, by the early eighteenth century there were more young adult females than males in many New England towns. As the population expanded, some young men seeking opportunity, adventure, and escape from the narrow structures of Puritan life left for the frontier. Leaving for the frontier was not a viable option for young Puritan women. Most eventually married, but a few, like Rebecca Dickinson, lived lives outside the norm while remaining in their communities.

By the revolutionary era most whites living in North America had been born there, and the gender ratio in both the North and South stabilized. Although it may be legitimately argued that the American Revolution was a revolution much more of ideas and laws than of cultural or social practice, the war spurred social change. The boycotting of British goods and the absence of men from home during the war years forced many women to assume more responsibilities both within and outside their homes. In Chapter 2, Patricia Parker traces the story of Susanna Haswell Rowson, a woman whose life and writings reflect the greater autonomy experienced by some white females in the Early Republic. Rowson, an English immigrant to America, wrote about the difficulties women faced during the war, celebrated the new nation's patriotism, and lived a life that reflected the transition from the revolutionary era to the nineteenth-century women's rights movement.

Interestingly, as the world of white women developed in the New Republic, the opportunities for Native American and African American women also changed—but not for the better. By the eighteenth century Southern colonies had reduced the use of white indentured servants and turned to African slaves as the primary labor force. The majority of blacks in North America, both men and women, worked as field hands on Southern plantations. Whereas inheritance among whites passed through the father, black children inherited their mothers' status. This situation left black women subject to sexual exploitation by white male owners and further destroyed the power of black men. Slave codes became more restrictive, and the introduction of the cotton gin in the 1790s sparked the growth of the cotton kingdom. The consequence was a further expansion of slavery and the establishment of even tighter slave codes.

Similarly, for Native Americans the early years of the New Republic had a negative impact. Most important, it opened the door to further white encroachment in the West. President Thomas Jefferson's vision of an agrarian America could be realized only with the acquisition of more land. The 1803 Louisiana Purchase answered this need. Jefferson sent Meriwether Lewis, William Clark, thirty-four soldiers, ten male civilians, and one Indian woman guide (Sacagawea) on an expedition up the Missouri River, across the northern Rocky Mountains, and along the tributaries of the Columbia River to the Pacific Ocean. As Laura McCall explains in Chapter 3, on Sacagawea, the interpretation of this teenage mother's life has fluctuated over time. Therefore, although Sacagawea is one of the few Native American women mentioned by name in traditional American history texts, her story is complicated by the motives of authors who have celebrated or obscured her role in the Lewis and Clark Expedition. The details of her life indicate the difficulties faced by Indian women at the opening of a century that devastated traditional Native American ways of life.

1

Rebecca Dickinson
A Life Alone in the Early Republic

Marla R. Miller

"Too is better than one for if one [Should] fall the other can lift him up but i must act my Part alone."[1] When Rebecca Dickinson (1738–1815) penned these words in the summer of 1789, she had spent many hours just like this one, alone in the chamber of a weather-beaten red saltbox just across from the meetinghouse in Hatfield, Massachusetts. An evening at the home of her brother had put the diarist in an especially thoughtful mood. Henry Dodge, an old bachelor who had courted her sister Irene more than fifteen years ago, had also been visiting there that night. Irene had long since married, but Henry had not. "He appeared to sit by her and i belive he has never forgot her," Dickinson mused. Dodge's plight was, to the aging spinster, only too familiar: "How great the loss is to loos the Pardener of our life for in the beginning tha was made male and feemale . . . there is great need of the help of Each other through the jorney of life . . . but i must act my part alone . . . alone in a world where tha goe too and too male and female."[2]

On the evening she wrote these words, diarist Rebecca Dickinson was forty-nine years old, and she, like Dodge, had never married. She was born in rural western Massachusetts in 1738. Dickinson's single status, more than any other factor, shaped her experience as a woman in early New England. A "bullock unaccustomed to the yoke" of spinsterhood, Dickinson recorded to her journal the rabblement of emotion her life alone evoked. Referring to herself as a "fish out of water," a "gazing stock," a "cat on a roof," a "sparrow alone on a rooftop," she was clearly aware of nothing so much as her own aberration: "How oft tha have hissed and wagged their heads at me," she wrote, "by reason of my Solotary life."[3] Her manuscript—four sewn gatherings of foolscap containing nearly five hundred entries written between July 1787 and August 1802, discovered tucked in the garret of her home some eighty years after her death—preserves the difficult "journey of life" of a woman struggling to "act her part alone."

In a society where marriage was nearly universal, Dickinson wrote that her "story frights half the women of the town." But hers is not the story of a village outcast. Evidence apart from Dickinson's own record paints a very different picture of her place among Hatfield citizens. Surviving recollections suggest that Dickinson was indeed a loved and respected member of her community. In his history of Hatfield, Daniel Wells records that "as she travelled from house to house about her work [gownmaking] . . . she acquired a fund of information concerning her neighbors that was unequalled by any other person. A gift for pithy, epigrammatic remarks caused her to be regarded as something of an 'oracle.'" Samuel D. Partridge, a lifelong resident of Hatfield, remembered Dickinson from his boyhood as a "very intelligent woman" whose sayings "were frequently repeated" by townspeople. Another woman recalled her as "Aunt Beck, it being the habit in those days to call single women who were loved by that community title, and Aunt Beck was well-liked by all." Nineteenth-century Hatfield historian Margaret Miller's research (Miller first brought the diary to public attention after its discovery in the 1890s) suggests that Dickinson indeed achieved at least the outward appearance of grace: "To old people who remember her," Miller wrote, "or knew her by hearsay she was a 'Saint on Earth,' a 'marvel of piety.'" Others remembered her as the "most industrious woman that ever lived."[4]

If some contradiction exists between Dickinson's sense of herself as an anomalous, even outcast, member of her community and other accounts of a village figure "well liked by all," that apparent discrepancy only mirrors other tensions that run through this complex text. Dickinson used the pages of her journal to express (and then lock away, literally, and perhaps figuratively as well) mounting concerns that she had been deservedly "cast out from the Peopel." Here she examined "how it Came about that others and all in the world was in Possession of Children ad frinds and a hous and homes while i was So od as to Sit here alone."[5] Yet, at the same time, Dickinson's journal hints that the diarist found attractions in her single status—attractions that she herself could barely admit. This text tells a tale of both shame and satisfaction, and it is in that very contradiction that the meaning of singlehood for early American women lies. Like other women offered no viable social role outside marriage, Dickinson nevertheless carved one out and bore the social and psychological costs of that struggle.

Dickinson's journal is an exceptional source for historians, not least because so few personal testimonies of never-married women exist. Personal writings of this type vary greatly in purpose and content. As windows into the past, their clarity depends upon the view we seek. Vast differences, for example, distinguish Dickinson's diary from that of her neighbor and client Elizabeth Porter Phelps. The two women were roughly the same age and lived on opposite sides of the Connecticut River; on Sundays after church meeting both women bent over their respective journals. But Phelps's text is an accounting of the social life and work activities that shaped life on the large farm of her politically and socially important family. She noted the text of the Sunday sermon but devoted the bulk of her energies to recording the comings, goings, and activities of friends, family, servants, and artisans. Whereas Phelps often lamented her little opportunity for contemplation, in contrast, Dickinson's was "a life full of self-reflecttion."[6] The difference between the manuscripts each woman produced is perhaps best illustrated by the fact that, although Rebecca Dickinson was a skilled gownmaker, almost nothing of her work can be gleaned from her own journal. If one seeks to study the trade of rural Massachusetts needlewomen, then Phelps's diary, which records the work performed by the artisans and domestic servants she hired, is a better source than Dickinson's own, more meditative text.

In her diary, Dickinson searched for ways in which to understand her place in the world. Small remarks by neighbors reverberated in the diarist's mind; in her journal they were turned over, reexamined, challenged, internalized, in prose so painfully unreserved that the reader can almost feel her reddening blush, the hairs rising on her burning neck as she encounters the tacit or declared reproach of her neighbors. At other times, the loneliness seems more than she can bear:

> About Dusk or the Edge of the evining Set out to Come home to this lonely hous where i have lived forty nine years lonesome as Death. . . . Came home Crept into my window and fastened up my rome neeled Down by my bed and after a Poor manner Commited my Self to god but not with that thankfull heart as i aught to have had o my god my Poverty and my leanness my Poverty as to the things of time when other Peopel are a Seeing there Children rejoicing with one another im all alone in the hous and all alone in the world a most wicked and Sinfull thought which makes me Cry o my leanness how Poor those Souls are who have there Portion in this life i am ashamed to Call god my father and to Complain the want of any thing.[7]

A young woman whose "mind was stored with Poetry" when she began to keep a journal, probably in the 1760s, Dickinson wrote through the dramatic decades of revolution and nation-building, years of political and social turmoil in Hatfield as elsewhere. But the summer of 1787 (while Congress hammered out the Federal Constitution in Philadelphia) found her burning those earlier, too-temporal quires. On July 22, 1787, Dickinson began the new diary, which survives today. She rededicated her writings to the state of her soul. The first half of that year had been especially difficult, and part of the significance of and motivation for these surviving pages lies in the months immediately prior to their opening. That summer, Dickinson grieved the loss of two close companions, Lucretia Williams and Elizabeth Alver, both of whom had died not long before. "This Sommer has stripped the[e] of all thy acquaintences. More precias than fine gold has thy friends been to the[e]." Without her companions, Dickinson was not simply lonelier, but more cognizant of her own aging, her own mortality, and the increasing likelihood that she would endure it all alone. Now, she wrote, "the world wears a difirent face."[8]

Other evidence of the ebb and flow of life was surely on Dickinson's mind about that time as well. As she approached fifty, the diarist had likely just passed or was passing through menopause, confronting the reality that, whether or not she would ever "change her name," no children would take care of her in her old age. "What Shall i do or where Shall i gow with whoom Shall i live when old and helpless"—uncertainty tore at her peace of mind. "This summer has given me a Sight of myself," she wrote at the close of that painful season; in a spirit of both resolve and despair she declared that "there is no hope for me in the things of time"—and hence all "the more need of Sending all my hopes to the heavenly world."[9]

Apart from these pages, little record of Rebecca Dickinson survives. She was the eldest daughter of Hatfield farmer and dairyman Moses Dickinson and farmwife Anna Smith Dickinson. Throughout Rebecca Dickinson's life, the population of her thriving farming community along the Connecticut River hovered at about eight hundred. The 1790 census reports 103 houses in the village and surrounding countryside; ten years later, just 20 more had been added. When Yale president Timothy Dwight passed through in 1797, he described Hatfield as a town where the "inhabitants have for a long period been conspicuous for uniformity of character. They have less intercourse with their neighbors than those of most other places . . . an air of silence and retirement appears everywhere. Except travelers, few persons are seen abroad besides those who are employed about their daily business. This seclusion probably renders them less agreeable to strangers, but certainly contributes to their prosperity. Accordingly, few farming towns are equally distinguished either for their property or their thrift."[10]

Rebecca's father, however, was distinguished neither for property nor thrift; tax and probate records show that he was a man of average means in the community, producing mostly grain on about 15½ acres of land and operating a dairy. As the eldest child, Rebecca surely helped raise her younger sisters and brother. By Rebecca's eighteenth birthday, Anna had given birth to five more children: Samuel, Martha, Miriam, Anna, and Irene. In time, each of these married. Martha moved seventy miles north, to Bennington, Vermont, and Anna left for Pittsfield, Massachusetts. Irene and her husband went to Williamsburg, a town set off from Hatfield lands, while Samuel and his wife Mary moved just over the Hatfield line to Whately and continued in the dairy line. Miriam remained closest, moving just a few doors south to the tavern owned by her husband, Silas Billings.

Meanwhile, Rebecca remained in the house in which she had been born. At some point, probably around the age of twelve, she was sent "to learn the trade of gownmaking." Through the years, she worked at her trade, helped with her siblings, and generally remained active in the "busi scenes of life," all the while passing gradually beyond the usual age of marriage, about twenty-three for Anglo women in eighteenth-century rural New England. Then, when it seemed that she should have a chance finally to "change her name," she felt the "bitter blow" that "robbed her hopes" for marriage, a family, and a home of her own. Gradually, what had seemed unthinkable in her teens and twenties came to haunt her thirties and forties and was, on the eve of her fifties, a grim reality.

Fortunately for Dickinson, and unlike most of her contemporaries, she enjoyed the benefits of a marketable skill: gownmaking. In her diary she frequently mentioned "invitations" to work in surrounding Hampshire County towns, suggesting that she had no need to solicit clients. In addition to simple tailoring and the occasional making of stays, Dickinson produced women's better garments: gowns of silk and taffeta for Sunday worship and special occasions, such as the garments rendered on that August afternoon she spent "at Sister bilings to fix Patte Church and Bets Huntinton for the we[dding reception] of oliver hastings," or the dark brown ducape gown in which Hadley gentlewoman Elizabeth Porter married Charles Phelps. Other clients included the wives and daughters of the so-called River Gods, members of the seven interrelated families who wielded the lion's share of political, economic, and ecclesiastical authority in the towns of the Connecticut River Valley through most of eighteenth century. That Dickinson was entrusted to create important gowns for prominent members of the local aristocracy suggests that she was sufficiently trained and talented to secure the patronage of the area's leading families.

Dickinson gratefully acknowledged the benefits of her marketable trade. Following a visit by the widow Catherine Graves, Dickinson wrote, "She began the world with me wee went together to learn the trade of gown making which has been of unspeakable advanta[g]e to me but of no Servis to her." Dickinson's suggestion that Graves's apprenticeship had been of "no Servis" refers to Catherine's subsequent marriage to Moses Graves, a man thirty-seven years her senior. Graves's income plus the raising of her six new stepchildren probably made taking in needlework unnecessary, if not impossible. Without husbands to provide for them, single women largely depended on the largess of male relatives for their maintenance. Dickinson enjoyed the benefit of her father's home, but she provided her own day-to-day expenses. Craft skills meant that she did not to have to appeal to any family members for necessities, much less for small luxuries like her silk gloves or her looking glass.[11]

Still, Dickinson recognized the trade's pitfalls. She frequently bemoaned the sporadic nature of the work and the threat that slack periods posed to her security. "How times vary with me," she noted one November afternoon, lamenting "how hurried [she] was formerly at this Season of the year." The pronounced seasonal variation of the clothing trades typically produced, for both tailors and gownmakers, months of complete unemployment broken by times of extreme overwork. The effect of this seasonality is captured in the lines of a character (who, like Dickinson, was an unmarried laborer) in one eighteenth-century drama: "What a present is mine, and what a prospect is my future. Labour and watchings in the busy season—hunger in the slack—and solitude in both."[12] This irregularity of employment, from season to season or year to year, proved stressful to Dickinson, who as her own sole source of support could ill afford time away from her needle. Once, while eagerly anticipating a visit from her sister Martha and her children, Dickinson wrote: "I Shall be glad to see them i hope to be at home when tha Come to town which makes me at a loss about going [to Hadley] but my daily bread depends upon my labour." Torn between readying her home for anxiously awaited guests and "imploy for her hands," Dickinson chose the latter.[13]

As she grew older, Dickinson's anxiety over her income mounted. Some years in the past, she wrote in 1787, she had been "hardly too scared to walk too miles afoot," but now, she fretted, "old age has Crept up" on her. As her geographical range necessarily narrowed, so too did the range of potential clients. Sickness also threatened her income, and apprehension over her recurrent bouts with the "Collick" caused much concern. During the following winter, Dickinson found herself "Distressing ill." She tried diligently to carry on, but her "Physick overdoing" finally caused her to faint. Alone in the house, she took to her bed, but this infirmity only produced panic over her fragile finances: "Have had an invitation to goe to Hadley to work but no Strength to move and must be Content with what is ready earnt by me since my health and my Strength is gon i would beg of god that my Estate may be a comfort to me now in the time of old age."[14]

Whether this "estate" refers to some security she received following the death of her father in 1785, or to some amount of money she was able to set aside after fulfilling her own fiscal obligations, is not clear. At the time of his death, Moses Dickinson provided equally for each of his daughters, bequeathing "the sum of sixty six pounds thirteen shillings and four pence of silver money what I have advanced to each of them to be accounted as part thereof the remainder to be paid by my son Samuel in two years after my decease." Despite Rebecca's unmarried status (at forty-seven), Moses' will made no special provisions for her welfare. In 1780, Moses had given Rebecca seventy acres of land in nearby Williamsburg. If the gift was intended to serve as potential income to be converted to cash at some later date should she find it necessary, that would suggest one way in which Moses acknowledged his daughter's need for support. Perhaps she rented the land to a Williamsburg farmer, drawing steady income from the property. Moses' decision not to allocate to her in his will greater resources than to his married daughters may also suggest that she was faring fairly well on her own.[15]

Whatever the actual state of Dickinson's finances, apprehension over security invaded her consciousness both day and night. Once, for example, she was "awaked by a dream i thought that i had Stole from mrs hurberd but knew my Self to be innocent but my Credit was a going." Dreaming she had been reduced to stealing from her friend, local innkeeper Lucy Hubbard, she pleaded that God spare her that humiliation and protect her soul from transgression. Elsewhere she sighed, "God has in great mercy this Summer back given me work he heard my Cry and has sent imploy for my hands the god who heard my Cry has given me work."[16]

Dickinson's "Cry" is understandable: over time she had ample opportunity to witness the precarious economic states other unmarried women endured. Without husbands and children, elderly single women were housed, fed, and clothed only as the generosity of others allowed. Dickinson knew what such dependence could mean. In the fall of her forty-ninth year, she noted the death of a thirty-year-old spinster who "was Driven from one brother to another and lived with her Sisters Some of the time." On another occasion she noted her own good fortune: "When i Compare my life with many of my acquaintences i am Content and well i may be there is no unmaried woman who has a hous to Shelter my goods in when others run from Place to Place not knowing where to goe nor what to Do."[17] Never-married women, Dickinson well knew, shuttled from place to place, wherever they were most needed or least underfoot.

Despite her own comparatively stable living situation, Dickinson knew that since she was without title to her home, any change in the family's circumstances could dramatically alter her own. She constantly anguished over the looming possibility that her aging mother would die, prompting her brother, who stood to inherit the property, to sell the Hatfield. "What Should i Doe was it not for this old hous it is a Safe Retreat from troble"; "the Winter is Comming on when there will be no rome for me"; "tha will put me where tha please who have the care of me"—passages such as these regularly mark Dickinson's text, pointing up her sense of vulnerability, her awareness that her hold on that "Safe Retreat" was tenuous at best.

Dickinson's journal is so filled with her sense of being alone in the world that it would be easy to forget the important role her family played—apart from her sense that her eventual fate lay in their hands—in shaping her day-to-day life. And yet they, like her trade, proved sources of both comfort and concern. In the eighteenth century, as today, family caregiving was primarily ascribed to women, and especially to unmarried women, who without husbands or children to look after were perceived to have fewer competing obligations. Like many single women, Dickinson was assigned and assumed the role of caregiver for infirm family members, in this case both her elderly mother, Anna, and her "feeble" nephew, Charles. These responsibilities both mitigated and exacerbated aspects of her life alone.

Charles Dickinson, born in April 1779 to Samuel and Mary Dickinson, was a "poor weekly boy who has never been well," given to "fits." It is possible that Samuel and Mary placed their son with his childless aunt in the hope that he would be a help to her (perhaps also he was of little use on Samuel's farm). But it seems likely too that the "feeble" eight year old was placed with Rebecca so that she might keep a watchful eye on a young boy who, despite his frailty, managed to cultivate a "mischeavous disposition."

In addition to her nephew, Rebecca also assumed much responsibility for the care of her elderly mother. Dickinson's mother arrived each fall to spend the winter with Rebecca and departed each spring to her "other house in the woods," probably Samuel's home in Whately. One might expect that such an arrangement would have provided both women with companionship and care in their advancing age. Widowed in 1785, Anna may have turned to Rebecca for care and support, and Rebecca may have gained a friend and companion no longer bound by the needs of her own family. But Dickinson's journal does not suggest that these two women enjoyed a particularly close relationship. Though at times Rebecca seemed to regret her mother's departures, she also expressed a certain vexation at her return. Loath to shirk her responsibility, her utmost concern was "my Duty to my aged Parent." One winter, even as she longed to travel to Bennington, Vermont, to stay with Martha and her family,

Dickinson maintained "my greatest Scrupel has been on my mother's account." Presented with this opportunity a second time, she again was "confounded between" her "schemes" and her "Duty."[18]

Family caregiving, a function legitimized by society, enabled Dickinson to participate vicariously in the traditional nurturing aspects of marriage and motherhood, perhaps easing her sense of uselessness. But if she did derive satisfaction from these duties, she did not record it. Instead it seems that the care of her mother proved emotionally and physically exhausting. In October 1787, when her mother returned after an absence of several months, Rebecca wrote, "We have Set up housekeeping one time more [though] how we are to live i Cant See." Just two weeks later, her nerves frayed and patience exhausted, Dickinson expressed her complete exasperation: "My mother Seventi five years of age not able to take Care of herself in a Pusseling [puzzling] fit broke my Specticles a great loss to me for tha Suted me So well that 1 ginny [a guinea was a coin of high value] should not have bought them out of my hand."[19]

As she aged, Dickinson's own illnesses aggravated her frustration. Each fall after she reached forty, Dickinson was plagued with a few weeks of serious illness. In fact, a "most distressing Collick" had confined her during the same week in which her mother underwent the "Pusseling fit." Although she "gained ease" after the local physician opened a vein, Dickinson commented, "how Sad to be Sick" when there was "no one to Doe the least kind offis." Anticipating yet another bout with her illness, she declared, "I Cant be Sick i wont be Sick there is none of my fellow being to Show me the least kind offis . . . my mother near eighty as Stuped as Can be [and] a litel feble boy Charls and my body in Sore distress." Her patience at an end, she fumed, "How Can the Stupid world not know my trobles no one from my brothers hous have been here but a boy ten years of age after a great many words by me."[20]

One can only imagine the tension of this scene: Rebecca, already exhausted and feeling unappreciated, pleaded with her brother and sister-in-law for some assistance in caring for Samuel's mother and son Charles. To her dismay, they responded by sending their ten-year-old son Moses, clearly more to assess the situation than to provide care. The added burden of her mother's arrival was apparently simply more than Rebecca could bear, as she later remarked, "Wee was too feeble to help one another i thought i had better be in the hous alone." Dickinson constantly bemoaned her lack of companionship, yet preferred solitude to responsibilities she felt she could not shoulder. Perhaps it is no wonder that after Anna's departure she wrote, "My mother has been gone five weeks tomorrow and Sweet Content has Crouned every Day."[21]

Dickinson's family, like their nineteenth- and twentieth-century counterparts, thought unmarried women like Rebecca, without husbands and children to attend to, had ample time and energy for childcare, nursing, or help with housekeeping. Singlehood strained her relations with members of the family in other ways as well. In 1792, English author Mary Wollstonecraft observed that "when the brother marries . . . [the unmarried sister] is viewed with averted looks as an intruder, an unnecessary burden on the benevolence of the master of the house and his new partner. . . . [The wife] is displeased at seeing the property of her children lavished on a helpless sister."[22] Consistent with observations like Wollstonecraft's, Rebecca and Samuel's wife, Mary, enjoyed a less than cordial relationship. Mary's reluctance to travel to Hatfield to care for Anna, Rebecca, or even her own son Charles, suggests the discordant perceptions that characterized Dickinson's relationship with her family. Mary suspected Rebecca of exaggerating her need while Mary herself had a whole household to run; for her part, Dickinson described Mary as "the most unhappy of the Daughters of Eve She is Pashanate Covetous jellous Sordid no love for her husband mean as the Dirt . . . what a tryal She has been to me."[23] With so much family authority vested in her brother, this tense relationship with his wife must have been a cause of concern for Rebecca as she looked toward an uncertain future.

Dickinson's discussion of her family points up one of the ways in which her actions sometimes belied her words. Despite her real sense of lonesome vulnerability, Dickinson herself engineered her solitary residence in the Hatfield home, requesting that she retain the house after Moses' death rather than move in with a sibling or have one of them with their families move in with her. Her desire to gain or retain an independent existence—in spite of an abiding loneliness—is striking. Luckily, her family was disposed both financially and temperamentally to accede to her request. Her life alone there, she concluded, was both "ordered of god as well as Contrived by myself."[24]

Dickinson also made this choice in full light of her belief that her neighbors "hissed and wagged their heads" at her "Solotary life." And her sense that her situation drew comment among her neighbors was not mere paranoia: notice of her solitary life *was* publicly taken. One summer, for example, she passed a pleasant evening in the house of her minister. Visiting there was Lydia Lyman Peck, and old friend of Rebecca's who herself had married late in life. After the guests had shared their conversation and tea, as Dickinson was making her exit, Lydia followed her to the door and blurted out that "she Could not bare to have me Come to this hous alone." Momentarily dumbfounded, Dickinson replied, "not So lonesome as the grave," but she "wondered after i Came home wether i was rite to give Such an answer how i must look in the eyes of the world."[25] The startled spinster had risen quickly to her own defense, but she acknowledged privately that her situation was bound to elicit comment and concern, if not outright censure. While Dickinson was in Bennington, her tentative effort to join the household of her sister Martha was crushed when, in a similar incident, a stranger asked her how it was that she had never married. "Thunderstruck," Dickinson again retorted, "my affairs might be in a worse order," but she abandoned her planned move and raced home, where her situation was less likely to prompt new inquiry.

In eighteenth-century Europe and America, singlehood invoked an interlacing set of implications. In essence, of course, an "old maid" was a woman who had failed to marry. From that fact followed a set of attendant assumptions. Older single women were often looked on with suspicion and derision as observers guessed reasons for their plight. Often, at least in parodies of the day, "old maids" were accused of pridefully declining reasonable proposals of marriage while they held out for the better offer that never came. Thus, a certain fastidious, finicky quality was often ascribed to the stereotypical old maid. Meanwhile, because sex outside of marriage was strongly discouraged by both social mores and religious doctrine, the reproductive potential of unmarried women of all ages was forever untapped. Of course, women violated prescription—and often—but never-married women were, at least publicly, presumed virgins. As historian Lee Chambers-Schiller suggests, since early American conceptions of womanhood were constructed around biology, "the misuse, or disuse, of those functions proved cause for concern." Permanent celibacy then carried with it a vague scent of decay, of withering organs and soured spirits. Finally, without in-laws and subject to the dearth of gainful occupations for women, the old maid remained, at least in theory, dependent on her family of origin and so perpetually, if artificially, "immature," no matter how advanced in age. In short, the old maid, according to one 1790 satire, was "one of the most ill-natured, magotty, peevish, conceited . . . censorious, out-of-the-way, never-to-be-pleased, good for nothing creatures."[26]

Given the general severity of scorn and ridicule heaped upon women who did not marry, and Dickinson's acute feelings of vulnerability and constant loneliness, the sources of her singlehood become all the more curious. As voiced by another young woman in 1762, when Dickinson was twenty-four years old, "The appellation of old Made . . . I don't believe one of our sex would voluntarily Bare."[27] What circumstances, then, led Dickinson to her life alone? Was the appellation involuntarily borne?

Certainly in Hatfield, demographic pressure reduced every woman's chances to obtain a mate. As fewer men moved into Massachusetts and greater numbers migrated westward, the proportion of men to women shrank. Midcentury warfare also took its toll. Britain's continuing effort to eject France from North America drew numbers of eligible men off to war, some of whom inevitably did not return. Though estimates vary, women outnumbered men in Massachusetts by at least the 1760s. In 1772 (when Dickinson was thirty-four) essayist William Gordon numbered the "excess" women in Massachusetts at 5,665. Gradually, the proportion of never-married women "grew from 9% for families formed between 1700 and 1759, to 12% among daughters whose parents married 1760–1774, to nearly 15% for those marrying 1775–1799."[28]

In Hatfield, as elsewhere, women hoping to marry were caught in a demographic bind. Dickinson was sixteen when the Seven Years War reached Hampshire County. The continued settlement of outlying villages in the 1760s and 1770s, when she was in her twenties and thirties, removed more men from the immediate community. The statistical probability of entering into marriage was decreasing during Dickinson's lifetime; and at least a dozen area women roughly contemporary to Dickinson remained single throughout their lifetimes. Moreover, that estimate probably represents just a fraction of the true number.

But Dickinson did not perceive her singlehood to be the result of broad social forces; instead, she pointed toward a single act, a "stroke which mowed down [her] earthly hopes." That phrase seems to indicate that the "appellation of old Made" was indeed involuntarily borne; however, other evidence suggests that her singlehood was not altogether without design. The truth, in other words, is probably somewhere in between. Although Dickinson often attributed her singlehood to one defining moment, in fact, she considered a variety of explanations, with sources in both the temporal and the eternal. For New England Calvinists, adversity—in this case Dickinson's lack of a husband, home, and children—was welcome evidence that God was sufficiently concerned with the state of one's Soul to send useful calamities: "It is good to be sick it is good to be afflicted for thereby i have learned to keep thy Commands." In denying her the comforts of family life, God had protected her soul from competing temporal interests. With "no children no grand children no house no land" to distract her from her faith, Dickinson was free to achieve the highest measure of devotion.[29]

But that same sense of divine intervention also carried with it an implied criticism, that her poor spiritual state required chastening. After much reflection, Dickinson determined that it was "vile idollatry" of the "things of time" that doomed her to a solitary life.

Hoping to quiet rising resentment at another evening alone, she wrote, "It is the will of god Conserning me no other Place would Doe to Cure me of my Pride and to wean me from the world." "How Can i quarel with the government of god who has witheld nothing from me which would have been for my good," she asked, "for what is all the gratification of this life to a Sure belief that our name is writen in heaven[?]" If she failed to seize this opportunity—to be "so recluse and get no more good by it"—the consequences were dire: "What a Sad thought to be so miserable here and tormented in the world to Come."[30]

If we cannot test her thesis about divine intent, we can examine her assertion that it was this "bitter blow" that put her on the solitary path. She no doubt experienced the event that so haunted her, but was it the cause of her singlehood? Although Dickinson claimed so, she may have adopted this explanation—consciously or unconsciously—as an acceptable one, the jilted lover being one of the few "scenarios" available to eighteenth-century women to explain a failure to marry. William Hayley's 1786 *Philosophical, Historical and Moral Essay on Old Maids,* for example, urges the never-married woman, "whenever she has occasion to speak of the nuptial state, to . . . represent her own exclusion from it, not as the effect of choice, arising from a cold irrational aversion to the state in general, but as the consequence of such perverse incidents as frequently perplex all the patterns of human life[.]"[31]

To be sure, Dickinson represented her singlehood, "not as the effect of choice," but as the consequence of a "perverse incident" revealed in subtle clues throughout her text. The first comes in an entry recording the events of the previous evening at her sister Miriam's home. Dickinson noted the presence of Jesse Billings, who, she wrote, "put those Sad thoughts into my mind." She returned home and "lited no Candel for the Darkness of my mind was beyond the Darkest Dungin there was no hope for me in the things of time." That night, she had a "Strange Dream": "I thought i was on a jorney with jesse billings mare with one rein of my bridle broke my Self lost entagled among horses where i had to lead the Creture rather than have any Servis from her my Desire was to gow to meeting but was not able to find the way."[32] That this encounter produced such sorrow, fear, and confusion suggests that Billings was the source of her disappointment.

Moreover, in October 1790, Dickinson reflected on the mind's inability to "forget" pain, musing "the Soul or thinking Part will remember[.] Some sorrow of the mind which was twenti years Past is more fast on my mind then the Pain [the colic] which i felt the week back." Twenty years earlier, in March 1770, Billings had married Rebecca's second cousin, Sarah Bardwell.[33] Although by then

Dickinson was already thirty-two, Sarah Bardwell was just twenty-seven; the women's age difference suggests that Dickinson could have reasonably entertained notions of marriage to Billings (whose age is unknown). Billings's blacksmith shop, just south of Miriam and Silas's tavern, would have provided ample opportunity for her to encounter Billings, and it was he who maintained her sewing tools.

Whatever did or did not occur in the past, even later, when presented with opportunities to marry, Dickinson was not desperate enough to choose "any match to avoid the reproach of having none." In April 1789, Dickinson recorded the death of Charles Phelps, whom she noted had once offered her his hand. Although Dickinson described Phelps as "a Person well lerned," she regretted he "knew too litel of himself . . . he was very great and very Small." Dickinson's assessment matches other accounts of a difficult man whose ambition exceeded his social and political savvy. Phelps eventually abandoned Hadley for the wilderness of the New Hampshire Grants. There Phelps channeled his considerable combative energies toward the fledgling government of what became the state of Vermont. Phelps's tenacious, if futile, battle to resist state authority ultimately resulted in his imprisonment. At the close of his life, Charles Phelps's health—physical, emotional, and financial—lay in ruins. It is little wonder that Dickinson concluded, "[I] have lived better than i Could have lived with him for the last ten years of my life."[34]

In 1788, fifty-year-old Rebecca received another proposal, from Dr. Moses Gunn of Montague. "He was more agreable than i Could think of," she wrote, "he would Doe if he was the right one but i Shall never Change my name i really belive there will alwais be a bar in the way." Perhaps she found the fact that Gunn had lost a leg "by a fit of Sickness" distasteful or the twenty-mile move to Montague unappealing. Reluctance to alter her lifestyle to accommodate the unknown trials of matrimony when she was at this time beyond her childbearing years may also have contributed to her decision, as marriage could no longer produce children who would care for her in her old age. But perhaps the "bar in the way" meant here, as elsewhere, her own "Stubborn Heart," that is, a general disinclination to marry. Whatever the reason, Rebecca accepted full responsibility for her fate, saying, "Tho i have no home may it be on my mind that today i have had the offer of one."[35] In the almost five hundred journal entries extant Dickinson repeated the phrase "here again in this old hous alone" more than one hundred times. Yet she chose that life, again and again.

On good days, Dickinson saw her way clear to a positive view of singlehood: "My bou[g]hs have been trimmed of[f] but the tree is not hurt . . . [though I] look not like the rest of the trees yet my mounten Stands Strong." In fact, God would "surely bring [her] feet to the gate of heaven" through singlehood. "There is a great many family blessings i know nothing of," she wrote in the spring of 1788, "but the gifts of time alwais bring Sorrow along with them a numirous family and a great Estate bring a great Consern upon the minds of the owners more than a ballence for all the Comfort that tha bring." Throughout life, Dickinson struggled to cling to that insight, to look at a neighbor and conclude that "she has her fortun i mine very different and both right."[36]

Dickinson's craftwork played no small role in the formulation of both her public and private assessments. Her artisanal skill enabled her to fend off the poverty so often associated with singlehood, to withstand the loneliness and sense of purposelessness that she battled daily, and to turn down offers of marriage when she found the overall situation disadvantageous. It may well have been her skill with shears, needle, and pins that permitted, or even encouraged, Dickinson to resist offers of marriage and to find a positive role in her community—"Aunt Beck," as she came to be known—contrary to the title of "old Made," which she did not like.

Dickinson's text may also reflect increasing ambivalence toward women alone in the New Republic. As scholars studying women's lives in the nineteenth century have noted, singlehood became an increasingly necessary and viable option in the quarter century following the Revolution. In the words of historian Mary Beth Norton, "In the years after the war [women] started to dispute, in tentative fashion, perhaps the most basic assumptions of all: that marriage was every woman's destiny." For single women, "Republican Motherhood"—a term historians have coined to denote the role offered women in the New Republic, encouraging women to accept civic duties (surrounding the raising of good citizens) rather than political rights—offered a more abstract conception of motherhood, one that enabled women such as Rebecca Dickinson to carve new roles for themselves as cultural custodians at large.[37] Over the first half of the nineteenth century, a "Cult of Single Blessedness" emerged, as increasing numbers of women embraced independence and voluntarism and consciously chose to remain single. The abolitionists and suffragists of the nineteenth century were the first prominent beneficiaries of that new mode of thinking. More than once, Dickinson "wondered what i was made for," insisting, if uncertainly, that "there is Surely Some thing for me to Doe in the world."[38] Decades later, she might have found an answer in the antislavery or suffrage movements, in settlement house work, or any one of a host of reform efforts; in late-eighteenth-century Hatfield, however, her choices were more circumscribed.

Yet, if demographic upheaval, economic exigency, and new currents of republicanism eventually eased (though by no means eliminated) long-standing hostilities toward the never-married, these shifts were in ideology and circumstance of which Rebecca Dickinson was at best but dimly aware. A product of her own culture, Dickinson shared the beliefs and assumptions of the society in which she lived. She understood herself and others according to established, available definitions. The result was a series of disjunctures between the negative attributes ascribed never-married women and her own positive sense of herself. That discrepancy between her private and public identity is in part an artifact of the sources themselves. As students of journal keeping often observe, the cathartic function of personal writing produces a skewed picture of an author; only some aspects of a person's character find themselves projected into permanence in the pages of a journal. Few of us would want to be known exclusively by the pages of our journals, but that is the only way we can now know Rebecca Dickinson. At the same time, however, the disjunctures that characterize this text reflect a tension *within* Dickinson's private identity, as she struggled to reconcile competing evaluations of singlehood provided by her religion, her community, popular culture, and her own observations and experiences.

At the throne of her God, for whom she ultimately kept this journal, Dickinson was not an old maid, but simply another penitent soul, striving toward heaven. "My days glide quietly along," the aging artisan wrote in the summer of 1794. Dickinson, "found in the spirit of thy holy day," rededicated herself "to live in the light of Spiritiall life hopeing waiting doeing gods will to the end of my mortal life is the Desire of rebeca Dickinson." "I Should never have [lived] through So many Storms," she wrote, "had it not been for the hope of heavenly things." Eventually, the elderly aunt moved into the home of her nephew Joseph and his family, and it was there, in the twilight hours of 1815, that Rebecca Dickinson left behind the storms of singlehood and perhaps found some comfort in heavenly things. "Ever tending toward that land of Promise," she finally gained admittance to the one place "where tha never marry nor are given in marriage but are like the angels of god."[39]

Notes

1. Rebecca Dickinson, Diary, June 1789, Memorial Libraries, Deerfield, MA, 108.

2. Lacking less pejorative terms, I occasionally employ the most familiar words that currently connote both never-marriedness and the opprobrium attached to it: spinster and spinsterhood. The word "spinster" did not come into its contemporary usage, however, until the nineteenth century, "old maid" being the usual term in Dickinson's lifetime.

3. Dickinson, Diary, September 22, 1787, 23.

4. Daniel White Wells, *History of Hatfield*, Massachusetts (Springfield: F. C. H. Gibbons, 1910), 205, 256; Partridge and Miller are quoted in Margery Howe, *Deerfield Embroidery* (New York: Charles Scribner's Sons, 1976), 62.

5. Dickinson, Diary, August 20, 1787, 12.

6. Ibid., October 21, 1788, 88.

7. Ibid., August 22, 1787, 9.

8. Ibid., September 2, 1787, 12.

9. Ibid., August 12, 1787, 4.

10. Timothy Dwight, "Journey to the White Mountains," in *Travels in New England and New York,* vol. 2, ed. Barbara Solomon (1821; Cambridge, MA: Belknap Press of Harvard University Press, 1969), 35.

11. Dickinson, Diary, September 26, 1787, 24; Hampshire County Hall of Probate, box 48, no. 37, Northampton, MA.

12. Dickinson, Diary, November 22, 1787, 36; Krishna Gorowara, "The Treatment of Unmarried Woman in Comedy from 1584–1921" (Ph.D. diss., Glasgow University, 1961), 322.

13. Dickinson, Diary, September 5, 1787, 17.

14. Ibid., September 5, 1787, 17; November 1787, 35–37.

15. Ibid., September 10, 1787, 20.

16. Ibid., September 28, 1788, 82; April 26, 1789, 102; June 21, 1789, 110; September 10, 1787, 20.

17. Ibid., July 3, 1789, 117; September 13, 1787, 21; June 8, 1788, 58.

18. Ibid., December 2, 1787, 38; July 14, 1788, 66.

19. Ibid., October 26, 1787, 33; November 15, 1787, 34.

20. Ibid., November 21, 1790, 137–138.

21. Ibid., November 21, 1790, and July 3, 1791, 151.

22. Mary Wollstonecraft, *Vindication of the Rights of Woman* (1792), reprinted in Bridget Hill, *Eighteenth Century Women: An Anthology* (London and Boston: Allen and Unwin, 1984), 131.

23. Dickinson, Diary, June 29, 1794, 200.

24. Ibid., August 12, 1787, 4.

25. Ibid., October 1787, 29.

26. Lee Chambers-Schiller, *Liberty, A Better Husband: Single Women in America: The Generations of 1780–1840* (New Haven: Yale University Press, 1984), 159; Dickinson, Diary, July 25, 1787, 1; and June Sprigg, "Women's Everyday Lives in Eighteenth-Century America" (master's thesis, University of Delaware, 1977), 57.

27. Sally Hanschurst to Sally Forbes, 1762, Sally Hanschurst Letterbook, miscellaneous manuscripts, Library of Congress, as quoted in Terri Premo, *Winter Friends: Women Growing Old in the New Republic, 1785–1836* (Urbana: University of Illinois Press, 1990), 75.

28. Gloria Main, "Gender, Work and Wages in Colonial New England," *William and Mary Quarterly* 51 (1994): 65 n 91.

29. Dickinson, Diary, end of October 1790, 136 ff.; May 3, 1789, 103.

30. Ibid., August 20, 1787, 7; September 25, 1787, 25; August 12, 1787, 4; March 30, 1788, 50.

31. William Hayley, *A Philosophical, Historical and Moral Essay on Old Maids* (London: T. Cadell, 1786), 7–9.

32. Dickinson, Diary, October 20, 1790, pp. 136 ff.

33. Dickinson, Diary, October 30, 1790, 136 ff.; Wells, *History of Hatfield*, 372.

34. Dickinson, Diary, April 19, 1789, 101.

35. Ibid., October 3, 1788, 84.

36. Ibid., August 12, 1792, 172 (from Psalms 30:7); May 31, 1794, 194.

37. Mary Beth Norton, *Liberty's Daughters: The Revolutionary Experience of American Women, 1750–1800* (Boston: Little, Brown and Co., 1980), 239.

38. Dickinson, Diary, ca. November 3, 1787, 34; May 25, 1788, 57.

39. Ibid., August 3, 1794, 206; September 2, 1787, 12; and June 1789, 108.

Suggested Readings

The manuscript diary of Rebecca Dickinson is owned by Memorial Libraries in Deerfield, Massachusetts, and is in generally good condition. Page numbers given after quotations correspond to a typescript prepared from a photocopy of the manuscript, also in Deerfield's Memorial Libraries. In this essay, Dickinson's original spelling and punctuation have been maintained, though in cases where her style impedes easy reading of the text, spelling has been corrected and words or letters have been added in brackets. As a whole, however, Dickinson's hand, if not her spelling and punctuation, is clear and consistent, and the original text quite readable. The diary of Elizabeth Porter Phelps was published in consecutive issues of the *New England Historical and Genealogical Register* between 1964 and 1968.

The most thorough treatment of never-married women in early America remains Lee Chambers-Schiller's *Liberty, A Better Husband: Single Women in America: The Generations of 1780–1840* (New Haven: Yale University Press, 1984). Chambers-Schiller's articles about single women in the nineteenth century pursue several of these themes; see in particular "Woman Is Born to Love: The Maiden Aunt as Maternal Figure in Ante-Bellum Literature," *Frontiers* 10 (1988): 34–43; and "The Single Woman: Family and Vocation among Nineteenth-Century Reformers," in *Woman's Being, Woman's Place: Female Identity and Vocation in American History,* ed. Mary Kelley (Boston: Hall Publishers, 1979), 340–342. A related work is Terri Premo's engaging study of aging women in early America, *Winter Friends: Women Growing Old in the New Republic, 1785–1836* (Urbana: University of Illinois Press, 1990). An excellent overview of women's lives before the Revolution can be found in Carol Berkin's book *First Generations: Women in Colonial America* (New York: Hill & Wang, 1996). The standard works on women's experiences surrounding the American Revolution remain Mary Beth Norton, *Liberty's Daughters: The Revolutionary Experience of American Women, 1750–1800* (Boston: Little, Brown & Co., 1980); and Linda Kerber, *Women of the Republic: Intellect and Ideology in Revolutionary America* (Chapel Hill: University of North Carolina Press for the Institute of Early American History and Culture, 1980).

Finally, for further insight into diary keeping in early America, consult Suzanne L. Bunkers and Cynthia A. Huff, eds., *Inscribing the Daily: Critical Essays on Women's Diaries* (Amherst: University of Massachusetts Press, 1996); and Steven E. Kagle, *American Diary Literature, 1620–1799* (Boston: Twayne Publishers, [1979]). Mary Moffatt and Charlotte Painter discuss the cathartic function of journal keeping in their anthology of personal writing, *Revelations: Diaries of Women* (New York: Vintage Books, 1984). Williams Andrews's edited collection of women's writings, *Journeys in New Worlds: Early American Women's Narratives* (Madison: University of Wisconsin Press, 1990), provides both the text of several diaries and critical analyses of those texts.

2

Susanna Haswell Rowson
America's First Best-Selling Author

Patricia L. Parker

Susanna Haswell Rowson (1762–1824), author of America's first best-seller, lived through the tumultuous time of the American Revolution. Afterwards, when the war-weary public longed for entertainment, she helped introduce the popular theatrical arts to the New Republic. Then as America became interested in women's education, she opened Boston's first schools for girls and young women. Throughout her lifetime, Rowson continued to write popular novels for and about women. Thus, her life paralleled the rise of the arts in the New Republic and the growing concern for women's rights and education.

At the age of five, Susanna Haswell had her first sea adventure when she traveled from England with her father, William Haswell, a lieutenant in the British navy. Susanna had been born in Plymouth, England (probably in February 1762). Her mother, Susanna Musgrave Haswell, had died shortly after Susanna's birth, so as a young child she lived with relatives. But in October 1766 she said good-bye to the family she had known and to the bustling port town of Plymouth. She, her father, and a nursemaid boarded a ship bound for the colony of Massachusetts Bay. Having grown up in a family of naval men, the child Susanna relished the idea of her first sea voyage, but anticipation and delight soon turned to fear as the ship encountered a storm. Twenty-five years later, the memory remained vivid enough for Susanna Rowson to recount it in her novel *Rebecca; or, The Fille de Chambre:*

> A fair wind presently took them out of the channel, and they flattered themselves with a prosperous voyage; but these flattering appearances were soon reversed, for the wind suddenly changed, rising almost to a hurricane, so that it was impossible to pursue their intended course or return to port, and they continued tossing about in the Atlantic till the latter end of December, and then had not half made their passage, though their provision was so exhausted that they were obliged to live on a very small allowance of bread; water and salt and meat they had, and a few pease, but of these they were extremely careful.[1]

Ten long weeks later, the crew sighted and flagged down a ship to plead for food. But they received no answer and the crew and passengers again faced death by starvation. Ten days later another ship passed. This time a sympathetic captain and his sailors fed their own dinners to the hungry passengers and equipped them with provisions for the remaining journey to Boston. *Rebecca* movingly describes the kindness of the sailors and their captain, who refused recompense.

Susanna's first sea experience had not yet ended, however. As their vessel entered Boston Harbor, it was hit by wind, sleet, and snow that froze the ropes and obscured the lighthouse at the harbor entrance. Her father dared not let his daughter descend the icy rope ladder to the waiting boat, nor did he trust himself to carry her, "lest a false step or slip might destroy them both."[2] An old sailor suggested tying the child around the waist and lowering her down the ship's side. Like a bundle of straw, Susanna Haswell arrived for the first time in America. Small wonder that shipwrecks and dangerous sea adventures figure in six of her later novels. Harrowing voyages had been the experience of many colonists who settled in America, and such scenes in Rowson's novels appealed to many who had suffered similarly.

Compared to the traumas of her arrival, the young Susanna enjoyed a peaceful childhood. Her father remarried, to American Rachel Woodward, acquired a little property, and settled on the Nantasket Peninsula, south of Boston. The nature of his work remains unclear, but he may have served as a customs officer. Susanna's two half-brothers, Robert and William Jr., were soon added to the family. Susanna learned to read and enjoyed the benefits of her father's small library, which included Homer, Spenser, Dryden, and Shakespeare. Though boys might attend a local grammar school and then a preparatory school, girls in colonial New England usually learned to read and do sums from parents at home or from a local dame school. A neighbor, the controversial patriot James Otis, called her his little pupil and often engaged Susanna in conversation. This rural idyll was broken, however, by the onset of the American Revolution.

The Haswells' war experience was typical of many families labeled "Tory" by their neighbors despite attempts to maintain neutrality. Lieutenant Haswell's employment with the Royal Navy placed him under suspicion by his American neighbors, who accused him of communicating with British ships nearing Boston Harbor. In the fall of 1775 the family was forcibly removed from its home and placed under house arrest in Hingham, on the south shore of Boston Harbor, about twelve miles by land from the city. Cut off from his employment and salary, Lieutenant Haswell was promised public assistance for food and firewood, but both sympathy and relief were in short supply during these tense times. Two years later the family was forced to move further inland, to Abingdon, where both Lieutenant Haswell and his wife grew ill. They relied upon young Susanna to find and chop firewood and cook their meager meals. By spring 1778 the Massachusetts legislature had negotiated a prisoner exchange and sent the Haswells to Nova Scotia, where they were allowed to board a boat for England. Susanna Haswell's American childhood had ended, leaving her with memories both bitter and sweet that would find their way into her later novels.

At the age of sixteen, Susanna Haswell and her family joined hundreds of American war refugees in London, waiting for the war to end so that they might either return to their homes and property or gain recompense for it from the British government. Her father, at age forty-four, felt physically and psychologically defeated. His third son, John Montresor, was born while the family lived in London. As years passed and Lieutenant Haswell continued to try to claim retirement pay and compensation, he relied upon his daughter for financial support. But as a young woman in eighteenth-century England, Susanna Haswell had few wage-earning avenues open to her. Women could be seamstresses, hatmakers, ladies' maids, or governesses. All placed women in vulnerable positions, and none earned enough to support a family of six. In her later novels Susanna's fictional heroines face similar situations, forced to seek employment to support themselves and sometimes their aging parents. Despite the apparent hopelessness of their condition, these characters regard work as a valuable, indeed ennobling, middle-class virtue. They enter the working world with pride and enthusiasm. With equal pride and determination they meet its disappointments.

No evidence exists, but it may be supposed that Susanna Haswell became a governess. Her skills qualified her for teaching. She could conduct herself with propriety, converse with charm and intelligence, sing, and sew plain and fancy needlework. She loved books and was as well read as any self-educated woman blessed with a father's moderately good library. Most important, she had a genuine interest in education, especially of girls. In the 1814 preface to *Rebecca; or, The Fille de Chambre*, the author described as autobiographical the scene in which young Rebecca becomes the maligned governess. If Susanna Haswell did take up a position as governess, she did not keep it for long, because her immediate interests rested elsewhere.

In 1786, Susanna Haswell did what many women of the coming decades did to earn money: she wrote a novel. Four years earlier, Fanny Burney had earned £250 for her novel, *Celia*, though more common were the 5- and 10-guinea amounts most booksellers offered authors, especially women. Haswell may have been acquainted with the few women writers in England at the time: Ann Radcliffe (1764–1823), Elizabeth Inchbald (1753–1821), Maria Edgeworth (1767–1849), and Hannah Moore (1745–1833), to name the best known. From the successful writer Samuel Richardson they learned to draw upon the world of the middle class and its values and virtues. Between 1770 and 1800 these women's novels dealt with the world of the home, the farthest reaches being the French convent or a debtors' prison. Haswell's first novel was *Victoria, a Novel. In Two Volumes. The Characters Taken from Real Life, and Calculated to Improve the MORALS OF THE FEMALE SEX, by Impressing Them with a Just Sense of THE MERITS OF FILIAL PIETY* (1786). The plot follows the adventures of young Victoria Baldwin, daughter of a deceased naval officer. Following a standard female-tragedy plot in which seduction is followed by pregnancy and abandonment, the book includes at least five subplots and several brief stories within stories, all of which reinforce the theme of filial piety. Haswell's first publication thus followed recently established conventions of the new genre of fiction. Susanna Haswell had begun what would become a long writing career.

But having been ill treated by the bookseller who bought her manuscript, Haswell found another career more immediately appealing. She was drawn by the lure of the stage. Eighteenth-century London offered a rich variety of popular entertainments, such as the acrobatic exhibitions at Sadler's Wells and Astley's Amphitheater and the pleasure gardens of Vauxhall and Ranelagh. Young Haswell wrote songs for the vocalists at Vauxhall and Ranelagh, discovering in herself a quick talent for light lyrics. More appealing, however, were the theaters, especially Drury Lane and Covent Garden, where American refugees most frequently attended productions. For a shilling or two, Haswell could enjoy a performance that lasted from three-and-one-half to five-and-one-half hours, beginning with music, followed by a five-act play, entr'acte entertainment, and finally an afterpiece of farce or pantomime. Haswell grew intimately acquainted with these theaters and their performers, so intimately that in 1786 she married a minor singer, actor, and trumpeter, William Rowson. The heroine of Haswell's autobiographical novel *Sarah; or, The Exemplary Wife* (1813) describes her decision to marry without love:

> I found I must accede to his proposals, or be thrown on the world, censured by my relations, robbed of my good name, and being poor, open to the pursuits and insults of the profligate. One thing which encouraged me to hope that I might be tolerably happy in this union was—though my heart felt no strong emotions in his favor, it

was totally free from all partiality towards any other. He always appeared good-humored and obliging; and though his mind was not cultivated, I thought time might improve him in that particular.[3]

Though great marital unhappiness lay ahead of her, life with William Rowson at first offered new excitement in a career as public performer. Evidence exists that Susanna Rowson performed with a company of London actors at Brighton in the summer of 1786, and it is likely that she, William, and his sister Elizabeth performed with provincial companies when they could not find opportunities in competitive London. "Strolling players," as they were called, affiliated themselves with towns such as Bath, Norwich, York, Liverpool, Manchester, Bristol, or Newcastle, all under royal patent. Wages ran about thirteen shilling sixpence a week, which compared favorably with those of a laborer, who might earn an average of eight or nine shillings a week, but which seemed paltry in contrast to the hundreds of pounds earned by the favorites of the great London stages.

Neither Susanna nor William evidenced great talent, though of the two, Susanna performed more frequently and in more-significant roles. She supplemented her rather average ability for acting, singing, and pantomime with a conscientious effort to learn her parts and regularly attend rehearsals, behavior that distinguished her from the other performers. Provincial actors were notorious for their inability to act and their disinclination to work, although the demands of learning and performing up to twenty roles at a time might have taxed even the most conscientious. Susanna Rowson refused to stoop to the behavior of most actors, who laughed or swore at the audience and ad-libbed to draw attention to themselves. She made known her standards as well as her evaluation of the most popular performers of the day in her second publication, a thirty-page, lighthearted poem entitled "A Trip to Parnassus" (1788). In couplets of anapestic quatrameters, Rowson describes the approach to Apollo's throne of some thirty-four actors and writers. Without mercy, Apollo either welcomes them with bay leaves and laurels or casts them aside as undeserving of praise. The book shows clearly Rowson's standards of honesty, conventionally moral living, and clean language and behavior on stage. She preferred a natural approach to acting rather than the overly rhetorical and heavy-handed lack of realism that marked most performances at the time.

Four more novels followed: *A Test of Honour* (1789); *Mentoria, or the Young Ladies' Friend* (1791); *Charlotte, a Tale of Truth* (1791); and *Rebecca; or, The Fille de Chambre* (1792). None earned her much money, and the reviews did not encourage her. She continued to act, performing at least once in London in a minor role in 1792. The following year, Susanna, William, and Charlotte, another of William's sisters, journeyed to Edinburgh, where they joined the Theatre Royal company, but the company, beset by competition and financial problems, performed little. The future looked bleak.

In 1793, the Rowsons met Thomas Wignell, who had come to England from the United States to recruit actors for his new Philadelphia theater. The war between England and its colonies had closed American theaters, but by 1793 many had reopened, and Wignell sensed a growing market as a population long deprived of luxuries clamored for entertainment. He hastily enlisted the Rowsons and about fifty others; all boarded a ship scheduled to arrive in Philadelphia that fall. This time, Susanna Rowson's journey was uneventful, but she and the others arrived to find the entire city of Philadelphia shut down with a yellow fever epidemic. Rerouted to New Jersey, the company eventually debuted in Annapolis, Maryland, and finally moved on to Philadelphia in January 1794.

Susanna Rowson took to her new job with the energy that characterized her entire career. She learned and performed thirty-five different roles in the first four-and-one-half-month season. She found American audiences more responsive and enthusiastic than British audiences; Americans threw eggs or rotted fruit when they disliked a performer, and they often interrupted a dull song with demands for "Yankee Doodle." Managers constantly needed new material to provide variety for audiences, who attended several performances a week. Rowson contributed both plays and songs. Music was an inherent part of these stage productions, and Rowson skillfully and quickly wrote lyrics. With her genuine affection for America and its people, she set patriotic themes to rhythmic, catchy lines. Her "America, Commerce, and Freedom" became a popular song for a ballet pantomime.

Rowson also wrote plays. In her first year with the New Theater, as it was called, Rowson wrote two plays based on current political issues, *Slaves in Algiers* and *The Volunteers*. In *Slaves in Algiers* she capitalized on public anger toward Algerian pirates capturing American ships. Though she set the play in Algeria, she had less interest in Algeria than in the subject of tyranny. And Americans, still feeling boastful about their success over Britain's tyranny, responded with enthusiasm. The key word to popularity with such audiences was "liberty," and Rowson stressed it.

> Who barters countrymen, honour, faith, to save
> His life, tho' free in person, is a slave.
> While he, enchan'd, imprison'd tho he be,
> Who lifts his arm for liberty, is free.[4]

With memories still vivid of Americans' fight for liberty, and with feelings about the French Revolution still running high, such lines generated positive reaction. But audiences also responded to Rowson's bold feminism, which she effected by turning the topic of Algerian tyranny to the subject of the tyranny of women. "Woman was never formed to be the abject slave of man. Nature made us equal with them, and gave us the power to render ourselves superior. . . . A woman can face danger with as much spirit, and as little fear as the bravest man amongst you."[5] The character of Fetnah the slave asserts that women, as well as men, love freedom. Fetnah has been a part of the Dey's harem, but once informed of the principles of liberty, she rejects forced "love." She makes fun of the Dey, saying, "He looks so grave and stately, that I declare, if it was not for his huge scymitar, I shou'd burst out a laughing in his face."[6] The phallic symbolism makes clear the forced nature of the sexuality, and the play plainly speaks against tyranny based on sex.

Although Rowson was not the only woman to speak up for women, most people were unaware of intellectuals such as Mary Wollstonecraft, whose *Vindication of the Rights of Women* had been · published in Philadelphia shortly before Rowson's play appeared, or of Abigail Adams's 1776 private request to her husband to "remember the ladies" when forming the new American government. Although *Slaves in Algiers* continued to attract audiences, at least one critic expressed strong objections to it. William Cobbett, an Englishman who had spent some years in France before emigrating to the United States the same year that Rowson arrived, became known as a vitriolic political pamphleteer. His targets included Benjamin Rush, Thomas Paine, Benjamin Franklin, Albert Gallatin, Edmund Randolph, James Monroe, and Susanna Rowson. Cobbett objected to Rowson's overuse of the word "liberty," as well as her grammar and figures of speech. But clearly his real objection lay with her feminism, particularly the couplet from the epilogue:

Women were born for universal sway,
Men to adore, be silent, and obey.

He anticipated, he said, a House of Representatives constituted entirely of women. To discredit Rowson, he intimated that people in the theater behaved adulterously.

Rowson had a defender, however little she may have approved of his defense. John Swanwick, congressman from Pennsylvania, although personally unacquainted with Rowson, wrote a retaliatory pamphlet denying Cobbett's qualification as a critic and insisting that the distinctions between the sexes were primarily based on custom and that a male education would qualify a woman for any of the duties of a man. But Rowson could not have been happy with Swanwick's assertion that Rowson's play was merely "a sally of humor, intended to create a smile, and not to enforce a conviction of women's superiority."[7] Rowson saved her reply for the preface to her next novel, *Trials of the Human Heart* (1794), where she called Cobbett a "loathsome reptile" and his allegations "false and scurrilous." She obviously strenuously objected to his assertion that her patriotism was less than genuine. She felt "equally attached" to both Great Britain and the United States. She declined to reply to Cobbett's objections to feminism, perhaps feeling that her drama had achieved its purpose.

Little remains of the other plays Rowson wrote for the Philadelphia company. *The Volunteers,* performed in 1794, dealt with the Whiskey Rebellion in southwestern Pennsylvania, when farmers resisted the federal excise tax. In defiance of Cobbett's objection to her overuse of the word, the thirteen extant songs for this play exuberantly celebrate "liberty." Also in the same year, the Philadelphia company performed Rowson's *The Female Patriot; or, Nature's Rights,* whose title certainly suggests continuation of the feminist theme begun in *Slaves in Algiers.* Unfortunately, the play has been lost. Two years later the company performed Rowson's *The American Tar; or the Press Gang Defeated,* also now lost. But the list of characters indicated that Rowson wrote parts for her husband and sister-in-law.

Although Rowson gained a small reputation as actress and playwright in Philadelphia, she enjoyed greater prestige as a novelist. Republication of three of her English novels might not have generated much income, but it did provide Rowson with a growing audience. *Rebecca; or, The Fille de Chambre,* apparently without appeal for English audiences, struck a responsive chord in American readers. Perhaps citizens of a youthful country liked the story of a heroine's coming of age, an initiation novel in which the heroine achieves maturity and knowledge of the world. At a time when cartoons and literature depicted the young United States as a woman cast off by a cruel and abusive parent, this story of a young woman abandoned by both her real mother and her female patron aroused nationalistic interest. And possibly the Massachusetts interlude and references to hardships suffered during the American Revolution added further interest for American readers.

But Rowson's greatest success proved to be *Charlotte.* One hundred sixty-one editions have been documented, and the book has remained in print since its 1794 publication. One reason for the novel's success was Rowson's choice of publisher. Mathew Carey had been a publisher and bookseller on Market Street in Philadelphia for six years and had developed effective distribution techniques. Long distances between towns and poor or nonexistent roads had effectively restricted readership of newspapers, magazines, and books. By 1794 communications networks had improved, thereby expanding audiences for all such publications. And among the growing American middle class, women were becoming increasingly literate and even finding a few hours a week of leisure, despite the chores required for family survival or home industry.

Part of *Charlotte*'s appeal is its simple plot. Charlotte, a fifteen-year-old girl in a Chichester boarding school, is persuaded by her dissolute French teacher, Mademoiselle LaRue, to run away to America with a dashing young army officer, Lieutenant Montraville, who claims to love her. Once in New York, Montraville ignores his promise to marry Charlotte and soon falls in love with the beautiful and wealthy Julia Franklin. But his guilt over Charlotte prevents his proposing marriage to Julia. Montraville's false friend, Belcour, who would like to have Charlotte as his own mistress, treacherously convinces Montraville that Charlotte is unfaithful and persuades Charlotte that Montraville has left her for another woman. Pregnant and abandoned, Charlotte is turned out of her lodging and struggles through a snowstorm to seek assistance from her former friend and French teacher, LaRue. But LaRue has found a new lover and refuses to jeopardize her home and social position by helping Charlotte. Finally taken in by some poor servants, Charlotte gives birth to a daughter and goes insane. Her father arrives from England just in time to forgive her before she dies, and he brings home to his heartbroken wife, not their lost daughter, but their orphaned grandchild, Lucy. The novel ends with Belcour's death in a duel, LaRue's dying penniless and alone, and Montraville "to the end of his life subject to fits of melancholy."

The plot thus follows the conventions of the eighteenth-century sentimental novel. It also follows convention by purporting to be "a tale of truth," as fiction still faced opposition among many who thought all literature should be educational and edifying. Those opposing fiction protested that novels were often tales of seduction and incest, hardly "suitable subjects" for young unmarried women, who were assumed to constitute the primary reading audience. Newspapers, magazines, and often the prefaces to novels carried arguments denouncing this claim. Defenders argued that stories of seduced maidens served as moral lessons, severe warnings of the perils posed by the male sex. Others countered that novel reading detracted from hours better spent at spinning, sewing, cooking, or even praying.

In the preface to *Charlotte*, Rowson attested that the story had been told to her by a woman acquainted with a real-life Charlotte and that she as author had merely "thrown over the whole a slight veil of fiction." In none of her previous works had Rowson insisted upon the truth of her fiction, and when she did, many believed her. Fans of the novel soon concluded that the heroine was one Charlotte

Stanley, daughter of the eleventh earl of Derby, and Montraville was in real life John Montresor, Rowson's cousin. Rowson herself never commented upon the veracity of such claims. But evidence does support the conclusion that the character of Montraville derived from the life of Montresor. Within the first year of publication, Mathew Carey issued a second edition. Readers liked it and sometimes bought tickets to the New Theater just to see "Mrs. Rowson." But her success as an actress would never rival her achievement as author of *Charlotte Temple,* as the novel was renamed in 1797.

By 1796 Rowson realized that the New Theater was in financial trouble. Though Wignell continued to meet payrolls, he was beset by a competing theater in the same city, yellow fever outbreaks that closed the theaters, and expenses incurred by the production of operas rather than ordinary plays. Rowson wrote to her half-brother Robert Haswell, who lived in Boston, for advice about the theater prospects there, and soon the Rowsons joined seven other actors in a defection from Philadelphia to a Boston company. Rowson's books had already earned her a reputation in Boston. Her work with immigrant musicians, who often moved from city to city giving lessons, holding concerts, writing music for theatrical productions, and opening music stores, meant that she had friends and connections awaiting her. In Boston she found the right combination of opportunities, people, and shared interests to hold her there for the remaining twenty-seven years of her life. She worked with Williamson's Federal Street Theater Company for only a year, performing and writing songs and at least one more play, before resigning from the theater forever in 1797 and turning to a new career—women's education.

Having experienced the atrocities of war during the American Revolution, Rowson spent her mature years enjoying the benefits of that war and suffering the social upheaval it caused. One effect was a change in the position of women. During the war, women had, of necessity, breached decorum and taken over family businesses or farms for absent or dead husbands. Many women discovered new capabilities and interests but, unable to inherit property or businesses, felt shackled by restrictive laws that gave them virtually no rights. After the war, women's diaries, letters, poems, essays, and plays such as Rowson's asked for "freedom," "liberty," even "equal rights." Such requests generated discussions of women's inferiority, equality, or superiority, which led to debates about women's educability. Into this discourse entered Susanna Rowson. But Rowson did more than talk: she acted.

Boston in 1797 had no schools for girls. Many girls still learned to read and write at dame schools. The Boston Act of 1789 stipulated that girls and boys be taught the same subjects, but girls were required to attend school for fewer hours per day and fewer months per year than boys. Yet the public desire for education for females had been shown just two years earlier, when the American Philosophical Society sponsored a contest on the topic of American educational improvements. Every submission had included a proposal for universal free education, that is, education open to all white men and women. Bostonians were ready for a woman's academy, and in November 1797 Rowson launched "Mrs. Rowson's Young Ladies' Academy." The school opened with three pupils; in a year it enrolled one hundred.

Despite the controversy over women's education, public opinion still held that intellectual accomplishments were inappropriate and perhaps unattainable for women. Many feared that a woman educated as a man was educated would abandon her proper sphere; a female pedant would never be a careful housekeeper. Few defied such assumptions outright. Even the most radical, such as the outspoken character of Mrs. Carter in Charles Brockden Brown's novel *Alcuin* (1797), never assumed that women should give up making puddings and nursing babies. But Rowson felt strongly about women's need to learn practical subjects, and her first curriculum consisted of reading, writing, arithmetic, geography, and needlework. Girls' schools founded later in other cities might include "accomplishments" such as painting on velvet and singing in Italian, but Rowson sought a more serious education for her girls. Still, her love of music and her desire to attract daughters of the best families led her to add lighter and more enjoyable subjects to her curriculum. In 1799 she bought a pianoforte, an instrument still exotic enough to merit newspaper notice, and called upon her theatrical colleague, Mr. R. Laumont, to teach music. She added dancing lessons and sometimes joined her students in the classes, where they found her "a light and pretty dancer." Rowson moved her academy several times, first to Medford, then to Newton, then back to Boston, each time improving and enlarging her facilities.

Rowson's love of performance led her to hold "exhibitions," public demonstrations of her students' talents. Students displayed their maps and needlework and read aloud their own poems, dialogues, or essays or they read works written by Susanna Rowson. These exhibitions were open to parents and the public and indeed became so popular that Rowson profited by charging fifty cents admission. The *Boston Weekly Magazine* reviewed the events. By 1811 the most popular part of the program had become the "female biographies," in which each student recounted a memorized account of a woman from ancient or modern history. Each woman's life exemplified her equality with, if not superiority to, men. The students looked forward to these annual presentations. Although women speaking in public often met with disapproval, Rowson offered no apologies and continued her student exhibitions throughout the history of the academy. She collected some of these demonstration pieces and published them as *A Present for Young Ladies.* The book characterizes the school as an institution where girls and young women learned self-respect, the importance of education, and confidence in the abilities of women.

Throughout her lifetime, Susanna and William remained married, even though William seldom held steady employment and the academy pupils often laughed privately at his obvious drunkenness. William's debts and the mortgage he took on the Hollis Street property caused Susanna Rowson grief and worry during her last years, as she was unable to pay the mortgage. The couple never had children, but some evidence exists that Susanna raised William's illegitimate son. Although childless herself, she informally adopted at least one girl and cared for her pupils as her own. She was fondly remembered by her pupils, whose letters describe her as a strict but caring headmistress.

No matter how great the other demands on her, Rowson always found time to continue her writing. In addition to novels and poetry, Rowson published textbooks. *An Abridgement of Universal Geography* (1805) included her own moral judgments of peoples, religions, and cultures, for no student, teacher, or critic at the time would have valued objectivity in the study of history or geography. She expressed disapproval of slavery, both in the United States and elsewhere; tyranny, whether religious (as in the Catholic Church), political, or otherwise; laziness, induced by warm climates; and immoral behavior, especially among political leaders. She included a section of "Geographical Exercises" reflective of her own fascination with navigation, with graduated exercises designed to teach girls rudimentary principles such as how to find the latitude and the longitude of a place and how, given the latitude and longitude of a place, to find it. Clearly, Rowson expected her students to learn more than mending and simple arithmetic. Even her youngest pupils, the audience for her *Youth's First Steps in Geography* (1818), were expected to learn maps of their state, country, and the world, as well as elementary navigation principles.

Rowson's *Spelling Dictionary* (1807) shows a pedagogical approach remarkably ahead of her time. She wanted to help students associate ideas and to think, not merely memorize. She sought to keep each lesson short and to help students see the rationality for learning, not simply feel forced to learn. Her *Exercises in History, Chronology, and Biography* (1822) included biographies of women, which shows that Rowson read history to find role models for her students. Her last text, *Biblical Dialogues* (1822), written when she had become ill and increasingly interested in religion, placed complex Bible stories within a narrative framework designed to appeal to young readers.

Though Rowson's later fiction never achieved the popularity of *Charlotte Temple*, she continued to entertain her reading audience with *Reuben and Rachel; or, Tales of Old Times* (1798) and a serialized novel, *Sincerity* (1803–1804). A sequel to *Charlotte Temple* appeared posthumously as *Charlotte's Daughter; or, The Three Orphans* (1828). But nothing touched the hearts of the American reading public like *Charlotte Temple*. Nineteenth-century editions added illustrations, including portraits of Charlotte and scenes from the novel. Some illustrations even depicted scenes that were not in the novel, such as a young woman leaning against a tombstone. Readers known as the "Charlotte cult" believed in the literal truth of the novel, as newspapers printed portraits of Charlotte and popular lore identified her house in New York on the corner of Pell and Doyers Streets. Charlotte's gravesite in Trinity Churchyard became the object of pilgrimages for the romantic. Nineteenth-century dramatic versions, such as one published by Charlotte Pixley Plumb in 1899, freely omitted much of the plot, added and deleted characters, and changed both action and dialogue. The novel remained in print for well over a hundred years. Today it is still available in paperback and continues to hold the interest of students in college literature courses.

Rowson died March 2, 1824, after a two-year illness. She was interred in the Gottlieb Graupner family vault in St. Matthew's Church, South Boston. When the church was demolished in 1866, her remains were transferred to Mt. Hope Cemetery in Dorchester, Massachusetts, and a granite monument was erected later in Forest Hills Cemetery, Roxbury, by her descendants, Mary and Haswell C. Clarke and Ellen Murdock Osgood. After his wife's death, William Rowson again mortgaged the Hollis Street house and land, remarried, and lived until 1843.

Susanna Rowson was a prolific writer, producing over her lifetime ten novels, six theatrical works, six textbooks, two collections of poems, and countless songs. As she lived during a crucial period during the nation's history, her writings reflect the taste and interest of the people of the new American Republic, who struggled to decide how to live with their acquired independence. Her life also demonstrates the way in which people who earned their livelihoods in the arts during this early federal period crossed boundaries freely from one field to another, considering themselves artists and entertainers, not merely playwrights or actors, novelists or lyricists. And Rowson's career change from entertainer to headmistress epitomizes the popular emphasis on women's education that characterized American debate at the turn of the century. Rowson thus seems a transition figure, a bridge between women of the colonial period and women of the nineteenth century. Though she never achieved wealth or great fame in her lifetime, she continues to hold reader interest today.

Notes

1. Susanna Haswell Rowson, *Rebecca; or, The Fille de Chambre* (Philadelphia: H. and T. Rice, 1794), 161.
2. Ibid., 116.
3. Susanna Haswell Rowson, *Sarah; or, The Exemplary Wife* (Boston: Charles Williams, 1813), 4.
4. Susanna Haswell Rowson, *Slaves in Algiers; or, A Struggle for Freedom* (Philadelphia: Wrigley and Berriman, 1794), 1.
5. Ibid., 9, 47.
6. Ibid., 39.
7. Susanna Haswell Rowson, *A Rub from Snub* (Philadelphia: Wrigley and Berriman, 1795), 76.

Suggested Readings

Letters from Rowson's family and students are found in the Barrett Collection at the University of Virginia, Charlottesville, Virginia. A complete bibliography of Rowson's writings was published in 1933 by R. W. G. Vail and the American Antiquarian Society in Worcester, Massachusetts. Vail documents 161 editions of *Charlotte Temple*. Most recently the novel has been edited by Cathy Davidson and published by Oxford University Press (1986). Of all Rowson's writings, only *Charlotte Temple* and *Charlotte's Daughter* are in print today. The only book-length biography, with an accompanying bibliography, is Patricia Parker's *Susanna Rowson*, published in Boston by Twayne (1986). There is another book-length study, Dorothy Weil's *In Defense of Women*, published by Pennsylvania State University Press (1976). Earlier biographies include Francis W. Halsey's Historical and Biographical Introduction to *Charlotte Temple: A Tale of Truth*, by Susanna Rowson (New York: Funk and Wagnalls, 1904), and Samuel Lorenzo Knapp's "A Memoir of the Author" in *Charlotte's Daughter; or, The Three Orphans. A Sequel to Charlotte Temple,* by Susanna Rowson (Boston: Richardson and Lord, 1828). Critical articles include Cathy Davidson's chapter, *"Charlotte Temple,"* in *Reading in America: Literature and Social History*, ed. Cathy Davidson (Baltimore: Johns Hopkins University Press, 1989); Blythe Forcey's "*Charlotte Temple* and the End of Epistolarity," in *American Literature* 63 (1991): 225–41; and Klaus Hansen's "The Sentimental Novel and Its Feminist Critique" in *Early American Literature* 26 (1991): 39–54.

3

Sacagawea
A Historical Enigma

Laura McCall

In 1804, Meriwether Lewis and William Clark hired Toussaint Charbonneau to serve as an interpreter for their epic journey up the Missouri River, across the Rocky Mountains, to the Pacific Ocean, and back. Charbonneau was a forty-five-year-old French Canadian who had lived in Indian country for at least ten years. He had many shortcomings but could interpret the languages of the river tribes: the Mandan, Arikara, Hidatsa, and Sioux.[1] With him was his fifteen-year-old pregnant wife, Sacagawea (ca. 1788 or 1789–1812, 1869, or 1884), whom he had either purchased from her captors or won in a game of chance.

Sacagawea, a Lemhi Shoshone, became an indispensable member of the Corps of Discovery and was essential to its success. At opportune moments, she acted as a guide, and without "her services as a translator, the expedition would have failed." As sister to Shoshone chief Cameahwait, she enabled the corps to obtain the horses needed to cross the Rocky Mountains and fostered cordial relations between Lewis and Clark and her people. She assured the safety of the group on numerous occasions because "her mere presence, with her baby, was a guarantee to strange Indians that this was not a war party."[2] She foraged for food when the corps was starving and, in less desperate times, supplemented their carnivorous diet with roots and berries. Without Sacagawea, the men of the Lewis and Clark Expedition would have either perished or been forced to turn back and the history of the United States could have been significantly different.

Sacagawea is one the few historical actors widely recognized by the general public. *Collier's Encyclopedia* (1976) calls her "a national heroine; there are more statues [erected] to her than to any other American woman." Gary Moulton, one of the premier scholars of the expedition, proclaims Sacagawea "the most famous member of the party after the two leaders themselves."[3] She is the first woman after Susan B. Anthony to be depicted on a U.S. coin.

Laura McCall wishes to thank James Drake, Stephen J. Leonard, John Monnett, and Katherine Osburn for comments on an earlier draft.

Despite her popular renown, Sacagawea remains an enigma. Although volumes crowd library bookshelves and she is beatified in novels and film, she is chronicled only in the writings of expedition members whose journals are extant. The academic community debates the spelling, pronunciation, and precise meaning of her name. Etymologists and historians accept Sacagawea; novelists prefer Sacajawea; inhabitants of the Dakotas favor Sakakawea. In the Hidatsa language, the word means Bird Woman. In Shoshone, it means Boat Pusher or Boat Launcher.[4]

Sacagawea is rarely named in the journals but instead is referred to as "the Squar" or "the Indian woman." Patrick Gass, who produced two lengthy and detailed logs, was uninterested in Sacagawea—he never mentioned her by name and called her only "the interpreter's wife." Gass failed to recount Sacagawea's heroic efforts when the flagship of the expedition nearly overturned, referring only to "the men who had been on board." He overlooked the incident when Sacagawea identified moccasins foreign to her people as well as the two occasions when Sacagawea fell gravely ill. On June 29, 1805, when Clark, Charbonneau, Sacagawea, and her infant, Jean-Baptiste, nearly perished in a flash flood, Gass merely described "another heavy shower of rain" after which Captain Lewis returned to camp, "drenched with rain." Gass passed over Sacagawea's remarkable meeting with her brother. On November 8, 1805, when several of the men and Sacagawea became ill while crossing a bay, he wrote, "Some of our men got sea sick, the swells were so great."[5] How could a voyager who was in daily and close contact with the only woman on the expedition be so detached and indifferent?

The other chroniclers responded similarly. Sacagawea is most often described in relation to her usefulness to the Voyage of Discovery—she saved precious instruments, gathered food, recognized important geographical signposts, interpreted on numerous occasions. With few exceptions, the diaries reveal little about her opinions, personality, or character. Rarely do her thoughts, feelings, or reactions to the journey surface. Sacagawea essentially lacks her own voice.

Some of this omission is owing to the nature of the expedition and the primary purpose of journal keeping. Even though William Clark regarded the corps as his "Band of Brothers," this voyage was not conducted for male identification, and rarely do any of the journals display deep introspection or ruminations about personality and character. Sacagawea was not the only member of the expedition about whom scholars know painfully little. The French engagés—men who signed on as guides, translators, and hunters—also received scanty attention.[6] This was the Age of Enlightenment, not Romanticism; the chroniclers were gathering scientific data and ethnographic information about Native Americans while attempting to establish trading networks. The general tone in these journals is clinical, not sentimental. Sacagawea was born in 1788 or 1789 in present-day Idaho within the shadows of the Continental Divide. Little is known about the lifeways or culture of her people, for prior to Lewis and Clark, their only contact with Euro-Americans had been indirectly with the Spanish to the south.

Meriwether Lewis recorded contradictory impressions about Lemhi women: Although the men "treat their women but with little rispect, and compel them to perform every species of drudgery, . . . [the] women are held more sacred among them than any nation we have seen and appear to have an equal Shere in all conversation, which is not the Case in any other nation I have seen."[7]

Demitri Shimkin, who studies the Eastern Shoshone, reports that a young woman's marriage was arranged "shortly after menarche." Her relatives "sought a good hunter, a stable and reliable although often much older man." Lewis reported similarly. Infant daughters were promised to grown men or "to men who have sons for whom they think proper to provide wives. . . . the girl remains with her parents until she is conceived to have obtained the age of puberty which with them is considered to be about the age of 13 or 14 years. the female at this age is surrendered to her sovereign lord and husband agreeably to contract." Sacagawea, a Northern Shoshone, had been promised before her capture and before "she had arrived to years of puberty. the husband . . . was more than double her age and had two other wives. he claimed her as his wife but said that as she had had a child by another man, who was Charbono [Charbonneau], that he did not want her."[8]

When Sacagawea was ten or eleven, members of her tribe ventured to the Three Forks region in present-day Montana, where a band of armed Hidatsa (Minitari or Gros Ventres) warriors launched an attack. Sacagawea later told Meriwether Lewis that the Shoshone braves, who were outnumbered and without guns, "mounted their horses and fled as soon as the attack began. The women and children, who had been berry-picking, dispersed, and Sacagawea, as she was crossing a shoal place, was overtaken in the middle of the river by her pursuers." Sacagawea dwelled with the Hidatsa until she was purchased or won by Charbonneau. The couple was living in the Mandan village in present-day North Dakota when Lewis and Clark decided to construct nearby Fort Mandan for their winter headquarters. On November 4, 1804, the captains and Charbonneau entered into a verbal arrangement by which the French trader would interpret among the Hidatsa. Later *Journal* entries indicate the interpreter's wife would translate for the Shoshone.[9]

On February 11, 1805, Sacagawea gave birth to Jean-Baptiste Charbonneau, "the indestructible baby," who would accompany the expedition across the continent and back. In the first detailed reference to Sacagawea, Captain Lewis observed that "one of the wives of Charbonneau was delivered of a fine boy. It is worthy of remark that this was the first child which this woman had born, and as is common in such cases her labor was tedious and the pain violent."[10] A scant two months later, the young mother and her sturdy infant departed on a seventeen-month journey that took them to the shores of the Pacific and back. Assessing Sacagawea's role in the Lewis and Clark Expedition remains the subject of lively debate. Perceptions of her significance have waxed and waned over the past two hundred years and have often reflected prevailing attitudes toward women. In the renderings of late-nineteenth- and early-twentieth-century scholars and during a period when the women's rights movement was in ascendance, Sacagawea directed Lewis and Clark across the Northern Plains and Rocky Mountains. As interpreter, guide, and ambassador to several Indian nations, she single-handedly ensured the success of the Corps of Discovery.[11] She thus provided feminists with a symbol of the strong, accomplished woman.

Mid- to late-twentieth-century scholars of the expedition, however, are not so favorably inclined. In their opinion, Sacagawea's service as a guide was minimal and that of interpreter was limited to a few specific incidents. She was an unessential member of the corps, which would have succeeded without her contributions.[12] The journals, however, indicate otherwise.

On May 14, 1805, for example, the flagship containing most of the corps's irreplaceable possessions filled with water and nearly overturned. On board were the papers, instruments, books, medicine, seed specimens, gunpowder, and culinary implements—in short, "almost every article indispensibly necessary to further the views, or insure the success of the enterprize in which we are now launched to the distance of 2200 miles." Sacagawea, in rapidly rushing and frigid waters and with her baby in tow, managed to catch and preserve most of the staples that were washed overboard. Lewis, who never warmed to Sacagawea, on this day ascribed to the "Indian woman . . . equal fortitude and resolution with any person on board at the time of the accident." Were it not for her alacrity and with "the essentials of their equipment lost, they would have had to turn back."[13]

Consider Sacagawea's contributions to the men's diet and health. The Corps of Discovery was in the wilderness, burning calories from exertion and cold and periodically on the verge of starvation. Sacagawea provided food on numerous occasions. On April 9, 1805, Lewis noted that "when we halted for dinner the squaw busied herself in serching for the wild artichokes which the mice collect and deposit in large hoards. this operation she performed by penetrating the earth with a sharp stick. . . . her labor soon proved successful, and she procurrd a good quantity of these roots." They were Jerusalem artichokes, strong perennials, but neither artichokes nor from Jerusalem. Also known as the Canada potato, they were one of the edible tubers widely cultivated by North American Indians.[14]

As historian Stephen Ambrose has observed, these roots were "welcome" because the expedition's hunters had been unable to procure meat. On April 30, 1805, Clark noted that "the Squar found & brought me a bush Something like the Current, which She Said bore a delicious froot and that great quantities grew on the Rocky Mountains." On May 8, "the Squar Geathered on the Sides of the hills wild Lickerish, & the white apple . . . and gave me to eat, the Indians of the Missouri make great use of the white apple dressed in differnt ways." In July, while at the Three Forks of the Missouri, Lewis saw where the natives had peeled the bark off the pine trees, upon which "the indian woman with us informs that they do to obtain the sap and soft part of the wood and bark for food."[15]

Sacagawea's foraging enabled the group to supplement their virtually all-meat diet and thereby prevent scurvy and other forms of malnutrition. On August 16, 1805, Joseph Whitehouse noted that the Indian woman "gathered a pale full [of service berries] & gave them to the party at noon." John Ordway declared they were "the largest & best I ever Saw." Sacagawea was also a fisherwoman. On at least one occasion, while recovering from a serious illness, "she has been walking about and fishing."[16]

At Fort Clatsop, Oregon Country, the corps spent a particularly miserable winter, cherishing a mere twelve days without rain and only six days of sunshine. Food was scarce and often moldy. So was their leather clothing, which was literally disintegrating off their backs. Sacagawea helped the men mend their old clothes and moccasins and tan leather for new attire. She relinquished her precious belt of blue beads for two otter skins. On November 30, 1805, she generously gave Clark "a piece of bread made of flour She had reserved for her child and carefully Kept untill this time, which has unfortunately got wet, and a little Sour—this bread I eate with great Satisfaction, it being the only mouthfull I had tasted for Several months past." On December 3, Clark twice recorded that after the marrow from the shank bones of an elk had been extracted, "the Squar chped the bones fine boiled them and extracted a pint of Grease, which is Superior to the tallow of the animal" and necessary for oiling boots and guns.[17] On Christmas Day, she bestowed upon Clark two dozen white weasel tails.

During the return journey, "Sahcargarmeah geathered a quantity of the roots of a speceis of fennel which we found very agreeable
food, the flavor of this root is not unlike annis seed." Clark reported
similarly on the same day and on May 18, 1806, wrote that the
"Squar wife to Shabono busied her Self gathering the roots of the
fenel Called by the Snake Indians Year-pah for the purpose of dry-
ing to eate on the Rocky mountains. those roots are very paliatiable
either fresh rosted boiled or dried and are generally between the
Size of a quill and that of a mans fingar and abut the length of the
latter." The men, who had been complaining of headache and intes-
tinal gas, found that these roots "dispell the wind . . . and adds much
to the comfort of our diet." On June 25, 1806, Clark remarked that
"the squaw collected a parcel of roots which the Shoshones Eat. it is
a small knob root a good deel in flavour and consistency like the
Jerusolem artichoke." Not only had Sacagawea again provided a
nutritious supplement to the corps' edibles, but she also brought a
new botanical item to the attention of the captains. As Gary Moulton points out, the "species was unknown to science at the time, and
Lewis collected the type specimen two days later." On August 9,
1806, Clark reported that the "Squar brought me a large and well
flavoured Goose berry of a rich Crimsin Colour, and deep purple
berry of the large Cherry of the Current Speces."[18]

Her skills as an interpreter merit greater recognition. Clearly,
Lewis and Clark recruited Charbonneau because Sacagawea could
converse with the mountain tribes and thereby assist in obtaining
horses. Her importance as a prospective translator was clearly
revealed when, on June 16, 1805, she fell gravely ill. Clark bled her
and Lewis gave her a mixture of bark and laudanum. In a telling
journal entry, Lewis expressed his selfish anxieties as to whether
she would recover and lead them to the Shoshone. Her indisposition
"gave me some concern, as well for the poor object herself—then
with a young child in her arms—as from the consideration of her
being our only dependence for a friendly negotiation with the Snake
Indians, on whom we depend for horses to assist us in our portage
from the Missouri to the Columbia River."[19]

On August 13, Lewis and his band encountered sixty warriors
including the Shoshone chief, Cameahwait. Sacagawea, traveling
with Clark, was not reunited with her people until the morning of
August 17. She first greeted Jumping Fish, who had received her
name while bounding across a stream to escape the Hidatsa in the
raid that captured Sacagawea. Their tearful reunion was cut short
by an impatient Meriwether Lewis, who needed horses and petu-
lantly called the "interpretress" into council. There she began to
translate from Shoshone into Minnetaree, Charbonneau from Minnetaree into French, and François Labiche (half French and half

Omaha) into English for the captains. Suddenly, she sprang up in astonishment. In one of the most remarkable reunions in history, she recognized her brother, Cameahwait. "[S]he jumped up, ran & embraced him, & threw her blanket over him and cried profusely."[20] They visited briefly before the resumption of negotiations.

At Cameahwait's village, Sacagawea confirmed through the translation chain that the crossing to the Pacific was going to be arduous and would require Shoshone horses and a guide. On August 25, Lewis learned from Charbonneau that Sacagawea had overheard her brother tell members of the tribe to prepare for travel to the buffalo country east of Lemhi Pass rather than help the corps portage west across the mountains. Had that happened, "Lewis and his men would have literally been left high and dry, halfway up Lemhi Pass, with only a dozen or so horses, and no guide for the Nez Perce trail." Lewis shamed Cameahwait into keeping his original promise, although, over the next several days, the price of horses rose precipitously.[21]

Sacagawea's interpreting skills proved unexpectedly invaluable while the group wintered in the Pacific Northwest. During a visit with the Walla Walla Indians and their chief, Yellept, the captains were, thanks to Sacagawea, able to parley in ways other than sign language. As Clark reported on April 29, 1806, "We found a Sho Shone woman, prisoner among those people by means of whome and Sah-cah-gah-weah, Shabono's wife we found means of Converceing with the Wallahwallars. We Conversed with them for Several hours and fully Satisfy all their enquiries with respect to our Selves and the Object of our pursute. they were much pleased." With the aid of Sacagawea's translations, Lewis learned that several members of the tribe required medical assistance. He treated a man seriously afflicted with rheumatism, another with a broken arm, and many with sore eyes. In return, the expedition left with twenty-three horses, most of them "excellent," and a shortcut that saved them approximately eighty miles.[22] Once more, Sacagawea had served them well.

Between May 14 and June 10, while in the company of the Nez Percé, the captains again benefited from Sacagawea's interpretive skills. In an almost daylong meeting, a young male Shoshone captive enabled the parties to communicate in a translation chain that tediously passed through Nez Percé, Shoshone, Hidatsa, French, English, and back. The captains explained to the principal chiefs "their intention of establishing tradeing houses for their relief, their wish to restore peace and harmony among the nativs, the Strength welth and powers of our Nation &c." Lewis concluded that "they appeared highly pleased."[23]

Although she was enlisted as an interpreter, Sacagawea inadvertently served the corps as ambassador and guide. On July 22,

1805, her abilities as a keen observer first emerged: "The Indian woman recognizes the country and assures us that this is the river on which her relations live, and that the three forks are at no great distance. this peice of information has cheered the sperits of the party who now begin to console themselves with the anticipation of shortly seeing the head of the missouri yet unknown to the civilized world." Four days later, the voyagers camped at the site of Saca-gawea's capture. On August 8, Lewis reported that "the Indian woman recognized the point of a high plain to our right which she informed us was not very distant from the summer retreat of her nation on a river beyond the mountains which runs to the west. . . . she assures us that we shall either find her people on this river or on the river immediately west of it's source; which from it's present size cannot be very distant. as it is now all important with us to meet with those people as soon as possible."[24] Sacagawea's percep-tive guiding came none too soon, for the weather was getting cold. In the days that followed, Sacagawea continued to assure Lewis and Clark they were in her country. She also provided critical geograph-ical information and confirmed they were nearing the headwaters of the Missouri and thus the Continental Divide, where they encoun-tered Cameahwait's band.

Why Sacagawea accompanied the expedition to the western coast remains unclear. Neither Lewis nor Clark alludes to the rea-sons for her continuation, and it seems odd she would leave her people after less than three weeks. No one anticipated that her interpretative services would be needed after the corps passed through the mountains with their Shoshone guide, Toby. Nor could she recognize any landmarks. Anthropologist Clara Sue Kidwell asserts that as "a captive and the wife of a white man, she no longer had a place within the social structure of her own tribe." Charbon-neau and the corps "were now Sacagawea's main reference points. Having been removed from her tribe, she could not go back; indeed, she may have chosen freely not to go back." Anthropologist Rayna Green surmises that a "good" Indian woman "must defy her own peo-ple, exile herself from them, become white, and perhaps suffer death." Stephen Ambrose, in contrast, speculates "that the question [of] whether she should stay with the expedition never came up, that she was by now so integral a member of the party that it was taken for granted that she would remain with it."[25]

Nevertheless, Sacagawea proved invaluable on this leg of the journey. While floating down the Snake and Columbia Rivers, both captains commented upon how Sacagawea's presence calmed the fears of the Northwestern tribes. During the second week of October, Clark attributed the Indians' sudden friendliness to the "wife of Shabono our interpetr [who] we find reconsiles all the Indians, as to our friendly intentions a woman with a party of men is a token of peace." On October 19, 1805, Clark recounted a mildly tense moment that was mitigated when Sacagawea appeared and the Walla Walla "immidiately all came out and appeared to assume new life, the sight of This Indian woman, wife to one of our interprs. confirmed those people of our friendly intentions, as no woman ever accompanies a war party of Indians in this quarter."

On their eastward return, Sacagawea unquestionably proved her value as a guide. When the corps reentered Shoshone country, she was the first to orient and confirm they were on the right trail. On July 6, 1806, John Ordway noted that "our Intrepters wife tells us that She knows the country & that this branch is the head waters of jeffersons river &C. we proceeded on down the branch." Clark reported that "the Indian woman wife to Shabono informed that she had been in this plain frequently and knew it well that the Creek which we decended was a branch of Wisdom river and when we assended the higher part of the plain we would discover a gap in the mountains in our direction to the Canoes, and when we arived at that gap we would See a high point of a mountain covered with snow in our direction to the canoes. . . . The Squar pointed to the gap through which she said we must pass which was S. 56° E. She said we would pass the river before we reached the gap."

On July 13, 1806, in what is now southwestern Montana, William Clark had to decide between Flathead and Bozeman Passes. Sacagawea recommended the latter and better choice—Bozeman Pass is lower—and she earned Clark's praise: "The indian woman who has been of great Service to me as a pilot through this Country recommends a gap in the mountain more South which I shall cross."[26]

In the following month, the Lewis and Clark Expedition descended to the Mandan village, where, on August 17, Sacagawea, Charbonneau, and Jean-Baptiste parted with the Corps of Discovery. Charbonneau was paid $500.33. Sacagawea, who had been far more useful, received nothing except a few revealing compliments from William Clark. In a letter thanking Charbonneau for his services, Clark recognized Sacagawea's importance when he commended "your woman, who accompanied you that long and dangerous and fatiguing route to the Pacific Ocian and back, deserved a greater reward for her attention and service on that route than we had in our power to give her at the Mandans."[27]

In 1810, Charbonneau and Sacagawea moved to St. Louis, obtained property, and attempted to settle down. The restless Charbonneau transferred his lands to Clark and returned to the wilderness, where he served as an interpreter and purveyor. He died in the early 1840s.[28]

Jean-Baptiste, whom Clark affectionately referred to as Pomp or Pompey, was educated in St. Louis, traveled through Europe in the 1820s as the protégé of Prince Paul of Württemberg, and came back to America in 1829 fluent in German, French, Spanish, and English. He returned to the West, where he served as a hunter, trapper, guide, and excellent cook. Sources place his death in Oregon in 1866 or Wyoming in 1885.[29]

After Charbonneau's departure from St. Louis in 1810, Sacagawea's life clouds. The most widely accepted theory has her accompanying her husband up the Missouri River and dying in childbirth in 1812 at Manuel Lisa's trading post in present-day South Dakota. A second hypothesis asserts Sacagawea was killed near Glascow, Montana, in 1869 during an Indian skirmish. A man claiming to be her grandson testified "in open council where other Indians could hear and correct his story."[30]

The third version, derived from Shoshone oral tradition, describes an elderly squaw named "Sacajawea" or "Porivo" who had knowledge of minute details of the Voyage of Discovery. According to this rendition, Sacagawea separated from Charbonneau after he wed a Ute woman while the couple was living in the Southwest. Sacagawea joined the Comanche and married a warrior named Jerk Meat. The Nez Percé attest that after his death in battle, she made her way back to Fort Washakie on the Wind River Shoshone Reservation in Wyoming and settled with her adopted son, Bazil. She died on April 9, 1884.

According to the Shoshone, Jean-Baptiste died in 1885. Bazil, who died the following year, was buried with papers purportedly proving that the woman who died in 1884 had accompanied the Lewis and Clark Expedition. When his body was exhumed in 1925, the evidence had decomposed.[31]

Even in death, therefore, Sacagawea remains a mystery. The exact timing and placement of her demise, however, provide historians with another issue for further study. As Americans approach the bicentennial of this pathbreaking journey, interest in Sacagawea and her fellow voyagers will most likely intensify. Along with the renewed curiosity are debates within the profession regarding the use of oral history as valid historical evidence.

Many scholars dismiss Native American oral traditions because they are not part of a written record, are often not arranged in a linear fashion, can be recited decades after the events under scrutiny, and do not "conform to Western standards of historical analysis and writing." Yet as Dakota scholar Angela Cavender Wilson observes, students of Native American studies need to "understand the power of the spoken word and to incorporate native oral traditions into American history." Wilson describes the vigorous and extensive training required of youth as they assume the task of preserving the stories of their people, concluding that "the ability to remember [and verbalize those memories is as much] an acquired skill" as is the white ability to record.[32] The precise placement of Sacagawea's death provides historians with an opportunity to ponder the validity of oral history.

A serious question for feminist scholars concerns the cultural baggage the expedition's journalists carried with them to the Far West. Were their judgments of Native American women informed by attitudes toward white women, such as the colonial helpmate, the "republican mother" of the Revolutionary era, or the true woman of the early nineteenth century? Were their points of view influenced by stereotypes of Native American women, which included the enchanting princess or the degraded squaw?[33] Although the chroniclers commented upon the various Native American women encountered on their journey—they were particularly interested in their dress, their physiques, their sexual customs, and their work habits—in these respects they were mysteriously silent about Sacagawea.

Their reticence merits analysis. Her proximity made her the perfect ethnographic study, but they did not turn her into a specimen. Had the young wife and mother taken on a human form? Were they protecting this unique individual from intense future scrutiny? Whereas they could generalize about the anonymous men and women whom they briefly visited, Sacagawea lived with the corps for one and one-half years. She fed them, translated for them, provided gifts for some, and assured the safety of all. Did they come to care for her?

Two illustrative incidents occurred when the corps reached Oregon. In the first, the captains had to decide whether to build their winter stockade near the soggy coast or farther upriver. In an unusual move, they put the decision to a vote. Clark registered the opinions of every member of the party, including his slave York and Sacagawea, whom he affectionately called Janey. At Fort Clatsop, the corps learned that a whale lay beached on the shores of the Pacific. A party of a dozen men made preparations for the five-day journey, and Sacagawea insisted upon going. "She observed that She had traveled a long way with us to See the great waters, and that now that monstrous fish was also to be Seen. She thought it verry hard that She Could not be permitted to See either (She had never yet been to the Ocian)." She "was therefore indulged."[34] Sacagawea's ability to have her way reveals her power and agency. This episode not only illustrates her assertiveness but marked recognition on the part of the men—they knew they owed her for her innumerable contributions.

Finally, can modern-day analysts reasonably blame or credit Sacagawea for the opening of the West to white settlement? In 1905 in Portland, Oregon, Susan B. Anthony lauded "the assistance rendered by a woman in the discovery of this great section of the country." Anna Howard Shaw termed her a "forerunner of civilization." Eva Emory Dye claimed she "led the way to a new time. To the hands of this girl . . . had been entrusted the key that unlocked the road to Asia." In 1942, Donald Peattie credited Sacagawea with adding five stars to the American flag.[35] Donna Kessler, in her intriguing book *The Making of Sacagawea*, hints at evidence that potentially holds Sacagawea responsible for, or at the least a major actor in, the opening of the West to white settlers, soldiers, and traders. Had it not been for Sacagawea, the mission most likely would have failed.[36] How would that have affected the status of the Oregon Country, which was simultaneously claimed by Great Britain, Russia, and the United States? How does this square with the "legacy of conquest" theories of the New Western Historians, who accuse rapacious whites of sundering native cultures? How does their revisionist model account for the possibility that a Native American woman participated in the opening of the West?

Clara Sue Kidwell contends that "Indian women were the first important mediators of meaning between the cultures of two worlds. . . . Explicitly, their actions led finally to the loss of Indian land and to destructive changes in Indian culture. But implicitly, they acted from motives that were determined by their own cultures."[37] Native American women served as intermediaries between their own tribes and others, often deciding the fate of captives and entrusting them to their care. Thus, it was only natural for women to serve as central agents in the fur trade, providing white men with important entrées into their tribes and ensuring male success through female labor and diplomacy. Sacagawea's essential assistance to Lewis and Clark was an extension of this intermediary role.

The year 2005 will mark the bicentennial of the meeting between Lewis, Clark, and Sacagawea. Considering all that has been written and filmed about this extraordinary woman, what do scholars actually know? She is not self-defined but described through others. Her name is in dispute. So, too, are the time and place of her death. Why have scholars underplayed her important contributions to the expedition? Is it valid to hold a fifteen-year-old Native American woman responsible for the opening of the West, the destruction of tribal ways of life, and environmental degradation? Was she, like Christopher Columbus, merely the first? If she had not lent her assistance to the expedition, would someone with comparable abilities have? Or were her myriad skills—as a food gatherer, interpreter, guide, and symbol of peace—unsurpassable and unmatchable? Sacagawea compels us to ponder these questions.

Notes

1. Irving W. Anderson, "A Charbonneau Family Portrait," *American West* 17 (March–April 1980): 4–13, 58–64.

2. Sacagawea was a member of the Lemhi Shoshone, who lived on the Montana-Idaho border near present-day Salmon, Idaho. The Shoshone were also known as the Snake. Gary Moulton, ed., *The Journals of the Lewis and Clark Expedition*, 9 vols. (Lincoln: University of Nebraska Press, 1983–1997), 3:328; 5:85; Ella E. Clark and Margot Edmonds, *Sacagawea of the Lewis and Clark Expedition* (Berkeley: University of California Press, 1979), 1; Harold P. Howard, *Sacajawea* (Norman: University of Oklahoma Press, 1971), 62; John Bakeless, ed., *The Journals of Lewis and Clark* (New York: New American Library, 1964), 211 n.

3. Clark and Edmonds, *Sacagawea*, 1; and Moulton, *Journals*, 3:3, 229.

4. Howard, *Sacajawea*, 16; John Logan Allen, *Lewis and Clark and The Image of the American Northwest* (New York: Dover, 1991), 221 n; Allen's book is a republication of *Passage through the Garden: Lewis and Clark and the Image of the American Northwest* (Urbana: University of Illinois Press, 1975).

5. Carol Lynn Macgregor, ed., *The Journals of Patrick Gass: Member of the Lewis and Clark Expedition* (Missoula, MT: Mountain Press Publishing Co., 1997), 94, 107, 148.

6. "Appendix A: Members of the Expedition," in *Journals*, ed. Moulton, 2:509–12.

7. Bernard DeVoto, ed., *The Journals of Lewis and Clark* (Boston: Houghton Mifflin, 1953), 208, 218; Demitri B. Shimkin notes a different paradox among the Eastern Shoshone: "On one hand, women were socially subordinated to men. . . . On the other hand, women possessed critical skills in plant gathering, household crafts, household transportation, child care and other areas." Shimkin, "Eastern Shoshone," in *Handbook of North American Indians*, William C. Sturtevant, general editor, vol. 11, *Great Basin*, ed. Warren L. D'Azevedo (Washington: Smithsonian Institution, 1986), 311.

8. DeVoto, *Journals*, 207; Shimkin, 312–13.

9. Moulton, *Journals*, 3:206–07; Clark and Edmonds, *Sacagawea*, 7–8; Moulton, *Journals*, 3:3; DeVoto, *Journals*, 63, 73, 85, 92–94.

10. Bakeless, *Journals*, 118; John Bakeless, *Lewis and Clark: Partners in Discovery* (New York: William Morrow and Co., 1947), 156.

11. The dissemination of this view into the popular imagination was a result of the fictional treatment of Sacagawea in Eva Emery Dye, *The Conquest: The True Story of Lewis and Clark* (Chicago: A. C. McClurg and Co., 1902); Grace Raymond Hebard, *Sacajawea: A Guide and Interpreter of the Lewis and Clark Expedition, with an Account of the Travels of Toussaint Charbonneau, and of Jean Baptise, the Expedition Papoose* (Glendale, CA: Arthur H. Clark Co., 1932).

12. The chief detractors include C. S. Kingston, "Sacajawea as Guide: The Evaluation of a Legend," *Pacific Northwest Quarterly* 35 (January 1944): 2–18; Ronald W. Taber, "Sacajawea and the Suffragettes: An

Interpretation of a Myth," *Pacific Northwest Quarterly* 58 (January 1967): 7–13; and Allen, *Image of the American Northwest,* 211–12.

13. DeVoto, *Journals,* 110, 147; Bakeless, *Lewis and Clark,* 190; Moulton, *Journals,* 4:2; Stephen E. Ambrose, *Undaunted Courage: Meriwether Lewis, Thomas Jefferson, and the Opening of the American West* (New York: Simon and Schuster, 1996), 225.

14. Ambrose, *Undaunted Courage,* 212; DeVoto, *Journals,* 93; Norman-Taylor, ed., *Taylor's Encyclopedia of Gardening,* 4th ed. (Boston: Houghton Mifflin, 1961), 620, 1180.

15. Ambrose, *Undaunted Courage,* 212–13; Moulton, *Journals,* 4:89, 128, 403.

16. Ambrose, *Undaunted Courage,* 223; Reuben Thwaites, ed., *Original Journals of the Lewis and Clark Expedition,* 8 vols. (New York: Dodd, Mead, 1904–1907), 7:134–35, cited in Macgregor, *Journals of Patrick Gass,* 239 n; Moulton, *Journals,* 4:318.

17. DeVoto, *Journals,* 312; Moulton, *Journals,* 6:97, 106–07; Clark and Edmonds, *Sacagawea,* 52.

18. Moulton, *Journals,* 7:264–65, 270, 286, 8:52 n, 286; DeVoto, *Journals,* 410; Clark and Edmonds, *Sacagawea,* 73.

19. E. G. Chuinard, "The Actual Role of the Bird Woman: Purposeful Member of the Corps or Casual 'Tag Along'?" *Montana, The Magazine of Western History* 26 (Summer 1976): 18–29; Ambrose, *Undaunted Courage,* 187; Clark and Edmonds, *Sacagawea,* 15; Bakeless, *Journals,* 188.

20. Ambrose, *Undaunted Courage,* 255–56; Moulton, *Journals,* 5:109–16; 8:161, 279, 305; Bakeless, *Lewis and Clark,* 250; Nicholas Biddle, *The Story of the Expedition under the Commands of Captains Lewis and Clark* (Philadelphia: Bradford and Inskeep, 1814), cited in Ambrose, *Undaunted Courage,* 277.

21. Ambrose, *Undaunted Courage,* 280–83; Moulton, *Journals,* 5:165.

22. Moulton, *Journals,* 7:178–80; Ambrose, *Undaunted Courage,* 359.

23. Moulton, *Journals,* 7:244; Ambrose, *Undaunted Courage,* 362–65.

24. Cited in Gunther Barth, *The Lewis and Clark Expedition: Selections from the Journals Arranged by Topic* (Boston: St. Martin's Press, 1998), 68–69; Moulton, *Journals,* 5:59.

25. Clara Sue Kidwell, "Indian Women as Cultural Mediators," *Ethnohistory* 39 (Spring 1992): 101–02; Rayna Green, "The Pocohontas Perplex: The Image of Indian Women in American Culture," *Massachusetts Review* 27 (Autumn 1975): 698–714; Susan Lobo and Steve Talbot, eds., *Native American Voices: A Reader* (New York: Longman, 1998), 185; Ambrose, *Undaunted Courage,* 285.

26. DeVoto, *Journals,* 249–50; Moulton, *Journals,* 5:268, 305; 9:331; 8:167, 180.

27. Thwaites, *Original Journals,* 7:134–35; and Howard, *Sacagawea,* 141–42.

28. Moulton, *Journals,* 3:228–29 n; Bakeless, *Lewis and Clark,* 454–55.

29. Albert Furtwangler, *Acts of Discovery: Visions of America in the Lewis and Clark Journals* (Urbana: University of Illinois Press, 1993), 221–22; Bakeless, *Lewis and Clark*, 454; Moulton, *Journals,* 3:291 n.

30. Irving Anderson strongly believes that Sacagawea died in 1812 and that later sightings were cases of "mistaken identity." Anderson, "Probing the Riddle of the Bird Woman; How Long Did Sacajawea Live; Where and When Did She Die?" *Montana, The Magazine of Western History* 23 (1973): 2–17; James P. Ronda, *Lewis and Clark among the Indians* (Lincoln: University of Nebraska Press, 1984), 258; Moulton, *Journals,* 3:171, 229; despite the title, Blanche Schroer's, "Boat Pusher or Bird Woman? Sacagawea or Sacajawea?" *Annals of Wyoming* 52 (1980): 46–54 focuses almost exclusively on the debates surrounding Sacagawea's death and favors the 1812 version; Clark and Edmonds, *Sacagawea,* 105–06; Bakeless, *Lewis and Clark,* 455.

31. Bakeless, *Lewis and Clark,* 456; Clark and Edmonds, *Sacagawea,* 144, 115, 128; Howard, *Sacagawea,* 154–62; Moulton, *Journals,* 3:229.

32. Angela Cavender Wilson, "Power of the Spoken Word: Native Oral Traditions in American Indian History," in *Rethinking American Indian History,* ed. Donald L. Fixico (Albuquerque: University of New Mexico Press, 1997), 102–04.

33. Sherry L. Smith, "Beyond Princess and Squaw," in *The Women's West,* ed. Susan Armitage and Elizabeth Jameson (Norman: University of Oklahoma Press, 1980), 63–75.

34. Moulton, *Journals,* 6:83–84, 168–72.

35. Cited in Clark and Edmonds, *Sacagawea,* 94–96; Chuinard, "Bird Woman," 20.

36. Donna J. Kessler, *The Making of Sacagawea: A Euro-American Legend* (Tuscaloosa: University of Alabama Press, 1996), 26–27, 29, 43, 47, 60–1, 89–90, 101.

37. Kidwell, "Indian Women," 97–98.

Suggested Readings

The few primary sources include the journals of Meriwether Lewis, William Clark, John Ordway, Joseph Whitehouse, and Patrick Gass; manuscript collections housed at the Missouri State Historical Society; and oral histories collected by Grace Raymond Hebard.

Relatively complete journal collections begin chronologically with Nicholas Biddle, ed., *The History of the Expedition under the Commands of Captains Lewis and Clark,* 2 vols. (Philadelphia: Bradford and Inskeep, 1814); Elliot Coues, ed., *History of the Expedition under the Command of Lewis and Clark,* 4 vols. (New York: Francis P. Harper, 1893); Reuben Gold Thwaites, ed., *Original Journals of the Lewis and Clark Expedition,* 8 vols. (New York: Dodd, Mead, 1904–1907); Donald Jackson, ed., *Letters of the Lewis and*

Clark Expedition (Urbana: University of Illinois Press, 1962, rev., 1978); and Gary Moulton, ed., *The Journals of the Lewis and Clark Expedition*, 9 vols. (Lincoln: University of Nebraska Press, 1983–1997).

Historical monographs of the Lewis and Clark Expedition include but are not limited to John Bakeless, *Lewis and Clark, Partners in Discovery* (New York: William Morrow and Co., 1947); Bernard DeVoto, *The Course of Empire* (Boston: Houghton Mifflin, 1952); John Allen, *Passage through the Garden: Lewis and Clark and the Image of the American Northwest* (Urbana: University of Illinois Press, 1975); James P. Ronda, *Lewis and Clark among the Indians* (Lincoln: University of Nebraska Press, 1984); Albert Furtwangler, *Acts of Discovery: Visions of America in the Lewis and Clark Journals* (Urbana: University of Illinois Press, 1993); Stephen E. Ambrose, *Undaunted Courage: Meriwether Lewis, Thomas Jefferson, and the Opening of the American West* (New York: Simon and Schuster, 1996). The Lewis and Clark Trail Heritage Foundation of Portland, Oregon, publishes a journal devoted to the expedition entitled *We Proceeded On.*

Book-length studies of Sacagawea include Grace Raymond Hebard, *Sacagawea: A Guide and Interpreter of the Lewis and Clark Expedition, with an Account of the Travels of Toussaint Charbonneau, and of Jean Baptiste, the Expedition Papoose* (Glendale, CA: Arthur H. Clark Co., 1932); Harold P. Howard, *Sacajawea* (Norman: University of Oklahoma Press, 1971); Ella E. Clark and Margot Edmonds, *Sacagawea of the Lewis and Clark Expedition* (Berkeley: University of California Press, 1979); and Donna J. Kessler, *The Making of Sacagawea: A Euro-American Legend* (Tuscaloosa: University of Alabama Press, 1996).

For fictional treatments, consult Eva Emery Dye, *The Conquest: The True Story of Lewis and Clark* (Chicago: A. C. McClung and Co., 1902); and Anna Lee Waldo, *Sacajawea* (New York: Avon Books, 1979).

II

The Mid–Nineteenth Century
The Era of the Common Woman

Using Andrew Jackson's career and presidency as the starting point, many U.S. history texts label the mid–nineteenth century as the "era of the common man." Although it took America's bloodiest war to outlaw slavery and, at least in theory, guarantee basic political rights to all adult male citizens, by the mid–nineteenth century democracy reached more men in America than in any nation in world history. Of course, Native American and Asian immigrants did not benefit from these changes. Furthermore, in later decades the failures of Reconstruction reversed the short-lived advances for black males. And women were not granted the same national political status as men until ratification of the Nineteenth Amendment in 1920. Black women, mired in the bonds of slavery in antebellum America and then by racial segregation, both de facto and de jure, did not gain full legal and civil rights until long after.

Nonetheless, the ideals of citizenship absent gender distinctions took a distinctly American tone at the birth of the U.S. women's rights movement in 1848. In other words, the seeds of change were planted by dramatic economic, political, and social shifts fueled by the industrial revolution, westward expansion, and new reform movements of the mid–nineteenth century. American women expressed their political opinions in partisan and activist ways, even though their citizenship did not include the right to vote. Moral reform and home life and women's proper role in each became subjects of popular debate. The stories of Elizabeth Cady Stanton, Susan B. Anthony, Harriet Tubman, Sojourner Truth, Elizabeth Beecher Stowe, and other female activists have received much attention from women's historians. But how did the dramatic shifts of the mid–nineteenth century affect "ordinary" women?

In literary circles, Transcendentalists, such as Ralph Waldo Emerson, Henry David Thoreau, and Margaret Fuller, helped to shape the shifting ideas about democracy, abolitionism, women's rights, and the complexities of an expanding nation entering the industrial revolution. But as Helen Deese explains in Chapter 4, not all female Transcendentalists marched in lockstep with other female activists or the women's rights movement. Caroline Healey Dall, the author of a prominent book on "the woman question," worked "in the front ranks of the feminist movement," although her story is unknown to many students of women's history and Transcendentalism. Dall believed in the equality of the sexes, but she did not follow the path prescribed by feminist leaders such as Stanton or Anthony. Looking for alternative models, Dall faced many obstacles as she strove for increasing independence and public roles for women in the era of the common man.

Jean Silver-Isenstadt, in Chapter 5, tells the interesting story of another nineteenth-century pioneer, Mary S. Gove Nichols. Nichols, like Dall, was a passionate advocate of women's rights. Nonetheless, Nichols did not focus her attention on obtaining women's equality through legal and civil means. Instead, she believed that good health was the essential element to obtaining equality. Nichols's personal experiences with the difficulties of childbirth coupled with her views on women's rights make her a progressive medical advocate. She chose to marry. But Nichols's choice of reform topic, professional career, association with radical intellectuals and artists, eventual divorce, and unconventional marriage made her a controversial figure whose life discloses much about the gender-related debates taking place in the mid-nineteenth-century United States.

Eliza Johnson Potter was another strong woman who did the unexpected. As slavery increased in the cotton South and state laws placed even greater restrictions on the freedom of African Americans, Potter's exceptional spirit and talents enabled her to lead an usual life. She lived as a free woman, traveled around the world, owned her own business, and became a recognized social critic. Slavery was certainly the common experience for most black Americans in the antebellum period. Nevertheless, when light is shed on the lives of free women such as Potter, the complex nature of race during slavery's heyday becomes apparent. As Wilma King aptly shows in Chapter 6, Eliza Potter was an extraordinary woman with a unique perspective on the growing racial crisis in America and beyond.

Westward expansion was also a significant trend in the lives of many ordinary Americans during the nineteenth century. Diaries of the westward migration have been a popular resource for scholars. Nonetheless, historians have generally overlooked the many army officers' wives who traveled and lived in the frontier West. In Chapter 7, Michele Nacy's careful analysis of Ada Adelaine Adams Vodges's life spells out the perpetual physical danger, separations of spouses, significant deprivation of creature comforts, and life marked by frequent relocations faced by wives who followed their husbands to isolated western military outposts. Unlike Dall, Nichols, and Potter, who lived outside the middle-class ideal, Vodges worked to turn her unusual environment into one more mainstream. She adapted in unique ways to the dominant nineteenth-century "cult of domesticity" and "ideal of true womanhood," which celebrated women's piety, purity, submission to men, and roles as wives and mothers. In addition, Vodges's letters offer insight into her attitudes about Indians and the social relationships among women living on the frontier.

Teresa E. Wooldridge Ivey also wanted to live up to the cult of domesticity and ideal of true womanhood. But like Vodges, Ivey had to create a public image somewhat different from her actual experience. Angela Boswell, in Chapter 8, skillfully uncovers Ivey's hidden story through various state court records. Born on a plantation in Georgia, Ivey married, separated, and divorced, having reinvented herself on the way as a "widowed" mother living on the Texas frontier. A shrewd businesswoman and clearly an independent person, Ivey publicly attempted to live up to the nineteenth-century ideal of true womanhood. Her efforts to conform to a public image of piety, purity, submission, and domesticity contradict many of the realities of her life. Even for many elite Southern females, the mid–nineteenth century marked an era of increasing female independence hindered by cultural ideals embraced by many women as well as men.

4

Caroline Healey Dall
Transcendentalist Activist

Helen Deese

Caroline Healey Dall (1822–1912) was not an ordinary woman. Only the fickleness of human fame and the vagaries of history enable us to treat her as such, for certainly the name of this nineteenth-century American reformer has been largely forgotten. Yet in her day she made her mark as a pioneer, playing a leading role in the women's movement in its early decades, a role that even recent historians of the movement have overlooked. Caroline Dall was, as far as she knew or as can be confirmed, the first woman to preach in Unitarian pulpits. The first Boston woman to give public lectures in that city, she was a founder and longtime officer of the American Social Science Association. Simultaneously, she lived out a poignant and in some senses tragic personal life. Her story is instructive as a revelation of some of the limits and strictures common to a woman of her time and place, even one so extraordinarily talented and educated as Caroline Dall.

Caroline Wells Healey was born to wealth and privilege in Boston, but the wealth was new and, as it turned out, unstable, and the privilege distinctly narrowed by her gender. Mark Healey, a self-made East India merchant and investor, had risen to the presidency of the Merchants' Bank of Boston by the time his daughter Caroline was a young woman. She was the oldest of eight children to survive infancy. Lacking formal education himself, Mark Healey nevertheless valued it highly and provided an excellent private education for his daughter through governesses, tutors, and private schools. He also demanded and expected great things of her; she was "bred and brought up," she later wrote, to be a literary woman. Before Caroline was ten, father and daughter were spending the evenings discussing literary, political, religious, and philosophical questions. By the time Caroline was thirteen, she had begun her attempt to fulfill his expectations by writing novels, publishing translations, and contributing short homilies to the *Christian Register*, a Boston Unitarian weekly.

Helen Deese is grateful to the Massachusetts Historical Society for permission to quote from the Dall Papers and to Tennessee Technological University for support for this project.

Caroline's hunger for the love and approval of both her parents, and her perceived failure at achieving either, is a constant theme of her teenage journals. Her extraordinary relationship with her father came at the expense of a close bond with her mother, Caroline Foster Healey, who (almost constantly involved with childbearing) suffered depression and even in her well moments saw little use in her daughter's literary efforts. Not surprisingly, the daughter identified with her father rather than her mother. However, Caroline, as the focus of her father's attention, had to struggle to fulfill his expectations. Even her precocious writing activities did not satisfy him. He particularly disapproved of the increasingly religious tenor of her work: "I had become devotional—he wished me—to become *literary*—He never said it—but I could see it."[1]

Caroline Healey's formal schooling was cut off at age fifteen. Though such an abbreviated education was not unusual for daughters even of the most aristocratic families, Caroline was surprised and bitterly disappointed to be removed from school. If Caroline had been male, there is little doubt that she would have attended Harvard (as did her only brother to reach adulthood) and that she would have become a minister. As it was, she had to satisfy herself with being a regular observer at Harvard exhibitions, class days, and commencement exercises, and with engaging in discussions of theological questions and practical religion with the young ministerial students who were her colleagues in church-sponsored classes. The likeliest explanation for her curtailed formal education (in addition to her being female) is the beginning of a serious financial crisis for Mark Healey, who was eventually forced into bankruptcy in the aftermath of the panic of 1837. At first unaware of her father's precarious situation, Caroline continued her studies on her own and was intensely engaged in teaching and charitable activities associated with Boston's fashionable West Church, the Unitarian church that her family attended, and with missions to children in poor neighborhoods.

Dall's early association with and her education by the Transcendentalists further set her life's course on a track of idealism and self-reliance, providing her with nontraditional role models and introducing her to the world of organized reform of the Boston abolitionists. Transcendentalism, an intellectual movement that involved a number of the most distinguished Boston-area writers, thinkers, and reformers from the 1830s to the 1850s (including among others Ralph Waldo Emerson, Henry David Thoreau, Margaret Fuller, A. Bronson Alcott, Theodore Parker, and Elizabeth Palmer Peabody), held that human beings are essentially good and can find truth through their own intuition, a truth transcending that which can be learned through the senses. At the age of eighteen, Caroline Healey came under the influence of one member of this circle, the remarkable Bostonian Elizabeth Palmer Peabody. Scholar, critic, educator, and businesswoman, Peabody, who was twice Healey's age, had just opened a bookstore that became a center for Unitarian and Transcendentalist writers and thinkers. Healey was awed by the foreign publications that Peabody carried and even more by the character of the proprietor herself. She was scholarly, enthusiastic, and a more than willing mentor to Healey. Although for several years Healey had been sitting in various public halls and Unitarian churches listening to lectures and sermons by male Transcendentalists, it was Peabody who provided her entrée into their circle. In 1841, Peabody recruited Healey for a series of conversations directed by Margaret Fuller, who four years later published the groundbreaking *Woman in the Nineteenth Century*. This group was heady company indeed for an eighteen year old; Ralph Waldo Emerson was among the distinguished participants. Despite Healey's sense that Fuller did not like her, she always considered this a key experience of her life, and Fuller her most important role model. At the same time that she attended Fuller's conversations, Healey was absorbing the preaching of the iconoclastic Transcendentalist minister Theodore Parker, whose radical theology she found unsettling but ultimately convincing. Never an uncritical disciple, she wrote Parker frankly about her objections to his use of what she considered shock tactics. He responded to her criticism without condescension, as if she were an equal. Parker became another significant mentor of Healey, particularly in his commitment to social reform.

When Caroline Healey was nineteen, she met and fell in love with Samuel Foster Haven, a widower sixteen years her senior. A noted scholar, Haven was librarian at the American Antiquarian Society in Worcester, Massachusetts. The budding relationship foundered, however, when, with most unfortunate timing, Mark Healey's bankruptcy occurred. In order to contribute to the family income, specifically to pay for her younger sisters' education, Caroline looked for work. She found a suitable position as vice principal of the exclusive Miss English's School for Young Ladies in Georgetown (District of Columbia). There, in exile from family, friends, and church, worried about her father, heart-broken at Samuel Haven's silence, she was vulnerable to the attentions of a visiting young Unitarian minister, Charles Henry Appleton Dall. Dall ministered to the poor in Baltimore and must have seen in Caroline, who already had a long history of charitable activities in Boston, the perfect helpmate. After having been in each other's company for only a few days and carrying on a correspondence for a few weeks, they became engaged. A year later they were married and settled in Baltimore.

Charles Dall's American pastorates, however, were all to be notably brief. Within a year, with Caroline pregnant, the couple moved in with her parents in Boston and Charles did "supply" preaching in the area. After the birth of William Healey Dall in 1844 they moved to Portsmouth, New Hampshire, where Charles was again involved in a short-lived ministry-at-large. After another period of filling in at vacant pulpits, Charles accepted a pastorate in the rural town of Needham, ten miles from Boston, in 1847. Here Caroline gave birth to a stillborn child and then to a daughter, Sarah Keene Dall, in 1849. After three years in Needham, Charles was once again forced to move, this time accepting a position in Toronto. Caroline and the children followed the next spring.

After their move to Toronto, Caroline was desperately homesick, as the city was at that time a far cry from the cultured mecca of Boston. The Dalls scarcely had enough to live on, and Caroline's father, in response to her appeal, agreed to help only on the condition that she give up all antislavery activities. For some time, Caroline had been associated with the Garrisonian abolitionists, and in Canada she helped distribute aid to fugitive slaves from the States. Unhesitatingly, she refused to accede to her father's demand. As the months passed, she became happier in Toronto, making friends and attracting the intellectual elite of the city. She also developed a deep affection for a young man in her husband's congregation who eventually boarded in their household. To John Patton, an English china importer with a scholarly penchant, Caroline Dall's education and her association with the luminaries of Boston made her unlike any woman he had known. He was fascinated and devoted, and she gratefully received such unaccustomed adulation. Simultaneously, the Dalls' marital relationship began to cool. The first ten years of their marriage had been a struggle with poverty and Charles's limited success. Yet they were for the most part happy, Caroline devoted to domestic duties and child care and supportive of her husband. Now, Charles came to resent Caroline's strength and she to resent his weakness. In the wake of a serious illness that Caroline described as "brain fever," Charles suffered an apparent emotional breakdown and became hostile to his wife. There was a reconciliation, but Charles was forced to resign his pastorate, move the family back to the Boston area, and once more look for work. He finally managed to solve several problems at once, though his solution created a new set of problems for Caroline: he decided, without asking the counsel of his wife or inviting her or his children to accompany him, to become a missionary to Calcutta. For the next thirty-one years Charles lived there, returning home at approximately five-year intervals.

Suddenly, at age thirty-two and with children aged five and nine, Caroline Dall found herself adrift in a sea with few markers.

She faced an economic and vocational crisis, to say nothing of the devastating personal implications of Charles's leaving. She was still a wife, but she could hardly count on the moral and emotional support of a husband. Her sense of duty and loyalty made her determined to remain a wife, even a supportive one, but she never got over her sense of having been abandoned by her husband. The portion of her husband's salary that was directed to her was insufficient. It was only with the greatest difficulty that Caroline Dall, although a woman of superior gifts, could translate her talents into economic rewards. Over the next twenty-three years (until the death of her father, when her financial situation was substantially improved) she supplemented her meager income by taking in boarders, teaching private classes, giving public lectures, and writing. She published literary criticism, children's fiction, biography, personal reminiscence, and religious and reform works. These strategies were generally more successful in helping Dall to establish a new identity than in meeting the financial needs of the family. There was periodic and often humiliating recourse to her father's sometimes generous, sometimes grudging, help. Nevertheless, as the years passed, despite her resentment that Charles seemed to be more dedicated to Hindu children than to his own, Caroline came to the point that she did not want him home. Difficult as her life was, it would in all likelihood have been much more frustrating and the forging of her own identity much more problematic if Charles Dall had stayed at home and played the traditional role of head of the household. His few visits proved traumatic for them both and must have caused Caroline privately to be thankful for his absences, in which she had managed to find meaningful work, a certain amount of fame, and a sense of herself. Thus, there was a certain freedom that she gleaned from her nontraditional marital arrangement.

Nevertheless, Caroline Dall's freedom was fraught with perils. She was after all a product of Brahmin Boston, and she, like the society that had shaped her, placed a high premium on respectability. She defined herself to a large degree by her religion and her role as mother, thus abhorring any hint of scandal. Her dilemma went far beyond the fact that she was not free to follow her heart and marry the man with whom she was doubtlessly in love. As a woman who took to the pulpit and the lecture platform and spoke in revolutionary terms of women's rights—and who did not live with her husband—she invited association in the popular mind with advocates of free love. As a matter of fact, Dall's radicalism never extended as far as the overhaul of the marital relationship, and she held to conventionally moral positions on sexual matters. Predictably, she did attract personal innuendo, most notably in the Orthodox religious paper *Boston Recorder*. Even her old mentor, Elizabeth Peabody, took exception to the frankness of Dall's lectures, writing to her that she would not wish to be in the audience in the company of a gentleman. Dall's unconventional marriage, combined with her advanced position on the woman question and with her public role (a flagrant breaching of the traditional woman's sphere), made vulnerable her equally prized roles as mother, church member, and lady.

Dall had begun her engagement with the woman question several years before Charles Dall's departure. In 1849 the *Liberator* published her first article on the topic. In the mid-1850s she wrote for and helped edit (with Paulina Wright Davis) the women's rights newspaper *Una*, probably the first such publication in the country. After Charles's departure for India her involvement in the movement intensified. She was active in a number of early women's conventions, including the Boston convention of 1855, over which she presided. Three years later she delivered a landmark address advocating woman suffrage before a committee of the Massachusetts state legislature, and in 1859, Dall spoke along with Susan B. Anthony and other leading reformers at the Women's Rights Convention, in New York City. In the late 1850s and early 1860s she took her message to the lecture platform, repeatedly delivering four different formal series of lectures in Boston and surrounding areas.

As a public lecturer in mid-nineteenth-century New England, Dall subjected herself to scrutiny and criticism of not just her oratorical skills and the style and substance of her lectures but also her appearance, dress, marital status, and lifestyle. On one occasion she was attacked for being conceited and presuming, for thinking she knew more than anyone else, and above all for wearing a dress that was deemed too short. After a published attack on her character, the committee sponsoring her next lecture asked for several items of documentation to allay their qualms: a recent letter from her husband to prove that they had never been separated; a volume of the works of Dr. William Ellery Channing, a revered Unitarian clergyman, to establish that someone else respectable thought highly of Mary Wollstonecraft (the British women's rights advocate); and the lecture itself to be read in advance by the committee to ensure that it did not advocate free love. Such demeaning treatment went with the territory for a woman in Dall's situation. Other less personal challenges she took as opportunities: she made her own arrangements for advertising her lectures, printing tickets, and hiring her lecture hall, although she had, she noted, male friends who would have been glad to take care of these business matters. She insisted on performing such tasks herself because she wished, as she said, "to make all business thoroughfares comfortable for women."[2]

Dall's use of the lecture platform to advocate women's rights met with a mixed reception. Most reviews were favorable, but many of them were written by friends. Her audiences varied from one thousand in East Boston to only five in Boston itself on a January night in which she described the city as having its worst weather within memory. For Dall, lecturing was not really a money-making proposition. Though she does record occasions in which she took in more than twice as much money as had been promised, more typical was her experience at the end of four weekly lectures in Boston: Dall totaled up her accounts to discover that she had just about broken even. It was fortunate that Dall's primary motivation was always the cause rather than the financial reward. When someone asked her whether she would give up lecturing if her father would wholly support her, she quickly answered no; she had done it long enough to believe that she had a God-given talent for it and that her message would do the world good. She also in time thrilled to the spectacle of the "excited human faces" of her audience turned toward her, "all wrought up—all with kindled eyes."[3]

With a view to disseminating her message more widely, Dall turned her lectures into publications: *Woman's Right to Labor* (1860), which won the Hovey Prize, endowed by a Boston philanthropist to support reform causes; *Woman's Rights under the Law* (1861); and her capstone work (its publication delayed by the self-imposed moratorium on the women's movement during the Civil War), *The College, the Market, and the Court: or, Woman's Relation to Education, Labor, and Law* (1867). This last publication incorporated the material in the two earlier titles with her lectures on education. In all these works, Dall's approach was closely reasoned and logical, her careful documentation of women's oppression supporting an intellectual appeal for equality. It was an appeal that relied on moral suasion, but moral suasion buttressed by hard facts. Dall's research into women's wages, her surveys of opportunities in higher education open to women, her reports on her own visits to such schools as Oberlin, Vassar, and Antioch, and her careful examination of women's property rights and other legal positions differentiated her from earlier reformers or those who were contemporaneous with her work. Dall's method looked forward to the "scientific" approach that came to characterize reform movements in the latter part of the century.

In her writings, Dall articulated a basic theoretical foundation for the women's movement in America (expressed thus in the *Liberator*: "We believe that no faculty has ever been developed in any man, which has not been, or might not be, equally developed in some woman, and we believe such development intended by God"); she then urged specific applications of the theory for contemporary society. In effect, Dall took Margaret Fuller's basic premise that a woman should be able to develop her own nature, whatever that nature might be, and made it practicable in antebellum and post-bellum America. Whereas by the time of the publication of *The College, the Market, and the Court,* Susan B. Anthony, for example, primarily focused her efforts on suffrage, Dall recognized that there were also major and equally crucial battles to be fought in the marketplace and educational arena. Her fundamental critique of women's economic role anticipates the work of such later writers as Charlotte Perkins Gilman. Indeed, Dall's perspective is remarkably modern. She observed that history, largely written by men who view women as inferior, simply reflects and validates male prejudices. On the economic front, she argued that women's labor should be valued at the same rate as men's. She sympathetically portrayed the lot of prostitutes, whose only choices often were, in her words, "death or dishonor." She encouraged women of means to become entrepreneurs: "Now I should rejoice," she wrote, "to see a large Lowell mill wholly owned and operated by women."[4] She suggested an early version of temporary-employment agencies. And she looked forward to a (somewhat romanticized) era of dual career couples: "Such marriages as I can dream of,—where, household duties thriftily managed and speedily discharged, the wife assumes some honorable trust . . . ; while the husband follows his under separate auspices! Occupied with real service to men and each other, how happily will they meet at night to discuss the hours they lived apart, to help each other's work by each other's wit, and to draw vital refreshment from the caresses of their children!"[5]

Dall was also one of the earliest practitioners in the field of women's studies in the country. In her *Una* articles (many of which were republished in *Historical Pictures Retouched,* 1860) she scrutinized history for instances of overlooked, suppressed, or maligned women of intelligence, independence, and virtue. Not content with simply highlighting the work of such figures as Margaret Fuller and Mary Wollstonecraft, she reread in a favorable light some of the female pariahs of male-written history—Aspasia, for example, the reputed courtesan who caused Pericles to leave his wife and family. She "retouched" the portraits of these figures—that is, she took the known facts and showed how they could be reinterpreted in a way favorable to these women, whom history had thus far read in the least sympathetic light or simply ignored. In response to a popular series of lectures by Transcendentalist Ralph Waldo Emerson entitled "Representative Men," Dall crafted a "Representative Women" lecture featuring Fuller, Wollstonecraft, Charlotte Brontë, and Lady Sydney Morgan.

These works made Dall a reformer of national stature. The publication of *The College, the Market, and the Court* was generally considered a major event in the American women's movement. It was widely reviewed, from New England to New York to San Francisco to London. In 1868, Elizabeth Cady Stanton wrote to Dall that she had been empowered to choose "some half dozen of our most distinguished" women to be featured in a chapter on the women's rights movement and added, "As from your literary ability you rank first, you must be one of the six."[6] A decade later, in honor of Dall's achievement, Alfred University awarded her a doctorate of laws (LL.D.), probably the first honorary degree granted to an American woman.

Yet Dall's role in the women's movement faded from the record in the last quarter of the nineteenth century. In Stanton, Anthony, and Gage's three-volume *History of Woman Suffrage,* Dall's work is very nearly ignored. In the chapter "Women in Boston" in Justin Winsor's *Memorial History of Boston* (1881), Caroline Dall's name is simply never mentioned. That was hardly an accidental oversight, since Dall's work was concentrated in the Boston area, and since a childhood friend of Dall's, Ednah Dow Cheney, wrote that chapter. Several reasons account for Dall's being dropped out of the history of the women's movement. Personal conflicts and jealousies were a primary cause, as the circumstances of her exclusion from the New England Woman's Club illustrate. Dall saw herself as having paved the way for the public roles of a number of Boston friends and acquaintances, including Caroline Severance, Julia Ward Howe, and Ednah Dow Cheney, all three prime movers in the 1868 founding of the Woman's Club. Dall, surprised to hear of the organization of this society without her knowledge, was then stunned to learn that she had been blackballed from membership. She never recovered from this blow, delivered by the very women whom she felt that she had enabled and with most of whom she attended church. It was perhaps the major reason that she essentially dropped out of the women's movement. Why would these "friends" have turned on her? The Woman's Club women told a friend of Dall's that it was "because [she] *al*ways had *led* everywhere—& always would!"[7] There is no question that Dall had a controlling personality and a lifelong history of unwittingly offending people. The result seems to be that some of those whom she had offended wrote her out of the history of the women's movement systematically. A rather obvious reason that Dall's contemporaries, in these later accounts, minimized her role was her essential abandonment of the women's movement. No doubt she would have said it the other way around, but the effect was the same.

But Dall did not abandon reform. Far from it. In 1865 she was one of the founders of the American Social Science Association, an organization that studied and attempted to improve prison conditions, the treatment of the insane, public health, and education. As a member of countless committees of this organization, Dall traveled extensively to examine and report upon conditions in prisons, asylums, and factories. All manner of issues affecting the poor, sick, or disadvantaged commanded her attention, ranging from lodging houses for women in cities to the purity of milk. So Dall's place in the women's movement was obscured later in the century partly because she was now identified, as she now identified herself, with a different reform movement.

As a reformer, Caroline Dall clearly had her limitations. Primary among them was her inability to work well with other strong women. Perhaps she does not deserve a place of eminence in the history of the women's movement if one views it from the limited perspective of organized political action. She was an idea woman, not an organization woman. But her true and crucial role was to foster what historian Gerda Lerner has called a "feminist consciousness," an enhanced awareness of woman's potential, of her marginalization by society, and a sense of connection with great women of the past.[8] The political branch of the movement built upon this consciousness.

Dall lived out the last thirty-four years of her life largely retired from active reform work, though she continued to hold an office in the American Social Science Association. In 1878 she moved to Washington, where her son, who had become famous as an explorer and author on Alaska, was building a career as a naturalist at the Smithsonian Institution. She also made extended visits to her daughter, who had married Josiah Munro, a successful businessman in Buffalo, New York. Dall's life in Washington only partly revolved around her son and her grandchildren, for she became the friend of political and scientific luminaries, the intimate of First Lady Frances Cleveland, the leader of a reading group for young women, and a well-known hostess. She also wrote for newspapers and magazines and occasionally published books on a wide variety of topics—from Shakespeare to her journey to California to theology.

In Dall's late years she recognized that the period of her young womanhood in the Boston area had been no ordinary time, and she felt an obligation to preserve her own record of it. In the 1890s she made arrangements to leave her journals (which already covered more than sixty years) and other papers to the Massachusetts Historical Society. In addition to this private contemporary record that Dall realized would not be tapped until after her death, she turned to publishing recollections and interpretations of the Transcendentalist movement and its participants. In 1895 Dall published her transcription of the Margaret Fuller conversation series that she had attended in 1841, *Margaret and Her Friends*. It remains the fullest and best contemporary record of those sessions. In the same year she delivered in Washington a lecture that she published two years later as *Transcendentalism in New England: A Lecture.* When she gave this lecture, Dall was nearly seventy-three years old. She could easily have used the stores of her memory and her journals to produce an entertaining talk filled with personal anecdotes of the celebrated Transcendentalists. But she was speaking before the Society for Philosophical Enquiry, and she aimed to be more than entertaining. Instead of telling after-dinner tales, Dall undertook to construct a revisionist interpretation of the movement, an unabashedly feminist one. The Transcendentalist movement began and ended, Dall asserted, with a woman. Its history "stretched along two hundred years," from the Puritan rebel Anne Hutchinson to Margaret Fuller. Hutchinson was banished from the Massachusetts Bay Colony as a result of her Antinomian beliefs emphasizing the conviction that the divine spirit is immanent in human beings and that its guidance should take precedence over men's laws. Dall's designation of Hutchinson, the very earliest eminent New England woman, as a foremother of Transcendentalism is a bold stroke of revisionist interpretation. Furthermore, Dall's contention for the centrality of Margaret Fuller's role in the Transcendentalist movement is a corrective to most nineteenth-century and, until recently, twentieth-century depictions of the movement.

The extraordinary life of Caroline Healey Dall, a pioneering reformer, a public lecturer and sometime preacher, an associate of the great and famous, was balanced and complemented by an ordinary life. This ordinary life was marked on the one hand by the frustration of her need for love, the failure of her marriage, the difficulties of single motherhood, the shame of personal innuendo, the pain of rejection, and on the other hand by the fulfillment made possible by her work. There is a sense, of course, in which the extraordinary life could not have been lived without the ordinary one. For it was at least in part these difficulties that brought Dall face to face with the reality of women's limited opportunities and severely restricted economic and political power and that led her to imagine and champion new paradigms for women's lives. Hers is the compelling human story of a woman whose uncommon background and education and opportunities combined with her all too ordinary failures and misfortunes to create an effective advocate for the powerless. In this sense her life story is as important a legacy as what she would have called her "work."

Notes

1. Letter to Charles Henry Appleton Dall, February 22, 1843, Caroline Dall Papers, Massachusetts Historical Society.

2. Manuscript Journal, November 11, 1858, Dall Papers.

3. Manuscript Journal, March 10, 1873, Dall Papers.

4. *The College, the Market, and the Court; or, Woman's Relation to Education, Labor, and Law* (Boston, 1867; [Memorial Edition], 1914; New York: Arno Press, 1972), 364.

5. Ibid., 208–09.

6. Stanton to Dall, February 29, 1868, Dall Papers. In the end there were fourteen "Champions of the Women's Rights Movement," including Dall, in the volume *Eminent Women of the Age*, ed. James Parton, Horace Greeley, T. W. Higginson, J. S. C. Abbott, James M. Hoppin, William Winter, Theodore Tilton, Fanny Fern, Grace Greenwood, and Mrs. E. C. Stanton (Hartford, CT: S. M. Betts, 1869).

7. Manuscript Journal, January 28, 1869, Dall Papers.

8. Gerda Lerner, *The Creation of Feminist Consciousness* (New York: Oxford University Press, 1993).

Suggested Readings

No published monograph on Dall exists. The most useful general biographical account is Stephen Nissenbaum, "Caroline Wells Healey Dall," in *Notable American Women 1607–1950*, ed. Edward T. James, 3 vols. (Cambridge, MA.: Harvard University Press, 1971), 1:428–29. Gary Sue Goodman's dissertation, "'All about Me Forgotten': The Education of Caroline Healey Dall, 1822–1912" (Stanford University, 1987), analyzes Dall's life from birth to age eighteen. Barbara Welter's "The Merchant's Daughter: A Tale from Life," *New England Quarterly* 42 (1969): 3–22, the first consideration of Dall by a women's historian, is hardly sympathetic. Rose Norman, "'Sorella di Dante': Caroline Dall and the Paternal Discourse," *A/B: Auto/Biography Studies* 5 (1990): 124–39, deals with Dall's depiction of herself in certain autobiographical writings. Dall as a reformer is treated in Howard M. Wach, "A Boston Feminist in the Victorian Public Sphere: The Social Criticism of Caroline Healey Dall," *New England Quarterly* 68 (1995): 429–50; William Leach, *True Love and Perfect Union: The Feminist Reform of Sex and Society* (New York: Basic Books, 1980). Dall's relationship to Transcendentalism is the subject of several articles by Helen R. Deese: "Caroline Healey Dall," in *Biographical Dictionary of Transcendentalism*, ed. Wesley T. Mott (Westport, CN: Greenwood Press, 1996), 60–62; "'A Liberal Education': Caroline Healey Dall and Emerson," in *Emersonian Circles: Essays in Honor of Joel Myerson*, ed. Wesley T. Mott and Robert Burkholder (Rochester, NY: University of Rochester Press, 1996): 237–60; "Tending the 'Sacred Fires': Theodore Parker and Caroline Healey Dall," *Proceedings of the Unitarian Universalist Historical Society* 33 (1995): 22–38; "A New England Women's Network: Elizabeth Palmer Peabody, Caroline Healey Dall, and Delia S. Bacon," *Legacy: A Journal of American Women*

Writers 8 (Fall 1991): 77–91; and "Alcott's Conversations on the Transcendentalists: The Record of Caroline Dall," *American Literature* 60 (March 1988): 17–25. Dall's writings on Margaret Fuller are considered in Joel Myerson, "Caroline Dall's Reminiscences of Margaret Fuller," *Harvard Library Bulletin* 22 (October 1974): 414–28, and "Mrs. Dall Edits Miss Fuller: The Story of *Margaret and Her Friends*," *Publications of the Bibliographical Society of America* 72 (1978): 187–200. Although there is no comprehensive twentieth-century history of Transcendentalism, the best starting point for research on the movement and its major figures is Joel Myerson, ed., *The Transcendentalists: A Review of Research and Criticism* (New York: Modern Language Association of America, 1984).

5

Mary S. Gove Nichols
Making the Personal Political

Jean Silver-Isenstadt

According to her friend Edgar Allan Poe, Mary Gove Nichols (1810–1884) was a short, articulate woman, "somewhat thin, with dark hair and keen, intelligent black eyes." In an 1846 article in *Godey's Magazine and Lady's Book*, Poe included her among his select "Literati of New York." He described Mary as "a Mesmerist, a Swedenborgian, a phrenologist, a homoeopathist, and a disciple of Priesstnitz [*sic*]—what more I am not prepared to say."[1] How could one briefly characterize this radical woman who had extricated herself from a bleak and abusive small-town marriage only to gain independent fame in New York City as a shameless lecturer to ladies? Born Mary Sargeant Neal in Goffstown, New Hampshire, in 1810, Mary might easily have contented herself with the domestic ideal of womanhood common in mid-nineteenth-century America: raising obedient children in a religious home, maintaining a peaceful and nurturing haven for her working husband, and being a model of submissiveness and piety. Had her first spouse proven tolerable, perhaps Mary's rebelliousness would not have been so strong. But Hiram Gove repulsed and horrified his wife. "Every time he approached me, or laid his hand on me," wrote Mary, "a convulsive spasm ran over my whole system, giving me indescribable pain. I could not overcome it." Unable to support a family, intolerant of Mary's reading and writing, and unrelenting in the bedroom despite his wife's protests, Hiram led Mary to recall her first marriage as "burning prairie."[2] Mary was pregnant five times during her marriage to Hiram. All but one pregnancy ended miscarriage or stillbirth. One child, Elma Mary Gove, was born to them.

Between 1831 (when she married Hiram) and 1841 (when she left him), Mary was transformed from a conventional young schoolteacher into a notorious advocate of women's rights—particularly of the right of every woman to understand and control her own body. The majority of antebellum women in comparable marriages found themselves crushed by the experience, but the seeds of Mary's personal mettle had been sown early. Mary was the third child of Rebecca and William Neal, who each possessed a strong will. In different ways, the Neals taught their daughter to question tradition.

Rebecca Neal was a practicing Universalist, having adopted a religion that rejected the notion of Hell and posited instead an all-merciful God. Most residents of Goffstown considered the sect heretical. Even worse, William Neal dismissed God altogether. He considered himself a "Freethinker" and enjoyed rhetorical debate. Neal prodded his daughter to defend her views with intellectual rigor, not received wisdom. Mary—a sickly, unattractive, cerebral, clumsy, and shy child, who considered herself an acute disappointment to her mother—found solace in books, pets, and conversations with her father.

When Mary was twelve years old, her beautiful, but mocking, twenty-year-old sister succumbed to tuberculosis. Mary had never felt close to her sister or elder brother, but Rebecca and William Neal were devastated and decided to leave Goffstown. They moved the family to Craftsbury, Vermont, a remote town near the Canadian border. There, Mary experienced her first profound religious attraction—a transient wave of faith that soon led her to a fascination with Quakerism, a sect she had encountered in her voracious reading. She had never met an actual Quaker, but the sect's history enthralled her. At the age of fifteen, Mary declared herself a member of the Society of Friends. (That her father considered Christians "a poor sect," but the Quakers "the best of the bunch," likely influenced her decision.)[3] In keeping with Quaker doctrine, Mary sought plainness in her dress and speech. It proved an early experiment in setting herself apart from those around her; it also led to her acquaintance with Hiram Gove.

A well-meaning uncle in Goffstown introduced twenty-year-old Mary to his friend Hiram Gove. Hiram was thirty-one and eager to marry. With no Quaker marriage prospects back in Craftsbury, where she had become a schoolteacher, Mary accepted Hiram's pleading proposal. She immediately began to regret the decision. Yet because she perceived a broken engagement as both sin and cruelty, Mary felt bound to her word and resigned herself "to be sacrificed."[4] After Hiram and Mary married, they and settled in Weare, New Hampshire, Hiram's hometown. Elma was born the following year.

To Mary's dismay, it quickly became apparent that Hiram, trained as a hatter, lacked the skills to earn a living. Mary was thereby forced to sustain the family by teaching, doing needlework, and writing stories and poems for small magazines. Meanwhile, she withstood Hiram's religious intolerance of her creative writing as well as his contempt for her personal correspondence. At times, Hiram even burned his wife's personal letters before she could read them. Mary also endured the four failed pregnancies as well as the regular, physical agony of what today would be considered marital rape. It was during these years of suffering that Mary developed an impassioned interest in the study of anatomy and physiology, a science generally considered inappropriate for female consideration. Her elder brother, a medical student, had once chastised her for perusing one of his textbooks. Yet esoteric knowledge of the body seemed to provide solace—and perhaps some sense of control. As a married woman in the 1830s, Mary Gove had no legal right to resist her husband's advances or to divorce him for making her miserable. Desperately, she borrowed every medical book available.

When the Goves moved to Lynn, Massachusetts, in 1837, Mary opened her own school and began for the first time to teach anatomy and physiology. Hiram's dependence on Mary's income naturally limited his opposition to her activities. Indeed, he legally took possession of all her earnings, requiring her to beg for funds even for necessary school supplies. Mary described Hiram as a jealous, controlling man who resented her friendships and impeded her social life. Even Mary's attendance at antislavery meetings and popular lyceum lectures required "unwomanly" self-assertion.

It was at a Lynn lyceum that Mary first encountered the teachings of a man who changed the course of her life. On a rainy night in 1837, a former minister and advocate of temperance named Sylvester Graham delivered a lecture on health reform. Graham had already drawn considerable public attention; in fact, many considered him a fanatic. (He is best known today as the Graham behind the graham cracker.) Relying on physiological arguments rather than moral or religious language to influence personal behavior, Graham presented an extremely rigid doctrine of self-control as a means of disease prevention. Believing that stimulation enfeebled the body, Graham advised a purely vegetarian diet free of spices, caffeine, and alcohol. He taught that temperate behavior would ensure physical resilience. Perhaps most compelling to Mary, however, was Graham's extreme caution regarding sexual intercourse: he recommended indulgence no more than once every four weeks. Mary considered him brilliant and soon opened a boarding school based on his system. In the late summer of 1838, the Ladies' Physiological Society of Boston invited Mary to deliver a series of lectures.

Only twenty-eight years old and almost entirely self-taught, Mary wrote and delivered fourteen physiological lectures. The advertisement read: "Physiological facts of a delicate nature and which many ladies would not bring themselves to hear from a gentleman, but a knowledge of which is of great importance to the well being of society and individuals, will be brought to view. . . . The course . . . will be given to LADIES and to LADIES ONLY."[5] The entire series cost one dollar.

Mary Gove covered topics ranging from the formation of bone to the physiology of respiration, from the muscles of the eye to diseases of the spine. Interweaving well-established medical facts (such as the structure of the heart) with popular theories of health reform, Mary sought to alter her listeners' practices as well as to broaden their minds. Though ostensibly speaking about management of the body—what to eat, what to wear, and why—Mary delivered the political message that restriction was destroying women's health. She railed against the wearing of corsets (then a popular fashion that compressed women's lungs and limited physical motion) and explained the need for fresh air, easy circulation, freedom of movement, clean skin, pure food, regular exercise, and, most important, education. "Let woman once know her own organization, and she will tremble at the thought of sacrificing herself, for she will know that she is doing it," assured Mary.[6]

By demonizing women's ignorance rather than attacking any human enemy, Mary had developed a socially palatable package for the message that women should take more control over their own lives. Health—the source of happiness—required both physical freedom and mental stimulation. "If girls are taught to reason," argued Mary, "they will not spend their days reading fictions, and their nights in morbid dreams of love. . . . God has given us various faculties. All should be cultivated."[7] She regularly spoke to audiences of four to five hundred women. When Mary repeated her lecture on tight lacing at no charge, she drew a crowd of two thousand. Surely, many came for the novelty of hearing a woman speak in public, particularly about such a daring topic as female anatomy (which Mary illustrated with a French mannequin). But the flowering of Mary's reputation as a valuable teacher could not have relied on shock value alone. For the next several years, she traveled throughout the Northeast, repeating her series of lectures in New York City, Albany, Providence, Worcester, Haverhill, Nantucket, Bangor, Portland, Philadelphia, and Baltimore. Public speaking was an almost unheard of occupation for an American woman in the late 1830s.

Although Mary Gove had achieved fame, many did not respect her bold abandonment of "woman's sphere." The popular *New York Morning Herald*, for example, publicized her lectures by announcing, "This extraordinary woman, saint, savante, serpent, or whatever else she may be, (for we have hardly decided whether she is more of heaven than of hell) began a new series of lectures."[8] And in 1839, Mary found herself excommunicated from the Society of Friends, whose authorities disapproved of her public speaking on worldly matters. Rejected by her religious community, Mary cultivated ties with liberal-minded male physicians, who endorsed the efforts of "Mrs. Gove," freely lending Mary scientific textbooks and anatomical specimens for demonstration in her lectures, providing access to their dissecting rooms, and writing personal letters of reference. Unwittingly, the editor of the widely respected *Boston Medical and*

Surgical Journal (now the *New England Journal of Medicine*) even published three of her anonymous articles in the winter of 1839–1840—short pieces that followed the similarly anonymous publication of her first independent medical manuscript, *Solitary Vice*, a pamphlet devoted to the dangers of masturbation.

Impassioned with the noble cause of women's salvation, Mary had gained many friends. Women attending her lectures lingered afterwards to confide all manner of personal hardships to this rare educator who seemed intuitively to know their suffocating plight. From the podium, Mary shared many vignettes of women's unspoken afflictions. One lecture in her regular series was open only to married women. Little more than endurance and prayer seemed available to many women caught in bad marriages, desperately striving to project the female ideal of domestic bliss. Often superficially blessed with luxurious homes and "respectable" husbands, most of Mary's grateful audience members still lacked education, social mobility, personal income, and legal autonomy. Mary offered these women more than sympathy: she provided a vision of health reform that legitimized their craving for more equity in the world and more substance in their education. By emphasizing the physical and intellectual aspects of the female experience, Mary countered a romanticized and very limited cultural portrait that neglected a woman's intellect, ambition, or passion.

In Mary's own home, however, things had not changed very much. The strain between husband and wife continued. And to make matters worse, Mary suffered from repeated attacks of tuberculosis. These episodes terrified her, reminding her of her elder sister's final days. Rather than undermine the persuasiveness of her medical advice, however, the severity of Mary's own illness seemed to demonstrate the power of her teachings to preserve life in the face of morbid predisposition.

Realizing that involvement with Hiram only exacerbated her symptoms, in August 1841, Mary risked her reputation, took her nine-year-old daughter, and left Hiram for good. Much was at stake. Mary knew she was stealing her husband's child; the law considered Elma to be the property of her father. With the danger of losing Elma well in mind, Mary first returned to her parents' home. Although William and Rebecca Neal had known nothing of their daughter's marital troubles, William threatened to sue Hiram for payment of past debt if he refused to leave Mary and Elma in peace. The tactic worked. For several years, Mary relied on her father's protection. In 1842, to very favorable reviews, she published *Lectures to Ladies on Anatomy and Physiology*. And soon thereafter, an unexpected love affair further liberated Mary from any lingering sense of obligation to her husband.

Henry Gardiner Wright was a twenty-eight-year-old attractive British educational reformer who had left a wife and child in England. He had come to America hoping to establish with friends a "consociate family farm." (Whether he intended to send for his family later is not clear.) The 1840s gave birth to many experimental living arrangements, such as Brook Farm in Massachusetts and other utopian communities inspired by the writings of Charles Fourier. Fourier advocated equal rights for all people, considering the slightest oppression an obstacle to harmony.

Mary—who was particularly intrigued with Fourierism—met Henry Wright at a picnic in the autumn of 1842. Both vegetarians, the two felt an immediate attraction. Henry became a boarder in William Neal's home. Seeking an intellectual collaboration, he and Mary founded the *Health Journal and Independent Magazine*. In its early issues they promoted the idea for a new joint-stock community to be established in the West. They were probably looking for a living arrangement more private and less scandal-prone than the one in which they found themselves. Yet Henry, battling cancer in July 1843, returned to England and died soon thereafter. During his final months in America, he had committed himself to a medical treatment that would eventually dominate Mary Gove's future career: the "water cure."

The water cure, or "hydrotherapy," originated in 1826 with a Silesian peasant named Vincent Priessnitz and steadily gained popularity in Europe and America. Mary watched as Henry Gardiner Wright drank twenty to thirty glasses of pure, cold water each day and wrapped himself in cold, dripping bandages. The cure called for frequent and diverse baths, regular exercise, a mild diet, and abstinence from medication, alcohol, tobacco, and spices. For nonlocalized disease, hydrotherapists wrapped their patients in cold, wet sheets (leaving only the head free) and then in several blankets. Mary borrowed Henry's books describing these practices. Throughout the 1840s and 1850s, thousands of men and women sought treatment at the bucolic retreats, subscribed to hydropathic periodicals, and consulted private water-cure physicians. Women in particular stood to benefit by adopting the cure. In contrast to regular, "allopathic," medicine—which viewed women's bodies as inherently fragile and biologically predisposed to reproductive disorders—hydrotherapy did not pathologize natural processes such as menstruation and childbirth. Rather than perceive these physical events as crises of vulnerability, water-cure physicians taught that nature had made women strong. Sickness, they argued, resulted from poor choices in diet, dress, and self-management generally. Sickness, they argued, could be avoided. By preserving health, women could spare themselves and their families the cost and embarrassment of calling on physicians. Women could also begin to view themselves as more sturdy than porcelain dolls—and far more needful of activity.

On December 1, 1844, Mary's father, William Neal, died of consumption. Several months later, Mary decided to tour a range of experimental communities in Ohio, leaving Elma behind with her grandmother. Mary's trip was well publicized and Hiram decided to use the opportunity to reclaim his daughter. He no longer had William's threat to fear. On March 20, 1845, Hiram took thirteen-year-old Elma away from her grandmother to an undisclosed location. Mary spent the next three months in a tortured quest for her daughter. She consulted lawyers, pursued rumors of Elma's whereabouts, and slept little. To make matters worse, Mary and her mother also realized that they could no longer afford to keep their home. Having lost William, Elma, and their house, Mary and Rebecca moved in with friends.

Eventually, Mary learned by mail where Hiram had taken Elma. In desperation, she found some male friends willing to re-kidnap Elma. The men gained Elma's trust by giving her a letter from Mary and were able to reunite mother and daughter on June 16, 1845. Mary and Elma spent the next two weeks in hiding. Because the law forbade married women from suing or from being sued, Hiram pressed charges against one of the men who had kidnapped Elma. Mary paid for his defense, which dragged on, with appeals, for the next two years, and during that time she and Elma moved from one boarding house to another, seeking obscurity. In the same month that she was reunited with Elma, Mary had learned that a Dr. Robert Wesselhoeft had just opened a new water-cure establishment in Brattleboro, Vermont. In need of shelter, a remote setting, and income, Mary decided to go to Brattleboro and train as a water-cure physician. In return, she offered her renowned lecture series to Dr. Wesselhoeft's guests. Treatment protocols were individualized for every patient, taking into consideration a person's age, stamina, symptoms, and dedication. Catharine Beecher, who described her stay at the Brattleboro Cure in 1847, must have had a relatively strong constitution:

> At four in the morning packed in a wet sheet; kept in it from two to three hours; then up, and in a reeking perspiration immersed in the coldest plunge-bath. Then a walk as far as strength would allow, and drink five or six tumblers of the coldest water. At eleven A.M. stand under a douche of the coldest water falling eighteen feet, for ten minutes. Then walk, and drink three or four tumblers of water. At three P.M. sit half an hour in a sitz bath . . . of the coldest water. Then walk and drink again. At nine P.M. sit half an hour with the feet in the coldest water, then rub them till warm. Then cover the weak limb and a third of the body in wet bandages, and retire

to rest. This same wet bandage to be worn all day, and kept constantly wet.[9]

After three months in Vermont, Mary took a position at the New Lebanon Springs Water Cure, about twenty-five miles southeast of Albany, New York. As resident physician, Mary found her work physically demanding. By the end of the year, she was ready for a return to the relatively milder demands of teaching anatomy and physiology. Just before the New Year, Mary and Elma moved to New York City, the size of which Mary felt would discourage and possibly even prevent Hiram from any further pursuit. She and Elma moved into a large house at 261 Tenth Street, along with a handful of artistic and intellectual peers, all of whom shared an interest in vegetarianism, water cure, and diverse social reform movements of the day. Devoted to healthy living, the group established a small gymnasium in the house before buying furniture. To support herself and Elma, Mary taught classes of up to forty women in the parlor of the house and accepted a small number of inpatients where space allowed. She also began contributing regular columns to the *Water-Cure Journal and Herald of Reforms*. Elma, who would later become a noteworthy artist, began to take her first drawing lessons. Over the following three years, Mary developed a thriving private medical practice specializing in "female complaints."

In addition to her medical work, Mary also continued to write, often under the pseudonym "Mary Orme" (the significance of which remains a mystery). Between 1845 and 1849 she published a second edition of her lectures, as well as three novels, occasional poetry, and a series of stories in *Godey's Magazine and Lady's Book*, the *American Review*, the *Broadway Journal*, and the *U.S. Magazine and Democratic Review*. These were productive, invigorating years for Mary, who enjoyed the creativity, friendship, and intellectual vivacity of those who attended the regular parties held at 261 Tenth Street—among them Edgar Allan Poe, Horace Greeley, Albert Brisbane, and Herman Melville. Full of energy and ambition, Mary ignored the fact that back in New England Hiram was spreading rumors that she was keeping a brothel in New York. She even continued to send him money to pay off debts he had accrued prior to their marriage.

Thus, the bonds of indissoluble matrimony continued to pain Mary, but her anxiety over Elma's security diminished, as her daughter was no longer a child. The true anguish of her marital status soon came to revolve around her intensifying relationship with a young writer and editor named Thomas Low Nichols. Mary met Thomas at a Christmas party in 1847. Each had read and admired the other's writing. It was not long before the two were exchanging passionate letters and struggling to accept the limits of Mary's freedom. "I have already had hard things said to me for my acquaintance with you—," wrote Mary to Thomas. "For this I care not, only so far as it may affect my happiness with you, and my business. If I were simply a writer, and had a stipend that would support me, the world might edify itself after its own fashion. But my business, my darling profession of water-cure, must not go into other hands."[10] Mary's career depended on her reputation. Though she surrounded herself with liberal friends, she did not care to test the limits of their tolerance. Thus, it seemed a miracle when Hiram notified Mary in 1848 that he wanted a divorce; he had fallen in love with another woman.

Abruptly liberated from the worst mistake of her life, Mary hesitated to rush into a second marriage. Though she deeply loved Thomas, she feared permanent vows. Yet Thomas, who respected Mary's independence and encouraged her career, still wanted to spend the rest of his life with her. In her autobiography, Mary recalled her firm words of compromise: "In a marriage with you, I resign no right of my soul. I enter into no compact to be faithful to you. I only promise to be faithful to the deepest love of my heart. If that love is yours, it will bear fruit for you. . . . If my love leads me from you, I must go. . . . I must keep my name—the name I have made for myself, through labor and suffering. . . . I must have my room, into which none can come, but because I wish it."[11]

Thomas agreed to all. The two were married by a Swedenborgian minister in July 1848—only nine days after Elizabeth Cady Stanton, Mary M'Clintock, and Lucretia Mott had convened America's first Women's Rights Convention in Seneca Falls, New York. At that unprecedented meeting, participants signed the newly composed "Declaration of Sentiments," a remarkable document portraying human history as "a history of repeated injuries and usurpations on the part of man toward woman, having in direct object the establishment of an absolute tyranny over her."[12] Had Mary been less distracted with her personal life that month, she might have been more involved in the convention. Yet her belief in health reform as the most fundamental of all social reform also distanced her from overtly political women's organizations. For the rest of their lives, Mary and Thomas worked tirelessly to foster women's happiness and equity. They did not, however, involve themselves directly in the formal women's rights movement, which often struck them as too limited in its demands.

From the beginning of their relationship, Thomas Nichols encouraged Mary's quest for social influence and bolstered her confidence. A tall, self-assured journalist who had once spent a summer in jail for slandering powerful Buffalo politicians, he did not take oppression lightly. Thomas, who was a Fourierist and advocate of women's rights, felt drawn to Mary's strength. He was also increasingly taken with the health-reform movement—a crusade that rekindled a former interest in medicine. As a young man, Thomas had undertaken one semester of study at Dartmouth Medical School in Hanover, New Hampshire, before becoming inspired by Sylvester Graham and abandoning school for the lecture circuit. Soon after his wedding, however, Thomas returned to medical school. He completed his formal training at the University of the City of New York and earned his degree in March 1850. He then apprenticed himself to his wife and became a firm convert to hydrotherapy. That year, he and Mary each published new works describing the principles and practice of the water cure. Both also continued to write regular columns for the *Water-Cure Journal*. By September 1851, Thomas and Mary Nichols had opened the coeducational American Hydropathic Institute—the nation's first hydropathic medical school. Within two years of their wedding, the Nicholses had become nationally prominent leaders of the water-cure movement. They received hundreds of letters each week. And as if this were not adequate accomplishment, they had also become new parents.

In November 1850, Mary, already forty years old, gave birth to a second daughter. She and Thomas named the baby Mary Wilhelmina and called her "Willie." Elma was then eighteen years old. Willie, a child born of mutual love between her parents, represented a great deal to Mary, who had followed a strict hydropathic regimen throughout her pregnancy and delivery. Willie, raised hydropathically, would have the blessings of health, education, and happiness that Mary had been denied. To Mary and Thomas, their beautiful daughter symbolized God's endorsement of "passional attraction." It was a notion ahead of its time—one that seemed, with greater clarification, to cause only widespread consternation.

Significantly, in addition to water cure, the Nicholses had also become outspoken proponents of "free love." The phrase referred to a belief in the universal right to love—or not love—whomever one wished. One of its principal advocates, Stephen Pearl Andrews, had become a good friend of the Nicholses as well as a lecturer at the American Hydropathic Institute. The right to divorce—a centerpiece of the Nicholses' radical philosophy—alienated all but the most liberal thinkers of the day. After all, Mary and Thomas defined "adultery" as any instance of sex without love, outside—or within—the bounds of legal marriage. Thus, one might commit adultery with a spouse by succumbing to unwanted embraces, but experience pure love elsewhere by following one's passional attraction. It is perhaps unsurprising that many came to slander the Nicholses as promiscuous. Yet they were not. Mary and Thomas did not seek additional sexual partners; they sought freedom in, and from, love—a distinction that the majority of their contemporaries found imperceptible. Quite simply, Mary and Thomas demanded the right of every woman to "choose the father of her babe."[13] Indissoluble marriage they compared to slavery. In 1853, Thomas published a sexually explicit and politically loaded physiology textbook entitled *Esoteric Anthropology.* Hugely successful, it scandalized as many readers as it impressed.

The following year, the Nicholses coauthored a lengthy tome: *Marriage: Its History, Character, and Results; Its Sanctities, and Its Profanities; Its Science and Its Facts. Demonstrating Its Influence, as a Civilized Institution, on the Happiness of the Individual and the Progress of the Race.* They argued for an abandonment of traditional marriage. Mary wrote:

> When she is owned by a man who can maintain her, though he is loathsome almost as death to her; when she is utterly lost in bearing his children, and in being the legal victim of his lust; when her children are not hers, but his, according to inexorable law; when she has no power to work, and no means of subsistence but from this owner; when public opinion will brand her with shame, most probably, if she leaves her husband, and most certainly if she enter upon ever so true and loving relations with another man;—what is such a woman to do but to live a false and unholy life? . . . A new thought has dawned on the world—that of fidelity to one's self.

Thomas concurred, addressing himself directly to the "Ladies of the Woman's Rights movement" when he wrote, "You can have no right until you assert your right to yourselves."[14]

These political sentiments foreshadowed later developments in the women's rights movement, but at the time they were written, the notion of "free love" horrified even the more radical feminist activists—those who opposed women's taxation without representation, who challenged the limitations on women's property rights, and who vehemently condemned the lack of maternal (as compared to paternal) rights. Even the most progressive advocates of women's equity feared the implications of free love: a world in which liberal divorce would enable husbands and fathers to abandon their families legally in pursuit of stronger passions. Thus, Mary and Thomas found themselves isolated at the extremes of both health reform and political reform, two approaches to social change that they refused to disentangle.

Thomas argued in *Marriage:* "The whole train of what are called female diseases, are mainly caused by the legalized and sanctified brutalities of the civilized marriage."[15] Such views—combined with a determination to speak and write bluntly about the physical aspects of sexual passion—led to their rejection by prominent colleagues in the water-cure community. Russell T. Trall, editor of the

Water-Cure Journal and Herald of Reforms, ceased to publish their columns in 1853. In 1856 he even attempted to deny Mary's legitimacy as a water-cure physician—a ludicrous claim.

It was not only *Marriage* that hurt Mary's professional standing with New York's hydropathic community. In 1855, she had published her autobiography, *Mary Lyndon, or Revelations of a Life: An Autobiography.* It was an honest account of her life and loves, which the editor of the *New York Daily Times* denounced at great length in a review entitled "A Bad Book Gibbeted." Calling the author of *Mary Lyndon* "thoroughly and completely a sensual woman,—the slave of the coarsest lust," reviewer Henry Raymond went on to condemn her "unbounded self-conceit." Raymond concluded that the author's "experience of life has sharpened her intellect, exasperated her temper, inflamed her sensual appetites, augmented vastly her self-esteem, and made her ten fold more the 'child of hell' than she was before."[16] Accustomed to public censure by then, Mary continued to advance a vision of social harmony in which freedom would prevail. She and Thomas expressed these views in their own widely read periodical, the *Nichols' Journal of Health, Water-Cure, and Human Progress*, founded immediately after their exclusion from the *Water-Cure Journal*. There, they began to promote what they called the "Progressive Union," a voluntary association of like-minded individuals who shared an interest in preparing themselves for entry into a more harmonious society of the future. During this time, the language of "purity" became increasingly prominent in the Nicholses' writings. The more fiercely they were slandered, the more determinedly chaste they became.

In 1856, Mary and Thomas moved to Yellow Springs, Ohio, and purchased property adjacent to Antioch College, a newly founded coeducational school. The American Hydropathic Institute had closed in the wake of scandal surrounding the Nicholses' free-love doctrines. (Though short-lived, their school had trained many graduates who went on to teach and practice water cure throughout the nation; subsequent hydropathic schools survived for many years.) In Ohio, to the chagrin of Antioch's president, Horace Mann, the infamous Nicholses and about twenty of their followers established "Memnonia," a "harmonic home," intended to be a place of personal renewal for its residents as well as a model community. Members followed hydropathic regimens of bathing, diet, exercise, and recreation. They studied languages, learned to play musical instruments, took drawing lessons, and generally sought self-improvement and physical purification. They met regularly to discuss theories of social reformation. And to the surprise of many back east, sexual relations at Memnonia were allowed only for the expressed purpose of procreation, for Mary and Thomas were determined to be understood accurately, not portrayed as libidinous. As hydrotherapists, they had long believed in the need for moderation and balance in all aspects of life. Although condemned as boundlessly lustful, the Nicholses had to make a surprisingly small step from their prior defense of sexual "freedom" to their advocacy of chastity.

The decision to seek friendlier soil in Ohio had been influenced by what today would seem an unlikely source. In the mid-1850s, Mary, along with millions of other intelligent Americans, had become convinced of the reality of visiting spirits. Known as "Spiritualism," this faith in the ability of departed souls to communicate with the living via specially endowed "mediums" had won the respect of national leaders and the general populace alike. Seances became commonplace social events. Thousands found comfort and guidance in the messages conveyed from the spirit world. Although Mary had initially responded to spiritualists' claims with great skepticism, she soon found herself not only convinced but also personally receiving direct messages from spirits. Once settled in Yellow Springs, Mary conducted regular seances, where she encountered the spirit of Saint Ignatius Loyola, who advised her to convert to Roman Catholicism. Following considerable research, reflection, and consultation with Catholic leaders in the region, Mary, Thomas, Willie, and several other members of Memnonia converted to Catholicism in 1857. The news shocked conservatives and radicals alike. The experiment of Memnonia came to an abrupt end. The Nicholses spent the next four years traveling to Catholic institutions throughout the Midwest and South, offering lectures on water cure and health reform. Their conversion had required a blanket recantation of all prior writings that conflicted with those of the Church. Areas of difficulty related to free love and not to any medical doctrines. Indeed, at Memnonia, Mary and Thomas had already adopted a lifestyle conforming with the teachings of the Catholic church—and in some ways even more stringent.

Years of anatomical and physiological study had convinced Mary that God intended women as well as men to experience sexual pleasure. Yet intellectual belief could not overcome Mary's early and traumatic personal history. Neither radical social philosophy nor loving union with Thomas prevented Mary from reaching the ultimate conclusion that "marital union, only for wise and healthy birth, is the law of health and holiness for those who are to inaugurate physical and spiritual redemption." Mary's newfound philosophy regarding physical passion did not undermine her quest for social reform: "The sublimation of the sensual force; its use in giving health and material power . . . ; its use in producing harmonies of music, architecture, and painting, in the prophecy and teaching of inspired poets, in the living words of a divine philosophy—all, and the myriad multiplication of all, are contained potentially in the sensual life of man. This sensual force is the fertile soil which produces the highest beauty he can conceive and create."[17] For Mary, the destructive aspects of sexual attraction reflected the flaws of a diseased society. However, rather than continue to defend the natural and as yet unachieved possibilities of sexual happiness, Mary chose instead to promote sublimation and chastity. From the start of her professional career, she had been abused and misunderstood as promiscuous and shameless. Conversion to Catholicism surely offered a measure of peace.

After several years of travel, characterized by universally warm acceptance, the Nicholses returned to New York City, where they intended to open a water-cure establishment and found a new periodical. However, the start of the Civil War disrupted their plans. Rejecting violence and horrified by the firing on Fort Sumter, the Nicholses decided to leave the country. In 1861 they emigrated to England, never to return. Elma also left the United States to study art in Europe. She eventually married an Englishman, Thomas Letchworth, and had two children. Mary was very fond of her son-in-law and frequently saw her grandchildren.

For the rest of their lives, Mary and Thomas continued to write on the subject of health reform. Thomas gradually abandoned medical practice in favor of writing, but Mary continued to see patients until the month of her death, August 1884. The Nicholses' years in England were some of the most productive years of their lives—and also some of the saddest. In 1864, Willie died of bronchitis. She was only fourteen years old.

The loss of her daughter left Mary utterly distraught. Devotion to work could not stem frequent, uncontrollable fits of crying. In addition, in 1864, Mary began to develop cataracts, and she lost her sight entirely in 1868. A life devoted to the hydropathic principles of health preservation had failed to sustain Willie or to prevent Mary's blindness. The Nicholses believed that Willie had inherited a weakened constitution from her mother. After five years of guilt, grief, and physical incapacitation, Mary agreed to undergo two surgeries at the Nottingham Eye Infirmary. The procedures restored her sight and thus her ability to work. Full of gratitude and newfound strength, Mary threw herself into medical practice. Thomas meanwhile founded a new journal, the *Herald of Health*, and opened a shop in London called the "Health Depot," which offered a variety of hydropathic instruments for home use as well as health food. From 1867 until 1877, the Nicholses lived in Malvern, where they had established a residential water-cure facility. After ten years in the countryside, during which Thomas regularly commuted to London, they moved to South Kensington, where once again they welcomed residential patients into their large home.

The Nicholses remained Catholic and committed to women's equity, though they did not leave any explicit record of whether conversion had changed their views regarding marriage. Invited to an American women's rights convention in 1870, Mary responded: "I cannot come . . . , but my interest in the freedom of women has not in the least abated during thirty years of labour and prayers for her emancipation. I claim one right for Woman which includes all human rights. It is that she be free to obey the Divine Law of her own life—that she not be subjected to the lustful domination of one man, or to the selfish or unwise legislation of many."[18] Conversion to Catholicism had diluted neither the force of Mary's writing nor the core of her belief: that God intended all human beings to enjoy their innate capacities for work, for creativity, for love, and for pleasure. The promise of human perfectibility and faith in the possibility of universal harmony never ceased to inspire Mary's work.

From early adulthood until the month of her death, Mary Gove Nichols fostered a broad vision of women's capacities. Made radical by the very conditions that hampered her peers, Mary fought most strongly for every woman's right to happiness and good health. This right, she believed, encompassed all others. For Mary, reform of all social inequities hinged on health reform. And the pursuit of happiness necessitated social change. Mary's influence drew its strength from her firsthand knowledge of women's common afflictions. Like many others, she had suffered the loss of children; the limitations of financial dependence; the agonizing narrowness of domestic life; and unfulfilled cravings for education, self-expression, intellectual respect, social freedom, and physical fulfillment. The umbrella of "health reform" enabled her to demand all at once.

In 1853, Thomas Nichols had defined health as "a sound constitution, a pure nutrition, and a free exercise of all the organs of the body, and all the faculties and passions of the soul."[19] For Mary, attachment to this concept led her to escape a smothering marriage and to seek an intellectually and financially sustaining career, public influence, sexual freedom, motherhood, literary recognition, and even a measure of immortality. In 1839, as she was beginning her lecturing career, Mary wrote to a friend late at night, "The world misunderstands and abuses me but I shall yet have a name and a place among the benefactors of our race."[20] It was a determination that never flagged.

Notes

1. Edgar Allan Poe, "The Literati of New York City—No. III," *Godey's Magazine and Lady's Book* (July 1846): 16.

2. Mary Gove Nichols, *Mary Lyndon; or, Revelations of a Life: An Autobiography* (New York: Stringer and Townsend, 1855), 137, 119.

3. Ibid., 49.

4. Ibid., 121.

5. *Graham Journal of Health and Longevity* 2, no. 18 (September 1, 1838): 288.

6. Mary Gove, *Lectures to Ladies on Anatomy and Physiology* (Boston: Saxton and Peirce, 1842), 97.

7. Ibid., 284.

8. *New York Morning Herald* 5, no. 76 (April 10, 1839): 2–3.

9. Catharine Beecher, *Letters to the People on Health and Happiness* (New York: Harper Brothers, 1855), 117–118.

10. Nichols, *Mary Lyndon*, 362.

11. Ibid., 385.

12. *Report of the Woman's Rights Convention, Held at Seneca Falls, N.Y., July 19th and 20th, 1848* (Rochester, NY: John Dick, 1848), 8.

13. Thomas Low Nichols and Mary Gove Nichols, *Marriage: Its History, Character, and Results; Its Sanctities, and Its Profanities; Its Science and Its Facts . . .* (New York, 1854; reprint, Cincinnati: Valentine Nicholson and Co., 1855), 197.

14. Ibid., 119.

15. Ibid., 93.

16. "A Bad Book Gibbeted," *New York Daily Times* 4, no. 1221 (August 17, 1855): 2.

17. Mary Gove Nichols, quoted in Thomas Nichols, *Nichols' Health Manual: Being Also a Memorial of the Life of Mary S. Nichols* (London: W. W. Allen, 1887), 289, 287.

18. Letter to Paulina Wright Davis, 1870, Vassar College Archives, Poughkeepsie, New York.

19. Thomas Low Nichols, "Catechism of Water-Cure," *Nichols' Journal of Health, Water-Cure, and Human Progress* 1, no. 2 (May 1853): 11.

20. Mary Gove to John Neal, 1839, 5th day, night, 11 o'clock, quoted in Irving T. Richards, "Mary Gove Nichols and John Neal," *New England Quarterly* (June 7, 1934): 341.

Suggested Readings

Mary Gove Nichols was a prolific writer. Her works include medical texts, novels, short stories, poetry, pamphlets devoted to social reform, and dozens of columns in a variety of contemporary journals. She also cofounded several independent periodicals. To gain a sense of Nichols's voice and purpose, scholars might begin in the pages of the *Water-Cure Journal and Herald of Reforms*, a periodical readily available on microfilm and rich with Mary's contributions between 1849 and 1853. For Mary's medical writing, see also *Solitary Vice: Address to Parents and Those Who Have the Care of Children* (Portland, ME: The Journal Office, 1839); *Lectures to Ladies on Anatomy and Physiology* (Boston: Saxton and Peirce, 1842); *Experience in Water-Cure: A Familiar Exposition of the Principles and Results of Water Treatment in the Cure of Acute and Chronic Diseases, Illus-*

trated by Numerous Cases in the Practice of the Author; with an Explanation of the Water-Cure Processes, Advice on Diet and Regimen, and to Women in the Treatment of Female Diseases, with Treatment in Childbirth and the Diseases of Infancy (New York: Fowlers and Wells, 1850); *Nichols' Medical Miscellanies: A Familiar Guide to the Preservation of Health, and the Hydropathic Home Treatment of the Most Formidable Diseases* (Cincinnati: T. L. Nichols, 1856); *A Woman's Work in Water-Cure and Sanitary Education* (London: Nichols, 1874). Samples of Mary's fiction include: *Agnes Morris; or, The Heroine of Domestic Life* (New York: Harper and Brothers, 1849); and *The Two Loves; or, Eros and Anteros* (New York: Stringer and Townsend, 1849). For examples of Mary's autobiographical and reform monographs, see *Marriage: Its History, Character, and Results; Its Sanctities, and Its Profanities; Its Science and Its Facts. Demonstrating Its Influence, as a Civilized Institution, on the Happiness of the Individual, and the Progress of the Race* (New York, 1854; reprint, Cincinnati: Valentine Nicholson and Co., 1855); and *Mary Lyndon; or, Revelations of a Life: An Autobiography* (New York: Stringer and Townsend, 1855). For other leading voices of the American health-reform movement, see the works of William Andrus Alcott, Harriet N. Austin, Catherine E. Beecher, Eliza B. Duffey, Eliza W. Farrar, Edward B. Foote, Sylvester Graham, Samuel Gregory, Frederick Hollick, James Caleb Jackson, Thomas Low Nichols, Joel Shew, and Russell Thatcher Trall.

Additional biographical work on Mary Gove Nichols includes Dorothy Eleanor Battenfeld, "'She Hath Done What She Could': Three Women in the Popular Health Movement: Harriot Kezia Hunt, Mary Gove Nichols and Paulina Wright Davis" (master's thesis, George Washington University, 1985); John B. Blake, "Mary Gove Nichols, Prophetess of Health," *Proceedings of the American Philosophical Society* 106, no. 3 (June 1962): 219–34; Philip Gleason, "From Free-Love to Catholicism: Dr. and Mrs. Thomas L. Nichols at Yellow Springs," *Ohio Historical Quarterly* 70, no. 4 (October 1961): 283–307; Sarah Josepha Hale, *Woman's Record* (New York: Harper Brothers, 1855); Janet Hubly Noever, "Passionate Rebel: The Life of Mary Gove Nichols, 1810–1884" (Ph.D. diss., University of Oklahoma, 1983); Jean Lara Silver-Isenstadt, "Pure Pleasure: The Shared Life and Work of Mary Gove Nichols and Thomas Low Nichols in American Health Reform" (Ph.D. diss., University of Pennsylvania, 1997); Bertha-Monica Stearns, "Two Forgotten New England Reformers," *New England Quarterly* 6 (March 1933): 59–84, and "Memnonia: The Launching of a Utopia," *New England Quarterly* 15, no. 2 (June 1942): 280–95.

For commendable secondary sources related to American health reform, see James H. Cassedy, *Medicine in America: A Short History* (Baltimore: Johns Hopkins University Press, 1991); Norman Gevitz, ed., *Other Healers: Unorthodox Medicine in America* (Baltimore: Johns Hopkins University Press, 1988); Harvey Green, *Fit for America: Health, Fitness, Sport and American Society* (Baltimore: Johns Hopkins University Press, 1986); and James C. Whorton, *Crusaders for Fitness: The History of American Health Reformers* (Princeton: Princeton University Press, 1982). On women's medical history, see Rima Apple, ed., *Women, Health, and Medicine in America: A Historical Handbook* (New Brunswick, NJ: Rutgers University Press, 1992); Judith Walzer Leavitt, *Brought to Bed: Childbearing in America, 1750–1950* (New York: Oxford University Press, 1986); Judith Walzer Leavitt, ed., *Women and Health in America* (Madison: University of Wisconsin Press, 1984); Carroll Smith-Rosenberg, *Disorderly Conduct: Visions of Gender in Victorian America* (New York: Oxford University Press, 1986); and Martha H. Verbrugge, *Able-Bodied Womanhood: Personal Health and Social Change in Nineteenth-Century Boston* (New York: Oxford University Press, 1988). On the water cure, see Susan E. Cayleff, *Wash and Be Healed: The Water-Cure Movement and Women's Health* (Philadelphia: Temple University Press, 1987); and Jane B. Donegan, *"Hydropathic Highway to Health": Women and Water-Cure in Antebellum America* (New York: Greenwood Press, 1986).

6

Eliza Johnson Potter
Traveler, Entrepreneur, and Social Critic

Wilma King

"I do not like Iangy, though I have never seen her, they say she is so cross and proud . . . they say Iangy charges too high a price," said the woman to her hairdresser who listened patiently before responding: "Madam . . . I suppose Iangy has combed [hair] so long, that now she is getting old, and has a certain price; those who will give her this price she combs for, and those who will not, she won't comb."[1] Little did the patron know that she was indeed talking to "Iangy" about "Iangy." "Iangy" was the nom de plume the author had substituted for her own name when writing the brisk-selling *A Hairdresser's Experience in the High Life*, published in 1859. Who was its author? What shaped the writer's identity and social consciousness? Moreover, why would the gossipy *Hairdresser's Experience* be of interest to readers in the nineteenth, twentieth, or twenty-first centuries?

The Ohio-born Eliza Johnson Potter (1820–?), author of the behind-the-scenes narrative, recounted anecdotes about her customers that reflected her position as a confidante to well-placed women who spoke freely about any subject or person while she combed their hair. "Nowhere do hearts betray themselves more unguardedly than in the private boudoir, where the hair-dresser's mission makes her a daily attendant," wrote Potter. Clients believed their secrets were safe with her. After all, whom could she, a free black woman rendering a service to wealthy white women, tell? Who would believe her?

Potter was an "outsider," yet her clients either saw her as enough of an "insider" to talk freely in her presence or were uninhibited because they rendered her inconsequential and did not see her at all. Whatever the case, Potter was careful not to reveal their identities in *A Hairdresser's Experience*. Instead, she managed to recount their intimate disclosures and "tell all" about the women's conversations by using general descriptions of "Miss So and So," occasional blank spaces, initials, or pseudonyms. To further shroud their conversations in mystery, Potter ignored time. As a result, contemporary readers cannot accurately place people and locations with the moment of occurrence. Despite this shortcoming for historians, *A Hairdresser's Experience* is an underutilized commentary about facets of American culture in the antebellum North and South.

Through Sharon G. Dean's introduction to the 1991 reprint edition of *A Hairdresser's Experience,* readers learn that Potter was born in 1820, came of age in New York, and was a woman of middling height with brunette skin and auburn hair. Neither Dean nor Potter provides details about the hairdresser's parents, early childhood, or education. However, it is known that Potter was an upright member of Cincinnati's St. Paul's Episcopal Church, one who ostensibly avoided gossip and kept to herself. Potter's autobiographical 1859 publication is thought to tell more about elite white women than about the author, but it speaks volumes about Potter's self-esteem and how she, a traveler, entrepreneur, and social critic, defined her independence. When she wrote "being at liberty to choose my own course," she was saying that she alone made conscious decisions about her own behavior. Given the circumstances, it is no surprise that Potter, in her independence of thought and action, defied conventional expectations associated with gender, class, and race.

As someone who admitted to wanderlust, Potter intended to gratify her "long cherished desire" to see the western world. Following the presidential election of William Henry Harrison in 1840, Potter sailed to France with a family in the diplomatic corps to work as nursemaid for a young child. This voyage was a boon to Potter, who satisfied her own curiosity with frequent carriage rides or strolls through Paris with her "little responsibility" in tow. She was more than an ordinary sightseer, and the numerous fountains, beautiful statues, manicured lawns, majestic parks, and magnificent palaces, as well as the theaters, operas, concerts, balls, and hippodromes, captured her imagination.

In fact, Potter's intense desire to see the baptism of the Count of Paris led her to defy her employer, who had ordered Eliza not to leave the house during his absence. Of the employer, the impetuous Potter wrote, "He never seemed to recognize that *I* had any right to amuse myself or to be happy upon any occasion; but for this I invariable cared precious little." Needless to say, she managed to secure tickets and witness the baptism, which Potter declared was a scene of greater splendor than she had ever imagined and she did not believe it could be matched.

Because of her inquisitiveness and willingness to submerge herself in French culture, Potter readily gained facility with the language and enjoyed hearing the comments of passersby who wondered aloud about this woman of color as well as the child in her care. Of greater significance, the caregiver listened with fascination to their discussions without the slightest indication of understanding what they were saying. Perhaps it was in Paris that Potter first experienced the gratification of being an outsider in a social circle that was otherwise closed to her because of her race and class. She wrote: "Being a stranger among strangers. . . . They observed my embarrassed manner, and spoke. . . . I soon felt at ease and not at all like an intruder." That she was a poor black servant was not a serious disadvantage, since her ears and eyes visited places where the "I," Eliza Potter, was not welcomed.

After a salary dispute with her American employer, Potter worked for the European "Countess M." and made herself valuable to fashionable ladies by learning the art of hairdressing. Potter could ply that talent as easily in France as elsewhere. Therefore, when an opportunity arose for her to go to England for a short duration with the countess's daughter, "M'lle M.," Potter accepted eagerly. Her interest in England lasted longer than her employer's; consequently, Potter remained behind when "M'lle M." returned to Paris. By that time, Potter was familiar with the manners and lifestyles of the rich and well-born and could support herself as a hairdresser while fulfilling her desire to travel. Indeed, she "visited all the watering-places . . . saw the curiosities . . . and was delighted with everything."

By the end of her stay in Europe, Potter had seen the Queen of England aboard a royal cutter bound for Scotland, witnessed the baptisms of the Count of Paris and the Prince of Wales, "caught a glimpse of the Emperor Nicholas of Russia," and was among the spectators at funeral ceremonies held for the Duke of Orleans. That she happened to be present in London or Paris during these auspicious moments was no coincidence. She was no casual visitor but a connoisseur-in-the-making, who hungered to see and know as much about the "high life" as possible without respect for geographical boundaries.

Whether in Europe, Canada, or the United States, Potter was "perfectly independent of everybody" and went wherever she pleased. During the transportation revolution, which lasted from the 1790s to the 1840s, it was not uncommon for men to travel widely. By contrast, women were thought to have delicate constitutions and unable to endure travel over rough roads in stagecoaches, in crowded rail cars, aboard luxurious riverboats, or on horseback. Moreover, few white women were willing to ignore social customs and subject themselves to personal injury or damage to their character by venturing far from home alone. On the surface, it appears that Potter, a woman with a "vagabond disposition," was unfettered by these restrictions. In Potter's case, race and class were less a

barrier than gender. Otherwise, when she was "so inspirited" by seeing the royal cutter sail away, she would not have wished that she
was "a man and in her majesty's service." She would have been on
board.

To what extent was this behavior representative of her contemporaries? Scholar Cheryl Fish, who examined travel accounts published by Nancy Prince in 1850 and by Mary Seacole in 1857, free
black women in the nineteenth century who journeyed outside their
places of birth, the United States and Jamaica respectively, concluded that the two women were in search of some "field of usefulness." Ostensibly, Seacole and Prince were interested in matters
beyond their own self-satisfaction and economic security. Seacole
traveled to southwest Russia to offer her services as a nurse during
the Crimean War (1853–1856), and in 1836 Prince sailed to Jamaica,
where she engaged in missionary work among newly emancipated
slaves.

To be sure, Prince was enthusiastic about her calling in the West
Indies, but there was nothing nonutilitarian or benevolent about her
residency in St. Petersburg between 1824 and 1833 while her husband, Nero, worked as a palace guard. Beyond the benefits from her
husband's employment by the czar, she realized that there was a
great demand for children's clothes and promptly started a sewing
business. Prince employed a journeywoman and hired apprentices to
assist in what proved a successful venture. In fact, the Empress of
Russia ordered clothing for her children and herself. Of equal importance for Prince's enterprise, members of the nobility followed the
Empress's example in ordering garments, which Prince described as
"handsomely wrought in French and English styles."[2]

Aside from her work, Prince, like Potter, steeped herself in the
culture of her host country. The Emperor Alexander and Empress
Elizabeth received Prince when she first arrived and presented the
newly married woman with a wedding gift. Nancy Prince was well
positioned to observe the pomp and ceremony of the Russian Court
from within for nearly ten years. She also traveled about the countryside, saw the flood waters in St. Petersburg reach a dangerous
height in 1824, wrote about the succession crisis following Alexander's death, along with the coronation of a new emperor, but with far
less passion than did Potter, who strained above the crowd, under
trying circumstances, to see royalty first hand.

A comparison of Prince's and Potter's descriptions of their travels outside the United States shows that Prince chronicled her experiences in an unpretentious way, whereas Potter's textual flourishes
underscore her intention to let readers know she had indeed seen
faraway places and witnessed incidents in the high life that evaded
them. Mobility was liberating for Potter, and she flaunted it.

Despite the great sense of pleasure at traveling widely for more than a year and gaining new knowledge and skills while exerting independence, Potter became homesick and returned to the United States. She wrote: "On sped the vessel, with its precious freight of human life, each heart beating quicker as the distance from land, and home, and friends was shortened by the revolutions of the mighty wheels. How much of the happiness of this world is comprised in such anticipated meetings! and how miserable they must be who know nothing of such joys as these!" It is not clear if the expected happiness was that of people aboard the vessel or of those on shore contemplating the satisfaction of greeting loved ones.

Whatever the case, Potter's roaming ended, at least temporarily, in Buffalo, New York. Her journey "was suddenly arrested by a sort of ceremony called matrimony." Potter admitted that she "entered into [it] very naturally, and became quieted down under it for a length of time, just as naturally." Writing apologetically, Potter continued, "I have seen other persons do the same thing, and so, I suppose, I need not be ashamed to own having committed a weakness, which has, from the beginning of time, numbered the most respectable of the earth among its victims." Potter's love of liberty and autonomy, combined with her interest in traveling, appears stronger than the penchant to remain with her partner(s). Without learning further details about the marriage, which Potter mentions at the outset of *A Hairdresser's Experience*, readers find her in the next paragraph "alone in the world" in a form of "self-exile," away from her family and friends.

Setting herself apart from most women, black or white, of her day, the once-married Potter portrayed herself as a very happy unattached woman. She remained silent about whether her liberty resulted from divorce or the death of her spouse. There are no references to a spouse, with the exception of one or two slips of the pen. At one point Potter wrote about traveling from Buffalo to join her husband in Pittsburgh. On another occasion, she mentioned that her husband objected to allowing a newly freed woman to live in their household. It is never clear if these references are to the same person.

Nevertheless, the 1860 census listed Eliza Potter as the head of a household at 6 Home Street in Cincinnati, where she lived with her two Pennsylvania-born mulatto children, a girl and boy, who were eleven and nine years of age respectively. By her account, marriage circumscribed and threatened a woman's independence; however, if Potter held the same sentiments about motherhood and child rearing, she remained silent.

Despite her concerted efforts to downplay her personal story, it is evident that Potter was not a traditional woman who embraced accepted gender and social conventions. She wrote about her marriage with indifference and the absence of her husband with even less attention. Her dismissal of the "sort of ceremony called matrimony" reflects her overwhelming interest in preserving both her identity and independence. Ironically, she did not advocate abandoning the institution of marriage and was far from forgiving women, or men, who violated matrimonial vows.

In that same vein, the hairdresser looked askance at "placage," arranged unions between white men and black women, which were not uncommon in Louisiana. Much has been said about these nontraditional marriages as formal states of concubinage. Any moral condemnation of these relationships must be made against the backdrop of the colonial government's prohibiting Europeans from marrying persons of African descent in the Louisiana Territory and the Catholic church's frowning upon their living together. However, the absence of civil and religious approval did not stop the growth of these relationships in colonial or antebellum Louisiana.

Regardless of the circumstances of her marriage, Potter portrayed herself as solely responsible for her economic well-being. The ever-resourceful hairdresser also worked as a governess, made flowers, and developed dressmaking skills. Potter's keen eye for details is responsible for the descriptions of garments found in *A Hairdresser's Experience*. Her depictions help to contextualize the proficiency needed in nineteenth-century haute couture dressmaking. She rhapsodized about white, black, and pink silk gowns, with overdresses of elegant Swiss lace, fluted flounces, and costly trimmings. Richly woven fabrics in beautiful hues alone do not make fashionable garments. Style and creativity combined with skill are indispensable. The minute details in the trimmings, including the fluted flounces and pleats, required extra finesse, skill, and labor. Dressmakers, black and white, needed both creative and practical talent to build and keep a contented clientele, most of whom were fashion-conscious white women. Potter preferred looking at beautiful dresses rather than making them. Besides, "nothing but hair-dressing pleased [her] fancy for any length of time."

As a hairdresser, rather than a domestic or laundress—the occupations of most free black women in the nineteenth century— Potter supported herself in a manner that set her apart. "My avocation," she boasted, "calls me into the upper classes of society exclusively." Potter thrived because of the urban settings in which she lived and her ability to "comb" for women who frequented the theater, opera, and gala balls.

Moreover, the independent hairdresser maintained high standards and was quite vigilant about her profession. In addition to combing the hair of the individual customers whom she served in their homes, not "common boarding houses," Potter followed her clients to luxurious resorts to style their hair. In fact, she once claimed that she earned as much as $200 in a season. After more than fifteen years of experience in the trade, Potter also operated a successful school of beauty culture in Cincinnati. The enterprising woman probably earned additional income from boarding students in her home while they studied in her school. As a result of her creativity and hard work, Potter owned real estate valued at $2,000 and held $400 in personal property in 1860. This feat earned her a place among the black nouveau riche in antebellum Cincinnati.

Potter's primary income resulted from close interactions with whites, many of whom demanded that African Americans, enslaved or free, assume the "humble pose," a subservient posture. Blacks, legal conditions notwithstanding, had learned early on how to pay deference to whites publicly while privately maintaining their self-respect. The much-discussed "mask," a protective device for disguising personal convictions and steeling the psyche, facial expressions, and body language, was a significant factor in maintaining associations with whites whose patronage was critical to the economic survival of many black entrepreneurs.

According to Potter, she was not a subordinate to her customers and did not assume the humble pose. Instead, she exercised agency as a discriminating observer of white society who unleashed stinging criticism upon the social climbers, adulteresses, and "slaves to fashion" among her clients. Based upon her experiences in England, Potter declared that she had seen enough of the nobility and those who mingled with them to recognize members of the finer class "in any part of the world." She saved her greatest scorn for the nouveau riche. As the self-appointed voice of moral authority, Potter succeeded in ridiculing customers without losing their business because she spoke indirectly and sanitized the publication of anecdotal accounts. For example, when a client asked her for a definition of a "lady" in the midst of others, she responded eagerly: "Ladies, I can not tell you what I think constitutes a lady, and keep my seat. I must get up. I do not think all those are ladies who sit in high places, or those who drive round in fine carriages, but those only are worthy [of] the names who can trace back their generations without stain, honest and respectable, that love and fear God, and treat all creatures as they merit, regardless of nations, stations or wealth. These are what I say constitute a lady." Potter soothed listeners by addressing them as "ladies" and employed the rhetoric of true womanhood in extolling purity and piety. The hairdresser wagged a knowing finger to condemn those among her acquaintances who did not measure up to her standards. But she never mentioned a single name.

At other times, Potter spoke directly, but privately, to miscreants. For example, while combing the hair of a married woman whose gentleman friend visited and planned a rendezvous, Potter remained silent. When the lover left, Potter upbraided her client. She railed about the woman's behavior and attributed her superior air to wealth and education. No doubt the nonplussed customer was amazed at Potter's temper when she decried treating people with contempt in the presence of others. "There were many simple looking people, and poor people, who understood more than those who were speaking of them." The couple had conversed in French and assumed that the "simple looking . . . poor" servant would not understand their tête-à-tête. When offered money to keep quiet, Potter refused the woman's cash. Only kindness could seal her lips. Emotional "blackmail" would be more effective if clients respected Potter and vied for her approval, as she seemed to think they did. Certainly, a few well-placed whispers about the woman were sure to filter back to her husband.

Besides attention to the morality of her clients, Potter was also critical of people whom she labeled as "slaves" to fashions. Their interest in clothes was "carried to an extreme" and became, in her opinion, "positively vulgar." Although Potter claimed repulsion at the women's unusual penchant for clothes, she paid an inordinate amount of attention to what they wore. Consider her description of a ball gown:

> [made of] gold colored silk, of unusual brilliance, the skirt was plain and exceedingly full, with a train of half a yard, but sufficiently short in front to expose an exquisitely formed foot, encased in a silk gaiter, the precise shade of the dress; white point lace with buff cape pleatings formed the trimming for the drooping angel sleeves which were gracefully confined at the shoulder by a silk cord and tassel, displaying an elegant point lace undersleeve corresponding with the trimming of the neck, which was a la Pompadour, and long tassels which drooped gracefully upon the skirt from the waist and confined with white and scarlet ostrich feathers.

Was Potter's intention to titillate readers with minute details about garments or to whet her own appetite for fashions?

Her comments about social climbers who frequented luxurious resorts raise similar questions. She was of the opinion that "watering-places betray[ed] many characters, and much misery, that would never be found out, if people who certainly *know* they *must* cut a ridiculous figure, and make an entire failure of it, would only be wise enough to stay at home. Envy, hatred and malice all show themselves at watering-places." Did those whose interests in social mobility pique Potter's sensibilities because she envied their privileged positions? Or did it anger her because they did things—regardless of expediency—that she could not, because of her race and class?

These questions are not irrational, considering the fact that Potter spent "one night in a crowd" mingling with wealthy whites in a social environment. Her mulatto skin enabled her to bound over the racial divide between black and white; therefore, she moved through the horde of 1,500 merrymakers in Saratoga uninvited and unnoticed. Potter's knowledge of polite behavior in the high life made it possible for her temporarily to cross over the social barrier between the rich and the poor. Because she stood at the intersection of race and class, the "night in a crowd" provided the perfect opportunity for Potter to blend in and gaze at the social elites without their knowledge or objections. If Potter despised the behavior of so many of the elite women, why did she make this effort to observe them?

The keenly astute Potter could not always expose others without exposing herself. The "I" occasionally replaced the critical eye. For example, Potter criticized "slaves to fashion" in such a way that readers would think she paid no attention to stylish clothes, that is, until she wrote about a rail accident in which she lost her trunk. The lengths to which Potter went to receive compensation are remarkable. Had she become one of them? Even more revealing of the "real" Eliza Potter is the satisfaction she gained from the episode. She explained: "I was never more amused in my life, than at seeing the different railroad gentle men pick up my list, look at and shrink from it, as if it were an impossibility for a working woman to have such a wardrobe. One of them seemed quite horrified at the very idea of my having ten silk dresses with me; but it afforded me a good deal of pleasure to let him know I had as many more at home; but I told him that did not make any difference, as I had to get paid for what they in their carelessness, burnt up." In that same vein, Potter was critical of talebearing, but her *Hairdresser's Experience* was based largely upon private conversations never intended for publication. "I merely write them out for the amusement of those who may wish to indulge themselves," Potter explained. Of course, she had "no evil intent" in publishing the gentle gossip. Potter was more interested in readers' knowing there was no need to "go into alleys to hunt up wretchedness"; instead, it could be found "in perfection among the rich and fashionable." The social critic unmasked the "pretenders" and cast reflections upon the nouveau riche, who, in her opinion, were unwilling to acknowledge any shadows of imperfection.

Potter's overarching subject stands in sharp contrast to that of other free black women writers in antebellum America, including Maria W. Stewart, Harriet Jacobs, and Mary Ann Shadd Cary, who used their literary skills to advocate the abolition of slavery. They witnessed bondage from a distance but believed it was their social responsibility to use their pens in favor of abolition. In 1852, Frances Ellen Watkins proclaimed, "The condition of our people, the wants of our children and the welfare of our race demand the aid of every helping hand." She initially made this observation about education but also found it applicable to the antislavery cause. In either case, "helping hands" were essential in freeing blacks from ignorance and bondage. Watkin's popular poem "Eliza Harris," based upon a fugitive slave mother in Harriet Beecher Stowe's *Uncle Tom's Cabin*, appeared in William Lloyd Garrison's *The Liberator* and two other nationally distributed newspapers as a commentary on the vile act of separating families.

Of all free-born black women writers in antebellum America, only Potter had a close-up look at bondage. She, like Frederick Law Olmsted, witnessed slavery firsthand and wrote about it for Northern readers. The inspiration of Olmsted's *A Journey in the Seaboard Slave States* (1856), *A Journey through Texas* (1857), and *A Journey in the Black Country* (1860), followed by the condensed *The Cotton Kingdom* (1861), was their author's position as a special correspondent for the *New York Daily Times* between 1852 and 1854. Henry J. Raymond, editor of the *Times*, wanted to counter the portrayal of slavery as presented in *Uncle Tom's Cabin* and *The Liberator* with an unbiased account. He hired Olmsted without asking his position on slavery.

Potter's reason for being in the South was more circuitous. "I always had an inclination to travel, and was particularly desirous of seeing the sunny South," she wrote. "Having heard a great deal of New Orleans, I wanted to go there and to judge for myself of its perfections and imperfections." Seeing slavery personally was inevitable. Potter moved about freely in Memphis, where she heard the screams and groans of an enslaved women being severely whipped while tied to a tree. This alarmed the free woman, who was more interested in knowing why the slave was beaten than in bringing it to an end. This reaction should not be construed as a lack of sympathy for enslaved women and men.

While in the South, Potter raised questions about the paradoxical existence of slavery within a free society. "I have often wondered to myself how men can speak so much on the glorious cause of freedom and speak of this in the land of liberty, while they are daily and hourly trafficking in human beings," she noted. It was a legitimate observation. During the American Revolutionary War, Abigail Adams mused, "It always appeared a most iniquitous Scheme to me to fight ourselves for what we are daily robbing and plundering from those who have as good a right to freedom as we have."[3] One writer was black and the other white, and nearly one hundred years had passed between their comments, but the American paradox was troubling for both.

Potter's awareness of the tenuous nature of freedom within a slave society notwithstanding, she was more concerned about losing her life to cholera than losing her freedom to kidnappers. Most free blacks were more terrified at the potential loss of liberty than of the inevitability of death. Under the Fugitive Slave Act of 1850, authorities received $10 if they deemed an accused person guilty and only $5 if he or she were found innocent. It was a financial boon to declare any accused person guilty of running away. Such cases were not subjected to jury trials, and the accused persons could not testify in their own behalf; therefore, the possibilities of kidnapping free persons with the intent to enslave them intensified after 1850. Potter was not completely lackadaisical about her liberty. First, she had some protection from enslavement, since she traveled in the services of wealthy whites. Second, free blacks were anomalies within a slave society where it was assumed that all blacks were slaves. Perhaps she was included in this assumption. Potter traveled in cities where conditions were often fluid enough for slaves to pass as free and for fair-skinned blacks to pass as whites. Finally, incidences of kidnapping were not as common in the South as in the North after 1850.

Whether in the North or South, Potter tended to avoid conversations about slavery, but when "dragged into it," she expressed an opinion. In writing about a black woman from Cincinnati who had become a slaveholder in New Orleans, Potter called her the "most tyranical [sic], overbearing, cruel task-mistress that ever existed." Potter believed color was an important factor in the way the woman treated her slaves, explaining, "The propensities are the same, and those who have been oppressed themselves, are the sorest oppressors." Potter added, "It is a well known fact, those who are as black themselves as the ace of spades will, if they can, get mulatoes [sic] for slaves, and then the first word is 'my nigger.'"

This anecdotal evidence is not sufficient to portray black slaveholding women. It does not consider the reasons for ownership of chattel, nor does it take regional differences into account. In public records often "fwc," free woman of color, was appended to the name of a black slaveholding woman. The designation was distinctly different from "free black" or "free Negro," yet it tells little or nothing about the actual shades of her skin. In any case, skin color is less significant in assessing treatment than the reasons for owning slaves.

Potter was closer to the mark in another discussion about bondage with a proslavery advocate who argued that some slaves were well treated. Potter retorted with anecdotes about how badly others were handled. When told that slaves could not care for themselves, Potter maintained that if given an opportunity, they were certain to defy such assumptions. If the hairdresser spoke as honestly about slavery while in the South as she wrote about it when she returned to the North, it is unlikely that she plied her trade among slaveholding women or remained unharmed physically. In all probability, Potter assumed the humble pose temporarily.

Potter was clever enough not to divert the focus from her clients, many of whom would buy her book, to herself. Her story was secondary, and to hedge about her thoughts on slavery was by design. There are occasional lapses. For example, after witnessing the sale of slaves in the public market Potter admitted that she "left, feeling more heavily burdened than ever." The emotional wrenching prompted her to "vow and declare that [she] would never come another season to the South to earn the money that was made so hard by others." The sight and thought of humans being bought and sold distressed Potter to the extent that she "played sick" for several days to avoid clients. Why did the sassy independent woman refrain from speaking up and out?

Potter's reaction to the sale of slaves and how she reported it reveal only one facet of this complex woman. Where did she stand with reference to the abolition of slavery? Did she identify with her sisters in bondage? Potter wrote, "I don't like abolitionists, nor any that bear the name." Historian Waldo Martin Jr. asserts, "Whites became abolitionists out of choice," whereas "blacks were abolitionists out of necessity." Eliza Potter was not an abolitionist in the formal sense of the word, and the source of her disquiet was the notion that "so much injustice and wrong, and actually speculation" was done in "that name."[4]

A great number of unheralded individuals assisted slaves to gain their liberty. Without fanfare or membership in any formal antislavery organizations, they helped to destroy slavery whenever the opportunity arose. Potter told a male slave whom she met in Louisville all that she knew about Canada, including specific travel directions. Describing herself as the "humble means of unloosing the shackles of one upright and manly soul," Potter was arrested and tried as an accessory. When questioned, she did not deny complicity in "directing his footsteps to a new world." She was quite indignant at the charges against her. "I said in reply to those who examined me," wrote Potter, "that I recognized no crime in what I had done—meant none."

Unlike Harriet Tubman, Frances Ellen Watkins, Eliza Ann Parker, Anna Douglass, and many other black women who assisted fugitives, Potter went to jail for three months for "*this* . . . doing what I conscientiously felt to be a Christian deed," or her social responsibility. The loss of her own freedom was not a great enough threat to make her confess to any wrongdoing. Comparing herself to the biblical Job, Potter "adhered to [her] integrity to the last, preferring to be tried with, and die with [if necessary]," she wrote, "those who had killed . . . rather than shrink from owning that I had boldly aided in rescuing the soul of an oppressed fellow-being."

With the intent to "try to do right to all creatures," Potter, who portrayed herself as a humanitarian without biases against "slaveholders, free-holders, or any other kind of holders who treat all people right, regardless of nation, station or color," provided shelter for older emancipated women who found themselves without family and friends in Cincinnati. Of her response to their conditions, Potter said, "I sometimes think it strange how so many of these creatures fall into my hands."

What is even more "strange" is that Eliza Potter, the self-styled writer, has received so little attention from students of nineteenth-century history. To be sure, Potter intended to tell more about the "high life" than about "life among the lowly," yet *A Hairdresser's Experience* must be read for what it says and does not say about American society. The hairdresser's references to the Atlantic cable or the "great excitement all over the Union" following the Mexican-American War (1846–1848), when the expansion of slavery would no longer remain a marginal issue in nineteenth-century politics, are worthy of notice. The same is true of her commentary about the Underground Railroad, emancipated mulattoes migrating to Ohio, where they attended Oberlin Collegiate Institute, and the fugitive slave Margaret Garner. Garner, who ran away with her husband and four children in 1856, killed her infant daughter when the family was recaptured and returned to slavery. Toni Morrison's prize-winning novel *Beloved* is loosely based upon the Garner case.

Little escaped Potter's eye, and *A Hairdresser's Experience* does more than amuse others with a "little gossip." The autobiography has historical value as a firsthand account of American society, based upon the views of a traveler, entrepreneur, and social critic who understood what it meant to be an outsider as well as an insider.

Notes

1. Eliza Potter, *A Hairdresser's Experiences in the High Life* (1859; reprint, New York: Oxford University Press, 1991), 12–13; all direct quotations from Eliza Potter in this essay are from her book.

2. Nancy Prince, *A Black Woman's Odyssey through Russia and Jamaica*, ed. Ronald G. Walters (reprint of *A Narrative of the Life and*

Travels of Mrs. Nancy Prince [Boston: N. Prince, 1850]; New York: Markus Wiener Publishing, 1990), 32.

3. Charles Francis Adams, ed., *Familiar Letters of John Adams and His Wife Abigail Adams, during the Revolution. With a Memoir of Mrs. Adams* (Freeport, NY: Books for Libraries Press, 1970), 41–42.

4. Waldo E. Martin Jr., *The Mind of Frederick Douglass* (Chapel Hill: University of North Carolina Press, 1984), 23.

Suggested Readings

Historians of African American women in the nineteenth century have largely focused on women in slavery. A more comprehensive view is available in Jacqueline Jones, *Labor of Love, Labor of Sorrow: Black Women, Work, and the Family from Slavery to the Present* (New York: Basic Books, 1985), and the anthology edited by Darlene Clark Hine, Wilma King, and Linda Reed, *We Specialize in the Wholly Impossible: A Reader in Black Women's History* (New York: Carlson Publications, 1995). There is only limited scholarship on free women in antebellum America such as Susan Lebsock's *The Free Women of Petersburg: Status and Culture in a Southern Town, 1784–1860* (New York: W. W. Norton, 1984). Black abolitionists have also been a source of information on women's experience. Memoirs of black women include Harriet A. Jacobs, *Incidents in the Life of a Slave Girl: Written by Herself*, ed. Jean Fagan Yellin (Cambridge, MA: Harvard University Press, 1987), and Susie Baker King Taylor's *Reminiscences of My Life in Camp with the 33rd U.S. Colored Troops. Late 1st South Carolina Volunteers* (Boston, 1902), edited by Patricia W. Romero and Willie Lee Rose and retitled *Susie King Taylor: A Black Woman's Civil War Memoirs* (New York: Markus Wiener Publishing, 1988).

7

Ada Adelaine Adams Vogdes
"Follow the Drum"

Michele Nacy

Ada Adelaine Adams Vogdes (1842–1919) was born into an upper-middle-class family in Jacksonville, Florida, on May 10, 1842. There is very little known about her childhood or youth except that she moved with her family to New York before 1867. Ada was married to Anthony Wayne Vogdes on December 5, 1867. "Wayne" was a career army officer who spent his military career, until his retirement in 1904, at various outposts in the western Indian frontier Wyoming Territory. Ada's parents, Charles and Ann Adams, appeared happy with their daughter's marriage to Wayne, even though they realized that the marriage meant that their daughter would live far from them. Ada Vogdes, typical of many army officers' wives, spent her entire adult life traveling throughout the United States with her husband. Just as every aspect of her husband's daily life was subordinated to the army's mission, so was hers. That mission led to isolation, periods of separation from her husband, significant deprivation of creature comforts, a transient lifestyle, and a perpetual threat of danger and death. It also inhibited her ability to fulfill the nineteenth-century middle-class ideals of "true womanhood" and the "cult of domesticity."[1]

Ada was a product of a nineteenth-century Victorian upbringing, which stressed the idea that a "true woman" displayed the virtues of piety, purity, submissiveness, and domesticity. "True women" exerted their moral influence upon society by the establishment of a home that acted as a private safe haven, separated from the corruption and competition of the public world of men. But Ada Vogdes and other officers' wives lived within the institutional environment of the army and the isolation of the frontier. Therefore, she and her contemporaries altered the ideals of true womanhood, and by extension their notions of themselves, to fit the reality of their lives. For Vodges and other army wives who lived in the world of men, the line between public and private, home and work, was rather fluid. The army had extraordinary control over their physical environment. It provided quarters, furniture, and utensils to every officer and his family. Such provisions, however, constituted little beyond a place to live and its accoutrements; they did not make army quarters a "home" consistent with the middle-class ideal.

During the years she lived in the West, Vogdes wrote detailed letters to her parents about daily domestic matters, Indian affairs, and social relationships. Her letters were not intended for public scrutiny, and perhaps it is this uncensored honesty that provides a clear view of what life was like for a middle-class woman who had traded her well-disciplined, refined, and proper home for a nomadic lifestyle with the United States Army.

Shortly after Ada's December 1867 wedding, Wayne, then a lieutenant in the United States Army, was ordered to Fort Laramie, Wyoming Territory. For the next eighteen years, Wayne and Ada Vogdes lived a nomadic life, shuttling from Fort Laramie, to Fort Russell, to Fort Fetterman, and back. In 1866, General William T. Sherman urged all officers' wives to "accompany their husbands and to take with them all needed comforts for a pleasant garrison life in the newly opened country, where all would be healthful, with pleasant service and absolute peace."[2] Sherman undoubtedly thought that these women would provide the domestic haven he believed was needed to enhance the morale of his officers and soldiers. The general's portrayal of cozy army domesticity was, to say the least, overly optimistic, since the majority of wives who joined their husbands found themselves at a succession of isolated and usually primitive garrisons. In addition, their circumstances at these frontier locations were dictated by official federal policy. The experience was typical, but often overlooked by historians. In the twenty-five years following the Civil War, no less than 62 percent of the army was stationed at frontier posts during any given year. In many of the mundane particulars of daily life, Ada Vogdes experienced no more hardships than most frontier women of this period. But in many other significant respects—her relative isolation, frequent household moves, conflicted attitudes toward Indians, and lack of control over many of the details of her private life—Vogdes's connection to the army set her apart.

The geographical isolation of the frontier left Ada far from her family as well as significant numbers of like-minded women. Both political considerations and army strategy dictated this isolation. Put simply, during the late nineteenth century the United States Army's primary role was to control, restrain, and confine Indians living on the plains and in the mountains of the American West. Plans devised at a distance to achieve this goal determined officer salaries, troop strength, and military strategy. Such decisions often had consequences for army officers and their families.

Transfers to new assignments meant long periods of travel through "uncivilized" country under primitive circumstances, facing extreme weather conditions and constant physical danger. For Ada, with each change of station the impermanence of her domestic life became quite glaring. In May 1868 Vogdes wrote to her mother about an upcoming move from Fort Sedgewick, Colorado, to Fort Laramie.[3] She was very sad to be going farther away from her family in the East, and a bit leery about the new location. To reach Laramie they would travel to Cheyenne City and then find transportation "up the country" in order to go about four hundred miles more in army wagons. On the trip from Sedgewick, Vogdes experienced the "most fright" she had ever had in her life. They were crossing the Platte River in wagons, but the water was so deep that there was no proper place to ford the river and the driver drove into quicksand. The horses sank down into water nearly over their backs. Ada and another woman sharing the wagon "felt quite alone" and were sinking lower and lower into the water until the wagon was nearly on end. The officers accompanying Vogdes's wagon were in another wagon following about a quarter mile behind. When the second wagon was nearly within reach, it too got stuck in quicksand. Four mule teams went down. Because the tide was so strong, getting out of the wagons would mean drowning. At this point Wayne came to Ada's rescue by trudging through the river and freeing her from the sinking wagon. She had felt sure that she was going to die. She noted that her heart beat so fast the rest of the day that it was an effort for her to breathe. Dangers like these were not unusual and generally viewed as normal hazards of moving. It was quite a change for a woman like Vogdes.

Travel for any reason was dangerous, but sometimes officers' wives chose to take such risks. In August 1868, Ada decided that she could not bear to spend time without Wayne, so she traveled with him to a detached assignment at a camp about twelve miles from Laramie. She simply did not want to stay at home without him. Vogdes initially reported that she was very comfortable in a nice tent, with a table, chairs and a "large, beautiful green arbor built of cedar." It did not bother her to be the sole female at the remote camp, and she felt perfectly safe from Indian attacks because there were about one hundred soldiers within a quarter mile. But one evening horrifying noises coming from all around them frightened the group. Ada, Wayne, and some of the soldiers trudged out in a miserable rainstorm to look for the source of the noise, only to find that they were surrounded by coyotes. Ada, drenched by the storm, said that she felt like an old mat that had been rained on time and time again and never permitted to get thoroughly dry. Within her tent there was no means to dry or warm herself. Nevertheless, it seemed that no matter how miserable the situation, Ada was much happier if she was with Wayne. The Vogdeses did eventually return

to Fort Laramie, but the following month Ada found herself alone
again when Wayne left for detached duty at the same camp. Such
uncertainty is what most disturbed Ada about army life. Ada wrote
her mother that if she knew when the detached duty would end, she
could "better endure."

Occasionally, moves turned out to be positive. Early in 1869 the
army was beginning to reduce the number of officers on its active
roles, and Wayne expected to lose his commission. In April 1869, Ada
learned that the army was going to give her a mixed blessing. The
good news was that Wayne was to be retained as an officer. The bad
news, from Ada's perspective, was another move; this time from Fort
Laramie to Fort Fetterman—a place Ada considered to be an extreme outpost of the territory. Ada was quite concerned; she worried
especially about receiving mail at a spot so remote. She also had
great trepidation about the move because she feared trouble from
the local Indians. She had heard that a party of soldiers repairing the
telegraph wires outside of Fetterman had been attacked by Indians.
One soldier was killed and three were missing. The fact that she had
just gotten settled into new quarters at Fort Laramie added to Ada's
frustration. Within a matter of weeks, Ada had packed and unpacked
only to have to pack, move, and unpack again.

Her distress intensified as she heard more and more frightening
stories about Fort Fetterman. Indeed, she would not be allowed to
venture outside the post, because of possible Indian attacks. Ada
wrote to her mother: "Yesterday you should have heard that we were
to go to Fetterman, and it has saddened me, as I know you hate to
have me go there but what can I do, but to follow the drum." In addition, Ada did not look forward to the dangerous three-day trip to get
to Fort Fetterman. She knew that she would not sleep a wink. Happily, although long and arduous, the trip was uneventful.

Once she arrived at Fort Fetterman, Vogdes set about the task
of settling into her new home. Although the uprootings were never
pleasant, there was nothing quite so stressful and challenging as the
job of establishing a domestic space that would provide a "proper"
home in this hostile environment. Frontier conditions challenged
the domestic ideal on several levels. Most obviously, garrison life
was hardly known for the creature comforts and physical surroundings that defined middle-class domesticity. Facilities could consist of
one-half of a double house, an adobe hut, or even structures with
canvas walls and ceilings and dirt floors. As officers' wives became
accustomed to a frequent moves, they began to reassess their prior-
ities and modified their notion of what constituted an ideal home.
Practicality replaced ideology.

Vogdes was lucky, but generally she and other officers' wives
faced what many women in the East would deem wretched conditions. Middle-class women, regardless of their location, were expect-

ed to maintain a comfortable and efficient home. Silver serving pieces, fine china and crystal place settings, and delicate linens were part of the normal middle-class home. Curiously, officers' wives used these same symbols of a "proper" home in their mud huts and tents. Wives also provided nursing and medical care to their families and others in need. Any woman living on the American frontier found her daily tasks challenging. Garrison life further complicated the situation.

Vogdes had been introduced to the difficulties of housekeeping during her husband's first assignment at Fort Sedgewick in May 1868. Living in a tent outside the garrison until quarters became available, Vogdes wrote to her mother, "Every two or three days we have a most terrific *sand-storm*, which fills the house, and every thing in it, full of the finest sort of dust, and it is next to an impossibility to keep clean." High standards of cleanliness were a priority for middle-class housewives even if their "house" was a tent. Frontier conditions, especially at its extremes, made the maintenance of such standards difficult, if not impossible. By October 1868, Vogdes had moved into the garrison. There she had three "nice" rooms in an abode building, which she described as "quite comfortable." The rooms were thirty feet by thirty feet, and she thought they were a delightful size for a sleeping room. The bedroom had a large open fireplace, and there was a stove in the parlor. The bed consisted of gunnysacks (bags used to store corn), which also covered most of the floors. But Vogdes worried that she would be in the quarters only until Christmas because they were actually captain's quarters. If a captain wanted them, Ada and Wayne would have to move. Ada said she took the quarters knowing that she might have to give them up, although she explained that at least in the army there were plenty of men to help if moving became necessary. Nevertheless, the uncertainty of her circumstance must have been unsettling.

The army's practice of "ranking out," or as some called it, "falling bricks," was very controversial among the wives of lower-ranking officers. When an officer arrived at a post, he was able to select any set of quarters that were designated for his rank or below. So a major could come into post and choose any quarters for which he qualified—even if there was a family already occupying those quarters. If he did select occupied quarters, the residents would be forced to move out in a matter of days. The "outcast" family then selected quarters from those available for their particular rank, and thus the dominoes would fall. So, even when Vogdes was settled into her house, she had to concern herself constantly with the possibility of being "evicted" through ranking out.

Typical of many women, Vogdes took great pride in her home; no matter how temporary. A house in any format at least allowed her to assume the prescribed domestic role for middle-class women. In an 1869 letter to her father, Vogdes described the boiling water, foaming soap suds, and pungent vapor emitted from the steaming boiler as she scrubbed her new home. Ada said that she kept "house like a lady for the first time and [had] no care, or thought about anything, anymore." This carefree attitude can be directly attributed to a hired cleaning woman whom Ada described as "anxious to do cleaning and [took] the greatest interest in all affairs." Vogdes also had a cook and other hired help. For nineteenth-century middle-class women, keeping a house like a lady included having hired help to do the actual labor. Local frontier women or Indians cooked and did cleaning, mending, and other daily chores. Often Ada would also have at her disposal a "striker"—an enlisted soldier assigned to Wayne but given household responsibilities as well.

Nevertheless, no matter how settled the daily routine became, soon Ada was on the move again. In a May 1869 letter from Fort Fetterman, Vogdes explained that this time her new quarters were in a log cabin, "the interior of which is as pretty and as beautifully finished as any house." Her parlor was a "lovely room fifteen by fifteen square, the mantle piece [was] of oak finish, as [was] the bookcase." From her parlor she could go into her oak-finished bedroom, which had the prettiest bed she had ever seen." Not only did she have four nice-sized rooms, but she also had "a large yard back with stables, cows houses and chicken house." Ada adapted to her circumstances and was even able to bring a bit of enjoyment with her.

Throughout her time on the frontier and the rest of her life, Ada loved music and commented on how much others enjoyed her musical talents. Ada often asked her parents to send sheet music; for example, she requested "some new songs on the guitar" because she "tired" of the old ones. In a letter from Fort Laramie written in December 1868, Ada regaled her parents with descriptions of her theatrical performances. Very pleased with herself, she wrote how much she loved the beautiful little theater and greatly enjoyed performing because it gave her "confidence in public." At first she had been very nervous about singing in front of an audience. Indeed, Ada explained, she had been "in constant fear of something" since arriving on the plains, but performing helped remove this nervousness. As early as 1869, Ada was involved in a choir and musical group at Fort Fetterman and found herself constantly playing and singing for a few friends. At Fort D. A. Russell in the summer of 1873, she considered the rental of either a first-class parlor organ, which would cost her $5.00 per month, or a piano for $10.00. Ada chose the piano, and in January 1874 she entertained fourteen officers in her home. Ada also played and sang in local churches. Although she put much energy into her efforts, her performances remained within the acceptable private sphere as defined by middle-class standards of proper behavior.

By August 1874, Ada felt content that she had achieved the domestic standard, despite the difficulties of frontier and army life. Vogdes commented that many of the couple's callers had complimented her on their lovely quarters. Nevertheless, tranquility was never permanent. When General Sherman talked of "absolute peace," he failed to mention that such a peace might well be violated by those who shared the frontier with the army—American Indians. As noted earlier, officers' wives sometimes hired Indians to do menial household chores. Officers' wives might also see Indians riding magnificent horses and wearing beautifully beaded clothes. Wives' letters often commented on the beauty and attractiveness of the Indian warriors and their wives, whose "toilet" (that is, dressing or grooming, a common term at the time), as Ada phrased it, "was most beautiful to look at."

At the same time, Indians could also look pitifully hungry wrapped in government blankets or seem very menacing as warriors that threatened the very survival of whites. Therefore, depending on the current relations with a particular tribe, contact with Indians led officers' wives to hold conflicting opinions about just who these people were and what should be done with them. The many well-publicized cases of brutality against whites assumed legendary status and served to harden white attitudes. Descriptions of Indian "barbarity" aroused hatred, vengeance, and fear in the hearts of civilian and military frontier inhabitants. With each telling, the barbarism and terror grew. Moreover, many officers' wives personally or through their husbands experienced terrifying encounters with Indians that only lent credence to stories they had heard from others. Although brutality went both ways, it is not difficult to understand why officers' wives felt malice and hatred toward Indians. It is perhaps more difficult to understand the seemingly benevolent, almost humanitarian, attitudes toward Indians held at times by officers' wives.

In a series of letters to her parents, Ada reveals these contradictory feelings. Ada's first written reaction to Indians appeared in a March 1868 letter to her father. She described a new policy ordering officers to go to bed with their clothes on so that they could react more quickly to night alarms when Indians threatened the garrison. Vogdes said there had been only two night alarms since the policy had been issued, but that those two were quite enough. Her trepidation about the Indians continued when she wrote in April 1868 that a party of Indians drove off all the livestock just about a mile on the other side of the river. Even though this attack had been outside the garrison, Vogdes confessed that she thought of nothing else but Indians, and "in fact, we all have 'Indians on the brain.'" In May 1868, Ada wrote her mother that "the Indians have been very troublesome all around us, since I last wrote. Men have been scalped at the Post above us, only half mile from the Fort, and we have to be very careful indeed about going away from the Fort any distance."

Despite such "troubles," Vogdes was also in awe of Indians. In January 1869, Ada was present at an Indian Council held at Fort Laramie, Wyoming Territory. She watched the two hundred Indians that came into the fort and told her mother they were "young, bold, dashing, warriors, with squaws and papooses." Vogdes was particularly taken with one of the Blackfoot chiefs, Black Hawk, who was dressed in a beautiful full suit of buckskin that "was most elaborately embroidered in white, blue, and red beads, from his throat to his ankles, and his black woven hair with bright feathers." Red Leaf, another Blackfoot chief, also wore a full suit of buckskin worked with porcupine quills. Typical of her times, Vogdes wrote that she found it "difficult to realize that they are genuine savages because some of them have splendid looking faces." These Indians had come into post to return mules that had been stolen earlier in the year, and Ada was quite pleased that the return of the mules seemed to indicate that the Indians wanted peace. Ada was also quite excited about personally receiving an arrow from Chief Red Leaf, saying that she would prize it highly.

Peace could also bring out feelings of sympathy. In March the same year, Vogdes wrote her father that the garrison was full of Indians and that she could not possibly turn them away from her kitchen: "They were dreadfully hungry and starved looking, I cannot refuse them anything that I can possibly give." She was most surprised when a particular Indian came into her kitchen for food, and when she gave him something to eat, he "threw off his buffalo robe, down to his waits, and sat in his skin," as if the comforts of civilization were too hot for him. The next month, even though the Indians had nearly eaten her out of house and home, she wrote, "I cannot bear to turn them away, they have such a good opinion of me, that I do not wish to offend them." Perhaps her feelings of superiority as she supervised the care of the unfortunate gave her satisfaction. She believed that the Indians thought of her as Lady Bountiful. Or perhaps her religious beliefs in true "Christian charity" motivated her actions. Certainly Ada seemed to enjoy bestowing favors upon those she called the "genuine savages." Nonetheless, perhaps what is most striking about Ada's letters is the absence of any reference to the souls or moral salvation of the Indians. As a daughter who often referred to her minister father's sermons "in times of anxiety," it seems remarkable that Ada never discussed a moral or spiritual obligation to redeem the Indians or save their souls.

In particular, Ada viewed Indian women with both compassion and contempt, sometimes simultaneously. What she viewed as grotesque physical abuse of Blackfoot women had prompted her sympathy at Fort Laramie. She complained about the way Indian men treated their wives. "I wish you could see how these Indian men load down their squaws," Ada exclaimed to her father. "A mule when he is laden is nothing to be compared to a poor squaw." For Vogdes, a woman who had been raised with a particular understanding of the role of women and the nature of "true womanhood," the position of Indian women within their culture directly conflicted with her own notions about female roles. It is doubtful, however, that Ada Vogdes, or any other officer's wife, thought of Native American women as capable of being "true women."

Although prejudiced by white supremacy ideas, Ada considered herself something of an expert on Indians. Her father asked many questions about the frontier Indians, and Ada did not hesitate to respond. Charles Adams was particularly interested in the burial habits of the tribes. Ada told him that the Sioux and Cheyenne were the only Indians on the plains that she knew of who put their dead in trees. The Arapahos, she thought, buried bodies in the ground soon after death. She explained to her father that there was a marked distinction between the burial of a big chief and an ordinary Indian. But learning about Indian culture did not make her tolerant. She concluded that Indians were "a strange dirty set of people," who had "no good in them."

By July 1869, Ada had moved to Fort Fetterman. She continued to help Indians who came to the fort by giving them food, saying, however, that she did not like the Arapahos as much as the Sioux because she could not understand the Arapaho very well. But over time, things grew less congenial. In October the post was put on "thorough war footing," with cannons mounted on hilltops. The entire garrison was enclosed and heavy gates erected at each entrance. Ada could see the Indians on the bluffs watching every movement of the fort's inhabitants. At the end of October the fort was apparently less well protected because Ada actually had some Indian visitors. She was quite frightened by the intrusion and ordered her husband's striker to give the Indians something to eat so that they would quickly leave.

Ada continued to vacillate between hatred and sympathy. But gradually, her sympathy waned. Although she found Indians useful for housecleaning and domestic work, she described them as devious and dreadful thieves. Perhaps frustrated by growing tensions on the frontier between Indians and whites as more settlers moved west, Ada increasingly complained about individuals in the East who opposed fighting Indians. She wished that such people could come out to the plains and live "or have some relative scalped and then they would find the true and only way to deal with them is to kill, kill!!" Like that of many Westerners, Ada's attitude toward Indians was hardened by warfare. In February 1874, Vogdes implored her father to "say a prayer for [us] daily while these Indians are bent on destruction to the whites." The Sioux, Cheyenne, and Arapaho suddenly began attacking whites over a three-hundred-mile stretch. A Laramie officer on his way to detached duty at Laramie Peak, the same place Wayne Vogdes had been assigned a few years earlier, was killed by an Indian. The dead officer was not scalped, according to Ada, because the Indians would not scalp someone if he "showed courage to the last." Perhaps fearing her own possible widowhood, she was quite upset that the dead officer left a wife of less than a year and an unborn child. Ultimately, Ada decided that the government should take prompt measures. She felt that the Indians had given sufficient cause "to *exterminate* them, root and branch."

Although contact with Indians was somewhat unique to whites living in the West, other aspects of Ada Vogdes's life, such as her efforts to maintain a "proper" home, were similar to those of many middle-class women. Army officers and their wives shared with most men and women of middle- to upper-middle-class families the notion that "traditional obligations of husband and wife" were specific gender roles, which cast men as protectors and providers and women as cooks, nurses, and moral custodians of the family. However, even within these roles, army officers and their wives found themselves in circumstances that were rarely traditional in practice or condition. For example, most nineteenth-century middle-class American couples spent the majority of their time together; long separations were unusual. For Ada and Wayne Vogdes, separation was quite common. In addition, separation presented perils and dangers not experienced in the civilian world. Vogdes and other officers' wives attempted to accompany their husbands whenever possible. These efforts to follow their husbands suggest at least a relatively satisfying personal relationship among spouses. Emotional fulfillment was another necessary element in the middle-class domestic ideal.

In March 1868, upon arriving at Fort Sedgewick, Ada Vogdes, a relatively new bride at the time, wrote home extolling the many virtues that Wayne possessed and said how very happy he made her. Vogdes told her mother that Wayne was all that she could desire. Ada continued: "They say generally that people are disappointed in each other after marriage. In my case, all mine are agreeable ones in my sense of the world. Wayne is more polite, attentive and loving than he was as a lover. He gratifies my every wish, and is more devoted than ever in his life." Wayne would readily accept responsibility for domestic chores, she said, including making the bed and cleaning the house. She was sure that "in devotion, [and] usefulness . . . and in [sweetness of temper]" she could not have found anyone better than Wayne. She told her mother that "all is love and devotion in my house."

Wayne's assistance continued during their many moves. Upon leaving for Fort Fetterman in 1869, Ada again praised Wayne's helpfulness: "There is no one in the whole Army I do believe," Vogdes wrote, "who moves with as little trouble as myself. Wayne packs everything from clothes down to my work boxes [and] cleans them all out." Such expressions may seem counter to the separate spheres model described by some historians. But if a man's willingness to assume household responsibilities is a criterion for a good middle-class marriage, Ada and Wayne Vogdes were well on their way. This cooperation may have also been another example of the ways army couples adapted the ideal to fit the realities of their lives.

Indeed, as already suggested, army life redefined certain aspects of the domestic ideal and introduced some new ideas about women's role. For example, not all officers' wives wanted children. Ada Vogdes wrote her mother about the birth of another couple's baby. Although Vogdes was excited about the new baby, she was quite happy not having children of her own. "I hope to continue as barren as that fig tree of the Lord's," she wrote her mother. Perhaps her reluctance to have children was based on her dislike for the little creatures. She wrote her mother that she "hated children more and more every year she lived and [thought] they [were] the most disagreeable things that can come into a house." She did not think that a child was the "well spring of pleasure in a house." Indeed, many army career couples had no children. It is difficult to determine if this was a conscious decision. Vogdes seemed determined not to have children, but other officers' wives lamented their "barren" homes. Being on the frontier, however, made her circumstances more acceptable within the social ideal. Raising children on frontier posts was dangerous and difficult.

Another shift from the domestic ideal was Ada's desire for some financial independence. Indeed, although forever the loyal army wife, she chafed at what she perceived to be her inability to manage her own financial matters. Influenced by the growing women's rights movement, Ada Vogdes's desire for a modicum of autonomy seemed to increase the longer she remained on the frontier. In December 1873, Ada wrote to her mother about Wayne's dominant nature regarding money. "Wayne keeps all his money in the bank," she complained. She concluded her letter with a gloomy appraisal of woman's status. "WOMEN ARE AS MUCH KEPT DOWN IN THEIR SPHERES OF LIFE, AS THE SLAVES OF AFRICA, OR CUBA. I am telling you facts & what I see & know from experience . . . men feel complimented to know they have a sub. [subject] who must ask them for the 'Almighty dollar' when they need it."

Despite these "modern" ideas, Ada was also well aware that the community that she had joined, the United States Army, was a traditionally structured and class-conscious entity. Notions of class and breeding were quite important to her. Even on the desolate and isolated frontier, Vogdes judged the people with whom she lived. She and her contemporaries might have been separated from the middle-class society of their youth, yet they carried with them the class consciousness and haughtiness that was prevalent in the civilian middle- to upper-middle-class world of the nineteenth century. Officers' wives were aware of and commented on the various class differences, even among their own group. They considered themselves "ladies" of the highest social standing, true "thoroughbreds," as some referred to themselves, and the army reinforced this idea by providing officers and their families with privileges, pay, and authority commensurate with a higher station in life. Vogdes provides a particularly fine example of the haughtiness so often associated with those of comfortable means and lofty social position. Her friendships with the wives of senior officers also helped further Wayne's career. She even believed that owing, in part, to *her* friendship with the wife of one of his commanders, "Mrs. Colonel Dye," the colonel would be giving Wayne an important position. Vogdes believed that Wayne would do an excellent job but was sure that the position would be offered to please her and that the Dyes thought a great deal of both Vogdeses.

In her correspondence she often commented on her growing feeling that she was "getting more aristocratic every year [she] lived" and that she found it quite unpleasant to spend time with those who were beneath her. She said that she did not "cultivate those in the regiment who were neither congenial or high bred." Ada had always been close to the senior officers' wives, whom she found lovely and of great comfort. She particularly enjoyed the companionship of her congenial friends, "Mrs. General Potter and Mrs. General Hunt." The use of the title "Mrs. General" was a less than subtle way of informing others that the lady was of high rank because of her husband and therefore deserved certain courtesies. As the daughter of a general, Mrs. Potter undoubtedly provided Ada with a friend who was both sweet and "high bred."

In one of her first letters home after joining Wayne at Fort Sedgewick in 1868, Ada wrote that there was a divided society at Sedgewick. The garrison, it seems, was divided in half—with the aristocrats on one side and those of lesser station on the other. Ada decided early on that she belonged to and would be considered part of the aristocratic half of the garrison. She believed that some in the garrison were quite jealous of her, but that did not matter as long as she was accepted by the proper members of the society. She thought that this encounter with a divided garrison provided her with more education about human nature than forty years of living in a city.

Vogdes may also give insight into some of the attitudes officers' wives held for those who, as she phrased it, were "plebeian people . . . who are not up to the mark on all occasions and do the polite thing at the right time." In Ada's definition, plebeian people had "no money, manners, or position." The army's official system of rank placed all officers' wives in the same upper-class social position. Nevertheless, even official policy could not alter the traditional attitude of social superiority held by many officers' wives, who held their own ideas of class that they imposed upon army society.

Although Ada generally commented on people not of her class, she also passed judgment on other officers and their wives. When stationed at Fort Fetterman, Ada found the commanding officer and his wife, "Colonel and Mrs. Chambers," quite lacking in social graces. "Mrs. Chambers is too common for me to endure," she wrote her mother, and she thought Colonel Chambers unfit for command. After finding the Chamberses also lacking in social standing, Vogdes wrote a letter to her mother in which she expressed her intolerance for women who lacked what she believed to be proper etiquette and training. "There is something in early bringing up that sticks out like quills on a porcupine if that bringing up has not been of the first quality. She had on a brown silk, or poplin, with thread lace around the neck, & sleeve, & a lovely set of solitaire diamond ear rings in her ears. She smoothed her dress down in front, & her hands were so rough, they sounded like little curry combs over the dress." Undoubtedly, Mrs. Chambers was in an unenviable position, having to compete with Ada's previous commander's wife, Mrs. Dye—whom Ada dearly admired. Her highly critical judgment of other wives was unique only in its lack of subtlety. It is interesting to note that Elizabeth [Libby] Bacon Custer, the wife of George Armstrong Custer, continued to enjoy the status of her husband throughout her life, even after his death. In the army, a husband's rank and status defined a wife's position, but values from the larger society influenced personal interactions.

Ada was able to enjoy the status and position of her husband's rank for many years. After their initial postings on the frontier, Wayne Vogdes served with the Fifth Artillery at Fort Trumbull, Connecticut, and Key West, Florida. Subsequent assignments included duty with the Fifth Artillery in Charleston, South Carolina, and Atlanta, Georgia. Their army adventures included a tour of duty in San Juan, Puerto Rico. In October 1900, Wayne Vogdes became the commanding officer of the San Diego military district at Fort Rosecrans in Southern California, and the Vogdeses moved to San Diego, where they spent the rest of their lives. Wayne retired in 1904 with the rank of brigadier general. After Wayne's retirement, the couple became active in both the civilian and the military communities in the San Diego area. Brigadier General Vogdes was a fellow of the American Geological Society and a member of several Academies of Science. He died on February 8, 1923.

Ada Vogdes died on January 27, 1919, at the age of seventy-six. "Mrs. Vogdes" was remembered in her obituary as being "among the best known of the army people, not only of this city but also throughout the country. . . . Mrs. Vo[gd]es was socially well known and was an active worker in St. Paul's Episcopal church."

Examining the experiences of Ada Vogdes through her letters provides an opportunity to hear, in her own words, a middle-class woman's reactions to all the new, bizarre, and dangerous adventures she faced as an army officer's wife in the garrisons of the western frontier. She made moves in blinding heat and over desolate terrain. Vogdes saw evidence of savage attacks by Indians and yet felt sporadic compassion for the sick, hungry, and pitifully clothed Indians that came to her quarters begging for food. She took great pride in her well-kept homes, always knowing that if judged by the standards of her class in the East, she was living in a hovel. Ada was a woman who grew up in a society that supported the nineteenth-century ideology of true womanhood; yet she lived the majority of her adult life in a society that thwarted that ideology at every turn. Ada faced the challenges of frontier life within the unique world of the United States Army on the western frontier, and this institutional environment forced her to adapt mainstream models in order to create her own ideology and style of domesticity. She began her married life as a relatively ordinary woman who believed herself to be much like others of her class. But the diversity and richness of her experiences on the frontier present a picture of an extraordinary woman, one who adapted social ideals to fit her own needs.

Notes

1. Barbara Welter, "The Cult of True Womanhood, 1820–1860," *American Quarterly* 18 (1966): 151–74.

2. Martha Summerhayes, *Vanished Arizona: Recollections of the Army Life of a New England Woman* (Lincoln: University of Nebraska Press, 1979); this particular quotation of General Sherman's is used repeatedly in manuscripts, diaries, and books of various authors.

3. All quotations from letters are included in the Vogdes Family Papers Collection, Special Collections, United States Military Academy Library, West Point, New York; specific letter dates are cited throughout this essay; other information may be found in "The Journal of Ada A. Vogdes, 1868–1871," housed at the Huntington Library, San Marino, CA; quotations from

the journal cited here are from Donald K. Adams, "The Journal of Ada A. Vogdes, 1868–1871," *Montana: The Magazine of Western History* 13 (Summer 1963).

Suggested Readings

The primary source material for this work was found exclusively at the Vogdes Family Papers Collection, Special Collections, United States Military Academy Library, West Point, New York. There are 176 complete letters and 93 fragments in the collection. Ada Vogdes kept a journal during her assignments on the plains, which is owned by the Huntington Library. In addition, "The Journal of Ada A. Vogdes, 1868–1871," edited by Donald K. Adams, was published in *Montana: The Magazine of Western History* 13, Summer 1963.

Further information about the lives of army officers' wives can be found in several books written by these extraordinary women. Ellen McGowan Biddle, *Reminiscences of a Soldier's Wife* (Philadelphia: J. B. Lippincott Co., 1907); Frances Grummond Carrington, *My Army Life and the Fort Phil Kearney Massacre* (Philadelphia: J. B. Lippincott Co., 1910); Frances M. A. Roe, *Army Letters from an Officer's Wife* (New York: D. Appleton, 1909; reprint, Lincoln: University of Nebraska Press, 1981); Martha Summerhayes, *Vanished Arizona: Recollections of the Army Life of a New England Woman* (Salem, MA: Salem Press, 1911; reprint, Lincoln: University of Nebraska Press, 1979); and Mrs. Orsemus Bronson Boyd, *Cavalry Life in Tent and Field* (Lincoln: University of Nebraska Press, 1982), are all exciting firsthand accounts of the adventures and experiences of these women as they accompanied their husbands on their frontier assignments. Additionally, several historians have edited the letters of such women, for example, Shirley Leckie, ed., *The Colonel's Lady on the Western Frontier: The Correspondence of Alice Kirk Grierson* (Lincoln: University of Nebraska Press, 1989). Robert H. Steinbach's *A Long March: The Lives of Frank and Alice Baldwin* (Austin: University of Texas Press, 1989) examines the Baldwins' lives. Of course, the three books by Elizabeth Bacon Custer require close scrutiny: *Boots and Saddles* (New York, 1885; reprint, Norman: University of Oklahoma Press, 1961); *Tenting on the Plains; or, General Custer in Kansas and Texas* (New York, 1895; reprint, Norman: University of Oklahoma Press, 1871); and *Following the Guidon* (New York, 1880; reprint, Norman: University of Oklahoma Press, 1966). Libbie Custer's campaign to immortalize her husband made her possibly the most famous officer's wife of all time but also casts suspicion that her books were ultimately self-serving. Nevertheless, they provide us with a detailed and vivid picture of garrison life. See

Shirley Leckie, *Elizabeth Bacon Custer and the Making of Myth* (Norman: University of Oklahoma Press, 1993).

For a discussion of middle-class women's prescribed role during the nineteenth century, see, for example, Kathryn Kish Sklar, *Catharine Beecher: A Study of American Domesticity* (New Haven: Yale University Press, 1973), and Barbara Welter, "The Cult of True Womanhood: 1820–1860," *American Quarterly* 18 (Summer 1966): 151–74.

8

Teresa E. Wooldridge Ivey
Constructing an Ideal Southern Lady

Angela Boswell

Historians have reconstructed the lives of certain Southern women and the ideal of the "Southern lady" through the diaries, journals, and letters left by a few nineteenth-century women. Unfortunately, most women lived in relative obscurity and left behind no records. Their lives are more difficult to reconstruct. Teresa E. Wooldridge Ivey (1816–1890) was one woman whose story is almost forgotten. In the midst of a larger research project on women in Colorado County, Texas, Ivey appeared again and again in public documents as an interesting and often enigmatic character. But she left behind no letters, diaries, memoirs, or histories. Consequently, the significance of her life easily slipped into obscurity. From the Texas and Alabama courthouse records one can reconstruct Ivey as a woman who carefully portrayed herself as a "Southern lady," while breaking every social rule set up to guide Southern women's lives.

The Southern ideal in the nineteenth century was a world of separate gender spheres. Men should use their superior intellectual abilities to rule the public sphere of business, finance, law, and politics. Women's sphere, believed to be morally superior, should encompass the home, family, and children. Southern prescriptive literature described the woman's role as nurturer, caretaker, and the moral center of the family. Ideally, she was pious, pure, domestic, and submissive. She should use her influence and natural inclinations toward piety to guide her children and husband toward a good and moral life. Family disputes were to remain private, and marriage was for life. Before the Civil War, plantation mistresses had the additional role of guiding and even ruling over the slaves owned by their families. Finally, Southern ladies made their homes havens from the public sphere and at the same time entertained and made connections that would enable husbands to succeed in the public world.

What becomes immediately apparent is the fact that few Southern women could live up to this ideal. The vast majority of African American women in the South were slaves. They had no opportunity to rule over their home or inhabit a sphere separate from black men. Most slave women, like most male slaves, worked in the fields from sunup to sundown.

Poor white women had much more freedom to choose how their time was spent, but very few of these women's families owned slaves. Therefore, they had little leisure time to pursue "moral elevation." In Colorado County, for instance, only half the white families owned any slaves, and very few had more than twenty. Poor white women usually found themselves working in the fields alongside their husbands at the busiest time of the year, thus blurring the separation of male and female duties. This circumstance was especially true for white women living on the frontier—and there were several frontiers in the South before the Civil War. In the frontier South women's labor was essential for turning the wilderness into a productive farm or plantation. In most families, a frontier wife performed traditional "male" duties that ran contrary to the female ideal. Even slave-owning families faced numerous hardships that forced women to work alongside men, at least temporarily forsaking their domestic duties.

Despite the difficulties of Texas frontier life, Teresa Ivey worked very hard to fulfill the role of a true Southern lady. Ivey's 1890 obituary called her a "friend to the orphans and hospitable to those who visited her. She was a member of the Baptist church . . . and loved to entertain her pastors." The records, however, hint that Teresa Ivey's life was far from the ideal, although she maintained the outward appearance of genteel womanhood.

Teresa Wooldridge was born in Georgia in 1816. Her wealthy slave-owning family moved to Mississippi while she was very young. Like many elite Southern families, Teresa's probably found it necessary to move farther west, as the land her father owned was exhausted by overproduction of cotton. Longer life spans and the growth of the cotton kingdom led many younger men to move west for opportunity and new land. Teresa's family did well in Mississippi. They prospered economically and were well respected. Her older brother served as justice of the peace and later in the Mississippi legislature.

Although details of her early years are no more than sketchy, with this background Teresa probably acted the role of the belle. In the nineteenth-century South, parents did not choose their children's marriage partners. But interested parents worked to assure that their children would meet potential partners only within their own social class through balls, picnics, and other forms of "acceptable" entertainment. For a young Southern woman, this was the period in which she had the most control over her own life. Although she was given a fairly wide latitude in choosing a husband, her fate was virtually sealed to that of her spouse, once he was chosen.

Sometime before 1844, Teresa chose to marry Jesse A. Ivey of Pickens County, Alabama, an area just across the border from her parents' plantation in Mississippi. Her parents were likely pleased with Teresa's choice, since Jesse Ivey was a wealthy, successful planter. As in almost all elite Southern couples of the period, Jesse was older than Teresa, in this case by thirteen years. Fulfilling her role, Teresa had two children: Martha Ann Teresa was born May 6, 1846, and Susan Rebecca in 1851. Teresa lived up to society's domestic ideal by marrying a successful gentleman, bearing and raising children, becoming an active church member, and keeping her family free of any public scandal.

However, the marriage was an unhappy one. Even though it was contrary to the ideal for a Southern lady, Teresa could have divorced her husband. During the early nineteenth century, the growth of the ideal of companionate marriage put pressure on relationships to live up to higher expectations. Marriages were less likely than those in the colonial era to be business arrangements in which each partner played a particular role for the good of the family. The new model raised expectations concerning emotional fulfillment from marriage. Both husbands and wives expected love and affection to be the basis of their interactions with each other. As the ideal of marriage changed, so did the number of people dissatisfied with their circumstance, and divorce laws became more liberal throughout the United States. Changing assumptions about gender roles and marriage highlighted the injustice of virtuous women being forever tied to deserting or otherwise degenerate husbands. Although Southern seaboard states were slow to change laws allowing greater accessibility to divorce (South Carolina did not do so until the twentieth century), frontier states both north and south incorporated the need for greater availability of divorce into their new laws and statutes. In general, Southern states, which had previously required an act of the legislature to obtain a divorce, offered relief to women by moving the divorce process to the less intimidating local or judicial level. Many states shortened the period of time for divorcing on the ground of desertion, and cruelty clauses were added or enlarged in scope either by statute or by judicial opinion.

Of course, not all unhappy couples divorced. Husbands had sufficient opportunities to simply abandon their marriages. With the ever-expanding West, men could strike out on their own and disappear forever into the "wild" frontier. The West held special appeal to men wanting to cut ties to wives, children, or families in the East. Frontier Texas especially appealed to such men. William Dunlap, for instance, left a wife in the East and simply remarried again without obtaining a divorce from his first wife. John Hope moved to Texas, leaving his wife in Florida, and filed for divorce after the requisite three years, charging her with abandoning him. Even the first president of the Republic of Texas, Sam Houston, left a wife in Tennessee and only eight years later sought the first divorce in Texas history.

Although abandonment was one way short of divorce of ending a marriage, some couples remained married but agreed to separate living arrangements. Sometimes these situations were spelled out in legal documents giving the wife some control over property. Sometimes these arrangements were less formal and can be discovered only by historical accident. One very unusual deed in Colorado County, Texas, was signed by three sisters, "we the said Emily Gilbert and Charlotte Cherry and Sarah Dunford in consideration that our respective husbands have abandoned and deserted us and have left us without the means of support."[1] All three of these women knew the locations of their husbands, either within Colorado County or in nearby counties. Yet only one of the three ever received a divorce.

Separate living arrangements, of course, benefited the women most who had some means of supporting themselves without remarrying. Teresa Ivey fortunately had a means of support if she left her husband, which she did in 1852 when she returned to her parents' plantation. Although the West usually called to men escaping family ties, in November 1853, Teresa decided that what worked for men could work just as well for her. Teresa's brother Augustus decided to move his family to Colorado County, Texas, and Teresa accompanied him. Teresa's reasons for making this move are impossible to know for certain. Possibly her entire family moved to Texas. By 1861, her other brother, Thomas A. Wooldridge, was also in Texas serving as an itinerant Methodist minister in a county near Colorado. It is also possible that Teresa, like others who moved west, saw Texas as an opportunity to increase wealth and property holdings. Of course, she might have also seen Colorado County, Texas, as an opportunity to begin a new life far away from her estranged husband.

Teresa Ivey owned property, as an inheritance from her parents. She took approximately twenty slaves and a substantial amount of personal property, including a rosewood dresser and a full set of china (white trimmed with gold) with her to Texas. She also brought the first carriages to the area, "built on the style of the old stage coach, with folding steps on the sides, a booth for baggage at the rear and a seat in front on the outside for the driver. The cost of these vehicles was $1000 to $1200 each, the pair of mules or horses that pulled them say $400. The colored gentleman in the livery who held the reins over the team was $1200."[2] Ivey did not relocate to Texas empty-handed by any means.

However, Teresa Ivey was a married woman with no independent legal control over her property. By 1853, most Southern states had followed Mississippi's lead in passing laws granting married women the right to own certain types of property. No matter what property married women were allowed to own, they still had no right to sell, rent, or mortgage it. Therefore, although Teresa was hundreds of miles away from Jesse Ivey, he retained legal control of her property. In order to circumvent this handicap, Jesse Ivey executed a trust. In November 1853 "in contemplation of the removal of said Teresa E. from the state of Alabama to the state of Texas," Jesse transferred $20,000 worth of slaves and other property to Teresa's brother Augustus "in trust" for Teresa. The trust further stipulated that Teresa was to have full power "to use enjoy and to sell and dispose of said property in any manner she may think proper."[3] This legal contrivance gave Teresa a certain amount of power over her own property, although that was still subject to the cooperation of her brother Augustus. The value was probably equal to the amount of property that Teresa had brought to the marriage.

Augustus and his family settled in Colorado County, and Teresa moved to a home nearby at the Lavaca County line. In 1853, Colorado County, Texas, was no longer a true frontier area. There were a few small towns, and wealthy landowners had established large-scale cotton-producing plantations. Much of the farmland had been cleared. There were even certain elements of civilization, such as established churches, shops, debate societies, and societal balls held in the county seat of Columbus. However, in general, Colorado County probably lacked many of the accoutrements of civilization to which Teresa and her brother were accustomed.

When Teresa Ivey moved, she chose to keep marriage and separation a secret. Another citizen referred to her arrival as that of "a brother and a widowed sister."[4] Indeed, Ivey maintained her married name of Mrs. Teresa E. Ivey, telling people that her husband was dead. Admitting that she was separated would have tainted her reputation. Being a single woman at her age also carried a negative status. It may have seemed strange for a woman, even a widow, to move west without a husband. But arriving in Texas with her brother and his family removed any stigma that might have been attached to that situation.

Teresa's primary difficulty in maintaining her facade was her legal inability to control her own property. As long as her brother, the trustee of her property, was alive, she was able to rent, sell, and use her property as she wished. Augustus, however, died in October 1856, barely three years after moving to Texas. Without a trustee, control of the property legally reverted to Teresa's husband in Alabama. But Jesse never challenged her rights, so Teresa continued to act as she had while Augustus was alive.

A distant cousin who had recently settled in Colorado County also died within a year of Augustus's death. Alfred Smith had moved to Texas without his wife. He planned to get established and then send for his wife, who was living in Tennessee. In his short residency, Smith borrowed immense amounts of money in order to buy a plantation. He had little collateral other than a few slaves that he mortgaged in order to purchase the land. Upon his death, Smith's creditors rushed to recoup as much of their losses as possible by filing suits to foreclose on the land and slaves. Alfred Smith's widow, Mary M. B. Smith, along with her brother-in-law, H. H. Smith, quickly moved to Colorado County to salvage what they could. Under Texas law, Mary, as the widow, had the first right to administer her husband's estate. Nevertheless, to become the administrator of an estate or to appeal any lawsuits in court, Mary Smith needed to post a bond of $50,000 (twice the amount of the estate). Yet no one in the community knew Mary Smith or her brother-in-law, and she could not find any businessman willing to secure the bond.

Teresa Ivey, however, had sufficient wealth to sign as security on the bond for her deceased cousin's widow. Before the Civil War, it was very rare for a woman to act as security on a bond in Colorado County. Restricted by Southern ideals of womanhood, few women would venture into such a business concern unless under their husbands' management. In addition to social restrictions, creditors and businessmen were leery of business deals with women, whether married or single. Because married women had no control over their own property, a creditor entering into an agreement with a married woman took an enormous risk. Later she might plead "coverture," nullifying her responsibilities and leaving the creditor legally defenseless to collect the debt. Single women, although able to make legal contracts the same as men, also presented possible problems. Even when it was absolutely certain that a woman was single and able to make a contract, she could at any time get married, and the creditors or purchasers would then have to deal with the new husband instead of the woman.

In Teresa's case, Alfred Smith's creditors had a right to worry about their ability to hold Ivey's property liable for malfeasance on the bond. Since the trustee to Ivey's estate had died, Teresa had no legal ability to rent, sell, or mortgage her property. As a married woman, Ivey could not sue or be sued without her husband's permission and consent. Smith's creditors therefore challenged the bond in court, claiming that Teresa "was at the time of the signing of the [bond] and still is a married woman, and could not legally sign said bond."[5]

Perhaps this challenge inspired Ivey to seek a more permanent legal ability to control her own property. Whether it was Teresa's idea is not known; about the same time, Jesse Ivey filed for and quickly received a divorce in Alabama. Unfortunately, the court records in

Pickens County, Alabama, have been destroyed, so there is no record of the grounds Jesse cited in the divorce petition. But since it had been a little over three years, the necessary period of time to claim abandonment, that is probably the charge he made. Divorce in Alabama required not only the court's decision but also the legislature's approval. On February 5, 1858, the Alabama state legislature declared "that Jesse A. Ivy be, and he is hereby divorced from his wife, Teresa A. Ivy, pursuant to a decree of the chancery court."[6]

Three months earlier, in November 1857, Mary Smith argued in a petition to the Texas District Court that Teresa Ivey could sign a security bond: "If the said Teresa E. had ever been married she was laboring under no disability on account thereof at the time of the execution of said bond, for that the bonds of matrimony theretofore subsisting between her and her husband had been dissolved in the state of Alabama."[7] The court clerk made no official notation of the judge's ruling on Teresa Ivey's ability to sign the bond. Since the case proceeded, it is highly likely that the bond was indeed ruled acceptable.

In what was to become Ivey's long history in Colorado County, this one answer, well hidden in a District Court case, is the only hint that she was not a widow but instead a soon-to-become-divorced woman. The very oddity of a woman's signing a bond probably induced the creditors to inquire about Teresa Ivey's motivation and background. Teresa certainly did not volunteer the information, as the creditors charged that she had "fraudulently and falsely concealed" the fact from the chief justice.[8]

Being divorced in Colorado County was not an absolute stigma. The frontier state of Texas had passed one of the most liberal divorce statutes in the South. Abandonment, adultery, and cruelty (broadly defined) were grounds on which marriages could be dissolved, and only a ruling from the District Court was necessary to finalize a divorce. In Colorado County, Texas, before the Civil War fifty-three people, representing one of every eleven marriages, filed for divorce. This ratio was far lower than the late-twentieth-century divorce rate of almost 50 percent, but it is a significant enough number to make divorce in nineteenth-century Colorado County more than a despicable rarity. Many divorced women in the county continued to live respectable lives, including one who remarried and lived another forty years only two residences away from her ex-husband.

But divorce still carried a negative connotation, as it denoted a failure somehow to live up to the ideal of Southern womanhood. Teresa's husband, but also her two young daughters, complicated the situation. Although she had left her daughters in Alabama with Jesse, Teresa decided in 1858 that she wanted the girls with her in Texas. According to the stories passed down to her descendants, Ivey returned to Alabama to retrieve her daughters "and just quietly left with them."[9] Of course, after claiming that she was a widow, returning to Texas with two daughters would have raised suspicion. So Ivey insisted that they were her nieces. On November 1, 1859, in order to protect the rights of her children while preserving the fabrication of their relationship to her, Teresa Ivey officially "adopted" her own daughters as her legal heirs.[10] Regardless of their true relation to her, this action actually bolstered Teresa's image as a Southern lady in Colorado County, as she now, through raising children, added the role of domesticity to her responsibilities.

After the death of her brother, Teresa Ivey had a few choices. She could pack up and move near another male relative, remarry, or remain on her own. Ivey chose to remain independent. In one financial enterprise she bought a block of land and town lots in nearby Oakland, Texas, and continued building the town that A. C. Hereford had begun there. By encouraging town growth, she increased the value of the lots and her investment. Additionally, Ivey rented out some of her slaves to other plantation owners, and she raised cattle for market. Teresa Ivey succeeded in her business ventures and even after the Civil War was able to recoup her losses and rebuild a wealthy estate.

Nonetheless, despite being a shrewd businesswoman, Ivey was careful to cultivate her image as a Southern lady. She was an active member of her church and served as a gentle hostess for visitors to her community. In 1859, she hosted a picnic so social and sumptuous that it earned her a mention in the county newspaper. The editors "thanked Mrs. Ivey for making such ample provisions. . . . We take occasion to praise the dinner here. It was an excellent dinner; none would want a better. We believe we speak within the bounds of reason when we say that twelve baskets of fragments were taken up after the appetites of all were amply satisfied."[11]

Ivey successfully concealed her divorced status and her relationship to her daughters from the community and, apparently, from the daughters themselves. Descendants of Teresa's older daughter, Martha Ivey, still maintain that Martha was Teresa Ivey's niece. Teresa's younger daughter, Susan, married respectably and had at least two children, one of whom she named Ivy. The case of Teresa's older daughter is especially interesting because during the Civil War, Martha's life took a turn that would have benefited from her mother's shared experience. In 1860, Martha, at the age of fourteen, married Stephen Conner. Leaving her home "where she had been raised with much tenderness and well supplied with all the comforts of life," Martha was completely unprepared for what she faced. She moved into a large household with her husband's family. When her husband joined the army during the war, Martha felt mistreated and neglected by his family. She bitterly and frequently complained to her husband. On a furlough in July 1864, Stephen "expressed to her his intention not to live with her again, and sent to her an abusive message [stating] that they were finally separated, and [that] she could marry again and he would do the same."[12] The very young Martha Conner believed her husband. If she even knew about the necessity of legal proceedings in order to obtain a divorce, she did not know enough to ask to see the legal documents granting it. Martha then married another man, David Calhoun, and her husband Stephen Conner later won a divorce from her for adultery.

Teresa Ivey's descendants report that she never approved of Martha's second "husband." Ivey called David Calhoun lazy and an "Irish drifter." She had higher hopes and ambition for her daughter. Teresa Ivey probably also disliked Calhoun because he helped bring scandal to the family, contrary to the image Ivey had so carefully cultivated. As hard as Teresa Ivey had worked to conceal her own divorced status, her oldest daughter not only divorced, but did so under the shame of adultery.

The year Stephen and Martha's divorce was finalized, Teresa redoubled her efforts to become a model Southern lady. She reinforced her domestic role by becoming a virtual mother again to a four-year-old boy indentured to her care. In addition, Ivey proved her piety by donating two lots of land to the Oakland Missionary Baptist Church. A few years later, Ivey donated more land to the town of Oakland for the building of a college and for a freedmen's school. Ivey undoubtedly had multiple reasons for these magnanimous gestures. Schools and churches built in Oakland would greatly increase the value of her lots, as well as endear her to the community. In 1872, Martha died during the birth of her second child, Virginia (called Mattie after her mother). Teresa took on the role of mother once again for her grandchildren Mattie and John C. Calhoun. In June 1890, Teresa Ivey divided all her property between her two grandchildren. She died on October 3, 1890, after "a lingering illness of over a month. . . . A large concourse of friends and neighbors followed the remains to their last resting place."[13]

Teresa Ivey's life was far from ordinary in many ways. She moved west without her husband or children, divorced, never remarried, later became a single parent several times, and was a shrewd businesswoman. Nevertheless, this circumstance was not so unusual as popular tradition might suggest, even for a "Southern lady." This history, like the details of Teresa Ivey's life, has remained hidden. Southern states increased the availability of divorce because people found divorces necessary as expectations about family life changed and economic conditions fluctuated. In addition, many widows did not remarry, especially in the years following the Civil War.

Twenty-five percent of Southern white men had perished during the war. Teresa Ivey was not the only single woman with children managing her own business. And a few married women even sought more control over their own property.

Teresa entered the public sphere of law and business, maintained her independence from any male, and at least as far as the community believed, never had children of her own. Although she obviously breached many expectations of the ideal of the Southern lady, Teresa became a model "lady" in her community by fabricating an acceptable past. Despite her choices to leave her husband and to live independently instead of submissively, Teresa still strove to live up to the ideal of the Southern lady, at least in her public image. She kept her divorce a secret, performed the hostess and domestic duties of a lady, tried to remain pure and pious, and attempted to steer her family in that direction as well. Teresa might not have agreed with every prescription of the ideal of domesticity, but nevertheless living up to the ideal as closely as possible was very important to her.

Teresa Ivey's life demonstrates the power of social ideals concerning womanhood. The ideal was so pervasive that most wealthy women, even a woman as independent as Teresa Ivey, remembered as "a remarkable woman for energy, perseverance and industry," endeavored to live up to its tenets.[14] But at the same time, Ivey's life also demonstrates that the ideal was only an ideal. The "Southern lady" was prescriptive, not descriptive. Many women living in the nineteenth-century South, maybe most, could not be described as true Southern ladies. But most attempted to live up to that ideal. Indeed, the ideal was so pervasive that everyone involved, Teresa Ivey, her community, and her descendants, believed the illusion that Ivey created.

Notes

1. Deed Records Transcribed, May 19, 1856, Office of the County Clerk, Colorado County, Book J, 54 [hereinafter CCCC].

2. Letter of James W. Holt (originally appeared in the *Weimar Mercury*, May 14, 1915), reprinted in "Looking Backward: Letters to the *Weimar Mercury*, 1915," *Nesbitt Memorial Library Journal* 6 (January 1996): 57.

3. Answer, *Mary M. B. Smith v Henderson and Tooke*, November 11, 1858, Docket File No. 1221, Colorado County District Clerk's Office [hereafter, CCDC].

4. Ibid.

5. Motion to quash bond, *Mary M. B. Smith v Henderson and Tooke*, November 4, 1857, Docket File No. 1221, CCDC.

6. *Digest of the Laws of Alabama*, 1857–58, 421.

7. Answer, *Mary M. B. Smith v Henderson and Tooke*, November 11, 1857, Docket File No. 1221, CCDC.

8. Ibid.

9. Telephone interview with Marjorie Bock Miller, Halletsville, Texas, February 12, 1996.

10. Deed Records Transcribed, November 1, 1859, Book K, 387.

11. *Colorado Citizen*, September 3, 1859, 2; Petition, *Martha A. Conner v Stephen Conner*, September 30, 1864, Docket File No. 1788, CCDC.

12. Ibid.

13. *Weimar Mercury*, October 11, 1890.

14. Ibid.

Suggested Readings

Although there are no private documents extant from the life of Teresa Ivey, her life can be pieced together from "public documents." For Teresa Ivey, the pertinent public documents in Colorado County, Texas, include Bond and Mortgage Records, Deed Records, Marriage Records, and records of the Probate Court, kept in the County Clerk's Office. Invaluable information about Ivey was also hidden in petitions, answers, and depositions contained in the District Court files, often in lawsuits where Teresa Ivey herself was not named. Of course, contemporary newspaper articles further illuminate her life, and reminiscences of Colorado County citizens both published and unpublished record more details. Although the relevant court documents in Alabama were destroyed by fire, the acts of the State of Alabama record Teresa and Jesse Ivey's divorce. The remainder of information about Teresa Ivey and her family comes from local histories and, of course, the U.S. census, one of the most valuable tools available to a historian of ordinary women.

Barbara Welter first identified the special expectations of nineteenth-century women in "The Cult of True Womanhood: 1820–1860," *American Quarterly* 18 (Summer 1966): 151–74. The best exploration of the development of this ideal of separate spheres is Nancy F. Cott's *The Bonds of Womanhood: 'Woman's Sphere' in New England, 1780–1835* (New Haven: Yale University Press, 1977). For information on Southern women in the nineteenth century, including the special expectations of women, see Joan Cashin, *A Family Venture: Men and Women on the Southern Frontier* (New York: Oxford University Press, 1991); Catherine Clinton, *The Plantation Mistress: Woman's World in the Old South* (New York: Pantheon Books, 1983); Drew Gilpin Faust, *Mothers of Invention: Women of the Slaveholding South in the American Civil War* (Chapel Hill: University of North Carolina Press, 1996); Elizabeth Fox-Genovese, *Within the Plantation Household: Black and White Women of the Old South* (Chapel Hill: University of North Carolina Press, 1988); Suzanne Lebsock, *The Free Women of Petersburg: Status and Culture in a Southern Town, 1784–1860* (New York: Norton, 1984); Sally G. McMillen,

Southern Women: Black and White in the Old South (Arlington Heights, IL: Harlan Davidson, 1991); and Anne Firor Scott, *The Southern Lady: From Pedestal to Politics* (Chicago: University of Chicago Press, 1970). Finally, changes in laws affected married women in many ways from the ability to own and control property to divorce. See Norma Basch, *In the Eyes of the Law: Women, Marriage, and Property in Nineteenth-Century New York* (Ithaca, NY: Cornell University Press, 1982); Jane Turner Censer, "'Smiling through Her Tears,': Ante-Bellum Southern Women and Divorce," *American Journal of Legal History* 25 (January 1981): 24–47; Richard H. Chused, *Private Acts in Public Places: A Social History of Divorce in the Formative Era of American Family Law* (Philadelphia: University of Pennsylvania Press, 1994); and Glenda Riley, *Divorce: An American Tradition* (New York: Oxford University Press, 1991).

III

The Late Nineteenth and Early Twentieth Centuries
Inventing the New Woman

Although mid-nineteenth-century feminists were disappointed that the Fourteenth and Fifteenth Amendments did not include female suffrage, women continued to take on more public roles during the Gilded Age and Progressive Era. Somewhat ironically, the "ideal of true womanhood" and "cult of domesticity" celebrating women's assumed superior morality and greater responsibility for affairs within the domestic sphere eventually expanded acceptable female roles beyond the home. Rapid industrialization and urbanization created great wealth for some, but cities also experienced social problems associated with unregulated growth: rising poverty, disease, high infant-mortality rates, political corruption, increasing social stratification, and crime. Women reformers such as Frances Willard, Jane Addams, and Florence Kelley worked with other like-minded females and with men to shape the social and civil reforms of the Gilded Age and Progressive Era. "Ordinary" women joined clubs, served as volunteers, and became professional social workers.

During the same period the number of female wage earners rose from less than 10 percent of the labor force in 1880 to nearly 22 percent by 1930. Although the 1882 Chinese Exclusion Act virtually ended Chinese entrance to the United States, other newcomers from Europe, the British Isles, and Japan contributed to a rising flood of immigration from 1880 until passage of the restrictive National Origins Immigration Act of 1924. Except for the Irish and the trickle of Chinese who came to America after 1882, male immigrants outnumbered female immigrants, but female newcomers filled many of the low wage jobs open to "working girls" in the expanding industrial economy. Racial discrimination hindered black and Hispanic women from being offered industrial jobs, so many worked as domestics and in agriculture. In the American South, sharecropping became common for both blacks and poor whites. At the same time more and more daughters from the growing middle class attended the nation's first women's colleges and postsecondary schools. Many of these young women filled "pink collar" positions: clerical workers, teachers, and nurses. Some traditionally male jobs opened to women with the onset of World War I. But social and legal barriers kept most women from working as doctors, lawyers, and in other traditional male professions. A growing minority of women, about 10 percent by 1920, chose career over marriage, and the birthrate declined to 3.5 births per woman. Nonetheless, marriage and motherhood remained the most significant career choice for the vast majority of women across all racial, class, and ethnic lines.

Westward migration continued, and mining areas went through raucous boom and bust cycles. The last "free" Indians were forced onto government reservation lands, and the 1890 census led the Census Bureau to declare that there was no longer a frontier. The West became an interesting mix of cultures, ethnicities, and the first states and territories to implement female suffrage. The Gilded Age and Progressive Era, highlighted by the passage and ratification in 1920 of the Nineteenth Amendment, granting national women's suffrage, produced the "new woman."

Margaret Breashears's story of Gertrude Osterhout (Chapter 9) shows the choices and controversies facing the first generation of women to attend college in America. Osterhout's breadth and depth of knowledge and interests in the world marked her as a "new woman" able and willing to express opinions on topics previously reserved for men. Her parents' and Osterhout's own expectations about education and life choices are revealed in the many letters that she exchanged with her family.

Margaret Olivia Slocum Sage used her advanced education as a stepping stone to a lucrative marriage. Ruth Crocker (Chapter 10) found that Olivia, as "Mrs. Russell Sage," was able to muster social and, upon her husband's death, economic influence. When Russell Sage died at the age of ninety in 1906, Olivia gained control of $75 million. No longer subject to her husband's miserly habits, Olivia launched into an astonishing philanthropy, spending about $35 million. In addition, in 1907 she founded the Russell Sage Foundation with $10 million. Through newspaper stories about paired couples such as Russell and Olivia Sage, readers could contemplate a division between selfish accumulation of wealth by men and the selfless benevolence of philanthropy by women. Philanthropy made possible a varied and surprising activism for elite women.

Middle-class club women were also active in various causes. In Chapter 11 Katherine Osburn tells the story of a white woman, Nellie Wiegel, who became a radical activist for Ute Indian autonomy. She eventually uncovered a scandal involving sexual misconduct, rape, and bribery. Wiegel's response to these events challenged the male power structure of the Bureau of Indian Affairs and resulted in her removal from positions in the Colorado Federation of Women's Clubs and the Colorado Indian Commission. The process of Wiegel's radicalization also suggests that encounters with people of a different culture could drastically alter Anglo women.

Sue Fawn Chung's Chapter 12, on Ah Cum Kee and Loy Lee Ford, also deals with cultural interaction and shows that there was no set formula for "living between two worlds." Born in Carson City, Nevada, in 1876, Ah Cum Kee was at ease in the Euro-American community and eventually lived more in the mainstream American culture than among Chinese Americans. Loy Lee Ford, born in Sacramento, California, in 1882, always retained strong ties to the Chinese American community and traditional values. Ah Cum Kee and Loy Lee Ford lived parallel lives in many ways. They were both forced to adapt to a mainstream American culture and struggled to integrate their children into American life, but mainstream culture often rejected them because of their race. Each chose a slightly different path, adapted to their backgrounds and environments within and outside of their families.

One of the most visible legal changes for women in the Progressive Era was the passage and ratification of the female suffrage amendment to the Constitution in 1920. Carole Stanford Bucy traces the controversial legal battle for ratification by examining the life of Tennessee suffragist Catherine Kenny in Chapter 13. As chair of the state campaign committee for the Tennessee Equal Suffrage Association, Inc., Kenny organized local suffrage leagues across the state and traveled extensively, giving speeches and holding rallies. Tennessee became the cornerstone in the almost century-long debate over female suffrage when in August 1920 it became the thirty-sixth state to ratify the Nineteenth Amendment, thereby making women's suffrage part of the U.S. Constitution. The life of Kenny, a white Roman Catholic married to a successful Chattanooga businessman, also illustrates the complex problems of religion and race for women in the turn-of-the-century South. Discriminated against in Chattanooga's high society because of her religion, Kenny was among the first in the Democratic Party to recognize the significance of the African American vote at a time when most black voters remained loyal to the Republican Party. Kenny spent much of her time building cross-racial, regional, and religious coalitions. Her life and the lives of the other women included in this section provide interesting pictures of the impact of rapid social, cultural, and economic change on the lives of ordinary women in the Gilded Age and Progressive Era.

9

Gertrude Osterhout
"I Am Independent"

Margaret Breashears

Gertrude Osterhout (1862–1920) came of age in an era of rapid social and economic change. Referred to as the Gilded Age and Progressive Era by historians primarily interested the phenomenal industrial, political, and economic modernization of the period, the late nineteenth and early twentieth century also gave rise to "the new woman." Gertrude Osterhout's life clearly shows the subtle shifts in gender roles among middle-class Americans that accompanied modernization in the United States. Born only fourteen years after the Seneca Falls Convention, Osterhout died the same year that the women's movement obtained its long-standing goal of national woman suffrage. Although she, like most women, was not a vocal women's rights activist, Osterhout benefited from the new opportunities and greater independence seen as acceptable for middle-class women.

Gertrude Osterhout, born to John P. and Junia Roberts Osterhout on January 7, 1862, spent the first eight years of her life in Austin County, Texas, where her father published a newspaper, the *Bellville Countryman*. The family moved to Belton, Texas, in 1870, when John was appointed by the Reconstruction Republican–controlled government as District Court circuit judge. Gertrude Osterhout's mother, Junia, generally stayed in Belton raising the couple's five children (three girls and two boys), keeping the house and twelve acres of land during her husband's absences on his two-hundred-mile court circuit. Infrequently Junia left Texas to visit relatives in Pennsylvania, sometimes taking her children with her. Gertrude, the oldest girl, was the second child.

Junia Osterhout's letters to her absent husband draw a clear portrait of Gertrude's childhood. In one letter Junia described nine-year-old Gertrude misbehaving as her mother sat writing. Including the commotion in her narrative, Junia remarked: "The children keep well and in good fussing order. Gerty has just pulled Paul's hair till he cryed [*sic*], and it has been just that way ever since you left first one and then the other till I don't know what to do with them." In some letters Junia complained to her husband about the children's dislike of their chores, especially weeding the garden. At other times she mentioned some special occasions when Gertrude and her brother Paul attended parties given by acquaintances of the Osterhouts. Junia even noted Gertrude's impatience with her mother's letter writing, commenting, "Gerty is all the time asking me if I am most done as she is tired of swinging the baby." Typically, nineteenth-century children helped with the chores. But John Osterhout's frequent absences probably made Junia more dependent than most mothers on her children's help. The girls cleaned house, washed clothes and dishes, ironed, tended the animals, and picked the vegetables and weeded the garden, and the boys plowed the fields, weeded the garden, made the necessary repairs on the farm equipment, and hauled produce to market.[1]

Gertrude entered Baylor College for Women in September 1880 at the age of eighteen. The college included a high school department, a female finishing school, and a college department offering courses comparable to those found in its male university division. Gertrude pursued the college curriculum. Comparing her chores at home to those she did in her first year at boarding school, Gertrude changed her mind about washing dishes, cleaning the house for company, and ironing clothes. In a letter to her younger sister, Ora, Gertrude scolds: "You must not complain about wiping the dishes. Sometimes I feel as if I would give anything to be back in the kitchen washing and wiping." To her mother, Gertrude confided: "We have to be so particular in housekeeping and bedmaking. Get demerits everytime [sic] there is a wrinkle on the bed or a particle of dust on anything." Disgusted with the strict marking of housekeeping demerits, Gertrude wrote home: "I got one demerit . . . because there was a little dust on the trunk. I think they are a little too particular, but, oh! when I get home there will be rest from the toils of the boarding house." After receiving the first set of washing she had contracted her first year at school, Gertrude wrote to her parents, "My washing has just come in and such a lot of mussed clothes you never did see, it almost makes me sick and wish I was home where I could do my own ironing." Although she prided herself on presenting a neat, starched appearance, Gertrude complained often of the difficulty in achieving such an appearance with the laundress the school hired.[2]

Gertrude's daily routine at school consisted of rising at 5 A.M., studying until 6, and then cleaning the room before breakfast. At 9 A.M. the girls went to the college for classes until noon, returning "as quick as we swallow our dinner" for more classes until 3:30 P.M. From afternoon class dismissal until the supper bell at 6:00 the students amused themselves. After dinner they studied another hour before going to bed. Comparing her days at school to jail, she bemoaned that the "poor girls have to stay imprisoned like convicts while the teachers gad about."[3]

Away from home and family for the first time, Gertrude noted that most of her classmates lacked the ladylike manners insisted on in her home. Emphasizing the neglect of etiquette among the girls in the boarding school, she wrote sarcastically, "This is a great place to learn refinement, where every other word you hear is slang such as 'dog gone, bless Lord, dog take it, bless jack,' and fifty other such expressions." The girls' table manners also bothered Gertrude. In a letter to her mother, she compared the girls to "hogs" who go after "swill . . . poured in the trough." Describing a dinner scene to her sisters near the end of her first year at school, Gertrude remarked, "I went down to the table, but the girls grabbed so for the food I got up and left without eating anything but a small piece of light bread." With an air of superiority, Gertrude finished: "I never have learned the grabbing business yet. I would rather starve than sacrifice my table manners in that way."[4]

Sharing a room with six other girls as well as hearing the constant din of someone practicing on the only piano available for thirty-five students made Gertrude long for the quiet of home. She wrote, "Of course it cannot be expected that it would be quiet among thirty-five girls, everyone wanting to speak at the same time." By January her first year, she added the duty of room monitress to her chores. She soon discovered that such a responsibility brought more problems: "I have more trouble and more duties to bear. . . . I have to be careful what I say to them [her five roommates] for fear of offending someone."[5]

Not everything about being at school displeased Gertrude, however. Growing up and meeting new people provided intrigue and news that she included in her letters home. For example, Gertrude ironically recounted with zest the lighting of a kerosene lamp by a roommate. "She carried the lighted lamp to the stove, unscrewed the burner and then stuck the stick of kindling in the bowl of the lamp." Referring to the Great Chicago Fire of 1871, Gertrude commented dryly, "It was equal to the Chicago woman taking the lamp into the milkshed, thereby causing such great destruction." In another letter Gertrude noted her addition of weight during the school year. When the girls went to town with their teacher in March 1881, Gertrude "stepped on the scales as lightly as possible hoping it would balance at one hundred and twenty pounds. But what was my astonishment when the merchant said, 'one hundred and forty three.'" She wrote, "[I] stepped off with a little more force than I got on with remarking that 'I knew those scales were not right.'" The same day at another store in town, she "mounted the scales again not feeling the least heavier than I did before, but-lo! I had gained one pound in fifteen minutes. I can now claim 144 pounds of live weight." Gertrude continually lamented the weight she gained through her college years in her letters to her family.[6] Besides going to town, recreation for the girls included picnics held about once a month on Saturdays. The chaperoned group went into the woods to pick hickory nuts and enjoy the outdoors. Gertrude also enjoyed listening to gossip, which generally centered around the "socials" held at the school, especially when the teachers decided to invite the college's boys to join the festivities. Dances during the Christmas season gave the girls an opportunity to become better acquainted with the boys. However, for Gertrude, the experience brought a sharp rebuke from her father, who strenuously opposed her attending, especially after the headmaster reported to him that Gertrude had actually danced at one. Her father's anger did not prevent Gertrude from attending future dances or from enjoying herself. She simply refrained from dancing herself. Gertrude later wrote her older brother that she and her friends "assembled in the hall and parlor to have a good time." They listened to a band and "were not disappointed" in the entertainment, for "the young men played and the girls danced to their hearts content." Gertrude took the opportunity to have "a pleasant little tête-à-tête" with the only member of the band she knew, a Mr. Voss. Although the Osterhouts did not approve of dancing, Baylor College for Women, a Baptist institution, regularly held dances in order to develop refinement in its female students.[7]

If no performance accompanied the social, Gertrude preferred to remain in her room, being either too shy or too modest to enjoy the mixed company with no family present. With the announcement of an expected social, she "primped" herself like the other girls, "before supper expecting to go into the parlor when the company came." But after supper, she confided to her family: "I did not feel as if I would enjoy myself among strangers. So I remained in my room." When chastised by her parents for withdrawing from society, she defended her choice, arguing that her retreat showed her obedience to the headmaster's instructions: "Perhaps I did wrong by not going in the parlor the night of the party. But Dr. Luther doesn't want the girls to get acquainted with the 'boys.'" To vindicate herself further, she described what the girls who met the company of college boys endured. The boys "are so hateful, they write on the bridge about the girls they know." Gertrude thought most of the behavior of the college boys frivolous and distasteful, observing from her third-story window on one occasion, "several of the university boys are out here flying kites now. Paul [her older brother] is not among them for which I am thankful."[8]

By the end of her second year, Baylor instituted "drawing room receptions calculated to teach the young ladies how to receive and entertain visitors. . . . The visitors are from the University." Apparently, the innovation failed to teach Gertrude the skill of conversation, even with gentlemen she knew through her brother. She wrote to her father that "the engineering corps" of the railroad "took sup-per here several nights ago. Among them was Mr. Higdon, (Paul's friend) and Mr. Tom Crane. I did not speak to any of them—kept quiet and took a back seat." Gertrude mentioned only once in her diary what she thought the ideal gentleman for her might be: "Gen-eral Hawthorne came. . . . I think in him I found my first beau ideal. He is tall with a commanding figure, in fact he looks every inch a soldier."[9]

Always serious about her studies, Gertrude achieved the highest ranking among the female students at the college by the time she graduated in 1883. Receiving a nearly perfect report that contained perfect marks in Spelling, English Literature, English Composition, Algebra, History, Latin, and a 97 in Reading, she bragged tri-umphantly to her father, "Of course I am proud of it [the report], because I was the only one in the whole school who got 100 in every-thing." She added, "You may rest assured that I am not getting vain if I am a little smart," as she continued on to explain the one demer-it she earned in housekeeping. Gertrude obviously did not consider her score in Reading a true estimation of her performance, since the flu had kept her from earning a perfect mark there also.[10]

During the course of her studies at Baylor, Gertrude read com-positions in front of students, recited lessons for the teachers, prac-ticed teaching lessons, and attended lectures given by visiting faculty. She described the preparation for one such teaching exercise to her sister, Ora. "I had to write my Normal teaching exercise. . . . We select some subject either from History or Geography and write all we can about it, memorize it, and write the principle [sic] parts on the blackboard and teach the other scholars." Gertrude chose to instruct her classmates on the ostrich. When a visiting professor lec-tured the girls on history, she recorded in her diary, the headmaster requested "us to carry blank books and lead pencils to the lecture for the purpose of taking notes, of course we carried them and wrote notes too—but mostly to one another."[11]

Although she always scored well on her exams, Gertrude hated every examination week, especially during her senior year. In a letter to her mother shortly before commencement that year, she complained, "A calamity fell upon us in the form of general exami-nations." Questions "from the histories of every nation, Civil Gov-ernment, Geography, Mental and Moral Sciences, the Natural Sciences, and all branches of Mathematics" were included in the final exams, which began at 8:30 A.M. "under the watchful eye of a monitor."[12]

While still a student at Baylor College, Gertrude occasionally tutored the younger students or filled in for a sick teacher in her strongest subject, Latin. During her junior year the headmaster hired her to "'check' deportment, house-keeping, go walking, and . . . take charge of them [the girls] on Sunday" in return for waiving her tuition. She informed her father she "lost one half hour from study every morning," as she "had to visit every room, hear the report for the night before, and give them [the students] some instruction and warning in housekeeping and deportment." Ironically, she found herself in the position of meting out the demerits for the reports on housekeeping, inspecting each room at ten thirty in the morning. Realizing the weight of her new position, she wrote in her diary, "I feel now that I ought to set an example worthy to be followed by my roommates."[13]

After graduation in 1883, Gertrude returned to Baylor as a teacher. Of her students, Gertrude wrote, "The results of my examinations suggest a comparison to the Texas crops—there had been much sowing but little reaping. Sometimes I am utterly disgusted with trying to teach." These episodes occurred more frequently during the warm spring months when she too found it difficult to remain shut up in the classroom. Remarking to her cousin George, "These are days when one longs to stay out of the house, to seek the shade and solitudes of the woods." She complained of the difficulty of teaching Latin, mythology, and modern literature when the weather did not force the students to remain inside: "One's spirit is out of harmony with Caesar's campaigns and Cicero's invectives against Cataline. Ancient mythology and modern literature have no charm in the budding time of the year." Considering the almost impossible task of maintaining her students' interest and attention after March, she thought the appropriate solution in an "ideal school" very simple: "There will be no lessons to recite in April and May." Always looking forward to each break and recess in the school calendar "to recuperate," she wrote relatives that "this one will surely use" the short Christmas break "to advantage. So when you think of me during the holidays . . . know that I am either sitting by the fire intensely interested in some book or dogging lazily on the lounge."[14]

Confiding in her cousin George, she wrote that she took no pleasure in the usual entertainments for the faculty. Gertrude mentioned that other faculty members often considered her antisocial. In an attempt to overcome her natural preference to read in her room rather than socialize, she proposed a course of action: "I have determined to sacrifice my own feelings and mingle with the other people for a little while" by attending the literary club "for an hour or two one evening in the week." However, most of the time Gertrude found it easier to curl up with a book in her own room, as "there are so many books that I want to read this year that I am using all my spare moments. I buy one or two books every month hoping in this way to have a small library of my own."[15]

Between school years, Gertrude enjoyed traveling about the country with her sisters or teacher friends. These experiences clearly reflect her growing independence in an era of "the new woman." During a trip to visit relatives in 1884, Gertrude attended a "Wild West" show featuring Buffalo Bill, concluding that "the performance was very good," thanks largely to the entertainment from "the Indians and Cowboys." That same summer she also visited Niagara Falls and wrote home: "The falls are far grander than I had ever imagined. We visited all the interesting points there." Opting only to view the sights, she reassured her family that "none of us went under the Falls."[16]

The desire for new experiences fueled some of Gertrude's summer wanderings. The summer of 1891 found Gertrude and her sister Ora in Colorado traipsing through the mountains, picnicking out in the woods. Although Gertrude enjoyed the trip, she commented that the prices Colorado charged for room and board to tourists amounted to "wholesale robbery of tourists." In 1899 she visited a teacher friend living near San Antonio. Taking the opportunity to "see the U.S. fishermen and to dip my hand in the beautiful San Marcos River," she drove nine miles from Kyle to the Fish Station, "a very interesting place. The situation is high and the grounds beautifully kept. There were many fish of all sorts and size. From this place the rivers of Texas are stocked with the finny tribes."[17]

Certainly, Gertrude felt travel was exciting. During a stay with her grandparents in Pennsylvania, Gertrude witnessed a fire that destroyed her grandfather's old house. According to Gertrude's letters, her Uncle Joe sounded the alarm. By that time, "the fire had made such headway that it was impossible to put it out. The heat was so intense and the flames reached so far that all access to the spring was cut off after carrying about half a dozen buckets of water." Reacting to the horrors of the night, she wrote, "Oh! it was terrible to see that old house go—just licked up by the flames in less than an hour." Traveling by herself from one set of relatives to another in the summer of 1884, she left the train station situated closest to her Aunt Lizzie's house and walked to her relative's home. Recounting the incident saucily: "Just as I got to the spring, Aunt Lizzie stepped out on the stoop and seeing me said, 'why we were not looking for you.' I said, 'no I am independent—come when I please and go when I please.' This is the third time I have been here and they have never had to meet me yet."[18]

Even though Gertrude styled herself as a free spirit and her correspondence contained an unfettered frankness, especially with her brother Paul and her cousin George, she remained within the constraints placed on her by the turn-of-the-century society. She resided at home with her family during the vacations too short for traveling and boarded with other female teachers at the school.

Gertrude differed from most women of her time only in her spinsterhood. Teaching provided an acceptable livelihood. Even for the limited periods during summer vacations away from her home, she conformed to the proprieties of her society in deportment and manners, traveling in a group of women or escorted by a male relative.

Gertrude Osterhout's correspondence to her family and relatives reveals the development of her feminine independence. Shortly after her graduation from Baylor in 1883, the twenty-two-year-old Osterhout informed her family that she was an independent woman. Later letters, especially to her brother and cousin, illustrated the continuing process of her maturation and independence. Gertrude Osterhout's life demonstrates the shifting roles for turn-of-the-century New Women. She chose to remain unmarried, a choice becoming much more common as growing numbers of middle-class young women earned college educations. But at the same time, Gertrude Osterhout selected a profession that was becoming increasingly "feminized" and had gained the approval of most in the middle class. Gertrude Osterhout continued her life of feminine independence until her death at Baylor on November 25, 1902.

Notes

1. Letters, J. P. Osterhout to David Stunkard, June 5, 1899; Junia Osterhout to J. P. Osterhout, August 13, 1871; June 8, 1875; August 13, 1871: all in Osterhout Papers, Rice University, Houston, Texas [hereafter, OPRU].

2. Letters, Gertrude Osterhout to Ora Osterhout, October 11, 1880; Gertrude Osterhout to Junia Osterhout, October 15, 1880; Gertrude Osterhout to J. P. Osterhout, September 24, 1880: all in Osterhout Papers, Austin College, Sherman, Texas [hereafter, OPAC].

3. Letters, Gertrude Osterhout to J. P. Osterhout, September 24, 1880; Gertrude Osterhout to Junia Osterhout, November 13, 1881: both in OPAC.

4. Letters, Gertrude Osterhout to all at home, September 13, 1880; Gertrude Osterhout to Junia Osterhout, September 13, 1880: both in OPAC; Gertrude Osterhout to Ora and Junia (sister) Osterhout, May 11, 1881: in OPRU.

5. Letter, Gertrude Osterhout to all at home, September 13, 1880: in OPAC; Gertrude Osterhout Diary: in OPRU.

6. Letters, Gertrude Osterhout to J. P. Osterhout, February 10, 1881; Gertrude Osterhout to all at home, March 13, 1881: all in OPAC.

7. Letters, Gertrude Osterhout to Ora Osterhout, October 24, 1880; Gertrude Osterhout to Paul Osterhout, November 1, 1880; J. P. Osterhout to Gertrude Osterhout, January 1881; Gertrude Osterhout to Paul Osterhout, March 15, 1882: all in OPAC.

8. Letters, Gertrude Osterhout to Ora Osterhout, October 24, 1880; Gertrude Osterhout to Junia Osterhout, November 14, 1880; Gertrude Osterhout to Junia Osterhout, February 6, 1880: all in OPAC.

9. Letters, Gertrude Osterhout to J. P. Osterhout, February 26, 1882: in OPAC; Gertrude Osterhout Diary: in OPRU.

10. Letter, Gertrude Osterhout to J. P. Osterhout, April 21, 1881: in OPAC.

11. Letter, Gertrude Osterhout to Ora Osterhout, November 8, 1880: in OPAC; Gertrude Osterhout Diary: in OPRU.

12. Letter, Gertrude Osterhout to Junia Osterhout, April 6, 1883: in OPAC.

13. Letters, Geneva Cole to Gertie Osterhout, February 11, 1882: in OPRU; Gertrude Osterhout to J. P. Osterhout, February 26, 1882: in OPAC; Gertrude Osterhout Diary: in OPRU.

14. Letters, Gertrude Osterhout to George Osterhout, June 14, 1900; Gertrude Osterhout to George Osterhout, April 5, 1895; Gertrude Osterhout to George Osterhout, December 20, 1899: all in OPAC.

15. Letter, Gertrude Osterhout to George Osterhout, February 1, 1887: in OPAC.

16. Letter, Gertrude Osterhout to Paul Osterhout, September 14, 1884: in OPAC.

17. Letters, Gertrude Osterhout to George Osterhout, September 10, 1899: in OPAC; Gertrude Osterhout to family at home, August 5, 1891: in OPRU.

18. Letters, Gertrude Osterhout to J. P. Osterhout, July 30, 1884; Gertrude Osterhout to all at home, July 24, 1884: both in OPRU.

Suggested Readings

Sally G. McMillan's *Southern Women: Black and White in the Old South* (Arlington Heights, IL: Harlan Davidson, 1992) presents a good general work for women of the South prior to the Civil War. Ann Fears Crawford and Crystal Sasse Ragsdale, *Women in Texas: Their Lives, Their Experiences, Their Accomplishments* (Austin, TX: State House Press, 1982, rev. 1992); Fane Downs's article "Travels and Trubbles: Women in Early Nineteenth Century Texas," in the *Southwestern Historical Quarterly* (1986); and Margaret Swett Henson's "Anglo-American Colonization," in *The New Handbook of Texas*, vol. 1 (Austin: The Texas State Historical Association, 1996): 185–190, all provide information about early Texas women. For discussions on Texas women on the frontier, see Ann Patton Malone's *Women on the Texas Frontier: A Cross-Cultural Perspective* (El Paso: Texas Western Press, 1983); and Jo Ella Powell Exley, ed., *Texas Tears and Texas Sunshine: Voices of Frontier Women* (College Station: Texas A&M University Press, 1985). For life in Texas around the turn of the century, try Ada Morehead Holland's *Bush Country Woman* (College Station: Texas A&M University Press, 1989); and Mamie Sypert Burns, *This I Can Leave You: A Woman's Day on the Pitchfork Ranch* (College Station: Texas A&M University Press,

1986). Elizabeth H. Turner, *Women, Culture, and Community: Religion and Reform in Galveston, 1880–1920* (New York: Oxford University Press, 1990); Ruthe Winegarten and Judith N. McArthur, *Citizens at Last: The Woman Suffrage Movement in Texas* (Austin, TX: E. C. Temple, 1987); and A. Elizabeth Taylor, "The Woman Suffrage Movement in Texas," in Ruthe Winegarten and Judith N. McArthur, eds., *Citizens at Last: The Woman Suffrage Movement in Texas* (Austin, TX: E. C. Temple, 1987), cover Texas women and their efforts in politics. For sources on ethnic Texas women, look at Ruth Winegarten, ed., *I Am Annie Mae: The Personal Story of a Black Texas Woman* (Austin: University of Texas Press, 1983); and Vicki L. Ruiz and Susan Tiano, eds., *Women on the US-Mexican Border: Responses to Change* (Boston: Allen and Unwin, 1987). Biographies and stories of Texas women include Sandra L. Myers, "A Woman's View of the Texas Frontier, 1874: The Diary of Emily K. Andrews," *Southwestern Historical Quarterly* 86, no. 1 (1982): 49–80; Tom Lea, *Maud Durlin Sullivan, 1872–1944: A Pioneer Southwestern Librarian* (Los Angeles: C. Hertzog, 1962); Janet G. Humphrey, ed., *A Texas Suffragist: Diaries and Writings of Jane V. McCallum* (Austin, TX: E. C. Temple, 1988); and Suzanne Comer, ed., *Common Bonds: Stories by and about Modern Texas Women* (Dallas: Southern Methodist University Press, 1990).

10

Margaret Olivia Slocum, "Mrs. Russell Sage"
Private Griefs and Public Duties

Ruth Crocker

"Rags to riches," the promise of opportunity for all, was one of the most enduring parts of the American dream for nineteenth-century Americans, but no one imagined that it applied to women. Their "careers" (the word means path or trajectory) remained as they had always been and as they often are to this day, determined by their relationship to the men who were their fathers and husbands. However, widows sometimes achieved what Carolyn Heilbrun calls "a kind of old-age freedom for women."[1] This essay considers the career of Olivia Slocum (1828–1918), an ordinary Syracuse schoolteacher who became the wife of one of America's richest financiers and who on his death in 1906 inherited the extraordinary fortune of over $75 million and proceeded to spend $45 million in her eighties.

Olivia Slocum was born into a prospering middle-class family in Syracuse, New York, in 1828. It was a time of boom and bust, with the Erie Canal and the railroads bringing population and commerce as they linked upstate New York to the eastern seaboard. Joseph and Margaret Slocum, Olivia's parents, had been part of that westward migration, as had the numerous Sage family of Connecticut whose seventh son, Russell, was born near Troy, New York, in 1816. By the 1830s, Olivia's father was operating a line of boats on the canal and had acquired warehouses and stores as well as a considerable acreage of land. But the dark side of nineteenth-century success is often a story of ruin and disgrace. Economic ruin haunted Joseph Slocum and was to wreck his family's security. In 1836, when Olivia was nine, he was already selling his recently acquired property, and in 1841, when she was thirteen, he was forced to put five hundred acres up for sale to pay his debts.

Education was a class privilege in the nineteenth century, one that Olivia Slocum's parents could hardly afford. Despite this, she managed to attend Troy Female Seminary, thanks to a loan from a wealthy uncle. The seminary was one of a handful of institutions of higher education for women then in existence. There Olivia studied a wide range of subjects, and she came under the influence of its

147

founder, the powerful feminine educator and writer, Emma Willard (1787–1870). Like her contemporary, Catharine Beecher (1800–1878), Willard combined personal charisma and formidable respectability with religious orthodoxy. Though she condemned the women's rights reformers and called suffragists "hyenas in petticoats," her career in fact greatly advanced women's progress into the professions and toward a fuller citizenship. That occurred because the young women trained at Troy went out as teachers throughout the nation, frequently setting up their own schools based on the Troy seminary model. Emma Willard's Troy Female Seminary was thus at the center of what Anne Firor Scott has called an "ever-widening circle" of influence, helping to shape a national culture in which white Protestant women played a role as cultural leaders and moral arbiters.[2]

Emma Willard came to hold a dominant influence over Olivia, who saw in her own mother, Margaret Slocum, only a figure needing sympathy and protection. Willard, in contrast, was her model and her mentor. Graduating in 1847, Olivia entered a stage of waiting for the right man to marry, a period that lasted twenty-two years. She might have preferred to wait at home as housekeeper and companion to her mother, but the family's financial needs pushed her into teaching, and from 1847 until 1869 she served in a series of paid teaching positions in Syracuse and Philadelphia.

Meanwhile the family's financial situation went from bad to worse, as Joseph Slocum's business ventures involved him in deals with some men cleverer and less scrupulous than he. These included Olivia's husband-to-be Russell Sage (1816–1906), who was already a rich man with interests in wholesale produce, banking, grain, horses, and warehousing. Sage's business empire, which had started in upstate New York, had expanded westward and he was now looking for opportunities in the newly created state of Wisconsin.[3] Some time in 1849, Joseph Slocum entered into a business deal with Sage, joining a commission business in Milwaukee newly formed by Sage and a Scottish immigrant, Alexander Mitchell. Among the immediate payoffs of Slocum's association with Sage, it was said, was Slocum's election in 1849 to the New York State Assembly representing Onondaga County, District Three. The long-term results of his association with the Troy financier would not be so happy, however. The business partnership would end in financial loss for Slocum, and his attempt to recover his losses would bring only a protracted litigation that went all the way to the Supreme Court.[4] Although the lower court found that Sage had swindled his partners, Slocum and the other plaintiff were unable to recover their losses when the case eventually went on appeal to the Supreme Court,[5] because the original transaction had involved conspiracy.

After this disappointment, Olivia's father disappeared for several years, the family home was sold in 1857, and Margaret Slocum took refuge with her relatives in West Troy.

Olivia continued as a teacher and occasionally as a governess, that odd position of genteel poverty and humiliation, half paid worker and half guest in her employer's home. These experiences of paid work taught her an unforgettable lesson about women's dependence on men. Although she loved teaching, she realized it would not be the answer for single women as long as teachers' salaries were too low to guarantee a decent livelihood as a basis for economic independence.

When the Civil War broke out, Olivia was working as a governess in Philadelphia at the home of a wealthy family. The city offered her a vivid view of the Civil War behind the lines. She recalled, "When a carload of sick soldiers was brought to Philadelphia, the bells would ring, and all the women would know that it was a summons for them, and they would gather whatever they had in the way of needed supplies and go to the temporary hospital."[6] Her Civil War experiences included voluntary work in a hospital where many of the patients suffered from what today we would call post–traumatic stress disorder. Later, when the country was facing the aftermath of its war with Spain, she wrote, "I have seen and known so much of the awful reality of war that I cannot speak lightly of anything connected with it."[7]

Olivia's father had gone to Russia to demonstrate agricultural equipment; he would return only to die of tuberculosis in Syracuse in 1863. Her mother was still living with prosperous relatives in West Troy. It was here, during a vacation from teaching, that Olivia renewed an old acquaintance with Troy businessman-politician Russell Sage. Twelve years her senior, an ex-congressman and already a multimillionaire, Russell Sage was lonely, having lost his wife to cancer in 1867. He proposed to Olivia and she accepted. They married in November 1869. She was then forty-one. Later, in a column for the *New York Herald*, "Suppose They Had Married the First Man That Proposed," Olivia was quoted as having averred: "If I had married the first man who proposed to me I suppose I would now be on a farm. But I would not like that at all. It would be too narrow a life for me. I would prefer single blessedness."[8]

Marriage to Russell Sage transformed Olivia's relationship to money, moved her to New York City and a fashionable Fifth Avenue address, and gave her the status of wealthy matron. But it also brought a frustrating stalemate that her newspaper interview glossed over. Though not hated and feared like his partner and friend, railroad builder Jay Gould, Russell Sage was a tireless workaholic and miser, known in the press as "the skinflint of the great Yankee nation." Marriage to Sage made her fortune, but it also linked her to one of the most ridiculed men of the age. Seeking a voice and believing she had a moral mission, Olivia created a separate persona based on benevolence, the mirror image of her husband's persona as greedy accumulator. Public work was duty for Olivia, a devout, lifelong Presbyterian. Among her papers at the Emma Willard School (as Troy Female Seminary was renamed in 1895) is a fragment in her handwriting that sums up her beliefs: "Private greifs [sic] must not stand in the way of public duties."[9] Were those "private griefs" the result of a less than happy marriage or her family's financial ruin? We do not know.

Elite women like Olivia Sage were peculiarly positioned in late-nineteenth-century America: half of a ruling class who saw themselves threatened by immigrants and insurgent workers, they were at the same time voteless subjects of their husbands. Between her marriage in 1869 and widowhood in 1906, Olivia had plenty of time to analyze the difficulties of her position. From personal grievances she developed a conviction that women's advancement could reform and purify American society and politics. The key for women like Olivia was volunteer work, including organizing and fund-raising, studying public issues, holding meetings, and planning the "investment" of benevolent resources of money and time. Sage donated time to missionary and benevolent societies and was associated with the New York Exchange of Women's Work (a producers' cooperative founded in 1878) and the New York Women's Hospital. Such activities, labeled by society benevolence or charity work, masked a varied and surprising activism that many historians believe helped to propel the suffrage and feminist campaigns. This was certainly the case for Olivia Sage, who was soon calling for suffrage for "educated women," using the language of "social housekeeping" that was common in the 1890s.

Olivia's work with the New York Women's Hospital illustrates these connections between a search for personal fulfillment, volunteer work, and activism. Arriving in New York City in 1869, she soon became one of an association of upper-class "lady managers" for this, the first hospital specializing in the diseases of women. The hospital had begun in a private house on Madison Avenue in 1854. Olivia performed a variety of duties for the hospital: fund-raising, interviewing a new matron, checking on supplies from time to time, allocating beds among needy applicants, visiting the sick, and responding to calls for unusual supplies such as the superintendent's plea, "Champane [sic] is needed and I send John. This is for Mrs. Barker Sect. 3."[10]

A letter filed along with her husband's correspondence to New York Governor Edwin D. Morgan shows how seriously Olivia took her responsibilities at the hospital, and how such work led women to increase their expectations: "At the meeting of the Executive Board on Wednesday, Mr. Bell the [Hospital] Engineer, made a requisition for coal, and previous to the meeting I went into the cellar and saw that there was only enough for about ten days use," she began. "The traps that return the hot water to the boilers are too small to do the work, and consequently the hot water passes off into the cellar. . . . The hospital can hardly afford any waste in the present state of its finances," she concluded. "I know that the business of attending to the traps belongs to a committee, and I would not have mentioned it to you, only to explain the drain upon the coals, *and I trust in this connection I have not intruded upon a domain where ladies do not belong*" [italics added]. The letter shows how Olivia Sage was using Emma Willard's practical science teaching to claim competence about running an organization, modestly appealing to the conventional idea of the "woman's sphere" while in fact challenging men's right to run things. (Readers might recall historian Linda Kerber's insightful statements: "The evidence that the woman's sphere was a social construction lies in part in the hard and constant work required to build and repair its boundaries," and "All the talk about spheres [in nineteenth-century women's writing] is the sound of spheres breaking up.")[11]

The hospital experience provided a valuable apprenticeship in handling money. Sage was treasurer and also was involved in fundraising for the new building. It also demonstrated the overwhelming advantage men possessed in matters of policymaking, even in such a "women's institution" as the hospital. When the hospital was reorganized in 1888 over the opposition of the lady managers, Sage agreed to serve on the reorganized Board of Trustees; however, she recalled a few years later, "The male portion of the Board was made up of lawyers mainly, and at Board meetings the women were outargued by them and voted as they did."[12]

In the 1890s, Olivia enlarged her public role. She was among the founders in 1891 of the Emma Willard Association, an alumnae organization for Troy Female Seminary, and she supervised the collection of biographical data for the important volume *Emma Willard and Her Pupils*, which contains information on the lives of 3,500 of the more than 12,000 women who attended Troy from 1822 to 1872.[13] Sage would continue to refer to Emma Willard when speaking about women's power. In 1905, sixty years after Sage received her diploma from Troy, she led a campaign to have Emma Willard's bust put in the Hall of Fame commemorating great Americans, which was then being designed by architect Stanford White for New York University. Olivia was outraged that Emma Willard was not to be included among the immortals. Although she was over eighty, she handwrote fifty letters on pink paper to influential people, urging the nomination of "Emma Willard, Teacher." "She was not only a great teacher, but an educator, an author, and in a vital sense, a reformer," she wrote of Willard. "Few other women named upon the list can rank with her. Many of them entered their life-work [because of her], they rose on the foundation she had laid." She urged a vote for Mrs. Willard, "in loyalty to her memory, not my strong personal preference alone, but the united wish and estimate of the Association that bears her name."[14]

Olivia Sage also began to call for the suffrage. Parlor suffrage meetings that brought hundreds of women together in her New York home took politics indoors and made possible a kind of genteel activism as elite women joined the suffrage cause. Women should run their own organizations, Olivia declared at one such meeting, after a bill to allow women trustees to serve on the board of the Troy Female Seminary was vetoed by the governor. "If women could vote, they would decide the question of whether women should be members of the Board of Trustees of a girls' school, or whether men alone should be members."[15] Her calls for women's economic emancipation seem especially poignant if we read the newspaper accounts of Russell Sage's enormous gains and losses on Wall Street at the same time. For example, a financial panic in 1884 forced him to pay out $8 million to creditors in a few days!

In this period of her life, the identity of "educated woman" served Olivia well. It covered up her obscure class origins while providing a legitimate reason for her to speak out in public, then still a risky activity for a respectable woman. Described by one reporter as "a Puritan and a schoolteacher," Olivia rejected the identity of "leisured woman," criticized fashion and its follies, and embraced the idea of work and moral earnestness. "Now the woman of to-day has demonstrated the quality of her talent, courage, and endurance," she wrote. "Therefore there is no excuse for her not working."[16] Speaking as a "schoolteacher" (even though she had not worked as one for thirty years) allowed her to lecture men about the mess they were making of public life. By claiming women were more moral than men, Sage and her allies constructed a suffrage argument based on women's eternal preoccupation and traditional duty: cleaning up after men. "When women vote there will be a national housecleaning such as no nation ever saw," she wrote. "Once armed with the ballot, then the mop, the broom and the bucket will be decidedly more in evidence in the places in which they are most needed."[17]

The vote in presidential elections was only one of a wide range of reforms that women were seeking at this time. In 1900, Olivia Sage was one of three signers of a petition calling for New York suffragist

Lillie Devereux Blake to become president of the National American Woman Suffrage Association on the retirement of Susan B. Anthony (Elizabeth Cady Stanton and physician Mary Putnam Jacobi were the other two). The flier listed Blake's long and tireless suffrage activity, crediting her with passage of laws granting school suffrage to women, allowing joint custody in the case of divorce, enabling a woman to make a will without her husband's consent, providing for women to be trustees "in all public institutions where women are placed," and supplying seats for department store employees. The flier also credited Blake with other advances. Because of her, women had been appointed census enumerators in 1880; war nurses had been granted pensions for their service; women had gained admission to the civil service; and female police matrons were being appointed to courts. This list of achievements for women's rights marked a substantial advance for cautious feminists such as Sage. Perhaps as a notation for such progress, she signed the document, "M. Olivia Sage" instead of the usual "Mrs. Russell Sage." (The candidacy of Lillie Devereux Blake failed when Anthony designated Carrie Chapman Catt as her successor rather than Blake. The latter then withdrew her name before the voting took place in order to avoid a fight.)[18]

Though fond of her husband, Olivia became increasingly infuriated by his stinginess. It was only through a combination of moral suasion and feminine wiles that she maneuvered him into donating $50,000 to each of her favorite causes, the Emma Willard School in 1895 and the Woman's Hospital in 1898. Russell Sage, the multimillionaire who was too stingy to buy his own newspaper, who rode the streetcar to work and "didn't believe in" vacations, was a figure of derision in the press. As he sank into senility in 1903, Olivia began to make her first serious philanthropic donations on her own initiative.

Begging letters began to flood into her Fifth Avenue home, and fund-raisers began to circle like sharks smelling the first drops of blood. Henry MacCracken, president of New York University, was the most imaginative: he awarded Olivia an honorary M.A. degree in 1904.[19] Her letter accepting the honor shows surprise and genuine delight. "With great diffidence I take my pen in hand to reply to your letter of April 30th. That an Institution so famed should choose to give me a Degree was quite incomprehensible, hence my hesitation in replying, as an acceptance seemed doubtful. But my loyalty to my own Alma Mater and to its Founder Mrs. Emma Hart Willard, induces me to write my acceptance and to thank the Corporation of New York University for the great honor they have done me."[20] For MacCracken, the plan paid off. Only six weeks after Russell Sage's death in July 1906, Olivia Sage rewarded New York

University with a huge donation. But her gift of almost $300,000, intended for a women's college or women's buildings at New York University, was never applied to that purpose. Here, right at its beginnings, her philanthropy was being diverted from the uses she intended. When Russell Sage died in July 1906 at the age of ninety, a Troy newspaper commented, "In leaving his fortune to Mrs. Sage, Mr. Sage has left it to charity."[21] Now the ordinary woman had the extraordinary sum of $75 million at her disposal. And the schoolteacher who had reinvented herself as a figure of benevolence, who was called by the press a "philanthropist" even during the decades when she had nothing to give away except advice on morals and manners, had enough money to carry out all her wishes.

Or did she? There is a puzzling contradiction in her benevolence. Although Olivia spent over $45 million in the final eleven years of her life and left another $49 million in her will, mainly to charity, Sage money went to some surprising causes. For example, she gave to women's colleges, including Wellesley, Vassar, and Bryn Mawr, but she donated far more to Harvard, Yale, and Princeton, universities that excluded women. She supported religious missions and women's auxiliary associations, but again gave far more to male-dominated associations, such as the American Bible Society. She gave nothing to the settlement houses, but over $1 million to the Charity Organization Society.

What happened? Why did Olivia fail to use that "old-age freedom for women" to give some spectacular gifts to women's organizations? A study of the thousands of letters between Sage and the institutions and individuals that were in pursuit of her money reveals that her gifts often had multiple meanings. For example, when she purchased Constitution Island off West Point and gave it to the nation in 1908, her action had at least four motives. First, it was an act of patriotism, commemorating a Revolutionary War victory over English forces on the Hudson River; second, it saved the island home of Susan and Anna Warner, best-selling domestic novelists whose *The Wide, Wide World* (1850) had sold over one million copies, as many as the better-known *Uncle Tom's Cabin*. Plans for the commercial development of the site as an amusement park meant that Anna Warner, the elderly surviving sister, would lose her home. But Sage despised such plans and thwarted them by her purchase of the island. Finally, the area with its natural beauty had sentimental ties with her younger days. No one explanation would have sufficed for Olivia's gift.[22]

In other cases, though, Olivia was simply outmaneuvered and outwitted by advisers and fund-raisers alike, as she was by the New York University administration. In the end, she spent millions of dollars on *their* favorite schemes and left her own plans unfulfilled.

Isolated by deafness and suffering the physical limitations of old age, she was easily hoodwinked. And in the end her influence was less than it might have been because she succumbed to the temptation to support many thousands of worthy institutions and causes with modest amounts of money, rather than to make one or two really major contributions.[23]

Her largest donation, $10 million in April 1907 to set up the Russell Sage Foundation for Social Betterment, was shaped by her adviser Robert W. de Forest, a railroad attorney, former associate of her husband, and a philanthropist in his own right. De Forest guided the elderly woman's benevolence toward an institution that would become the flagship of social science research. Thus, Sage money helped to found modern social science and social work; very little of it went directly to poor people. Of the millions spent, only $10,000 a year went to needy persons in New York City, a sum that was carefully administered by the New York Charity Organization Society. Yet Olivia experienced a great pleasure in making the enormous donation to the foundation. She insisted that the foundation should bear only her husband's name, altering an early planning document by refusing to include her own. She reportedly exclaimed at the first meeting of the trustees of the foundation, "I am nearly eighty years old and I feel as though I have just begun to live!"[24]

During her last years, as she continued to spend on religious, civic, charitable, and educational causes, she remained mentally alert. Two documents from 1916, when she was eighty-eight, show where her heart was. In the first, a fund-raiser from Rutgers (at that time a male-only college affiliated with the Reformed church) complained of being turned away when he approached a representative of Sage for money. "I am sorry not to help you, but Mrs. Sage takes very little interest now in helping the education of men, and has told me repeatedly that she was going to do nothing more for men's colleges," he was told.[25] In the same year, Olivia gave $1 million to endow a new women's college, named, again, for her husband. It was entirely consistent with her long-held principles that Russell Sage College of Practical Arts in Troy should be designed for women's vocational education, with the goal of producing a generation of women that would enter the professions and business and achieve the economic and political participation that had always eluded its founder.

The terms of her will were extraordinarily generous. Like the private philanthropy of her final eleven years, they reflected competing claims of sentiment, influence, and ideology. Donations to churches, missions, and other religious causes exceeded donations to all other causes, except to universities. The legacy was divided into fifty-two equal parts. Of the eighteen colleges named in the will, fifteen received two parts, or about $800,000 each.[26] The Emma Willard School, the New York Woman's Hospital, the Children's Aid Society, the Charity Organization Society, the Metropolitan Museum of Art, the American Museum of Natural History, and Syracuse University received $1.6 million each. Of these, the Metropolitan and the Charity Organization Society donations were clearly prompted by Robert de Forest, as was the $5.6 million for the Russell Sage Foundation. Her donations to Syracuse University and the Emma Willard School were motivated by sentimental ties, in the first case to her birthplace and in the second to her adored teacher. Other large donations, however, reaffirmed sentimental and intellectual ties to the "woman's domain" of religious auxiliary societies. Several women's auxiliary associations were named. For example, the Board of Home Missions of the Presbyterian Church of America and the Women's Executive Committee each got a whopping $1.6 million. The Woman's Board of Foreign Missions of the Presbyterian Church also received $1.6 million. She left $400,000 to the New York Bible Society; the nondenominational New York City Mission and Tract Society (Woman's Board) received $1.6 million.[27]

If there is a lesson to be learned here, it is that in the nineteenth century, women's relation to money was crucial, though wealth was rarely within their control. The female philanthropist commanded respect without alarming conservative opponents of women's claims. In a gender system where women could still represent themselves as naturally benevolent, their philanthropy appeared ordinary: it was no more than the instinctive goodness of true womanhood (scholars call this "naturalizing" women's benevolence). Thus, such women as Olivia (Mrs. Russell Sage) and her younger friend, Helen Gould, daughter of Jay Gould, aroused little curiosity. As mirror images of the ruthless "robber baron," the benevolent woman allowed contemporaries to understand the economic transformations of the time as containing both change and continuity. Although newspaper stories about paired couples such as Olivia and Russell Sage might have led readers to contemplate a gendered division between selfish accumulation and selfless benevolence, the real story is more complicated. It suggests that at a time when money and the market became the measure of all things, women could sometimes wield power, not by earning money or by amassing it, but by giving it away. Using her husband's name, "Mrs. Russell Sage," and giving to many of the women's organizations she had supported as a volunteer during thirty-five years of marriage, Olivia Sage presents a fascinating puzzle to historians for the way she went about giving away the fortune her husband had spent his whole life to collect.

Notes

1. Carolyn G. Heilbrun, *Writing a Woman's Life* (New York: Ballantine Books, 1988), 127.

2. Anne Firor Scott, "'The Ever-Widening Circle': The Diffusion of Feminist Values from the Troy Female Seminary, 1822–1872," *History of Education Quarterly* 19 (Spring 1979): 3–25.

3. Paul Sarnoff, *Russell Sage, the Money King* (New York: Ivan Obolensky, 1965), 62–64; Russell Sage's correspondence with Edwin D. Morgan, New York Whig politician and businessman, begins to mention Wisconsin railroads at this time; Russell Sage to Edwin D. Morgan, December 4, 1856, August 27, 1857, Morgan papers, Box 11, folder 6, New York State Library (NYSL).

4. Joseph Slocum "was a successful food merchant who became a New York State Assemblyman through the good offices of his business associate, Russell Sage" (Sarnoff, *Money King*, 141).

5. *Wheeler v Sage*, 68 U.S. (I. Wallace) 518 (1863).

6. Margaret Olivia Sage, "Mrs. Russell Sage's Plea," *New York Daily Tribune*, August 8, 1898, II, 7, c. 3.

7. Ibid.

8. "Suppose They Had Married the First Man That Proposed," *New York Herald*, December 10, 1899.

9. Typically, she attributed the quotation to Emma Willard. Handwritten correspondence Margaret Olivia Sage, n.d., at Emma Willard School Archives, Troy, New York.

10. Superintendent [Women's Hospital] to Margaret Olivia Sage, January 6, 1886; January 27, 1888; January 30, 1888; February 8, 1888; March 1, 1888; Russell Sage Foundation (RSF), Box 97, folder 978.

11. Linda Kerber, "Separate Spheres, Female Worlds, Woman's Place: The Rhetoric of Women's History," *Journal of American History* 75 (June 1988): 9–39.

12. Margaret Olivia Sage, "Opportunities and Responsibilities of Leisured Women," *North American Review* 181 (November 1905): 719; the reorganized board had thirteen male and twelve female members.

13. Mrs. A. W. Fairbanks, ed., *Emma Willard and Her Pupils, or Fifty Years of Troy Female Seminary, 1822–1872* (New York: Mrs. Russell Sage, 1898).

14. Letter from Margaret Olivia Sage to the Honorable Edmund C. Stedman, LL.D., July 19, 1905; Margaret Olivia Sage to John W. Burgess, Ph.D., LL.D, July 19, 1905; Professor Burgess was the chair of Political Science at Columbia, Stedman Collection, Butler Library, Columbia University.

15. "Equal Suffrage for Women: Mrs. Russell Sage Gives Her Views on the Subject," *New York Times*, April 15, 1894, 8.

16. Margaret Olivia Sage, "Opportunities and Responsibilities of Leisured Women," 714. The article provides a summary of her views on how women's influence would reform society and clean up politics.

17. Untitled clipping, *New York Times*, February 4, 1909, RSF, Box 98, folder 995.

18. Alma Lutz, *Susan B. Anthony: Rebel Crusader, Humanitarian* (Boston: Beacon Press, 1959), 292.

19. Letter from "M. Olivia Sage" to Chancellor MacCracken, May 31, 1904. File: Honorary Degrees, New York University Archives.

20. Ibid.

21. *Troy Record*, July 28, 1906, 5.

22. Letter from Captain Peter E. Traub to unknown, May 28, 1908, United States Military Academy Archives, West Point, NY.

23. Kathleen McCarthy, *Women's Culture: American Philanthropy and Art, 1830–1930* (Chicago: University of Chicago Press, 1991), 174–75.

24. Robert W. de Forest, "Margaret Olivia Sage, Philanthropist," *The Survey* 41 (1918): 151.

25. Letter from Theodore Janeway, M.D., to President Demarest, March 8, 1916, in folder, "Mrs. Russell Sage (Margaret O. Sage)," Box 33, folder 33, RG 07/All/03, Rutgers University Archives.

26. These were Tuskegee, Hampton, Union College, Hamilton College, Amherst, Dartmouth, Barnard, Bryn Mawr, Smith, New York University, Yale, Princeton, Harvard, Williams, Wellesley; four received $100,000 (Park College, in Maryland; Middlebury, Rutgers, Syracuse University). The matter was complicated by the fact that the will contained a clause stipulating that the amount donated to any institution during Mrs. Sage's lifetime was to be deducted from the bequest; thus, Syracuse University, which had received $637,000 during her lifetime, was entitled to only $100,000 more in the will; "Mrs. Sage's Estate Worth $49,051,045," *New York Times*, November 14, 1918; the provision caused shock, disappointment, and a great deal of legal wrangling.

27. *Forty-Second Annual Report, Woman's Board of Home Missions, Presbyterian Church, USA*, May 1921, 65; "Mrs. Sage's Estate Worth $49,051,045," *New York Times*, November 14, 1918.

Suggested Readings

Very little has been written on Olivia Sage. Irvin Wyllie, "Margaret Olivia Slocum Sage," in *Notable American Women,* ed. Edward T. James, Janet Wilson James, Paul Boyer, 3 vols. (Cambridge, MA: Harvard University Press, 1971), 3:222–23, is a good, but brief, overview. Ruth Crocker, "From Widow's Mite to Widow's Might: The Philanthropy of Margaret Olivia Sage," *Journal of Presbyterian History* (formerly *American Presbyterians*) 74, 4 (Winter 1996): 253–64, is an up-to-date discussion and analysis of her philanthropy; it argues that Sage was typical of many nineteenth-century churchwomen who became involved in reform and institution building. Several books illuminate areas connected to Olivia Sage's life and career. A fascinating and important study of the New York Women's Hospital is Deborah Kuhn McGregor, *Sexual Surgery and the Origins of Gynecology: J. Marion Sims and His Patients* (New York: Garland Publishing Company, 1989). David C. Hammack details the establishment of the Russell Sage Foundation in David C. Hammack and Stanton Wheeler, *Social Science in the Making: Essays on the Russell Sage Foundation* (New York: Russell Sage Foundation, 1994), 1–34. Anne Firor Scott's "'The Ever-Widening Circle': The Diffusion of Feminist Values from the Troy Female Seminary, 1822–1872," *History of Education Quarterly* 19 (Spring 1979): 3–25, explains why Emma Willard and her seminary were so important for American culture. Unfortunately, the only study of Olivia's robber baron husband, written by money expert Paul Sarnoff, *Russell Sage: The Money King* (New York: Ivan Obolensky, 1965), though entertaining, is largely gossip and invention where Olivia is concerned.

Several contemporary sources are invaluable. The biographical dictionary published by the Emma Willard Association and organized and paid for by Mrs. Sage, Mrs. A. W. Fairbanks, ed., *Emma Willard and Her Pupils, or Fifty Years of Troy Female Seminary, 1822–1872* (New York: Published by Mrs. Russell Sage, 1898), includes much material about Willard and her seminary. Also revealing is Arthur Huntingon Gleason's "Mrs. Russell Sage and Her Interests," *The World's Work* 13 (November 1906): 8182–86. There is Olivia's own essay in which she states her views on everything from women smoking (she opposed it) to the vote, Margaret Olivia Sage, "Opportunities and Responsibilities of Leisured Women," *North American Review* 181 (November 1905): 712–21.

The main collection of Olivia Sage's unpublished papers are at the Rockefeller Archive Center, Pocantico Hills, New York, and at the Emma Willard School in Troy, New York. Other scattered papers can be found at the Butler Library, Columbia University; the New York State Library, Albany, New York; New York University Archives; the New York Public Library; Rutgers University Archives; United States Military Academy Archives, West Point, New York; and elsewhere.

11

Nellie Wiegel
"How About That?!"

Katherine Osburn

In 1925, Mrs. Charles W. "Nellie" Wiegel (dates unknown), the Colorado Federation of Women's Clubs (CFWC) chair on Indian Welfare, wrote a terse letter to Edward McKean, Indian agent on the Southern Ute Reservation in Southwestern Colorado. Wiegel began by noting that CFWC was "a great and powerful force and whether it is used for good or not so good remains to be seen." She assured McKean that although her group [did] "not want to cause trouble," they were "three and a half million strong and must be reckoned with." She credited McKean with integrity, writing, "I believe you have the best interests of the Indians at heart, that you are doing your best, and that you are the proper man for the place." She then presented a list of grievances concerning finances and the allocation of Ute resources. Wiegel was the voice of righteous indignation, exclaiming, "How about that?!" after every point she raised. "I can hear you swear and know what you will say about it all," she wrote in closing, "but never mind that at all! . . . Do the square thing by me and I am always, yours to command for a better understanding."[1] Wiegel was not clear in her letter why she was concerned about Ute finances, but it is likely that some Utes wrote to her knowing that they might get support from the CFWC: a white women's organization dedicated to education, cultural and civic improvements, political activity, and social welfare work.

McKean's reply soothed Wiegel's irritation. He thanked her for her interest and then refuted her charges, assuring her that the Utes' financial affairs were well taken care of by the Bureau of Indian Affairs (BIA). Wiegel seemed satisfied with McKean's response. Yet within two months she wrote Commissioner of Indian Affairs (CIA) Charles H. Burke demanding a further accounting of Ute funds. Burke responded with a lengthy explanation of Ute finances and proposed that rather than concerning herself with reservation finances, she devote her efforts instead to projects for the Ute women and children.[2] Wiegel, however, continued to agitate for the Utes' political and economic empowerment.

These confrontations were typical of Nellie Wiegel's relationship with the BIA between the years 1923 and 1941. During the late

161

nineteenth and early twentieth centuries, the BIA attempted to "civilize" Native Americans living on reservations, and women's clubs played an important supporting role. Nonetheless, tensions sometimes developed between the Indian Bureau and the CFWC. These problems were, in part, related to Wiegel's confrontational personality and her construction of her role as Indian advocate. Although she always maintained that she was only trying to assist the "proper authorities," Wiegel constantly challenged the actions of BIA personnel. They answered her queries and professed gratitude for her help, but many policymakers grew to resent Wiegel's "interference." Despite her repeated claims that she was not a "troublemaker," Nellie Wiegel raised an enormous amount of trouble for the Indian Service in her career with CFWC.

Wiegel's experiences as an Indian activist reflect several important themes in the lives of many well-to-do women in the early twentieth century, and research into these activities reveals the difficulties of writing the history of "ordinary women." An extended search of historical records in Colorado failed to locate any information on Wiegel's life other than her correspondence with the BIA, her reports to the CFWC, and a newspaper clipping about her collection of Indian Art, published in the *Rocky Mountain News,* a Denver newspaper, in 1938. Other than references in correspondence to her husband and a married daughter, Wiegel's personal life is invisible to historians; even the date of her death cannot be ascertained.

What is known is her controversial career as an Indian activist. A middle-aged woman in the 1920s, Wiegel had come of age during the Progressive Era, when women of all classes were active in reform. Wiegel was a wealthy Denver homemaker who, like many clubwomen, was engaged in civic affairs. She had the leisure and means to travel, and she used her social position to win appointments to committees that advised government officials on social policy. She chaired both the Indian Welfare Division for the CFWC and the Colorado State Indian Commission, a committee of volunteers appointed by the governor to oversee Indian Affairs in the state. Wiegel emphasized self-help for Native Americans, including education, employment opportunities, and citizenship—defined as voting.[3] In these goals, she was promoting a conservative social welfare agenda common to many Progressive Era campaigns.

In some respects, however, her activities reflected new cultural forces at work in the 1920s and 1930s, when appreciation for selected aspects of Native American culture became popular. Rather than insisting upon complete assimilation for the Utes, Wiegel devoted much of her energy to encouraging appreciation among non-Indians for unique and colorful Indian "traditions." This campaign also included encouraging the Utes to appreciate their culture. She told the *Rocky Mountain News*: "We should teach them [the Utes] to be proud of their Indian blood, proud of their heritage of bravery. It is a mistake to try to make whites of them."[4] Wiegel's concept of cultural pluralism, however, did not involve a cultural and political identity as a separate nation. Rather, she encouraged the Utes to assimilate to mainstream culture while maintaining nonthreatening aspects of Ute culture, such as arts and crafts, history, mythology, and ceremonialism. Her paradigm was to preserve Indian traditions within a new context—the Indian as an educated, self-sustaining American citizen. Wiegel dedicated countless hours to helping the Utes realize these goals.

Wiegel's construction of her identity as a reformer is also instructive. In some ways she continued a traditional woman's role. Although very active in public life, Wiegel never translated her volunteer work into a paid job, nor did she ever run for an elected political office. Instead she chose to remain a volunteer—a holdover from the era of "Lady Bountiful"—the well-to-do woman altruist of the late nineteenth century, who "uplifted" the "less fortunate" by helping them "improve" their homes. Framing her public advocacy in the traditional role of the homemaker as protector and moral guardian of society, Wiegel informed the Commissioner of Indian Affairs (CIA) in 1932, "As are the homes of the nation, so is the nation."[5] Perhaps seeking to derail possible accusations that she was "out of her place," she always conducted her activities under the auspices of male authority figures. Thus, in some respects, Wiegel represented a very "traditional" approach to women's reform work. Her actions in playing this role, however, reveal tensions over women's public identities in the early twentieth century.

In the 1920s and 1930s, women were increasingly turning volunteer work into paid employment as social workers and were struggling to construct professional identities for themselves. In their new vocation, women were enjoined against "putting too much of one's own prejudices, sentiments, loves and hates into one's job" and encouraged to be "rational" and "scientific."[6] As more women joined the ranks of professional social workers, they also endured popular stereotypes that characterized them as meddlers. It may have been to head off this kind of potential opprobrium that Wiegel stated her desire to "be a help and not a meddle." Moreover, she was apparently sensitive to possible gendered criticisms of her volunteer work as frivolous, for she occasionally asserted that she was no dilettante. Rather, she represented herself as a dispassionate and objective observer who could advocate on behalf of the Utes. Thus, Wiegel's life may be seen as a type of transitional figure between the homemaker-volunteer reformer of the late nineteenth and early twentieth centuries and the professional social worker or political

official of later decades. An examination of her activities with the
Southern Utes illuminates how she shaped this role.

The U.S. government first created a reservation for the seven
bands of Utes in 1868. Anglo greed for Ute lands, however, continually eroded its acreage. In 1880, four of the seven bands were relocated to Utah and the remaining ones—the Capote, Mouache, and
Weminuche, numbering about 807—were confined to the Southern
Ute Reservation, a narrow strip of land in the southwestern corner
of Colorado. The CFWC, founded in 1895, showed an interest in Indians immediately by sponsoring a campaign in 1898 to preserve the
prehistoric cliff dwellings at Mesa Verde, Colorado, near the reservation. The federation created a Committee on Indian Welfare in
1921; this committee became a division in 1925, and Wiegel became
its first chair in 1926. Immediately, she investigated conditions at
the Southern Ute Reservation, helped establish a State Commission
on Indian Welfare in the governor's office, and introduced a bill in the
Colorado legislature to erect a memorial to Ute chief Ouray in Mon-
trose, Colorado. For this work, Governor William Adams appointed
Wiegel chair of the new Colorado State Indian Commission.[7]

Wiegel's activities early in her career complemented BIA plans
to acculturate Native Americans. She established "a young women's
club through which good work is being done along the lines of the
Home Making and Better Homes clubs." This organization functioned to help "the young mothers who desire to make 'American
Homes' patterned after those of their white sisters [and] who wish
to raise their children to be good citizens, self-supporting and self-
sustaining." Her "Save the Babies" campaign taught Indian women
scientific methods of child rearing. Wiegel also promoted another
cause dear to the hearts of BIA administrators—citizenship. She
wanted "to merge [the Utes] into the citizenry of the Nation as self-
supporting, law abiding and EDUCATED citizens." To this end, she
encouraged the Utes to vote and "tried to busy the residents [near
the reservation] in the matter. If they want to do something to help
the 'poor Indian' let them do their duty as citizens to see that the
said Indian gets to the polls!"[8]

In keeping with her emphasis on self-help, Wiegel lobbied for
more federal funds for education and marketing Indian crafts. In
1926 she attempted to get congressional funding for an Indian cultural center in Durango, Colorado (near the reservation), where the
Utes and other tribes could sell handicrafts. She sent craft supplies
and secured Agent McKean's support. Writing to him about her
plans, Wiegel deferred to his authority over the Utes: "Without the
assistance of you and your force I realize I could do nothing; with
that hearty assistance, together we can do some splendid work. We
will set a pace for the other agencies to follow." Wiegel noted that

having McKean's backing meant she could now "drum up support" for the project.[9] Despite Wiegel's and McKean's enthusiasm, the center never materialized, probably because Wiegel was unable to raise the funds. Economic realities, then, sometimes limited her effectiveness, but she continued her advocacy undeterred.

Wiegel's construction of her role as the Utes' protector propelled her into a defense of Ute treaty rights. In 1931 she asked members of the Senate Committee on Indian Affairs to stop a proposal that would lease lands on the Ute reservation to Navajo shepherds for grazing. She appealed "to the friends of the Indians against a great injustice which may be done to my Utes—I say MY advisedly, because I have been adopted by them as a 'red sister.'" Wiegel feared that when the Navajo leases expired, whites would take the lands because they were "immensely rich in gas, oil, and coal." In closing she asked, "Are treaties, promises, agreements, acknowledgment of ownership, etc. again mere scraps of paper to be tossed aside when the white man begins to covet that which is the Indians [*sic*] by every known right?"[10] The proposed leases apparently were never enacted, but the direct impact of Wiegel's activism on this decision cannot be gauged.

Even as Wiegel assumed the role of the champion of the powerless, she was careful to portray herself as objective. In 1928, at the entreaty of a Ute father, Wiegel sought the whereabouts of Max Buffalo, a missing Ute policeman accused of murder. "The poor old fellow," she wrote of Max's father, "is heart broken. Max'[s] wife is 'carrying on' raising her baby and trying to keep her little batch of sheep together hoping that someday her man will come back to her. She is neat and clean and so sad looking. . . . This is sob stuff, maybe, a heart story and you know I have kept clear of that in my dealings with the office, but this is a peculiar case." The bureau promised to help, but the young man was never found. Wiegel's assertion that she shied away from emotional issues in her work reflected her image of herself as a professional whose work should be treated seriously.[11]

Wiegel's interactions with BIA officials were a delicate balancing act. She justified her behavior, including sharp criticism of BIA policy, as necessary for the defense of "her Utes." Yet, in most interactions, she claimed deference to BIA authority. In 1927, on behalf of several Utes, she raised a number of charges against reservation employees, including an allegation that Agent McKean and an agency farmer were skimming profits from Ute funds. The BIA investigation cleared McKean but found the farmer guilty of incompetence, and the bureau fired him. Commissioner Burke informed Wiegel of his decisions and noted that they could do little more, since she refused to name the Utes who had sought her assistance. Wiegel's reply expressed disapproval of Burke's decision, but she deferred to his authority: "I feel that you are making a grave mistake but of course the action taken by you is [a] matter for you to decide." Wiegel also defended her refusal to name her sources. "Knowing the power of a superintendent in his 'dominion,'" she wrote, "I did not think it just or honorable to expose anyone, either employee, Indian or resident of that locality to a vindictive retaliation for telling the truth." Wiegel concluded by restating her conservative conceptualization of her role as guardian. "Information came to me without my seeking," she wrote, "after verifying same to my satisfaction, I passed it on to the Bureau and there my duty ended. . . . Personally it is now a closed chapter."[12]

Nevertheless, Wiegel's failure to get what she wanted from the Indian Service also frustrated her, and expressing her exasperation sometimes offended government officials. Writing to BIA inspector H. H. Fiske, who had investigated the charges against McKean and the agency farmer, Wiegel noted, "I have about decided that all efforts by anyone in or out of the Service for the betterment of the Indians will have about as much effect on the powers in control in Washington as throwing pebbles against one of these old stone buildings. 'Was, is now, and ever shall be' applies and all the King's horses and all the King's men will not change the methods or minds of the great bosses back east. You see I am very much discouraged this morning." Fiske reacted to Wiegel's despondent letter by forwarding it to the commissioner and the Office of the Chief Inspector of the BIA with comments about how she was "a most 'difficult' person." He dismissed Wiegel as "a gabster, spreading her secrets wherever she thinks she may find a retentive ear. Foolish and to no purpose."[13]

Wiegel apparently knew she had been criticized, for in 1931 she asked Commissioner Charles J. Rhodes if his "oft repeated permission to go onto the reservation still holds. . . . If, for any reason, you would rather I stay away, kindly wire . . . and I will comply with your wishes. I believe in obeying rules and regulations." Rhodes replied that the bureau welcomed her "suggestions and cooperation in matters pertaining to the advancement of the Indians and while it is not always possible to accept and act upon them, nevertheless we are pleased to consider them." Wiegel then responded that she knew he approved of her work but that some Indian Service employees did not. In the same letter, Wiegel sounded quite bitter about her failure to get action from the Indian Service. She reported that although she had information about the new superintendent of the Ute agency, Edward Peacore, that indicated his unfitness to serve: "I have no report to make regarding same, no suggestions, no recommendations. . . . Whatever I say would only be 'considered' and not acted upon in any way, so why bother?"[14]

The CFWC, however, did not share Wiegel's disillusionment. At their annual convention in La Junta, Colorado, on September 22–25, 1931, the CFWC passed a resolution calling for an investigation of Peacore. Within two weeks, Wiegel informed Commissioner Rhodes that the CFWC was not "bringing accusations against any person or persons in the Indian service," but was placing evidence of "alleged mis-conduct and alleged mal-administration [by Peacore] before the proper authorities for immediate investigation." Wiegel explained that the CFWC had a duty to report its findings to the Indian Service because "we hold that when these Indian girls are taken from their homes and parents by the federal government and placed in the reservation school, that the Indian Bureau, through its representatives, is making itself a direct guardian of said Indian girls."[15] Wiegel and the CFWC, thus, felt obligated to help the BIA live up to its responsibilities to protect Indian girls from immorality and sexual exploitation. In this capacity, Wiegel contacted agency employees and people who lived near the reservation and collected testimony for the investigation.[16]

Various reservation employees accused Peacore of sexual misconduct, which set a low moral tone for the reservation. According to some reports, Peacore was guilty of having an affair with a teacher at the reservation boarding school and of threatening the jobs of Hattie Haren, school cook, and her husband Mack, the school engineer, "if she did not have guilty intercourse with him." Moreover, Peacore allegedly overlooked other immoral behavior on the reservation. Former agency employee Lottie McCall described how Eric R., visiting nephew of the reservation trader, seduced, impregnated, and abandoned Ruth C., a young Ute woman. Ruth agreed to have sex with Eric, but McCall felt Peacore should have taken steps to remove Eric and protect Ruth's morals. Peacore also failed to protect fifteen-year-old S. D., a Ute student who claimed she had been raped and held by the rapist in his home for several days. Lottie McCall testified that she and her husband had asked Peacore for help with this situation and he replied that he could do nothing unless they had "been caught in the act." S. D. was "now living with first one man and then another," McCall concluded, blaming Peacore for her ultimate turn to "immorality."[17]

The investigation of these incidents was intensely bitter, and Wiegel's activities became a focal point of the controversy. Special Investigator Roy Nash intensely disparaged her, accusing Wiegel of spreading "malicious slander . . . and gossip . . . before a meeting of the butcher, the baker, and the candlestick maker in a village the size of Ignacio!" Nash discounted her investigation by contrasting her methods with his. "Unlike Mrs. Wiegel," he reported, "I decline to interview cooks and servants in this matter"; instead, Nash questioned the boarding school faculty. On another occasion, Nash wrote, "The influence of this woman is wholly evil and must be terribly disorganizing, it is to everybody's interest that she be eliminated from the scene." Allison L. Kroeger, of the Colorado State Indian Commission, wrote to Governor Adams complaining that Wiegel had "upbraided" him for not investigating thoroughly. In defending his actions, Kroeger said that he, unlike Wiegel, was not a "scandal monger." Wiegel, he concluded, was not "interested in the welfare of the indians [*sic*] other than to use them to satisfy her own personal desires for power. She apparently is the wife of an employee of the Denver Rio Grande Railroad Company and therefore able to travel about on a pass and make trouble and try to rule and ruin." He urged both Adams and the BIA to remove Wiegel from Indian Affairs. Needless to say, Agent Peacore also maligned Wiegel.[18]

As a result of the altercation, the BIA cooled its relationship with Wiegel. In February 1932 Commissioner Rhodes wrote to the secretary of the interior, Ray Lyman Wilbur, urging him to try to curb Wiegel's influence in Indian Affairs. "It is better to have her as an active enemy than to compromise with her in an effort to work together," he wrote. "She apparently has no idea of the ethics of public work." He then sent Wiegel a chilly letter thanking her for her interest in the BIA and citing his support for Peacore, who was absolved of her charges but was transferred to another agency because of the negative publicity. Colorado Congressman Edward Taylor, representing the district containing the reservation, joined the anti-Wiegel faction and pressured Governor Adams to remove her from the state board. Governor Adams, however, stood by Wiegel.[19]

Wiegel reacted to the controversy in a letter to the secretary of the interior charging that "the so-called investigation of Nash was partial to Superintendent Peacore" and citing numerous commendations of her work by both the commissioner and the secretary of the interior. She noted that she had seen a preliminary copy of Nash's report and wondered if "any action [would] be taken by you against Mr. Nash for his vicious and public attack on me." Wilbur's reply was apparently noncommittal (it was not found in the files), for ten months later Wiegel was still requesting a formal copy of Nash's report and the official response in "vindication of the Governor's stand in my behalf and as my just right and due." This was the last letter from Wiegel on the topic found in the historical record, and it is unclear if she ever received the report.[20]

Although she was not removed from the Colorado State Indian Commission, Wiegel was forced out of her position as chairman of the Division of Indian Welfare in the CFWC in 1932. She claimed that "the wives of Congressman Taylor's Durango group . . . threat-

ened to withdraw the southwest district from the State Federation
. . . if I was continued in the chairmanship of Indian Welfare." Abhorring the controversy, Wiegel refused the renomination as chairman,
and noted that the new chair of Indian Welfare was "the wife of one
of the most active of Congressman Taylor's Durango group." She
despaired that the CFWC's Indian Welfare Division for the next two
years would be "all for Durango business interests, and who cares
for the Indians."[21] An examination of the circumstances surrounding
Peacore suggests that her cynical assessment of Colorado Indian
Affairs may have been accurate.

The Peacore scandal caused bitter factionalism. Irate citizens
from nearby communities petitioned the BIA for Peacore's removal,
and others wrote in his favor. Among the anti-Peacore faction were
the La Plata County Taxpayers League and Mayor R. R. Garrick of
Ignacio (a town on the reservation); the mayor of nearby Cortez, Colorado, sent a petition with signatures of twenty businessmen in support of Peacore. Ultimately, Peacore was found guilty of sexually
harassing Haren and making false statements during the investigation. He was given ten days to "show cause . . . why he should not
be dismissed from the Service, demoted or transferred."[22]

Peacore was then transferred to South Dakota and immediately
suspended. Bureau officials denied that his suspension was because
of Wiegel's charges, instead citing new charges uncovered in the
investigation that Wiegel had begun. Wiegel, however, knew she had
been vindicated, for Mayor Garrick informed her of the circumstances of Peacore's departure: "The great and noble Mr. Peacore is
gone. He left Saturday night when it was dark and he took his
sweetheart with him. . . . He was supposed to be in Denver at the
Brown Palace Hotel Monday evening. I would have liked to have followed him and see what assumed name he travels under."[23] In
departing the reservation, Peacore abandoned his wife and children,
apparently leaving with the home economics teacher Wiegel had
named as his mistress. Early in 1933 he left his new post and vanished. In the aftermath of his disappearance, the BIA discovered
that he had paid "an excessive amount" of money to Allison Kroeger
to survey the reservation, had used Indian funds to do county
roadwork, had given government supplies and favorable leasing
agreements to friends, and had hired other friends for lucrative construction work who were completely unqualified for the job.[24] Thus,
true to Wiegel's assertions, at least some of Peacore's support may
have been from people who profited from his administration.

Despite Peacore's disappearance in 1933 (which she viewed as
vindication of her position), Wiegel did not regain the chairmanship
of the Division of Indian Welfare until 1936. The CFWC and BIA
records are silent about her activities during those years and about

the circumstances of her reinstatement. Once back in her old position, Wiegel reactivated her campaigns to better the Utes' lives through self-help. This time, however, she also pushed to have people sympathetic to her goals appointed to the Senate Committee on Indian Affairs. In late 1936, Wiegel began a crusade to completely abolish "the stupendous, all-powerful machine called the Bureau of Indian Affairs . . . [in which] American Indians are held as 'wards' of the Federal Government with no rights to life or property except as granted or dictated by said Federal Government."[25]

Aligning herself with a group of Native Americans who sought political autonomy from the federal government, Wiegel began lobbying the Senate Committee on Indian Affairs for the discontinuance of the BIA. At the annual CFWC convention in 1937, Wiegel hammered through a resolution petitioning Congress to abolish the Indians' position as wards of the federal government. The proclamation noted that Indians had become citizens in 1924, but the Indian Bureau still hindered their "complete, full citizenship." The resolution did not call specifically for the abolition of the BIA, but it cited excerpts critical of the Indian Service from the annual report of the secretary of the interior. The report noted that many tribes had won claims against the government for broken treaty promises, but that government bureaucracy had hindered the payment of the settlements. The CFWC concluded that "even though tribes may have funds to their credit, under the existing laws they are still in the position of *incompetent wards with inheritances lying in the hands of a guardian.*" To Wiegel and her supporters this was unconscionable.[26]

Wiegel's new campaign represented a shift in her thinking. From her earlier paradigm that envisioned the federal government as a tool for Indian assimilation, Wiegel had come to believe that the government hindered Native Americans' empowerment. This belief became fairly commonplace among persons active in Indian affairs in the 1940s and 1950s; thus, Wiegel was on the "cutting edge" in Indian policy. Despite the growing popularity of this idea among policymakers (and the introduction of numerous bills in Congress), the campaign to abolish the Indian Service failed.

Nellie Wiegel's last public record was a handwritten note dated January 12, 1948, and addressed to "Dear Folks." She spoke of her husband's sudden death from a heart attack in June and complained of her difficulty in finding an apartment. She was still active in Indian affairs, writing: "Quite a stir about the Indians. The Bureau will get a bigger appropriation and the Navajos nothing." She noted that she wanted to sell her house so as to be able to "come and go as I please" without worry. A history of the CFWC listed her as chair of the Division of Indian Welfare until 1941, when the division became a standing committee under the Division of Public Affairs. With her disappearance from the public record, Wiegel's ultimate fate cannot be established.[27]

Wiegel's career began as an adjunct to the government's assimilationist agenda. She promoted education, citizenship, and middle-class homemaking skills—the very things the Indian Service was attempting to impart to Native Americans. She also organized voters and lobbied Congress for her goals. Her strategy, common to twentieth-century women reformers, enlisted the activist state to implement her welfare work. Through these actions, Wiegel clearly defined herself as a political player—head of a power bloc of politically organized women working through the "proper channels" in the service of Indian welfare. Wiegel's actions reflected a view held by most well-to-do women reformers—that the government was supposed to protect the weak and that women could organize as a political pressure group to ensure that it did.

In her role as protector of the disempowered, however, Wiegel was drawn into conflict with male employees of the Indian Service. The climax of this oppositional relationship came in the 1931 investigation of Agent Peacore. Nonetheless, her dispute with the bureau in this particular affair was on a small scale—Wiegel sought the removal of an individual whom she judged immoral. At that time, she did not offer a substantive challenge to the status quo. Gradually, however, Wiegel grew increasingly disillusioned with government bureaucracy. The temporary loss of her place in volunteer Indian work highlighted the linkage between volunteers and the Indian "establishment," which held ultimate power over Native Americans. This experience undoubtedly shaped her conclusions that the main obstacle to Indian empowerment was the Indian Service. Wiegel, therefore, called for a radical action on behalf of a conservative agenda. In her latter years, she abandoned all pretenses of working for established authorities and turned her attention on those authorities themselves. As always, she acted in the name of the Indians and under the auspices of their best interests: a traditionally selfless female role.

The question of power in Wiegel's activism is an intriguing one, for her relationship with power appears to have been ambivalent. At times, Wiegel publicly claimed or implied that she held substantial sway, both as a member of the CFWC and as an individual. In her first correspondence with a Ute agent she asserted that her organization was "three and a half million strong and must be reckoned with." Assistant Indian Commissioner E. B. Merritt gave at least lip service to that claim, telling Wiegel, "We need the sympathetic interest and cooperation of all good citizens of this country and especially of the organized womanhood." Allison Kroeger informed Governor Adams that Wiegel declared that "she is the personal representative of Governor Adams [and] a woman with a great deal of influence not only in Colorado, but also in Washington." He also professed that when Wiegel tried to provoke his resignation from the Colorado State Indian Commission, she informed him "that she had consented to our appointments, leaving the impression that the appointments were up to her." A letter Wiegel sent Kroeger confirms his interpretation of her as a woman confident of her power. She reminded him that in the investigation of Peacore she was "the chairman of this commission and you were suggested as the delegate from Durango." She then took credit for the appropriation of funds for the Ute hospital (which Peacore had been claiming) and instructed Kroeger to go to the reservation himself and look beneath the surface of the Peacore administration. "A word to the wise you know," she concluded. "And this is only for you as one of this commission—as yet." Kroeger interpreted this letter—most probably her remark "as yet"—as an example of Wiegel's desire to intimidate him.

Investigator Nash also saw Wiegel as a bully. He forwarded to the commissioner a copy of a letter Wiegel had sent the principal of the reservation boarding school regarding the Peacore investigation: "In any forthcoming investigation, as you value your future standing, be very careful that you 'tell the truth, the whole truth, and nothing but the truth, so help you God.' The truth is known and will be acted upon later and it will be just too bad, so I am informed, for the person not 'coming clean.' . . . You doubtless remember a certain principle [sic] of that school who served others than the government authorities for whom he was supposed to be working and what happened to him."[28] Although Wiegel's letter does not directly state that she will "bring down" Principal Harshbarger, she obviously felt that she wielded enough clout to intimidate him into cooperating with the investigation. Nash also contended that Wiegel claimed she had Agent McKean transferred from the Ute reservation in 1927; there are, however, no records of Wiegel's declaring this herself.

Thus, while insisting that she was simply gathering information to give the proper authorities, Wiegel often behaved quite assertively in reservation affairs; and despite her assurances that she was "not against anyone," she threatened action against people who she felt were uncooperative. Wiegel's repeated public assertions that she was not doing what she was clearly doing represents either self-delusion or a strategy (conscious or unconscious) to cloak her offensive with the mantle of submission to authority. In the absence of real power to effect change, Wiegel frequently adopted a passive-aggressive approach, a traditional ploy to appropriate power used by those who feel powerless.[29] In employing these tactics, Wiegel may have been responding to the rhetoric policymakers employed to reproach her. None of Wiegel's detractors directly accused her of forgetting her place as a woman, but their censure was phrased in derogatory gendered language used to rebuke "uppity" women: gossip, meddler, slanderer, foolish woman, and troublemaker. Her harshest critic, Congressman Taylor, went as far as to call her "evil." Wiegel's behavior was forceful and at times appears imperious, but the hyperbole in her critics' attacks suggests an anger at her activities that may well be connected to her gender. Bureau correspondence concerning Peacore never used such opprobrious language—even after he disappeared, leaving behind his family and evidence of betrayal of his oath as an Indian agent.

This use of language was probably not lost on Wiegel, for throughout the controversy she positioned herself carefully as an objective and discreet observer who went through the proper channels. She asserted that she had not instigated the investigation—that persons upset with Peacore contacted her and she simply gathered data, not evidence. She directly refuted the accusations of gossip and slander, claiming that she had not made public the charges against Peacore, but rather Peacore's defenders had done so. Although she wrote forcefully in her defense and took full credit for Peacore's dismissal, she continually stood behind male authority figures such as the governor and the mayor of Ignacio.[30] For all the anger directed against her as a troublemaker motivated by a will to power, her activism was one of influence (rather than actual power) wielded under the protection of male government officials.

Wiegel's penchant for hiding behind male authority figures may have reflected her reading of who held actual power in early-twentieth-century America, for she interpreted the actions of her female critics in light of male behavior. Wiegel implied that the CFWC women who opposed her were pawns of their husbands, and she saw her ouster from the Indian Welfare chair as a result of an attack directed by men. She wrote Commissioner Rhodes that they "took up the fight which that group of men has been waging against me for eight months or more." According to Wiegel, Congressman Taylor's clique informed her: "We Durango ladies care nothing about the superintendent's morals. We care nothing about the morals of the Indians. We are only interested in how much financial prosperity the Indians can bring to Durango." The handpicked successor for her post as Indian Welfare chair was, in Wiegel's account, "very keen [for the post] but after consideration informed me that her husband had a certain business deal under way, which, if she accepted the nomination, would not be consummated!" Her contempt for the women who allowed their husbands' business interests to override their concern for reservation morality was vehement. "Their methods," she wrote, "are despicable." Wiegel dismissed her women censors by blaming their husbands, but she did not excuse their behavior. Rather, she "resigned from all and every federated club of which I was a member."[31] Wiegel obviously believed women should stand firm in matters of morality, even if it meant contradicting their husbands. Her strategy for fighting the business interests that threatened the Utes, thus, was to seek action in both private and public realms. She blended the traditional idea that wives should bring about moral change by influencing their husbands at home with direct opposition to those men in the public sphere.

The history of women's experiences in constructing their public lives is compelling and complex. As women of the early twentieth century sought to enter civic life and effect real change, they wrestled with conflicting ideas about their roles in society. Nellie Wiegel, a dynamic woman who was unafraid to challenge government power structures, and yet who frequently camouflaged her affront beneath the cover of male authority, is a fascinating example of this process.

Notes

1. Letter from Nellie Wiegel to Edward E. McKean, Southern Ute agent [hereafter, SUA], November 27, 1925, Records of the Consolidated Ute Agency [hereafter, RCUA], 44014, Box 1, Folder: "Colorado Federation of Women's Clubs," National Archives and Records Administration, Rocky Mountain Region (NARA-RMR).

2. Letter from McKean to Wiegel, January 18, 1926; Letter from Wiegel to McKean, January 18, 1926; Commissioner of Indian Affairs [hereafter, CIA] to Wiegel, no date (refers to letter of March 1, 1926), all in RCUA, Box 1.

3. George Loomis, "Committee of Women's Clubs Looks after Indians," *Rocky Mountain News*, November 23, 1925, RCUA, Box 1; "Indian Art Treasures," *Rocky Mountain News*, October 28, 1938, in Clippings Files, Western History Department, Denver Public Library.

4. Loomis, "Committee of Women's Clubs Looks after Indians."

5. Letter from Wiegel to Charles J. Rhodes, CIA, June 18, 1932, in Roy Nash and H. J. Hagerman, "Report of Conditions at the Southern Ute Agency," 1931–1933, in 3 parts, CCF-CU, 154-55399; Part 1 [hereafter, Nash-Hagerman Report].

6. Daniel Walkowitz, "The Making of a Feminine Professional Identity: Social Workers in the 1920s," *American Historical Review* 95 (October 1990): 1051.

7. Virginia Donaghe McClurg, "Cliffs and Pueblos of Colorado," *The Clubwoman* 11 (June 1898): 76–78; letters from William Peterson, SUA, to McClurg, July 18, August 1, September 3, October 3, January 19, all 1904; and March 31, 1905, all in RCUA, 44013; letter from CIA to Wiegel, March 2, 1932, CCF-CU, 154-55399.

8. Mrs. C. W. Wiegel, "Indian Welfare," *The Colorado Clubwoman* 6 (September 1926): 6, 8, and 5 (March 1926): 9; letter from McKean to CIA, April 21,

1926; letter from Wiegel to McKean, May 28, 1926, RCUA, Box 1; Katherine Osburn, *Southern Ute Women on the Reservation: Autonomy and Assimilation, 1885–1934* (Albuquerque : University of New Mexico Press, 1998).

9. Mrs. C. W. Wiegel, "Division of Indian Welfare," *The Colorado Clubwoman* 8 (May 1929): 7; letter from CIA to McKean, April 30, 1926, RCUA, Box 1; letter from Wiegel to McKean, January 18, 1926; letter from McKean to Wiegel, January 21, 1926; letters from Wiegel to McKean, February 5, 1926, and March 16, 1926; letter from McKean to CIA, April 21, 1926, letters from Wiegel to McKean, May 8 and 28, 1926, RCUA, Box 1.

10. Mrs. C. W. Wiegel, typescript of unpublished article "The Ute's Last Stand" and letter from Wiegel to Senator Burton B. Wheeler and Senator Lynn J. Frazier, February 24, 1931, Records of the U.S. Senate, Record Group 46, SEN 83A-F9, Box 50, no. 10; Special File no. 224 [hereafter, Senate File 224], National Archives and Records Administration (NARA), Washington, DC.

11. Letter from Wiegel to CIA, June 1928; letter from CIA to Wiegel, June 28, 1928; H. H. Fiske, "Investigation of the Death of Joe Salt by Max Buffalo," June 3, 1927, both in CCF-CU, 821-4335; Wiegel reiterates her point that she is working in an advisory position for "betterment" in nearly all her correspondence.

12. Letters from CIA to Wiegel, September 16, 1927; Wiegel to CIA, September 21, 1927, in Senate File 224.

13. Letter from Wiegel to H. H. Fiske, BIA Inspector, May 4, 1927; letters from Fiske to CIA, May 11, 1927, and Fiske to J. F. Garland, chief inspector, Interior Department, May 22, 1927, CCF-CU, 154-44331.

14. Letter from Wiegel to Charles J. Rhodes, CIA, September 7, 1931; letter from Rhodes to Wiegel, September 23, 1931; letter Wiegel to Rhodes, September 29, 1931; Nash-Hagerman Report.

15. "Resolution Passed at Convention of Colorado Federation of Women's Clubs," La Junta, Colorado, September 22–25, 1931, Records of the U.S. Senate, R.G. 46, SEN 83A-FP, Box 50, no. 10, NARA, Washington, DC.

16. Letter from Wiegel to R. R. Garrick, mayor of Ignacio, CO, January 27, 1932; Nash-Hagerman Report, Part 3.

17. Letter from Peacore to Mr. A. L. Kroeger, member, Colorado State Indian Commission, Durango, CO, January 12, 1932, in Nash-Hagerman Report, Part 1; letter from Wiegel to CIA, November 24, 1931; letter from Peacore to CIA, November 17, 1931; letter from Lottie McCall to Wiegel, October 28, 1931; letter from McCall to Wiegel, October 28, 1931; letter from Peacore to CIA, November 17, 1931, all in Nash-Hagerman Report, Part 1; "Affidavit of Snow Deer Hamlin," Nash-Hagerman Report, Part 1; letter from McCall to Wiegel, October 28, 1931; letter from Peacore to CIA, January 12, 1932, all in Nash-Hagerman Report, Part 1.

18. Letters from Nash to CIA, October 19, 1931, and February 5, 1932, letter from Al Kroeger, Durango, CO, to Governor William Adams, Denver, CO, February 15, 1932, in Nash-Hagerman Report, Part 3; letter from Peacore to CIA, January 8, 1932, Nash-Hagerman Report, Part 1.

19. Letter from Charles J. Rhodes, CIA, to Secretary of the Interior Ray

Lyman Wilbur, February 27, 1932; letter from Rhodes to Wiegel, March 2, 1932; letters from Wiegel to CIA, July 5, 1932, and August 12, 1932; letter from Wiegel to Ray Lyman Wilbur, March 11, 1932; all in Nash-Hagerman Report, Part 3.

20. Letter from Wiegel to Ray Lyman Wilbur, March 11, 1932, in Nash-Hagerman Report, Part 3.

21. Letter from Wiegel to CIA, August 12, 1932, CCF-CU 40017-832; Yearbook Files of the CFWC, 1925–1962.

22. Wiegel to R. R. Garrick, mayor of Ignacio, CO, January 27, 1932, in Nash-Hagerman Report, Part 3; "Petition from the Concerned Citizens of Ignacio," January 14, 1932; "To Whom It May Concern," December 1931; "Petition from the Business Concerns of Cortez, Colorado," December 1931; J. W. Sower, president, La Planta County Taxpayers League, June 17, 1932; Nash-Hagerman Report, Part 1; letter from Rhodes to Peacore, April 1, 1932; Nash-Hagerman Report, Part 2.

23. Letter from Representative Edward T. Taylor to CIA, April 16, 1932, in Nash-Hagerman Report, Part 2; clippings from *The Denver Post*, June 12, 1932, and August 2, 1932; and *The Durango Herald*, June 13, 1932; letter from R. R. Garrick to Wiegel, August 9, 1932, all in Nash-Hagerman Report, Part 3.

24. Letter from CIA to Donald Wattson, SUA, February 3, 1933; memo from the La Planta County Board of Commissioners, February 4, 1933, CCF-CU, 52721-154.

25. Mrs. C. W. Wiegel, "Indian Citizenship," transcript enclosure to her December 1936 "Report to the CFWC," SEN83A-F9, Box 30, no. 6, NARA, Washington, DC.

26. James S. Olson and Raymond Wilson, *Native American in the Twentieth Century* (Urbana: University of Illinois Press, 1968), chap. 6; "Resolution Adopted at Annual Convention, September 17, 1936," SEN83A-F9, Box 30, no. 6, NARA, Washington, DC.

27. Letter from Wiegel to Dear Folks, January 12, 1948; SENAA-F, Box 30, no. 6, NARA, Washington, DC; *A History and Chronology of the Colorado Federation of Women's Clubs, 1895–1955* (Denver: The Colorado Federation of Women's Clubs, 1955), 79; my attempts to trace Wiegel past her last letter ended in failure; the last listing of her in the Denver City Directory was in 1939, and I have been unable to locate her death certificate; I wrote to every Wiegel in the Denver phone book and Denver metro area but received no replies; there is no further record of Wiegel in the records of the BIA, the CFWC, or the Western History Collections of the Denver Public Library.

28. Letter from Wiegel to McKean, November 27, 1925; Assistant CIA E. B. Merritt to Wiegel, no date, RCUA, Box 1; letter from Al Kroeger, Durango, CO, to Governor William Adams, February 15, 1932, in Nash-Hagerman Report, Part 3; letters from Wiegel to Kroeger, November 24, 1931; and Nash to CIA, October 19, 1931, both in Nash-Hagerman Report, Part 1.

29. Anne Campbell, *Men, Women, and Aggression* (New York: Basic Books, 1993).

30. Clippings from *Denver Post*, August 2, 1932; letter from Wiegel to Wilbur, March 11, 1932, both in Nash-Hagerman Report, Part 3.

31. Letter from Wiegel to CIA, August 12, 1932, CCF-CU, 40017-832; Yearbook Files of the CFWC, 1925–1962.

Suggested Readings

The literature on women in the early twentieth century is extensive. Recent studies emphasize the broad range of women's experiences according to the variables of race, class, and ethnicity. An excellent bibliographic essay that analyzes the interplay of these elements is Susan Tank Lesser, "Paradigms Gained: Further Readings in the History of Women in the Progressive Era," in *Gender, Class, Race, and Reform in the Progressive Era,* ed. Noralee Franklin and Nancy S. Dye (Lexington: University of Kentucky Press, 1991), 180–93. The classic works on the activities of middle-class clubwomen are Karen Blair's *The Clubwoman as Feminist: True Womanhood Redefined, 1862–1914* (New York: Holmes and Meier Publishing, 1980) and Anne Firor Scott's *Natural Allies: Women's Associations in American History* (Urbana: University of Illinois Press, 1991). There are many fine studies of women's political participation in the early twentieth century, including Carroll Smith-Rosenberg, *Disorderly Conduct: Visions of Gender in Victorian America* (New York: Oxford University Press, 1985); Christine Lunardini, *From Equal Suffrage to Equal Rights: Alice Paul and the National Women's Party, 1913–1928* (New York: New York University Press, 1986); Nancy Cott, *The Grounding of Modern Feminism* (New Haven: Yale University Press, 1987); J. Stanley Lemons, *The Woman Citizen: Social Feminism in the 1920s* (Urbana: University of Illinois Press, 1973); Susan Ware, *Beyond Suffrage: Women in the New Deal* (Cambridge: Harvard University Press, 1981); and Susan D. Becker, *The Origins of the Equal Rights Amendment* (Westport, Conn.: Greenwood Press, 1981). For a study of another middle-class woman's ambivalent relationship with power, see Elisabeth Israels Perry, *Belle Moskowitz: Feminine Politics and the Exercise of Power in the Age of Alfred E. Smith* (New York: Oxford University Press, 1987).

Most of the literature concerning women's activism on behalf of Native Americans focuses on women who worked in the Indian Service. See Helen M. Bannan, "True Womanhood on the Reservation: Field Matrons and the United States Indian Service," Working Paper No. 18 (Albuquerque: Southwest Institute for Research on Women, 1984); Lisa Emmerich, "To Respect and Love and Seek the Ways of White Women: Field Matrons, the Office of Indian Affairs and Civilization Policy, 1890–1928" (Ph.D. diss., University of Maryland,

1987); and Elizabeth A. McKee, "Civilizing the Indian: Field Matrons under Hoopa Valley Agency Jurisdiction 1898–1919" (master's thesis, California State University, 1982). Helen M. Wanken, "'Women's Sphere' and Indian Reform: The Woman's National Indian Association, 1879–1901" (Ph.D. diss., Marquette University, 1981), is a study of women's voluntary associations for Indian "uplift," and Lawrence C. Kelly's *The Assault on Assimilation: John Collier and the Origins of Indian Policy Reform* (Albuquerque: University of New Mexico Press, 1983) provides a discussion of the activities of the General Federation of Women's Clubs with respect to Indian policy.

Primary sources on Wiegel and the Federation of Women's Clubs include Mary C. Bradford, *History and Chronology of the Colorado State Federation of Women's Clubs, 1895–1931* (Denver: The Colorado State Federation of Women's Clubs, 1931); *Sixty Years of Achievement, 1890–1950, The General Federation of Women's Clubs* (New York: The General Federation of Women's Clubs, 1950); and Mary I. Woods, *Unity in Diversity: The History of the General Federation of Women's Clubs* (Washington, DC: The Federation, 1958). The Federation has published a guide to its archival resources, *Guide to the Archives of the General Federation of Women's Clubs*, ed. Cynthia N. Swanson and Lisa C. Mangiafico (Washington, DC: The Federation, 1992). Nellie Wiegel's articles, reports, and correspondence may be found at the Colorado State Federation of Women's Clubs offices in Denver, Colorado. They include: *The Colorado Clubwoman*, 1925–1932; Minutes of the Executive Board, 1914–1922; Papers of the CSFWC; and Yearbook Files, 1898–1934. Her letters to the BIA are in the Records of the Consolidated Ute Agency (RCUA), 44014, box 1, folder: "Colorado Federation of Women's Clubs," National Archives and Records Administration, Rocky Mountain Region. Further correspondence is located in the National Archives and Records Administration, Washington, DC, RG75, Records of the Bureau of Indian Affairs, the Central Classified Files, Southern Ute Agency, 1907–1922, the Central Classified Files, Consolidated Ute Agency, 1922–1934, and in Senate File 224.

12

Ah Cum Kee and Loy Lee Ford
Between Two Worlds

Sue Fawn Chung

A h Cum Yee Kee (1876–1929) and Loy Lee Ford (1882–1921) were not unlike many second generation, turn-of-the-twentieth-century women who lived between the two worlds of their American birthplace and that of the traditions and values held by their immigrant parents. Nonetheless, each woman's English-language abilities, interaction with the mainstream community as children and then as adults, preservation of aspects of Chinese tradition, including dress, language, and child-rearing practices, illustrate differences in the process of acculturation.[1] Influenced by their upbringing, husbands, and frontier Nevada communities, these two women combined their two worlds in different ways.

Ah Cum Kee

Ah Cum Yee was born in the Chinatown of Carson City, Nevada, in 1876.[2] Her father, Non Chong Yee, was better known in the Euro-American community by his adopted American name, Sam Gibson. As manager of the Quong Hing Company, Ah Cum's father was one of the prominent figures in the Chinese-dominated lumbering industry in the Lake Tahoe–Carson City area between 1870 and

The research for this study was funded by the Nevada Humanities Committee. Sue Fawn Chung is indebted to Rose Ford's son Richard Lym, Bessie Ford's daughter Cynthia Chow Squire, and Lillian (Anne) Ford's daughter Barbara Lee for many personal insights about their grandparents and to Ramona Ruiz O'Neil, whose grandfather, Norman Douglass Money, talked about the Fords in his memoirs. Chung and Ah Cum Kee's granddaughter, Shirlaine Kee Baldwin, provided much of the information about the Kees, including the family photograph album, letters, Charles Kee's memoirs, Chung Kee Store account book pages, the immigration papers of Nellie Louie and King Yee, and documents in Chinese and English. Jeffrey Kintop of the Nevada State Archives provided the plat maps of Carson City's Chinatown and the tax records for Ormsby County. The staff of the Central Nevada Museum was helpful in locating information about Tonopah and the Ford family.

1886. According to Carson City plat maps, Quong Hing Company owned one square block of Chinatown (Carson to Valley Street, Second to Third Street), and Ah Cum's mother and father separately owned a total of at least four buildings. Sam paid the required poll tax on Chinese aliens for several individuals. Prominent citizens, including Duane L. Bliss and Hume Yerington, knew Sam Gibson and his family.

However, by the late 1870s anti-Chinese sentiment had increased and led to numerous attacks on Chinese immigrants throughout the West. In 1875, Congress passed the Page Law, which essentially required Chinese women who wanted to immigrate to the United States to prove that they were not prostitutes. This resulted in a "bachelor society" for Chinese in America. In 1882, Congress passed the Chinese Exclusion Act to stem the tide of Chinese immigration, particularly Chinese laborers. Anti-Chinese activists then tried to drive out the Chinese already in the United States. In 1885–1886, anti-Chinese rioters burned much of Carson City's Chinatown and called for a boycott of Chinese businesses involved in the lumbering industry. Disgusted, Ah Cum's parents returned to Guangdong, China, with their two of their three children in 1886, leaving Ah Cum behind.

When Ah Cum reached school age, her parents decided to send her to live with a childless couple who were close friends, Hong Wai Chang (d. 1907) and his wife, Bitshee Ah Too (d. 1896). After Ah Cum's family left the United States, she regarded this couple as her foster parents. The couple owned a laundry in the new mining boomtown of Bodie, California, and sent Ah Cum to Bodie's small integrated public school. If Ah Cum had lived in San Francisco's Chinatown, she would have been required by law to attend a segregated Chinese public school. As a young teenager, Ah Cum worked doing household chores for several Euro-American families. As a result, she was fluent in written and spoken English and at ease with people of different ethnic backgrounds.

In 1888, Ah Cum's foster family moved to nearby Hawthorne, located in Esmeralda County, Nevada. Founded in 1881 as a freight station on the Carson and Colorado Railroad for such nearby mining towns as Bodie (to the northwest) and Aurora (twenty-eight miles to the southwest), Hawthorne had a relatively transient Chinese population of miners, railroad laborers, and stamp mill workers. In addition, the East Walker River arose from the Sierra Nevadas and furnished a limited amount of water to Hawthorne, thus allowing some dry farming. In 1900, Esmeralda County had only 27 of the 2,184 farmers then living in Nevada, making it one of the smallest agricultural production areas in the state. Consequently, farmers who were able to raise fresh vegetables and fruits in this very dry climate made an important contribution to the community.

Chung Kee, who was born Gee Wen Chung in 1847, was just such a farmer. He immigrated in 1860 or 1871, probably at the request of his brother or another relative who was already in the United States.[3] This "chain migration" was common among immigrants from all countries. According to Chinese business partnership records in the Pacific Region National Archives,[4] Kee also managed a small Chinese store in Hawthorne called "Chung Kee," from which he got his name. As a result, his last name became Kee in the United States.

In 1890 at the age of fourteen, Ah Cum married Chung Kee, who was twenty-eight years her senior. According to the 1880 U.S. census, Chinese men outnumbered Chinese women in the United States twenty-one to one (100,686 men to 4,779 women). By 1890 the ratio had increased to approximately twenty-six to one (103,620 men to 3,868 women). In 1880 Nevada the ratio was even higher: thirty-three to one (5,102 men to 314 women). Therefore, among Chinese Americans the practice of making a marriage contract between a well-to-do man and the parents of a young girl for a future wedding was typical because there were so few Chinese women. Moreover, Chinese tradition sanctioned marriage between older men and young females because of the importance of raising a large family and having male heirs to continue the family lineage.

The wedding was announced in the *Walker Lake Bulletin,* which described Ah Cum as "a pretty little Chinese damsel who can read, write, and speak English like a native" and Chung Kee as "the heathen who propels a vegetable cart about town."[5] Many Euro-Americans attended the wedding, which was the only social event in town that week. It is not clear if this was an arranged marriage, but Chung Kee was very traditional and in all probability a promise of marriage for young Ah Cum to Chung Kee had occurred before Sam Gibson returned to China and was the reason why Ah Cum was left in the United States.

Ah Cum's husband was well known in the Chinese and larger community. Chinese miners in the region, Euro-Americans, and Native Americans purchased supplies and other items from Kee's store. Miners ate at his boardinghouse restaurant. He knew many of the prominent Euro-American community leaders. The local newspaper frequently commented on which fresh vegetables Kee had available. He also was a Chinese labor boss for borax mining, and he leased mining land in Fish Lake Valley, near Hawthorne, from Benjamin Edwards. In addition, based on papers that he left to his descendants, Kee acted as a local "banker" for the Chinese community by keeping track of their money and loans, collecting payments for emigration ticket loans, helping send money back to China as well as pay American taxes, and negotiating the purchase and sale of property. Kee also sent money to his sister in China, donated funds toward the construction of the Ningyang Railroad Company, and supported education in the district of his birth in China. According to Bureau of Indian Affairs records and Paiutes at the nearby Walker River Reservation, Chung Kee and his family taught the Paiutes how to dry farm. This tremendously improved their economy.

Ah Cum and Chung Kee had six children, all born in Hawthorne, and they attended the local school: Yuen (Charles, 1893–1977), Ah Lon (May, 1895–1965), Ah Look (Florence, 1897–1919), Ah Moi (Myrtle, 1901–1986), Fon (Willie, 1903–1956), and Lin (Frank, 1906–1989). Since both parents spoke the same dialect, they communicated daily with each other and their children in Chinese. In addition, in keeping with Chinese tradition, shortly after the birth of each boy, Chung Kee submitted their names to the Chung (his real family name) clan genealogy in his birthplace in Kaiping (Hoiping), Guangdong Province, China. Undoubtedly, as was characteristic of the times, the local schoolteachers gave the Kee children their American names or their parents named them after close Euro-American friends and acquaintances. More often than not, they were the only Chinese American children in the Hawthorne public school.

Charles, who finished the sixth grade in Hawthorne, recalled being frequently taunted by the children in school because he had a queue (a traditional hair braid) and wore traditional Chinese clothing. Ah Cum quickly learned that this was unacceptable and by the early 1900s, her children wore American clothing and hairstyles to school. In a photograph taken in 1907, Ah Cum and her six children dressed in the latest American fashions. This change to Western dress was much earlier than that of the Chinese American women living in urban Chinatowns, such as in San Francisco and New York.

Ah Cum's socialization to Euro-American culture continued as the years passed. According to the 1900 census manuscript, there was one other Chinese family in Hawthorne: Dun and Ellen Chung, who also owned a "Chinese good store" and had five children approximately the same age as the Kee children. The couple married in 1889; Ellen had been born in California in 1868 so she had much in common with Ah Cum. However, by 1910 the Dun Chung family had moved away. Ah Cum had become good friends with Loy Lee Ford, who lived in nearby Tonopah. Ah Cum was not hesitant about traveling with her children to visit friends in other Nevada communities and in San Francisco, California. This independence was unusual: most Chinese American women needed "the protection" of a man in order to travel. In addition, because of her fluency in English, Ah

Cum made good friends with Euro-American women in Hawthorne and maintained these friendships for the rest of her life, regardless of where she lived. Thus, Ah Cum was not isolated from female friends, even though there were no other Chinese women living in her town.

After her marriage, Ah Cum and her husband had continued vegetable farming and running the boardinghouse. When Chung Kee died in 1909, Ah Cum took over all of these tasks with the help of her children and Kee's cousin. In the 1910 census manuscript, Ah Cum was the only Chinese female farmer in the state. According to county records, the plot of land, called "China Gardens," was valued at $1,000. The entire family worked on the farm and was assisted by one to four seasonal hired hands.

Although the Kees raised a variety of different vegetables, they were known for their stringless white celery, which was grown by covering the maturing plants with empty one-gallon tomato cans. In the sandy, alkaline-desert soil, the Kees used buckets suspended by a pole to hand water the vegetables. Precious rainwater was stored in cisterns and river water kept in wooden reservoirs. The Kees introduced dry farming techniques to other farmers in the area.

The Kees shipped their highly prized stringless white celery, a delicacy, to the St. Francis Hotel in San Francisco, the Utah Hotel in Salt Lake City, and other gourmet hotel dining rooms throughout the West. Like many Chinese vegetable growers, Ah Cum and her family also sold their products by peddling them in two baskets suspended by a pole and later by horse and wagon to the local and neighboring communities. In his memoirs, Charles recalled that as soon as he was old enough, he had to drive the wagon across the steep hills in order to get the produce to market in nearby settlements as well as to the train station for distant shipping.

Nevertheless, desert farming was difficult, and Ah Cum and her family struggled to survive during the years following Chung Kee's death. Known as a skilled cook and baker of breads, Ah Cum fed the Euro-American miners inside her boardinghouse restaurant and the Paiutes outside in the back. Many of the Paiutes learned to appreciate eating Chinese food from this experience. In turn, they gave her baskets and pine nuts, which she probably shipped to San Francisco, perhaps for sale in southeastern China. The economic relationship was also one of friendship: the Paiutes guided Ah Cum's children on fishing trips on Walker Lake. The fish was eaten at home and served at the restaurant. Ah Cum also canned fruits and vegetables and stored them in her cool, dark basement to supplement family and restaurant meals.

When the Southern Pacific Railroad relocated its station in 1906, there was an economic depression in Hawthorne. Between

1912 and 1919, Ah Cum and her children moved back and forth between Tonopah, Virginia City, and Hawthorne in search of work. However, Ah Cum had enough money to purchase a hillside home outside of Tonopah's Chinatown and maintain various properties her husband had owned. Among her close friends were the pioneering Tonopah families of George and Nellie Brissell and Billy and Loy Ford. In 1914, following her late husband's wishes, Ah Cum sent Charles to Guangdong, China, where he married a Chinese woman and had a son. Unaccustomed to traditional Chinese ways, Charles was unhappy in China and returned to the United States in time to be drafted into the army during World War I. For her other children, Ah Cum adopted a more practical, and therefore liberal, approach to dating and marriage. She realized that she could not prevent them from dating Euro-Americans, since there were so few Chinese in the town, region, and state. On August 30, 1915, the *San Francisco Chronicle, Carson City News,* and *Elko Free Press* carried the news that Ah Cum's second-oldest daughter, Florence, had married Rudolph Espinoza, of Basque descent. The couple was married at sea by a captain based in San Francisco because California and Nevada state laws prohibited interracial marriage. Although Charles objected to the marriage, the press reported that Ah Cum approved of the union; therefore, the sheriff, who had arrested the newlyweds for violating the miscegenation law, released them. Unfortunately, in 1919 Florence died from influenza while living in southern California.

In her own life, Ah Cum ignored Chinese traditions regarding the importance of loyalty to one's deceased husband. She became infatuated with a Tonopah Chinese restaurant owner, King Louie, who recently had immigrated, leaving his wife in China. In 1916, flaunting prevailing moral prohibitions, they had a daughter, Nellie, who was named after Ah Cum's good friend Nellie Brissell. In 1917 Louie's son, Fawn, arrived in Tonopah from China and Ah Cum moved her family and "stepson" (Fawn) back to Hawthorne. By 1920 she had moved to Reno, where Louie had opened a restaurant and herb shop. Louie also worked for George Wingfield, a wealthy and politically powerful man in Nevada. Ah Cum became involved in community activities and had her younger children participate in Reno's Fourth of July parades in their beautiful silk Chinese outfits. In the early 1920s, Louie returned to China, divorced his first wife, and unsuccessfully tried to return to the United States during the next two decades. Ah Cum moved to Oakland, California, where her youngest son Frank and his wife had settled. She died in 1929 and was buried in Oakland. During her lifetime, Ah Cum and her children became more and more assimilated to mainstream American culture. But she only had the freedom to do so after her traditionally oriented husband had died.[6]

Loy Lee Ford

Loy Lee Ford's experiences were different. Loy was born in Sacramento, California, in 1882.[7] Little is known about Loy's childhood, but she was probably raised in Sacramento's close-knit Chinatown. Urban centers that had large immigrant populations for which Chinese was the primary language, such as Sacramento's Chinatown, helped to preserve Chinese traditions. Confucian values stressing the importance of family, filial piety, and the duty of young women to marry and continue the spouse's family lineage through the birth of sons were an integral part of a female's upbringing. Like most Chinese American girls of that generation, Loy's contact with the outside world was very limited, and most of her spare time was spent at home in a protected environment. Loy undoubtedly contributed to the family's welfare through some kind of work, such as housecleaning, sewing, or assisting in some small way in a family business enterprise.

When she was sixteen or seventeen, a go-between approached her parents and negotiated a marriage contract for Loy and thirty-four-year-old Min Chung (1850–1922), then better known by his American name, Billy Ford. He was a Chinese labor boss for borax mining companies in Candelaria, Nevada. Arriving in San Francisco in 1865, Min Chung, came from Kaiping (Hoiping), Guangdong Province, the same place where Chung Kee was born. After a brief stay in San Francisco, fifteen-year-old Min Chung spent two years in Virginia City during its mining heyday. In a region with few women and discriminatory laws that prohibited Chinese from working hard-rock mining, Chinese male immigrants turned to cooking and laundry work for employment ("women's work" in the minds of most Euro-American men). After working as a cook in Virginia City, Min Chung eventually got a job in the borax mining industry, viewed as one of the most promising industries of the 1880s and 1890s. He eventually became a Chinese labor superintendent in borax mining and leased mines in Columbia Marsh, near Candelaria, Nevada. This position brought Min Chung into close relationships with Euro-American businessmen, engineers, and miners.

Perhaps his new career encouraged Min Chung to further Americanize and between 1870 and 1890 he adopted the American name of Billy Ford. Three memoirs of famous Nevadans give different accounts of how Ford got his American name. Norman Douglass Money, who considered himself to be a member of Billy Ford's family, recalled that when Billy moved to Chloride, California, and worked in a hotel owned by Thomas Kendall and William Douglass, Ford's employers and lifelong friends gave him his Americanized name. Jack Douglass said that his father, William Douglass, who had worked with Min Chung in Sodaville, Nevada, had "honored" his

Chinese friend by giving him the name "Billy," taken from William Douglass's own name. Another story was that Billy Ford worked as a personal valet for the famous sportsman, William Ford, and took this American name from his employer. Although Min Chung's Chinese name was recorded in the 1900 census manuscript, in the 1880s and 1890s the local community knew him as Billy Ford, and in 1910 and 1920 the United States census manuscript listed him as Billy Ford. When he purchased mining property, notably the Bricklode Mine near Tonopah, he signed his name as Billy Ford. Whatever the true story, Min Chung's name change indicates his desire to be accepted by the Americans as an "Americanized Chinese," as the *Tonopah Bonanza* called him in news stories published in September 1903 and April 1922.

By the late 1890s, Billy Ford had finally achieved the economic status enabling him to marry and support a family. Euro-American businessmen Thomas Kendall and William Douglass encouraged Billy in this pursuit and gave him funds to find a wife. However, the shortage of Chinese women of marriageable age in Nevada hindered his dream. Almost one-third to one-half of the Chinese men in the state were married, but the majority of them lived separately from their wives, or their wives were omitted from the census manuscript. The rest usually remained single because of the shortage of Chinese American women. In order to find a bride in the United States, Billy, like many men of his generation, sought the assistance of a go-between, who located Loy Lee in Sacramento and negotiated the marriage with her family. Brides from China, in general, were held in higher regard among Chinese men than American-born Chinese women: those from China were believed to be more traditional, and there was a larger pool from which to select a wife. But Billy probably did not have sufficient funds to make the trip to China and was too Americanized to want a traditional China-born woman. In keeping with centuries-old traditions, Loy's parents selected their daughter's mate, whom she probably never saw before her wedding day.

Accompanied by the go-between, Loy traveled by slow train from Sacramento, which was humid and green, to Candelaria, which was typical of Nevada's dry desert landscape. The trip between Reno and Candelaria alone took more than ten hours. In an unfamiliar environment, facing marriage to a stranger must have been a frightening experience for young Loy. One of the few Chinese women in the region, Ah Cum Kee, and her children traveled part of the way with Loy.

The weekly *Walker Lake Bulletin*, April 5, 1899, described the wedding as one of the most memorable social events in Candelaria. In preparation for greeting his seventeen-year-old bride, Billy had decorated his Chinatown home with brilliant colors, including red banners, symbolizing happiness. Laundryman Quong Wo and his wife of nineteen years, Kam Yup Wo, served as best man and matron of honor, but they were much older than the young bride. All the respectable citizens of the town turned out for the wedding. Ah Cum helped Loy dress in her traditional red Chinese wedding gown and showed her how to greet the numerous strangers at the reception. Firecrackers marked the conclusion of the wedding vows. As Americanized as he was, Billy, dressed in a traditional blue silk gown and pink sash, still clung to traditional Chinese customs for one of the most important events in his adult life—his marriage. The preservation of these traditions probably made Loy feel more comfortable, since she was raised in an ethnic Chinese atmosphere.

After the wedding, the Benjamin Edwards family "adopted" the young bride, gave her the American name of Lily Sue because she was like a delicate flower, and introduced her to Euro-American customs and family life. She and her children became close to the Edwards. The marriage increased the Fords' interaction with Euro-American families, and the couple underwent subtle changes in their attitudes and adjustments to their lifestyle as they learned about American child-rearing and domestic practices.

Loy knew the importance of having a son to carry on the family line. In December 1899, Timothy Tian Bon was born. To satisfy her husband, the baby had an American name, and to respect her traditional upbringing, he also had a Chinese name. But Billy, unlike Ah Cum's husband, did not register this or any subsequent baby's name in the clan records in Kaiping, China.

Upon the advice of Ben Edwards, Billy and Loy moved to the nearby new boomtown of Tonopah. In May 1900, Nye County official James Butler discovered rich veins in the San Antonio Mountains near present-day Tonopah. Reputed to be the "Second Comstock Lode," Tonopah's mines eventually produced $150 million worth of ore. The early months were bleak because of the town's inaccessibility, coupled with an outbreak of the black plague in January 1902. Tonopah was transformed from a primitive mining camp to a permanent town during that year. In 1903, Tonopah residents boasted that the area had over 3,000 new inhabitants, two newspapers, thirty saloons, at least two major churches, a gambling hall, three bands, an opera house, a stock exchange, livery stables, bakeries, merchandise stores, a number of doctors and lawyers, and all the other amenities of a boomtown. By mid-1904, the Tonopah Railroad connected the town to other Nevada communities and ultimately to the Southern Pacific Railroad (successor to the Central Pacific Railroad), and the town continued to grow rapidly until the depression of 1917.

Tonopah was unusual in that many of Nevada's top leaders came together there in its early years: Tasker Oddie, partner of Jim

Butler, future governor and United States senator; George A. Bartlett, Patrick McCarran, and Key Pittman, all future United States senators; William Douglass and Thomas Kendall, previously mentioned miners who became prominent businessmen; Hugh Brown, founder of the Nevada Bar Association; George Wingfield, influential businessman and political power broker; Benjamin Edwards, mining company vice president and future California financier, Chris Zabriskie, borax magnate; and William Shockley, wealthy borax mining engineer in China and Nevada, just to name a few. Billy and Loy Ford knew all these men and their wives and counted many of these prominent citizens among their good friends.

In Tonopah, Loy and Billy had six more children: James Butler (1902–1955), Rose (1905–1973), Bessie (1906–1995), George Washington (1906–1989), Lillian (1909–1936), and Alice (1915–?). Unlike their first child, none of these children had Chinese names and many of the births were announced in the local newspapers, an honor accorded to no other Chinese American family in Tonopah at this time. The Fords were the first Chinese family in Nevada to give all of their children American names from birth.

Chinese Americans like Loy Lee and Billy Ford had moved to Tonopah shortly after the town was founded. The Chinese inhabitants had established a Chinatown on Main Street a few blocks away from the center of town. Court records from 1903 indicate that the early Chinese residents originally came from Taishan and Kaiping, two of the "Four Counties" in Guangdong, the main emigration region of Chinese immigrants in America. The majority had lived in the United States for thirty or more years and worked as restaurant owners, grocers, merchants, cooks, laundrymen, wood packers, boardinghouse managers, vegetable peddlers, servants, gamblers, prostitutes, and laborers. As one of the few married women in Chinatown, Loy probably knew all of the men from her husband's home district, and because they spoke the same Chinese "Four Counties" dialect, she could easily communicate with them. This was not always the case in turn-of-the-twentieth-century Chinese American marriages.

Loy had the duties of caring for her own growing family and helping Billy's relatives. Billy Ford's cousin Charlie Chung (1850–1914) relocated from Sodaville to Tonopah by late 1900. Billy formed a partnership with Charlie Chung and opened a store and restaurant in Tonopah on a lot on Main Street next to Ramsey's saloon. There, in 1901, Billy Ford and Charlie Chung built the Barnum Restaurant and Boarding House, which, according to the *Tonopah Bonanza*, fed almost the entire populace. The two men also became very active in buying and selling land and mining properties. Unlike the California constitution, according to the Nevada constitution, resident aliens, even Chinese, were allowed to own, buy, and sell property and could purchase shares or interest in mines from Euro-Americans. However, Chinese immigrants never knew when the law would be changed, and many adopted the practice of putting deeds of land in the names of family members or friends who were American citizens by birth.

Because of the growing anti-Asian sentiment targeted at land-ownership in the West, Key Pittman, Billy and Charlie's attorney (who was also a senator from Nevada from 1913 to 1940), advised the men to "sell" the Barnum to Loy, a U.S. citizen by birth, in order to ensure that the property would never be taken away. The practical aspects of passing property in Nevada probably overcame any traditional Chinese prejudice against women owning property. For Loy this action was another major step in acculturation. In fact, for Chinese Americans the restaurant business was a family affair. Charlie Chung, Loy, Billy Ford, and their children all probably worked there.

Friendships with Euro-Americans also increased the Ford's acculturation and benefited the family. Billy and Loy, again using Loy's name, bought a home on Summit and Oddie, on the edge of Tonopah's Chinatown, from their old friend Ben Edwards, who had become the vice president of the West End Consolidated Mining Company of Arizona. Edwards expressed the feelings of respect other men had for Loy's husband when he said that Billy was a "completely trustworthy employee, and a loyal and devoted friend." In 1918, Ford helped Norman Douglass Money, whom Billy treated as a son, get a job in Sparks, Nevada, as a tool apprentice for the Southern Pacific Railroad. Money commented, "[This confirmed] the old concept that once a Chinaman accepts you as a friend, the friendship usually lasts a lifetime and is regarded as a responsibility." The Fords also had a special friendship with one of Nevada's famous power brokers, George Wingfield, who "always made it a point in later years while visiting [Tonopah] . . . to hunt up 'Billie' and see that he was not in need."[8] Loy and her children benefited from Billy's prominence. Loy became close to the wives of many of her husband's Euro-American friends. In addition, when Loy and Billy's son Timothy was studying electrical engineering, he stayed at the Wingfield home in Reno. The Ford's influential friends were an example of the traditional Chinese system of *"guanxi"* (connections, or "networking"). This situation worked well in both the Chinese and the American world, thereby helping the Fords to achieve prosperity and prominence.

There were also some less traditional advantages. For example, in September 1903 an anti-Chinese mob vowed to drive all the Chinese out of Tonopah. According to the *Tonopah Bonanza*, Billy had been forewarned and sent Loy and the two boys to the home of a Euro-American family for protection. However, the *Tonopah Miner* reported that the rioters found a very frightened Loy at home but realized that she was Billy's wife and left her alone. The violence led to the death of a seventy-year-old Chinese laundryman who shared a home with Charlie Chung. At the time, the local newspapers claimed that union leaders and workers wanted to rid the town of "cheap Chinese labor," but a story published in the *Tonopah Bonanza* on April 14, 1922, suggested that a number of future "Wobblies," members of the Industrial Workers of the World Union, had been staying at the Barnum Restaurant and Boarding House and owed a considerable debt. So these men probably initiated the anti-Chinese action as a way to defraud the Fords and Charlie Chung. The frightening experience had a positive impact upon Loy: she learned even more about American ways and values by spending several weeks in a Euro-American home.

Because the two local newspapers and prominent citizens of the town, including Jim Butler, severely criticized the actions of the rioters, the community developed a warmer feeling toward the Chinese living there. During the course of the preliminary hearing for the arrested men, Key Pittman requested that Billy serve as court interpreter, an important position. But because the rioters had stolen $86 from the Ford's home, the court chose instead to have George Quong, from Carson City, serve as interpreter. By the end of the year, the community leaders knew Loy and Billy. Furthermore, Loy learned that if anyone bothered her, she could count on help from the local sheriff by telling his wife, who had become a good friend.

The generally congenial atmosphere of Tonopah was in sharp contrast to the anti-Chinese hostility in the nearby mining town of Goldfield, which adopted a local ordinance prohibiting "Mongolians" from disembarking from the train and staying overnight in the town. Loy and her children violated both ordinances when they went to Goldfield on the invitation of a Euro-American friend (probably Mrs. George Wingfield). They stayed overnight at the Goldfield Hotel but, according to Loy's daughter Bessie, were afraid to leave the building because of the feeling of hostility and prejudice in Goldfield. Loy and her daughter were relieved to return to the friendlier atmosphere, which Bessie described as being like "warm sunshine," of Tonopah.

As noted earlier, Tonopah's population grew rapidly with the building of the railroad. An estimated 10,000 lived in Tonopah between 1905 and 1907. Thereafter, a series of fires, the panic of 1907, when two of the three Tonopah banks were forced to close, and the shutdown of depleted mines marked the beginning of the town's decline. By 1910 the population had dropped to 3,900. The 1910 census manuscript listed 44 Chinese adult males (27 married men and 2 widowers), 3 sons of Loy and Billy Ford, 2 married adult females,

3 daughters of Loy and Billy Ford, and 1 half-Chinese half-Shoshone female teenager (Bertha Coffey)—a total of 53 Chinese Americans. In this small community, everyone knew one another.

As the Ford children grew up, Loy became involved in their education and worried about their future marriages. Seeing the advantages of education and believing the Confucian adage "Education is the equalizer of mankind," Loy sent her children to school as long as the family could afford it. Often they were the only Chinese American children in the Tonopah school. In all the Ford children's class photographs, Loy and Billy's sons and daughters were among the best dressed. According to an interview with one of George's classmates, Edward Slavin, "We were all alike—recent immigrants or children of recent immigrants." Loy bought her children music lessons, got them a family dog, and sent them to the nearby Episcopal Church, all indications of her acculturation. As mentioned earlier, Tim lived in George Wingfield's home in Reno while studying engineering, and all the Ford children had at least an elementary, if not a secondary, education, an achievement for anyone of that time period, much less the sons and daughters of Chinese Americans. None of the Ford children ever learned to read or write Chinese, and each had only a limited speaking ability in Chinese. Furthermore, they seldom wore Chinese-style clothing; one time when Bessie did wear a traditional costume, she remarked how much she disliked it. Loy sent the children on visits to larger Chinese communities, such as those in Reno and Sacramento. She hoped that there they could date Chinese Americans. This might have been a reflection of her traditional beliefs, but it may have also been a practical recognition of prevailing antimiscegenation legislation. The children, with the exception of Jim, who remained single, did marry ethnic Chinese. Charles Kee's army service in World War I influenced Tim and Jim, as well as Willie Kee, to join the U.S. Army during World War II, and Bessie married a man who attained the rank of U.S. Army colonel. As adults living in Fresno, California, Tim and Jim, reasserting their Chinese identity, changed their names to Jeung (a variation of their original last name of Chung). However, young George, who briefly married a Chinese American girl, had a second marriage, to a Euro-American woman, which lasted more than forty years. He kept the name Ford. He achieved some fame as a martial arts instructor and technical adviser for the early segments of the television program *Kung Fu* and as a musician in California. In spirit and actions, Loy and her children preserved many Chinese traditions and beliefs while adopting Euro-American ways.

Nevertheless, in the mid-1910s the Fords faced a dilemma that many immigrant and native-born working-class families encountered during unexpected hard times. Tonopah's mining had collapsed, and the family was just making ends meet. Moreover,

Loy's health was declining, especially after giving birth to Alice in 1915. Loy and Billy realized that they could not adequately feed and clothe all their children, so the two youngest, both girls, were given up for adoption. A childless Chinese couple, Mr. and Mrs. Hong, adopted Lillian (who was two or three years old at the time) and changed her name to Anne, raising her in nearby Keeler, California. Lillian maintained contact with her birth family despite this early separation. The Fords contacted two Tonopah church women about finding a family to adopt their newborn daughter, Alice. These women contacted Donaldina Cameron of the Presbyterian Mission in San Francisco, who took four-month-old Alice for adoption by Mr. and Mrs. Sue of Oakland, California. But unlike the situation with Lillian, Alice and her new parents did not keep in contact with the Fords.[9] In an era before Social Security, this situation recurred among many poor immigrant mothers and even native-born mothers throughout the United States. Although not common, it was not unheard of for Chinese parents to give up a child for adoption because of the family's financial situation. Cameron convinced several Chinese families that the adopted child would be raised in a financially secure environment if given up for adoption. Besides, Loy was in no physical condition to protest this action if she objected, and her husband's advancing age and declining health also him left him with few alternatives.

Loy's health continued to deteriorate, and in 1920 she entered a hospital in Reno for medical treatment not available in Tonopah. Billy, who was seventy-one at the time, was working as a valet to an official of the Southern Pacific and traveled back and forth between Reno and Tonopah, where two of the Ford children, George and Rose, lived. Loy Lee Ford died in a Reno hospital on January 31, 1921. Her body was brought back to Tonopah for burial the next day. The *Tonopah Bonanza*, February 1, 1921, noted that the Ford children had gathered for the funeral. Tim and Jim, who were working in Sacramento at the time, and Bessie, who had been living in the San Francisco Bay Area, returned to join George, Rose, and Billy for the Episcopal services. Typical of the period, there was no obituary in the local paper for Loy Lee Ford. During the nineteenth and early twentieth century, few local newspapers published obituaries for women, native born or immigrant.

Just over a year later, on April 13, 1922, Billy Ford died of pneumonia and was buried next to Loy in Tonopah. He was warmly remembered by the residents of Tonopah. In an unusual tribute, the April 14, 1922, obituary published in the *Tonopah Bonanza* was entitled a "Real Pioneer [of] Southern Nevada, [Who] Was Honored and Respected Among Associates, RAISED A SPLENDID FAMILY,

Was Universally Liked and Demise is Regretted by the Pioneers of the State." It read, "In the passing . . . of Billie [*sic*] Ford, whose real name was Min Chung, southern Nevada lost its most beloved Celestial and a man who was as true an American as most of us who are born on our native hearth." During an interview in 1996, veteran Nevada newspaperman and editor Jack McCloskey, who was born in Goldfield in 1911 and worked for the *Tonopah Bonanza* in the 1920s, called Billy Ford "one of the influential men in the state." Unfortunately, Loy did not get the same recognition, although she had contributed much to the Ford family's success, as well as the development of Nevada.

Conclusion

In conclusion, Ah Cum Kee and Loy Lee Ford were not different from many other Chinese American women of their time and generation, but they also were not alike. Both benefited from living in a generally receptive environment that resulted from their husbands' prominent roles in their communities.

Raised in a relatively integrated setting and receiving a non-segregated public school education, Ah Cum was at ease among Euro-Americans. She adopted many aspects of mainstream American society while retaining some basic, selective Chinese values and traditions as well. When Ah Cum, at the age of fourteen, married a very traditional Chinese man, she followed his traditional ways as best she could. Her children and her work brought her back into the mainstream community; after her husband's death, she lived more in the American world than the Chinese one and expressed a greater degree of acculturation when, for example, she consented to her daughter's marriage to a non-Chinese.

Loy, who apparently was much more introverted, was raised in a transplanted traditional Chinese setting, and at age seventeen, past the major formative stage of her life, married a man who wanted to be "Americanized." Billy Ford opened new vistas for Loy. Furthermore, with the help of their children and Billy's Euro-American friends, Loy became even more Americanized, or acculturated. Because of Billy's importance in the community, Loy had to be a part of his larger world. She learned to speak some English. At the same time, she valued many Chinese traditions; among them were the celebration of Chinese New Year's and the insistence that her children not marry outside of the race. However, one of her sons and many of her grandchildren, being more at ease in a multicultural world, eventually followed a different path.

Most, if not all, of the Kee and Ford children felt uncomfortable in San Francisco's Chinatown, which seemed very "alien" to them because of the community's preservation of many Chinese traditions. The children of Ah Cum Kee and Loy Lee Ford chose to live in communities such as Oakland, Fresno, and Los Angeles, which had more Euro-American aspects. Despite their differing degrees of acculturation, Loy and Ah Cum lived between the two worlds of their ethnic traditions and the American mainstream so that their children would have even better opportunities.

Notes

1. For definitions of acculturation and assimilation, see the works of Robert Park, Milton Gordon, Oscar Handlin, Roger Daniels, Sucheng Chan, Ronald Takaki, and Elliott Barkan. When I began the research I did not know that Chung Kee's and Billy Ford's surnames at birth were the same as mine. I have found nothing that verifies they are my relatives, although it is possible.

2. The birth and immigration dates are from the U.S. census manuscripts for Esmeralda (later Mineral) County, Nevada, and Ormsby County Recorder's Office, *Miscellaneous Records*, Book 34, p. 398, dated April 10, 1926. Jeffrey Kintop of the Nevada State Archives provided the plat maps of Carson City's Chinatown and the tax records for Ormsby County.

3. Chung Kee (1847–1909) was also known as Chung Gee Wen, Jeung Kee, Gee We Chung, from Gawk Wun Lay Village, Kaiping (Hoiping) District, Guangdong Province, China; his family name is Chung, also romanized Jeung or Zhang; the latter date comes from the U.S. census manuscript, 1900, Nevada, Esmeralda County, Hawthorne; because he was so traditional, I favor the later date for his arrival.

4. National Archives, San Bruno, Immigration and Naturalization File RG 85, File 13561/278.

5. *Walker Lake Bulletin*, October 8, 1890. The newspaper carried several stories about Chung Kee between 1880 and 1909, but they were usually very brief.

6. Kee Family Papers, Asian American File, University of Nevada, Las Vegas, Special Collections Library. See also *Mineral County Independent*, September 25, 1974, on Charles Kee's visit to Hawthorne.

7. Norman Douglass Money, "Poker Bill and Mary Ann and Other Mining Tales: Recollections of Norman Douglass Money," ed. Ramona Ruiz O'Neil (mss, University of Nevada, Las Vegas, Special Collections Library, 44 and 53). See also Lorena Edwards Meadows, *A Sagebrush Heritage: The Story of Ben Edwards and His Family* (San Jose: Harlan-Young Press, 1972), 111–13, 116–18, 126, 131, 135–37, 163, and 181, which covers Ford's relationship with Edwards and the events in Candelaria. Jack Douglass, *Tap Dancing on Ice: The Life and Times of a Nevada Gaming Pioneer*, as told to William A. Douglass (Reno: University of Nevada Oral History Program, 1996), mentions Billy Ford

8. Meadows, *A Sagebrush Heritage*, 117.; Money, "Poker Bill and Mary Ann," 44; *Tonopah Bonanza*, April 14, 1922.

9. The adoption papers are on file in the Nye County Recorder's Office, *Miscellaneous Papers*, Book 1.

Suggested Readings

This study relied upon local newspapers, U.S. census manuscripts, Immigration and Naturalization Service files, Nye and Esmeralda County Recorder's Office land deeds, court records, birth and death records, Chung clan genealogy for Kaiping, unpublished and published memoirs, oral interviews, photograph collections, and other documents in Chinese and English. The Kee Family Papers are in the Asian American File, University of Nevada, Las Vegas, Special Collections Library.

For a general background on Chinese American women, see Huping Ling, *Surviving on the Gold Mountain: A History of Chinese American Women and Their Lives* (Albany: State University of New York Press, 1998); Judy Yung, *Chinese American Women: A Pictorial History* (Seattle: University of Washington Press, published for the Chinese Culture Foundation of San Francisco, 1986), and Yung, *Unbound Feet: A Social History of Chinese Women in San Francisco* (Berkeley: University of California Press, 1995); Sue Fawn Chung, "Their Changing World: Chinese Women on the Comstock, 1860–1910," in *Comstock Women: The Making of a Mining Community*, ed. Ronald M. James and C. Elizabeth Raymond (Reno: University of Nevada Press, 1997), 203–228; Sucheng Chan, ed., *Ethnic and Gender Boundaries in the United States: Studies of Asian, Black, Mexican, and Native Americans* (Lewiston, NY: Edwin Mellen, 1989), and Sucheng Chan, "Exclusion of Chinese Women, 1870–1943," in ed. Chan, *Entry Denied: Exclusion and the Chinese Community in America, 1882–1943* (Philadelphia: Temple University Press, 1991), 94–196; Benson Tong, *Unsubmissive Women: Chinese Prostitutes in Nineteenth Century San Francisco* (Norman: University of Oklahoma Press, 1994); George Anthony Peffer, "Forbidden Families: Emigration Experience of Chinese Women under the Page Law, 1875–1882," *Journal of American Ethnic History* 6, no. 1 (1986): 28–46; Harry Kitano and Wai-tsang Yuen, "A Chinese Interracial Marriage," *Marriage and Family Relations* 5, no. 1 (Spring 1982): 35–48; Janice Stockard, *Daughters of the Canton Delta: Marriage Patterns and Economic Strategies in South China, 1860–1930* (Stanford: Stanford University Press, 1989); and Yen Le Espiritu, *Asian American Women and Men: Labor, Laws, and Love* (Thousand Oaks, CA: Sage Publications, 1997).

13

Catherine Kenny
Fighting for the Perfect Thirty-Sixth

Carole Stanford Bucy

When the Tennessee General Assembly ratified the Nineteenth Amendment to the United States Constitution on August 18, 1920, many saw the event as the end of a long struggle for woman suffrage. Tennessee was the necessary thirty-sixth state to make women's right to vote part of the U.S. Constitution. For Nashville suffragist Catherine Talty Kenny (1874–1950), the victory signaled a new era in Tennessee politics. Kenny believed that women would not simply cast their votes but would also unite to pursue social reforms. Although some saw suffrage as an end in a struggle for justice, Kenny viewed women's enfranchisement as an important tool for direct political power and influence. Suffrage was a necessary step if women were to become full participants in Tennessee's public life.

Catherine Kenny's background was unique among the leadership of the Tennessee suffragists. Unlike Tennessee's Protestant suffrage leaders Anne Dallas Dudley, Abby Crawford Milton, and Kate Burch Warner, Catherine Kenny was an Irish Catholic. She was born in 1874 in Chattanooga, Tennessee, to Hugh and Bridget Cotter Talty. Catherine's father died in a Chattanooga yellow fever epidemic in 1878, leaving a widow and six children under the age of ten. Moving the family from one tenement apartment to another in a neighborhood known in Chattanooga as Irish Hill, Catherine's mother worked as a seamstress to support the children until they were old enough to work. At fifteen, Catherine was sent to Nazareth Academy, a Catholic high school attached to Nazareth College in Bardstown, Kentucky. Catherine attended the school for only one semester in 1889, however, and then returned to Chattanooga, where she worked for the next ten years in a variety of positions as a store clerk, stenographer, and cashier.

In 1899, Catherine Talty married John M. Kenny and moved from Chattanooga to Nashville, where John Kenny worked as a salesman for a wholesale coffee company. Like many other ambitious young men with Chattanooga connections, John Kenny obtained a charter from Benjamin Franklin Thomas for a Coca Cola franchise in Nashville. At this time the Atlanta-based Coca Cola had just begun creating independent bottlers in cities around the country.

Catherine Kenny's early years in Nashville were devoted to the typical domestic duties of a young Catholic wife. As the Coca Cola Bottling Works flourished and expanded, the family moved out of the minority Catholic neighborhood near the plant into a large house in the fashionable West End section of the city. Kenny gave birth to four children and cared for her mother, who lived with the family until her death in 1908. In numerous public statements made throughout her life, Kenny saw her role as mother as her greatest responsibility and the primary reason that she became involved with political causes. "I have the best job in the world," said Kenny, speaking to mill workers on an Atlanta street. She continued: "I am the mother of four children, and I'm trying to rear them as they should be reared. I wouldn't give up that job for any position that might be tendered me. But I do want to say something about the conditions under which those children shall be educated, the surroundings in which they must work and the manner in which the laws looking to the removal of temptations from their paths are enforced."[1]

At a time when many American Catholics opposed woman suffrage, Catherine Kenny, the only Catholic among the leadership of the Tennessee suffragists, was able to reconcile her religious beliefs as a Catholic with her political beliefs in equality and women's rights. When others criticized the Catholic church for the comments of various prominent American bishops in opposition to women's rights, Kenny defended the Church and pointed out that the Church had taken no official stand on the subject of woman suffrage, instead leaving the matter to the judgment of its members as to what they thought best.

John Kenny's success as a businessman offered his wife an opportunity to become involved in activities outside the parish community that largely confined other Catholic women in Nashville at the turn of the century. Kenny joined the Ladies Hermitage Association, one of Nashville's most prestigious women's organizations, and the Nashville Capitol Association, but anti-Catholic sentiment probably restricted her social connections. Therefore, Kenny turned her attention to the Nashville Equal Suffrage League.

The state suffrage association in Tennessee, which had not been active since the turn of the century, was reorganized in 1906 by a group of women from Memphis. For several years the Tennessee Equal Suffrage Association (TESA) had members only in Memphis. Although not a 1911 charter member of the Nashville Equal Suffrage League, Kenny was active in the organization by 1913. The local suffrage league enabled her to develop leadership skills. In addition, suffrage activities gave Kenny visibility as a leader and provided her numerous opportunities for personal growth. It brought her into contact with elite Protestant women who were increasingly politically active in the city. By the time Kenny became involved in the suffrage movement, she was among the economic elite of Nashville, even though her Catholicism continued to confine her socially. In the political arena, Catherine Kenny was able to forge an independent identity.

Kenny's interest in voting and politics led her to become a political ally of U.S. Senator Luke Lea (D) at a time in Tennessee history when the state Democratic Party was divided by a bitter power struggle. Lea, the publisher of the *Nashville Tennessean,* became the statewide leader of a group of progressive Nashville-area Democrats that vied with West Tennessee Democrats for control of the party. In 1910, Lea and other like-minded Democrats had forged an alliance with East Tennessee Republicans that elected Ben W. Hooper (R) governor that year. As Catherine Kenny became active in the suffrage league, she also became an active and influential member of Lea's progressive coalition.

In 1913, Kenny became the spokesperson for the local suffrage association and the state TESA. Her ties to publisher Luke Lea made her an excellent press chairman for the suffragists. Stories about woman's suffrage began to appear regularly in the *Tennessean* and other pro-suffrage papers as well as those opposed to giving women the vote. Kenny quickly began to identify activities and events that would gain positive publicity for the movement. Nashville's first suffrage parade was a personal triumph for Catherine Kenny. She presided over the event, the first in the South, held on May 2, 1914. Under her direction, the parade included decorated automobiles and an elaborate tableau staged at the parade's end on the steps of the Parthenon in Centennial Park. Favorable publicity led to an increased awareness of woman suffrage across the state, and local associations began to grow.

Nevertheless, about the same time, a power struggle developed within the state suffrage association. When TESA president Sara Barnwell Elliott resigned because of poor health in 1914, Memphis suffragists, who had founded the state association, attempted to retain control. But the statewide convention instead elected Lizzie Crozier French, from Knoxville, as its president. French had the support of Kenny and the Nashville league. To the delight of Kenny, French immediately announced that Nashville would be the site of the 1914 National American Woman Suffrage Association (NAWSA) convention, an act that further alienated the Memphis suffragists.

Two weeks before the opening of the NAWSA convention at Nashville's Ryman Auditorium in November 1914, the state suffrage association held its annual convention, in Knoxville. Conflict within the state association had not diminished. At this meeting, the association split, with the Nashville and Knoxville representatives forming a separate state association, the Tennessee Equal Suffrage Association, Inc. (TESA, Inc.). Lizzie Crozier French was elected president of the incorporated association; Catherine Kenny, home in Nashville recovering from an appendectomy, was elected vice president. The Memphis-based TESA elected Elinor McCormack as its president. For the next three years, that two statewide suffrage associations worked independently and competed with each other for members and support.

The NAWSA convention gave the Nashville suffrage league and its members national attention. Catherine Kenny was frequently quoted in newspapers about the meetings: "One thing we Nashville suffragists have clearly demonstrated . . . is our ability to handle affairs and that neither prejudice nor hard times could discourage a zealous, sincere and earnest body of women from handling with credit to themselves, their city and their state one of the largest and most representative associations of women in the United States."[2] Indeed, the NAWSA convention was a success for the Nashville league.

When the national convention ended, TESA, Inc., devised a plan to introduce a bill in the Tennessee General Assembly to amend the state constitution allowing female suffrage. The rival TESA supported a different bill, which called for a referendum to hold a constitutional convention to rewrite the state constitution, on the grounds that the existing constitution was so complicated that it would be very difficult and perhaps impossible to amend. When the General Assembly convened in January 1915, both associations were optimistic that some type of female suffrage legislation would pass in 1915. Tom Rye (D) had been elected governor with the support of both factions of the state Democratic Party, and party unity made conditions in the General Assembly more favorable for suffrage legislation. Nonetheless, the two state suffrage associations supported separate bills before the General Assembly. The Nashville suffragists went to Capitol Hill to lobby for their bill to begin the amendment process. Local president Anne Dallas Dudley, accompanied by Catherine Kenny, spoke for the suffragists. Kenny reported: "Mrs. Dudley set a new standard in lobbying. She gave to this disagreeable work that quality which has emphasized all of her suffrage activities, and which has done so much to allay prejudice in the minds of many men—her fine, womanly personality." Kenny noted that "the Governor, himself, said when we called on him the day before the vote was taken, that he didn't even know we were at the Capitol. So the misinformed Anti's, who expected to see the caricatured suffragists of song and story, were given the surprise of their lives, and of course you know what happened."[3]

Although Kenny did not speak, she clearly enjoyed lobbying. This direct method, designed to influence the male members of the state assembly, marked a turning point in the strategy used by the Tennessee suffragists. They were no longer content to influence through indirect means. Now they went directly to the halls of the legislature and addressed those who had the power to change the laws. The bill calling for the amendment to the state constitution passed by an overwhelming majority in both houses. According to the Tennessee constitution, the proposed amendment had to be reintroduced and voted on again in the 1917 session of the legislature before being submitted to the voters for approval. A photograph appeared on the front page of the *Tennessean* showing Governor Rye signing the bill with Dudley, Kenny, and other Nashville suffragists gathered in his office. The TESA bill for a referendum on a constitutional convention to be held in August 1916 also passed in the final days of the session.

Since the women of both organizations needed to work together for passage of the referendum for the constitutional convention, the week after the legislature adjourned, the leaders of the associations held a conference in Tullahoma to devise a plan for the joint effort. They agreed to organize a Campaign Committee with a cochair from each association. The TESA appointed Mary L. Kelso of Knoxville, and the TESA, Inc., appointed Catherine Kenny. When Kelso resigned, she was replaced by Abby Crawford Milton, a newcomer to suffrage, but the wife of influential Chattanooga newspaper publisher George Fort Milton. Although Milton's Chattanooga league was a member of TESA, she and Kenny worked well together, partly because Milton's husband was a political ally of Luke Lea.

When Lizzie Crozier French resigned as president of the TESA, Inc., in 1915, Kenny, the vice president-at-large, assumed the responsibilities of the president until the election of Anne Dallas Dudley at the 1915 state convention in Jackson. Kenny established a suffrage camp in Cheatham County where she hosted suffrage leaders from across the state and held strategy sessions for the passage of the referendum. Kenny and Milton continued the work of the Campaign Committee, organizing new leagues across the state and recruiting new members. Kenny saw the long-term possibilities of this committee. She and Milton created an effective grassroots network organized by Congressional districts that would be in place when a national suffrage amendment went before Congress. Kenny solicited political advice from the secretary of former governor Ben W. Hooper (R) and worked closely with Senator Lea (D). By the time the TESA, Inc., held its state convention in Jackson, the association had twenty-three member leagues. "Phoenix-like we have risen, and God Willing by the time we meet again in Annual Convention there will not be a village or hamlet in all our state without a suffrage organization," Kenny told the delegates in her convention address. In January 1916, there were thirty-five leagues in her association.

Nashville suffragists Catherine Kenny, Anne Dallas Dudley, Kate Burch Warner, Caroline Kimbrough, and Maria Thompson Daviess took an active part in the NAWSA convention held December 12–15, 1915, in Washington. Kenny was frequently quoted in the local Tennessee newspapers about the convention. The *Tennessean* carried an article entitled "Nashville Woman Arouses National Convention of Suffragists," which described Kenny giving the Tennessee report at the convention: "Mrs. John M. Kenny of Nashville, elicited great applause at the hands of the entire convention and created a most favorable impression."[4] Kenny accompanied Pattie Ruffin Jacobs of Alabama when Jacobs spoke before a Senate committee. At that hearing, Jacobs discussed the specific issues that suffrage could address: women's and children's labor reform, advocacy for better schools, and improved government. These progressive issues became a major part of Catherine Kenny's suffrage agenda. Clearly, Kenny and other suffragists wanted to use the vote as a tool for social change.

Throughout 1916, both state associations actively worked for state legislation. In keeping with the NAWSA strategy seeking bipartisan endorsement of suffrage, Anne Dallas Dudley and Catherine Kenny appeared before the executive committees of the state Democratic and Republican Parties, asking for suffrage planks in their platforms. The Dudley-Kenny partnership worked well. Anne Dallas Dudley became a well-known spokeswoman for suffrage, and Kenny remained a behind-the-scenes, grassroots organizer. As a conservative Southern woman, Dudley was able to reconcile woman suffrage and discrimination against blacks. Dudley spoke about the justice and fairness of enfranchising white women, since black men had the vote; Kenny formulated an agenda of social concerns that could be remedied by woman suffrage. Kenny's success as a suffrage organizer also provided excellent training for her political activities within the state Democratic party and in local Nashville politics.

Both suffrage associations in Tennessee experienced growth, but their efforts continued to be limited by the division between them. Average citizens could not distinguish the two associations except for the fact that Nashville women dominated the leadership of one association, whereas the leadership of the other association was largely from Memphis. In 1916 NAWSA president Carrie Chapman Catt held a conference in Memphis in an effort to bring the two groups together. Kenny rode in the automobile with Catt and Abby Milton in the suffrage parade held during the conference. Catt also privately met with Kenny and Dudley, representing Nashville, and Elinor McCormack, representing Memphis, to urge reunification of the two state suffrage associations. They agreed to work together for their common goal through the Joint Campaign Committee. Although the Nashville suffragists saw the referendum for the constitutional convention as their bill, the State Constitutional League, an all-male organization, led the fight for the convention. When the referendum for a state constitutional convention was held August 3, 1916, it was defeated. Consequently, the Joint Campaign Committee, although not the chief advocate of the defeated bill, failed to unite the TESA and TESA, Inc.

Although the two suffrage organizations remained divided, Kenny and Milton continued the work of the Joint Campaign Committee throughout 1916 and into 1917. TESA and TESA, Inc., again agreed to cooperate for passage of suffrage legislation when the Tennessee General Assembly reconvened in January 1917. Women from both associations addressed the January 17 meeting of the Tennessee House Judiciary Committee in support of a bill patterned on a successful Illinois statute. This legislation would give Tennessee women presidential and municipal suffrage, thereby instituting a strategy consistent with Catt's NAWSA "Winning Plan" partial suffrage goal. Catt believed that ratification of a federal amendment would be easier if most states had at least partial female suffrage. TESA, Inc., delayed its state convention until January 30, hoping to lobby for the bill during its meetings, but on January 31, the bill was tabled in the Senate.

The defeat remobilized the Joint Campaign Committee, which worked for the measure during the General Assembly recess in February. A gift of $500 from a Memphis suffragist enabled Kenny's association to hire four professional organizers to rally public support across the state. NAWSA paid the salaries of three additional campaign workers to help with lobbying, publicity, and the generation of grassroots support. When TESA, Inc., had its annual state convention, in Nashville, at the end of January, members elected Catherine Kenny chairman of publicity. Using the Joint Campaign Committee that she and Milton had established earlier, she developed a comprehensive statewide plan for publicity and succeeded in getting numerous newspapers to publish special suffrage editions. Kenny, Sue Shelton White, and Caroline Kimbrough also added the innovation of "street speaking" to the suffrage campaign. Speaking from busy street corners to whoever would listen, these women attracted attention to their cause. Kenny's photo appeared in the *Atlanta Constitution,* showing her addressing a group of workers outside a local Atlanta factory. When the Tennessee Senate returned from its recess, however, it again voted to table the bill without acting on it.

By the time the bill was tabled, the United States was on the verge of war. TESA offered Governor Tom Rye its services for the war effort at the same time that Carrie Chapman Catt offered NAWSA's support to President Woodrow Wilson. When the United States entered the war in April 1917, the suffragists agreed to devote their full attention to the war effort. Using the experience she had gained in the suffrage association, Catherine Kenny became the publicity chair for the Tennessee Division of the Women's Committee of the National Council of Defense. It was her responsibility to publicize and advocate women's contributions to the war. Kenny became the editor of the "Monthly War Bulletin," a newsletter. In the first issue she called on Tennessee women to support the war effort and expressed her desire for unity among the women of the state: "The supreme test of the nation has come. We must all speak, act and serve together."[5] When President Wilson's daughter, Margaret, came to Nashville, Kenny organized the visit and held a dinner in her honor. All suffrage activities in Tennessee came to a halt until the war ended. Kenny continued her efforts toward a lasting peace after the war was over and attended the Southern Congress for a League of Nations, an event hosted by former president William Howard Taft in Atlanta.

Despite the lack of direct action for suffrage in 1917, the war ultimately united the state suffrage associations. In 1918, Anne Dallas Dudley stepped down as state president of TESA, Inc., when she was elected to the national board of NAWSA as third vice president. Margaret Ervin Ford, the president of TESA, also relinquished her office, and the delegates from both associations elected Kate Burch Warner of Nashville as president of the reunited TESA. Catherine Kenny continued to work for suffrage, but she was already looking ahead to reforms that could be accomplished after women gained the vote.

When the war ended, the reunited state association again introduced a General Assembly bill for municipal and presidential suffrage. On April 3, 1919, House Speaker Seth Walker, a Democrat, left his chair as speaker to announce his conversion to female suffrage. That same day, the bill passed the House. With the outcome in the Senate in doubt, Kenny, having become the state chairman for publicity, spoke for the state association: "It will mean much to the women of Tennessee for their men to give them the vote. It will show them that their men are progressive and chivalrous as they have always been and stand stoutly behind the women and President Wilson." She continued: "If the Senate does not give us the vote this time, it will not make any definite difference because the next United States Congress is pledged to pass the federal amendment. This means that we shall have the vote pretty soon anyway. But we should like to have it from our men first."[6] Kenny's statement was a skillful attempt to appeal to the vanity of the male legislators so that Tennessee women would not have to wait for the federal amendment.

In the Senate, the measure passed on April 16 by one vote. Tennessee became the twenty-seventh state, and the first Southern state, to grant women the right to vote for presidential electors and in municipal elections. Kenny expressed her excitement to reporters: "It is a wonderful thing for Tennessee. And the women will show the men that they can measure up to these responsibilities. Municipal suffrage will make the women take an active interest in what is going on about them, and will train them in the work of voting, so that they will be ready for general franchisement when it comes." Suggesting her ultimate goal, Kenny speculated that the "first work of the Tennessee women, I think, will be to get behind the educational institutions of the state and to wipe out the illiteracy for which Tennessee has a reputation. The schools will have their most efficient support."[7]

Immediately after Governor Albert Roberts (D) signed the bill into law, Catherine Kenny became the first woman in Davidson County to pay poll tax: "I am very proud of my little slip of paper entitling me to cast my ballot. It is a matter of history. The State Board of Election Commissioners promised us the support of its members and I know we shall be treated splendidly."[8] Kenny and the other women who registered paid the late penalty, which had been waived for returning soldiers. John J. Vertrees, a lawyer, immediately filed suit in Chancery Court to get an injunction to restrain the State Board of Elections from permitting women to vote. Vertrees said that women were not eligible to pay the penalty and register. Although Chancellor James B. Newman issued a decision declaring the law unconstitutional, his decision was reversed the following month by the state Supreme Court. The Supreme Court opinion stated that women would have to pay the state poll tax before they could vote. Catherine Kenny, Anne Dallas Dudley, and Caroline Kimbrough appeared in the office of the county trustee to pay the tax, but the trustee refused to receive the money, on the grounds that state law exempted women from the poll tax. The women then filed suit in Chancery Court against the trustee. Again, the case was appealed to the state Supreme Court. This time the court ruled that women did not have to pay a poll tax in order to vote in 1919.

The reunited TESA held a victory convention in Nashville in June 1919 following the passage of presidential and municipal suffrage. In the midst of the meeting, word came that the U.S. Senate had passed the federal suffrage amendment, sometimes referred to as the Susan B. Anthony Amendment, in honor of the women's rights pioneer. "Excitement ran riot," and the women sang "Praise God from Whom All Blessings Flow." In an election free of conflict, Kenny's Joint Campaign Committee ally, Abby Crawford Milton, was elected president of the state association as the successor to Warner.

By 1919 Catherine Kenny had become actively involved in local politics as well as suffrage. Kenny forged a political relationship with Frankie J. Pierce and Mattie Coleman, two African American activists, to support reform candidates in the 1919 local Nashville elections. In return, Kenny promised support for Pierce's legislative agenda, a state vocational school for African American girls. Following the organizational pattern Kenny had established during her work on the Joint Campaign Committee, Kenny and Della Dortch, a member of the Nashville Equal Suffrage League, organized the Women Voters League of Nashville, composed of one representative from each city ward. In an effort to improve the quality of local public education in Nashville, Kenny and the Women Voters League supported a 25 percent pay increase for teachers. Kenny saw this partnership as one of her greatest successes and was eager to share her political success at the national convention the following year. Carrie Chapman Catt, still trying to placate Southern suffrage supporters on the race issue, told Kenny that the program was too full for a speech on the topic.

NAWSA held its victory convention in Chicago in February 1920, to coincide with the one hundredth anniversary of Susan B. Anthony's birth. Catherine Kenny was among twelve Tennessee women from across the state who received NAWSA's distinguished service cross. Upon returning to Nashville, state president Abby Milton appointed Kenny as Tennessee's suffrage historian. As historian, Kenny would submit the Tennessee chapter for the NAWSA's history of woman suffrage, to be edited by Ida Husted Harper. In addition, since Tennessee women now had at least partial suffrage, Kenny and Milton began making plans for the evolution of the Tennessee Equal Suffrage Association to the Tennessee League of Women Voters. Kenny explained her vision for the League of Women Voters to a reporter: "This precludes the idea that some people had that the women would form another party" (referring to Alice Paul's more radical National Women's Party). Instead, "we are urged by our President Mrs. Carrie Chapman Catt, to join either the Republican or Democratic party right away and work through them." Consistent with Catt's ideas, Kenny explained, "by 'working through' the parties I mean that in each the women will urge on the candidates their own platforms. In that way they will wield a tremendous influence for good government and clean politics."[9] For Kenny this meant that she would continue to remain active in the Democratic Party while at the same time maintaining nonpartisan activities through the League of Women Voters. The idea of being a nonpartisan political activist was, for many Progressives, the answer to factionalism. Kenny believed that she could distinguish between her political activities and her nonpartisan League of Women Voters activities.

Abby Milton was elected president of the Tennessee League of Women Voters in May 1920. The excitement expressed in the speeches at this meeting indicated that the Tennessee suffragists believed that ratification of the federal amendment was rapidly approaching. Kenny, who had made the local arrangements for the state convention, remembered her political debt from the 1919 municipal elections to African American women. Even though Nashville was still a segregated town, Kenny invited Frankie Pierce to address the meeting to tell the suffragists what African American women would do with the vote. Pierce told the convention that her sisters would use the vote to "uplift our people" and asked only for a "square deal." Ratification seemed a certainty to Tennessee suffragists, even though the thirty-sixth and deciding state was still in doubt. For some, this convention and celebration marked the impending end of a long struggle, but for Kenny and Milton it was the beginning of a new level of women's political involvement. Kenny and Milton saw the League of Women Voters as the organization that would bring women into the political arena. For them the league was an umbrella organization for all other women's groups. It would set a legislative agenda primarily focused on issues related to women, children, and good government. Kenny saw the league as the supreme union of women speaking with a united voice rather than one organization among many.

Shortly after the state convention the U.S. Supreme Court handed down its decision in *Hawke v Smith*, the case that questioned the Ohio constitution's requirement that federal amendments be voted on during a regular session rather than a special session. Tennessee's General Assembly could now be called into special session by the governor for the purpose of ratification. Anne Dallas Dudley and Abby Milton were scheduled to leave the state for the Democratic National Convention in June, but the special session had not been called. Before Dudley and Milton left for San Francisco, Milton named Kenny chairman of ratification for the League of Women Voters. Although Governor Roberts had been silent on the issue of a special session, because he was facing a very difficult battle in the state's August Democratic primary, Milton was confident that he could be persuaded to issue the call. She wanted to have Catherine Kenny, with her coalition-building skills, in place should the call come. When writing her own history of ratification, Milton gave Kenny full credit for the telegram that Roberts received on June 24 from President Wilson urging the governor to call the special session of the General Assembly. After receiving word of President Wilson's telegram, the state delegates at the Democratic National Convention issued an appeal to Roberts; he replied to the National Convention stating that he would call the session after the state's Democratic primary on August 7, 1920. As soon as Kenny learned the governor's response, she opened the league's suffrage headquarters at the Maxwell House Hotel in Nashville and immediately organized a letter-writing campaign to lobby members of the General Assembly.

Carrie Chapman Catt's greatest fear about the special session of the Tennessee General Assembly stemmed from the past divisions among Tennessee suffragists. When she wrote to Kenny to outline her suggestions for a plan of action for the campaign, Catt gently suggested that perhaps the League of Women Voters should consider a male lobbyist from outside the state. Catt realized that with Kenny and Milton actively supporting a candidate in the primary, the non-partisan stand of the Tennessee League of Women Voters would be questioned. When Catt became fearful that Governor Roberts would postpone the special session, she decided to come to Nashville to ensure that Tennessee women were united for ratification.

Catt's arrival in Nashville was quickly followed by the arrival of a strong antisuffrage contingency to fight ratification. Josephine Pearson, president of the Tennessee Division of the Southern Women's League for the Rejection of the Susan B. Anthony Amendment, established her headquarters at the Hermitage Hotel, the same hotel where Catt was staying. In addition, many antisuffrage men from around the country came to Nashville to pressure legislators to vote against ratification. Antisuffragists were committed to preserving the prevailing order and were fearful that a federal amendment would lead to increased national intervention in voting activities in Southern states. They argued that female political activism was "unwomanly" and would lead to the destruction of the home. Visible opposition to suffrage, as well as the presence of Carrie Chapman Catt, brought the Tennessee suffragists together for ratification.

By the time the legislators arrived for the special session on August 9, Tennessee had five ratification committees: the League of Women Voters committee, headed by Catherine Kenny; the governor's committee, led by Kate Warner; the Republican committee, headed by Minnie Beasley; a men's ratification committee, headed by former Tennessee Governor Tom Rye; and a special committee appointed by Catt, headed by Charl Orman Williams, a Memphis suffragist who was the vice chairman of the Democratic National

Committee. Sue Shelton White also came to Nashville as a representative of Alice Paul's Women's Party. With Carrie Chapman Catt at Nashville's Hermitage Hotel throughout the fight for ratification, these diverse groups worked together for the cause, keeping their personal differences in the background.

On August 13, the Tennessee Senate ratified the amendment by a comfortable margin of twenty-five to four. The suffragists knew that the vote in the House would be very close. After numerous delays, on August 18, the House finally voted on ratification. An unsuccessful vote to table the amendment was followed by a vote on the amendment itself. Speaker Seth Walker had changed his position again and spoke against the amendment. In a dramatic moment during the vote Representative Harry Burn (R) voted for the amendment, making the vote forty-nine to forty-seven. Although Speaker Walker then changed his vote to "aye" so that the amendment could be reconsidered, the vote held. The Tennessee House had ratified the Nineteenth Amendment, and Tennessee had become the thirty-sixth and deciding state to ratify. After a week of parliamentary and legal maneuvers, the ratification resolution was sent to Governor Roberts for his signature and then on to Washington, where Secretary of State Bainbridge Colby signed the proclamation making the Nineteenth Amendment part of the Constitution.

Even though legal battles lay ahead for the League of Women Voters, Kenny, Dudley, and Milton again returned to the political arena after ratification. By late September, it was apparent that Governor Roberts's campaign for reelection was in trouble. Fearful that a defeat of the Democrats would make Kenny's reform agenda more difficult to implement, Carrie Chapman Catt urged Kenny to support Roberts's campaign. Catt asked the Democratic National Committee to send a woman to Tennessee to work in the fall campaign and assured Kenny that she would help the Tennessee League of Women Voters get "on its feet again" after the election. Catt seemed to instinctively know how best to appeal to Kenny. If Kenny supported Governor Roberts in his campaign, Catt and the League of Women Voters would help her implement her legislative agenda. In spite of Carrie Chapman Catt's efforts to rally the suffragists behind the candidacy of Governor Roberts, he lost the general election, as the Republicans swept the state in what was a national Republican landslide.

After Roberts's defeat, many of the women who had worked for the ratification of the Nineteenth Amendment abandoned Kenny and her League of Women Voters. Anne Dallas Dudley's political activities were limited. Milton, the state president, became ill and was unable to give the organization needed energy and time. By 1921, the future of the Tennessee league was in doubt. Milton wrote to National League of Women Voters president Maud Wood Park for help. Park agreed to attend the state convention, to be held in Memphis October 24 and 25, but Milton resigned before the convention because of an undisclosed illness. The convention elected Kenny as state president.

By the time Kenny was elected state league president, Nashville's mayor Felix Z. Wilson (D) had named her to the City Hospital Commission. Kenny had supported Wilson and his reform ticket in the election and was being rewarded for her service. Her appointment shows that although Kenny was president of the nonpartisan League of Women Voters of Tennessee, she had no intention of limiting her own partisan political activities.

Kenny attempted to maintain a broad agenda of reforms for the league. The Tennessee League of Women Voters sponsored citizenship schools to train women on voting and held a Conference on Efficiency in Government called by Governor A. A. Taylor (R). The conference featured extensive morning and afternoon sessions on a wide variety of topics of interest to league members. Kenny presented a session on the 1921 Sheppard Towner Maternity and Infancy Act's application in Tennessee. Although the program addressed many important issues of concern to women, by the time the conference took place, membership in the League of Women Voters had declined. Money became a constant problem for the organization.

Kenny also suffered a major political defeat in 1922. The Nashville City Council voted Mayor Felix Z. Wilson out of office when an opposing faction gained control. Kenny became a political outsider in local government, even though she retained her seat on the City Hospital Commission. She continued to give speeches on the importance of voting and participation in government, but the support for her efforts continued to diminish: "You and I thought that when we had won the vote our work was over. And that grieved us. We have longed for the old days—the struggle, the comradeship, the thrill of working for freedom for the women of all ages. Ah, my friends, there are greater days ahead, unless our task fall from nerveless fingers, and our eyes fail to see the light. . . . We must try to take our woman citizens up to the mountain top and show them the kingdoms of this world of good government."[10] Those who had worked with her to win ratification did not share her vision for the league. The League of Women Voters was not able to lead women to the mountaintop. Although there was no real opposition to many of Kenny's programmatic goals, the women of the state did not follow her. The coalition that had achieved ratification was only a temporary alliance of convenience. The women in the coalition were committed to preexisting groups and exhibited a decided lack of political consciousness as Tennessee women.

When Kenny addressed the 1924 Buffalo national convention of the League of Women Voters, she discussed the importance of women in the Tennessee Democratic Party and expressed her frustrations with those who had abandoned political activism after ratification:

> The majority of Democratic women have an idea that the way to get the things they want in politics is to wait until they are invited to sit at the political banquet table and have their order served them on a silver platter. But my experience and observation lead me to believe that Mrs. Catt's advice is the only way. You must get inside, even waive the formality of an invitation, for they are not issued in well regulated Party Circles, and help *yourself* (cafeteria style), if you would, escape dying of *political Malnutrition*. . . . We must not be discouraged that the fetters of sex tradition still bind men. Four years have not been sufficient time to reconcile them to their political partnership. . . . I do know however, that our united efforts are needed now to secure the passage of a great number of reforms and laws.[11]

Kenny became increasingly frustrated by the difficulties she faced in promoting her legislative program. For example, she was unable to get the Tennessee General Assembly to ratify the 1924 federal Child Labor Amendment. But such difficulties were not necessarily hers alone. There was a national shift toward a conservative political climate in the 1920s. The Child Labor Amendment was never ratified.

A legislative council headed by the state president of the WCTU (Women's Christian Temperance Union) attempted to take the place of the League of Women Voters as an umbrella organization, but Kenny disliked the women in this group and found their methods unacceptable. In 1925, she resigned as state League of Women Voters president before the completion of her term.

Ultimately, Catherine Kenny was unable to sustain the momentum of woman suffrage and lead the women of Tennessee, united in the League of Women Voters, into the political arena. In an era when the national League of Women Voters struggled to create an independent identity, Kenny was not able to keep her progressive values alive. Personal problems demanded her attention and limited her political activities. Kenny's husband lost his business and moved to Louisville, leaving her in Nashville; her daughter had a serious illness. In 1927, her husband died in Louisville, and the year following his death, she moved out of the state. She traveled extensively with her son, a U.S. naval officer, but never moved back to Tennessee. Kenny died in New York City in 1950.

Catherine Kenny had been an excellent grassroots organizer and lobbyist, but her experience testifies to the difficulties in articulating a women's agenda. Although her ability to articulate a vision for women was not enough to persuade women to put aside their differences during the 1920s, her ideas remained alive. A later generation of women who, like Catherine Kenny, understood the importance of political coalitions pursued a comprehensive agenda. In a political climate friendlier to reform, many of her ideas were ultimately implemented.

Notes

1. Unidentified newspaper clipping, entitled "Intense Earnestness Characterizes Mrs. Kenny's Remarks at the Street Meetings Held Thursday Night," January 16, 1916, Kenny Scrapbooks, Catherine Kenny Papers, Tennessee State Library and Archives [hereafter, TSLA], Nashville, Tennessee.

2. *Nashville Tennessean* and *Nashville American*, November 15, 1914.

3. Catherine Kenny Speech, Tennessee Equal Suffrage League, Inc., Annual Convention, Jackson, Tennessee, October 1915, Kenny Scrapbooks, TSLA.

4. *Nashville Tennessean* and *Nashville American*, April 3, 1919.

5. "Monthly War Bulletin," vol. 1, no. 1, Kenny Scrapbook, TSLA.

6. *Nashville Tennessean* and *Nashville American*, April 3, 1919.

7. Ibid., May 16, 1919.

8. Ibid., May 15, 1919.

9. Ibid., February 20, 1920.

10. Catherine Kenny Speech, Kenny Scrapbooks, TSLA.

11. "Women in Party Conventions from the Viewpoint of a Democrat," Speech delivered at the Buffalo Convention, National League of Women Voters by Mrs. John M. Kenny of Nashville, President, Tennessee League of Women Voters, April 24–29, 1924, Kenny Scrapbooks, TSLA.

Suggested Readings

Catherine Kenny's two suffrage scrapbooks were donated to the Tennessee Historical Society in 1995 by Kenny's granddaughter, Lenore Selby, and placed at the Tennessee State Library and Archives (TSLA). These scrapbooks contain newspaper clippings describing Kenny's suffrage activities and a few of her speeches. All information about Kenny's personal life has been found in the records of the Church of St. Peter and St. Paul in Chattanooga, Tennessee, and the Nashville City Directory. There is no significant correspondence in the Kenny scrapbooks. The Carrie Chapman Catt Papers at TSLA contain numerous letters from Kenny to Catt as well as other correspondence in which Kenny's name is mentioned. The Catt Papers also contain the draft Kenny submitted for volume 6 of *The History of Woman Suffrage*, edited by Ida Husted Harper, as well as Margaret Erwin Ford's chapter on Tennessee ratification. Much of the correspondence in the Catt Papers details the fight between

Kenny and Ford over the writing of the official history of suffrage work in Tennessee. When volume 6 was published, Harper, acting on the advice of Catt, included both accounts. The TSLA also has taped interviews with Abby Crawford Milton in which Milton describes her work with Kenny and the Joint Campaign Committee. The League of Women Voters Papers at the Library of Congress contain additional correspondence between Kenny and the national league officers during the years following ratification. To date, the most comprehensive account of suffrage in Tennessee is A. Elizabeth Taylor's *The Woman Suffrage Movement in Tennessee* (New York: G. K. Hall, 1957; reprint, New York: Octagon Books, 1978), but Taylor mentions Kenny only twice in this book. Anita S. Goodstein's "A Rare Alliance: African American and White Women in the Tennessee Elections of 1919–1920," *Journal of Southern History* 64, no. 2 (1998): 219–46, provides a detailed account of Kenny's political activities.

IV
World War II and Beyond
Women Challenging
Modern America

The 1930s and 1940s were decades of crisis. High unemployment during the 1930s sent many people, especially men, on the road looking for jobs. Black Americans and members of other minorities were the last hired and the first fired. Some Mexican Americans were "deported" to Mexico whether they were immigrants or not. In general married women were fired from jobs in government, schools, and even private business if their husbands had employment. The Franklin D. Roosevelt administration's New Deal expanded the role of the federal government into the lives of ordinary citizens through job programs, housing assistance, and the Social Security Act. But many such efforts favored men and underscored the traditional role of wife and mother for women. Birth, marriage, and divorce rates fell during the 1930s as desertion, domestic violence, and homelessness became more common.

U.S. entrance into World War II, after the Japanese attack at Pearl Harbor on December 7, 1941, directly affected ordinary Americans. Japanese American men, women, and children living in the western United States were interned in "relocation" centers for much of the war. Almost eleven million American men and women served in the U.S. military during the war. The war also ended the Great Depression and opened the door to better employment for minorities and women. Women made up over 50 percent of the wartime labor force by 1945. And unlike most female workers in the past, a growing number of these women were married. The war years also stimulated a rise in marriage rates, which led to the postwar baby boom. By 1950 the median age at first marriage had fallen to 22.8 for men and 20.3 for women (from 26.1 for men and 22.0 for women in 1890). Life in the suburbs became the prescribed ideal of the postwar years. Nevertheless, this fact paralleled a rising divorce rate, and the 1950s and 1960s included the twentieth century's highest teenage pregnancy rates. Although many women left their jobs after the war's end in 1945, female employment steadily rose throughout the balance of the century, and at the end of the century women made up approximately 50 percent of the paid labor force.

The 1950s Civil Rights movement led to passage of the 1964 Civil Rights Act, thereby setting the stage for further legislation protecting workers against discrimination based on race, ethnicity, creed, or sex. In addition, women gained greater control of their reproductive capacity through the 1965 patent of the birth control pill and legalized abortion after the 1973 *Roe v Wade* Supreme Court decision. By 1990 life expectancy for women had risen to 78.1 years, meaning that for the first time in history, most women could expect to live nearly half of their lives beyond their reproductive years.

Using the records of the federal Fair Employment Practices Commission and general information about black Americans who migrated to Cincinnati in the years just prior to and during World War II, Andrew Kersten pieces together in Chapter 14 the extraordinary story of Willie Webb. Kersten argues that the simple bravery of working-class black men and women such as Webb helped to build the framework for the civil rights victories of the postwar years.

World War II also had a dramatic impact on many Americans living outside the United States. Ethel Tomas Herold was born in Montana in 1900. Herold and her husband became teachers and opened a business in the Philippines in the decades prior to World War II. The Japanese bombed the Herold's home on December 8, 1941, and took them, their two children, and five hundred of their neighbors prisoners just after Christmas. Theresa Kaminski argues in Chapter 15 that Herold's decision to become a teacher, even in the Philippines, was a fairly typical choice for an ordinary woman at the time. But Herold's patriotism and national pride served as a source of inspiration for others during the years she was a prisoner of war. Herold's work on behalf of her own family and the rest of the internees attests to the enduring, yet flexible, roles of womanhood present in American culture by the mid–twentieth century.

Paula Barnes notes in Chapter 16 that at first glance a political wife–first lady such as Betty Flanagan Bumpers may not seem to qualify as an ordinary woman. But Betty Bumpers went to great lengths to remain an "ordinary" wife and mother while living in a political fishbowl as wife of Dale Bumpers, Arkansas's governor and senator, in the postwar decades. Bumpers's life also shows how far wives and mothers could move into the public world of politics by the late twentieth century. Best known as an antinuclear activist and the founder of Peace Links, Bumpers became a very public player in the world of diplomacy during the volatile cold war years.

The Immigration Act of 1965 is related to the cold war and midcentury Civil Rights movement. This significant piece of legislation replaced the ethnically biased and racist national origins' quotas in the 1924 Immigration and Naturalization Act. Part of President Lyndon Johnson's Great Society agenda, the 1965 law opened the door to a new wave of immigration, increasing the number of people coming to America from South America, Mexico, Central America, the Caribbean, the Middle East, Africa, and Asia. Miguel Juarez's interview with borderland artist Mago Orona Gandara illustrates some of the challenges faced by women who straddle two distinct cultures in modern America. Gandara also discusses the difficulties faced by independent women artists or perhaps any "ordinary" woman of the late twentieth century.

14

Willie Webb
One Woman's Struggle for Civil Rights during World War II

Andrew Kersten

During World War II, African Americans fought for a double victory over fascist armies in Europe and Japan and over apartheid in the United States. The generals of the home-front campaign are well known. Over the last three decades, many books have been written about A. Philip Randolph, Walter White, and other leaders of national associations that sought to end Jim Crow. Less well known are the foot soldiers in the battles against American prejudice and discrimination. Their stories have generally not been recounted by historians. Nevertheless, it is possible to find some information about the common women and men who participated in the Civil Rights movements by using the records of wartime federal agencies. Within the papers of the President's Fair Employment Practice Committee (FEPC), for example, are testimonies of activists and workers who cooperated with the committee to eliminate job bias in defense factories. Complete biographies are rare in these records. Rather, the files offer a glimpse into the lives of workers and community leaders and provide a larger historical context for social movements and institutions. Such is necessarily the case with the subject of this essay, Willie Webb (dates unknown), an African American woman who fought for the right to use her skills as a welder to aid the "arsenal of democracy."

Until the 1940 and 1950 census manuscripts are opened, there will not be many details available about Willie Webb or her family. What we do know comes from the Fair Employment Practice Committee's public hearings held in Cincinnati, Ohio, in March 1945. There she told the FEPC and the audience about her employment experiences during the war and some details about her life. In 1940, Willie Webb married and moved with her husband to the Queen City. Although Webb's exact age is unknown, she and her husband were probably in their twenties, as almost 30 percent of all black wartime migrants were. Most likely the Webbs had come from the South. According to Henry S. Shryock Jr. and Hope Tisdale Eldridge of the United States Census Bureau, African Americans constituted 14 percent of all migrants leaving the South. They dominated some migration streams. In the early 1940s, roughly three out of every four persons leaving Mississippi for Illinois and Michigan were African American. Nevertheless, Webb's move was exceptional. During the early years of defense mobilization, it was mostly African American men who moved northward. The movement of women and families became more characteristic after 1942.[1]

Like thousands of wartime migrants, the Webbs were probably drawn to Cincinnati because of its booming economy. What did a war job mean? Kathryn Blood, a researcher with the United States Women's Bureau, argued that for black women it meant "security . . . against poverty and disease." African Americans also sought new homes in Northern cities to escape the omnipresent hardships of Jim Crow. During the war, Cincinnati's population increased from 810,000 to 860,000 (6.2 percent). One out of every six migrants was African American. Cincinnati's population did not rise as dramatically as other major cities such as Detroit, whose population increased by 8.2 percent; San Francisco, which grew by 25.9 percent; and Portland, which had 31.8 percent more people in 1945. Nonetheless, the newcomers' presence led to changes in Cincinnati's urban ecology, particularly residential patterns.[2]

By luck or by design, Willie Webb lived at 3114 Borrman Avenue, located in an eastern section of town known as Avondale. Her housing situation was better than that of most black Cincinnatians. In 1940, about three out of every four African Americans lived in the city's West End ghetto, which was 64 percent black. Living conditions there were terrible. The housing, once owned by Cincinnati's wealthy, was old and decrepit. Large mansions had been divided up into smaller tenement apartments. The greedy speculators who owned the buildings charged high rents and rarely improved the housing. In 1940, 87 percent of black housing in the West End needed major repairs. The West End was also congested. A 1923 housing survey reported that twenty persons lived in one three-room flat at 1131 Hopkins Street. In a nearby twelve-room tenement at 324 George Street, ninety-four African Americans made their home. Partly because of overcrowding, the ghetto was an unhealthy place: death rates there had been at times over one and one-half times the city average. For example, in 1924, the death rate in Cincinnati was 15.2 per 1,000. In the black community the rate was 26. Epidemic diseases ravaged the West End. African Americans made up almost 30 percent of all tuberculosis cases in Cincinnati during much of the early twentieth century. In 1940, the death rate from TB among blacks (255 per 100,000) was over six times that of whites (42 per 100,000). Like Willie Webb and her family, those who escaped the West End were undoubtedly better off. Many middle-class blacks, such as Pullman car porters, doctors, and teachers, lived in Avondale. That neighborhood housed roughly 20 percent of the city's black population. Like the Webbs, these families were progressing despite the unfair housing practices in Cincinnati.[3]

Although Willie Webb was fortunate to live in Avondale, away from the dire problems of the West End, Cincinnati was not a welcoming place for Webb or her husband. Almost every institution, from schools to hospitals to public recreational facilities, discriminated against African Americans. Worst of all prejudices, black educator Frank Quillin concluded, was "the one that strikes at the law of self-preservation, strikes indeed at one of the basic principles of our life, namely, that every man should be permitted to earn his bread by the sweat of his brow." According to Quillin, job bias in Cincinnati was worse than in many Southern cities. Why, then, would Willie Webb and her husband move to Cincinnati? Despite the continued presence of employment discrimination, the Queen City in 1940 offered more opportunities for blacks than it had during the 1930s depression decade, giving hope to some that the color line in employment would relax and new job openings appear.[4]

The lack of employment opportunities was a particular problem for blacks everywhere during the Great Depression. In 1930, black attorney and Cincinnati activist Theodore M. Berry surveyed the economic status of the city's African Americans and found job discrimination commonplace. Berry sent 475 questionnaires to Cincinnati employers and received answers from 234. One hundred and seven businesses (46 percent) openly refused to hire black workers. The other 127 Cincinnati businesses utilized some black labor, but as Berry noted, the questionnaire "seemed to provide evidence of a low occupational status for Negro workers." Over 80 percent of the black women workers were engaged in domestic service and had "very little opportunity" to work in industry. The only manufacturers willing to employ black women produced chemicals, forged metal goods, and leather clothing, all produced under very poor working conditions. Roughly 70 percent of black men worked as unskilled laborers, many of them as porters or janitors. A few found a place in some branch of industrial production, but these jobs were rarely skilled in nature and therefore were low paid. As the economic depression dragged on, the conditions that Berry described worsened. By 1940, blacks, who made up 8 percent of the labor force, accounted for 20 percent of the unemployed and 29 percent of those on government work-relief projects.[5]

The desperate situation, however, was not hopeless, as many migrants learned from labor recruiters and black newspapers such as the *Chicago Defender*. In the early 1940s two large Cincinnati firms, Wright Aeronautical (a subsidiary of Curtiss-Wright) and Cincinnati Milling Machine, opened their gates to thousands of black workers. Although managers kept black workers confined in segregated buildings, the employment policies of both companies were an auspicious sign of possible things to come. There were also educational opportunities for blacks. Willie Webb, who had completed the ninth grade and two years of night school, after her move to the city took several industrial training courses run by the National Youth Administration (NYA), which trained about 175 black Cincinnatians during the war. By March 1945, Webb had amassed 536 hours of training in electric spot, acetylene, and arc welding.[6]

Although she had now mastered a very marketable skill, the problem for Willie Webb and many other black Cincinnatians was that the employment prospects that had drawn them to the city never fully materialized, as job bias continued. Although some barriers fell during the war, employment discrimination remained an aspect of daily life for African Americans. The situation for black women was worse than that for black men. As historian Eileen Boris has shown, employment discrimination is a function not merely of racial prejudice but of "racialized gender." In other words, white notions about African Americans as well as about womanhood and masculinity worked together to keep black women from most industrial work. Overall, the economic position of black Cincinnatians did improve as defense mobilization began. In April 1940, one out of every twenty industrial workers was black. By September 1942, the ratio had increased to one out of thirteen, and by August 1944, the peak of wartime production in Cincinnati, one of every nine industrial workers was African American. Yet despite this progress in the job market, there were some troubling difficulties. One company, Wright Aeronautical, employed nearly half of all blacks engaged in war work. Most Cincinnati defense employers simply refused to hire black workers. The few that did often placed African Americans in unskilled, and thus lower paid, jobs. Black women faced the most discrimination. Although they represented over 10 percent of the city's female labor force, African American women were only 3 percent of the female employees working in war plants in 1944. This was well below the national average. At the war's peak, black women accounted for 8 percent of all war industry workers in the United States. White women fared much better. By 1944, they constituted roughly 40 percent of the workers in defense factories. Married white women made the most advances. Before the war they were 13.9 percent of all workers. In 1944, that percentage had risen to 22.5. The effect of the war on black married women such as Willie Webb was less pronounced, since it was not uncommon for black wives to work outside the house either before or after the war. These women remained about 25 percent of the workforce during the 1940s.[7]

Willie Webb's struggle to find wartime employment was typical for many black women. When Webb first signed up for industrial training run by the NYA, her instructor said that when finished she would get a job, not in Cincinnati, but at a military base located about sixty miles north of the city, Patterson Field, in Dayton, Ohio. Unwilling or perhaps unable to relocate or make the long commute, Webb sought employment within the city. Her chances should have been good. Although Cincinnati never experienced a labor shortage akin to those of other Midwestern cities such as Detroit, employers generally found it—in the words of the director of the local War Manpower Commission—"difficult to meet labor demands." Even so, Webb's job search was frustrating.[8]

In May 1944, Webb went to the local United States Employment Service office (USES) and received a referral card for a welding position at the Crosley Radio Corporation. Webb immediately went to the company's employment office. The receptionist provided an application but told her that there were not any openings for "colored girls." As per company policy, the receptionist gave Webb the telephone number of a company that was supposedly hiring African American women and men. Without protest, Webb left the Crosley office jobless, deciding to explore the new referral. Most likely Webb then went to the Wright Aeronautical Corporation, which by the spring of 1944 employed three-fifths of all black women who had war-related jobs. It is certain that she also went to Cincinnati Industries, another local manufacturer, which eventually hired Webb.[9]

Crosley officials believed that they had to turn away African American job applicants because the company's major union, the International Brotherhood of Electrical Workers (American Federation of Labor), Local 1061, opposed black employment. Union leaders and the rank and file, particularly white women workers, threatened to strike if blacks were hired in any but custodial positions. In early 1944, white workers made good on their threat and struck after the company employed a black Puerto Rican woman. After this display of solidarity, plant managers refused to hire any more black workers. With the plant completely engaged in the production of materials for the United States Army Signal Corps and United States Navy, Crosley's leaders, along with federal officials, wished to meet all production schedules without interruptions. Thus, during the war, there were only 6 black janitors among its 8,000 employees, over 60 percent of whom were white women. Nevertheless, company officials did not want to appear—in their words—"cold-blooded about this." Interviewers and receptionists were told to discourage blacks, particularly women, from applying and to offer alternate employment possibilities.[10]

Crosley was not the only major defense firm in Cincinnati to deny job opportunities to minority workers. Continuing the earlier pattern, discrimination against African Americans was widespread. The city's largest firms, including Baldwin, Cambridge Tile, F. H. Lawson, and Proctor and Gamble, all refused to hire black and, sometimes, Jewish workers out of fears that existing employees might protest through work stoppages or perhaps a race riot. In addition, USES officials, who supplied the city's war plants with workers, were accomplices in these unfair employment practices. They readily filled "white workers only" job orders from local companies. In the opinion of Dillard Bird, the manager of the Cincinnati USES, the employment of minority workers would create disruptions. Moreover, Bird believed that black men were qualified only for janitorial jobs and black women for domestic work. Thus, when African Americans inquired about jobs, they were often turned away. Such was the experience of Louise Boyd, an African American also living in Avondale. Boyd had read a circular from the local United States Employment Service office: "Women [are] wanted," it stated, "to work in defense industry." The job requirements listed a high school education, a height of at least five feet two inches, a physically fit body, and an age of at least seventeen years. Boyd applied but was rejected. As she later explained, "I met all the requirements but one . . . my face is black." When she complained to a USES official, she was told, "Sorry we have nothing for colored."[11]

Challenging such policies, some local activists had attempted to pressure the USES into ending its toleration of and collusion in these discriminatory practices. Focusing on the USES was a logical move, since most employers hired applicants referred by the federal employment service. In December 1943, a black women's wartime civil rights organization, the Double Victory Council of Cincinnati, led by Anne E. Mason, a Cincinnati reporter for the *Pittsburgh Courier* (a nationally distributed black newspaper), picketed the Cincinnati USES to protest job discrimination against black women. The march against the office resulted in a meeting between Double Victory Council's leaders and Bird's boss, James M. Baker, the War Manpower Commission's Cincinnati director. Baker told the black activists that the solution to discrimination was not protest or forced integration but "a well-planned educational campaign." Mason and her organization agreed to hold off any future public protests and await the results of the proposed educational program. However, neither the campaign nor the hiring of black women followed. When it seemed clear that direct action was not producing more jobs for black women, let alone men, the Cincinnati branches of the National Urban League and the National Association for the Advancement of Colored People (NAACP), in conjunction with the Double Victory

Council, began collecting complaints of discrimination, including that of Willie Webb. The group then sent the complaints to the only federal agency capable of fighting job bias, the President's Fair Employment Practice Committee.[12]

On June 25, 1941, President Roosevelt had issued Executive Order 8802, proclaiming it "the policy of the United States that there shall be no discrimination in the employment of workers in defense industries or Government because of race, creed, color, or national origin" and creating the FEPC to enforce the order. Glaringly absent from the enabling policy statement was the word "sex." Therefore, the FEPC did not have the power to investigate complaints of discrimination solely based on gender. However, in cases where it was clear that some sort of genderized racial bias was operating, the committee could take action, and after 1943, it increasing became concerned with the plight of African American women. The FEPC was an administrative agency originally consisting of about 20 members. At the peak of its operations in 1944, it had roughly 120 officials working in seventeen suboffices scattered across the nation. Because the committee lacked the powers to issue subpoenas, use federal courts, or fine offending parties, it carried out its functions in large part by holding public hearings, through which it used moral suasion to end job discrimination. At these hearings, the FEPC appealed to employers' sense of fair play and patriotism to end employment discrimination. In January 1945, the FEPC announced that it planned to hold a series of public hearings in Cincinnati to address sixty-two complaints of discrimination brought by sixteen black men and forty-six black women.

The Cincinnati hearings were held from March 15 to 17, 1945, in the City Hall. Willie Webb played a small but integral part in these hearings. The FEPC's goal was to cajole Cincinnati employers into adopting fair employment practices. With the help of Theodore Berry of the local NAACP, the FEPC built good cases against Crosley Radio, Baldwin, Cambridge Tile, F. H. Lawson, Kirk and Blum Manufacturing, Schaible, Streitmann Biscuit, and Victor Electric. Berry was the link between the complaints and the committee as he helped prepare the FEPC's witnesses for the hearings. The evidence that Berry helped to collect was so overwhelming that in early March, before the hearings, two companies, Schaible and Kirk and Blum, settled with the FEPC, promising to hire and upgrade black workers. The rest refused, hiding behind their labor unions, which threatened to strike if the plants became integrated.[13]

Over the three days in mid-March 1945, the FEPC held six separate proceedings involving those recalcitrant employers. The hearing with the Crosley Radio Corporation on March 15 was typical. The FEPC's examiner, Emanuel Bloch, began with the testimony of the manager of the Cincinnati office of the USES, Hubert J. Shank, who had replaced Dillard Bird in 1943. The USES manager knew intimately the employment policies of the local war plants to which he referred workers. He had been in contact with Crosley about its unfair employment practices since late 1943. The USES often sent black applicants to Crosley, which would return them jobless. Before contacting the FEPC about this, Shank tried to determine the position of both Crosley's management and union. Industrial relations director Carl T. Nearing told the USES that Crosley did not hire blacks, because it feared that its union would strike. To corroborate this testimony, Fred Ross, president of the International Brotherhood of Electrical Workers, Local 1061, at Crosley testified next. He reiterated the union's threat to walk out if blacks were employed and added that the purpose of the war was "to preserve the American way of life," which to Ross meant keeping "negroes [sic] in their place."[14]

After allowing Crosley's managers and union leaders to state their positions, the FEPC called its witnesses to the stand. The testimony of those who had filed complaints with the committee was a critical component of the hearings. These black workers served as compelling examples of how racism and discrimination squandered talent and limited the effectiveness of the "arsenal of democracy." Willie Webb was just one of several black women who gave their stories before the committee and audience of 150 people. Women such as Ruby Chapman wanted to work at Crosley in order to help their soldier husbands stationed overseas. Webb testified that she was simply an extremely qualified worker who was not allowed to show her competence as a welder. Despite her hundreds of hours of training, Crosley's managers had no use for her because of her skin color. Webb was on the stand for only a few minutes. Once her point was made—that Crosley discriminated against qualified African American women workers because of their race—she was excused. Judging from the hearing transcripts, the brevity of her appearance might have been a relief to Willie Webb, who seemed quite nervous and had to be continually asked to speak louder. Although Webb never spoke publicly about her fears of testifying, one can surmise that in an era in which African Americans did not regularly appear in court proceedings against whites and in which lynching was still all too common, her actions in this case could certainly produce anxiety. By the same token, Webb's testimony in light of these circumstances demonstrated her courage to fight for civil rights.[15]

On March 17, 1945, the Cincinnati FEPC hearings came to an end. Generally speaking, the FEPC had failed. Only three of the firms promised the committee that they would hire African Americans. Moreover, Crosley still refused to hire Willie Webb. At the time of the committee's proceedings, Webb was employed at Cincinnati Industries, a local manufacturer, where she worked as an instructor. But like many women (both white and black), Webb most likely lost her job after V-J Day. Cincinnati war plants, like those all over the United States, shut down after the end of the war, displacing thousands of workers. African American women and men were the first to be laid off and the last to be hired back. In the postwar years, minority workers generally lost their wartime employment gains and returned to traditional jobs such as domestic service, janitorial work, and unskilled day labor. Thus, Webb probably was fired from her job at Cincinnati Industries and found work as a domestic servant or perhaps moved again, seeking better economic opportunities.[16]

What then are we to think about Willie Webb's attempt at economic justice? Although the FEPC failed to satisfy Webb's complaint, the committees' actions did have a beneficial long-term effect. The wartime activities of the FEPC, along with those of civil rights and labor activists, moved the United States closer to a national equal employment opportunity policy. The early 1940s have been called the seedtime for the modern civil rights movement. In the 1960s this movement had a measure of success, with the enactment of several landmark laws, including the 1964 Civil Rights Act, which created the administrative grandchild of the FEPC, the Equal Employment Opportunity Commission (EEOC). Regardless of the recent debates about the effectiveness of the EEOC, it was nonetheless an important milestone in modern civil rights history; a history forged with the courage, dedication, and perseverance of not only government officials and politicians but also common people such as Willie Webb who were willing to fight for democracy at home. Although Webb lost her personal wartime battle for economic opportunity, her efforts helped bring a larger victory against racism and prejudice.[17]

Notes

1. "Estimates of Negro Population in War Production Centers, April 1, 1945," Microfilmed Papers of the President's Fair Employment Practice Committee (FEPC Micro), Reel 5; Testimony of Willie Webb, In the Matter of the Crosley Corporation, Case No. 72, Cincinnati, Practice, Records Relating to Hearings, No. 72–79, 1943–1945, Box 1, Cincinnati Historical Society (CHS); Charles S. Johnson, "Negro Internal Migration, 1940–1943: An Estimate," *Monthly Trends and Events in Race Relations* (August 1943): 10–11; Allan Winkler, "The Queen City and World War II," *Cincinnati Goes to War*, ed. Dottie L. Lewis (Cincinnati: Cincinnati Historical Society, 1991), 3; and Henry S. Shryock Jr. and Hope Tisdale Eldridge, "Internal Migration in Peace and War," *American Sociological Review* 12 (1947): 27–33 [hereafter, Webb Testimony].

2. Kathryn Blood, *Negro Women Workers* (Washington, DC: United States Women's Bureau, 1945), 1–12; and Beverly A. Bunch-Lyons, "And They Came: The Migration of African-American Women from the South to Cincinnati, Ohio, 1900–1950" (Ph.D. diss., Miami University, 1995).

3. Wendell P. Dabney, *Cincinnati's Colored Citizens: Historical, Sociological and Biographical* (Cincinnati: Dabney Publishing Co., 1926), 378–95; Florence Murray, ed., *The Negro Handbook, 1944* (New York: Current Reference Publications, 1944), 184; Gary P. Kocolowski, "The History of Avondale: A Study in the Effects of Urbanization upon an Urban Locality" (master's thesis, University of Cincinnati, 1971); Robert B. Fairbanks, *Making Better Citizens: Housing Reform and the Community Development Strategy in Cincinnati, 1890–1960* (Urbana: University of Illinois Press, 1988), 64–65; Robert B. Fairbanks, "Cincinnati Blacks and the Irony of Low-Income Housing Reform, 1900–1950," in *Race and the City: Work, Community, and Protest in Cincinnati, 1820–1970*, ed. Henry Louis Taylor Jr. (Urbana: University of Illinois Press, 1993), 193–98; and Charles F. Casey-Leininger, "Making the Second Ghetto in Cincinnati: Avondale, 1925–1970," in *Race and the City*, 235–51.

4. Frank W. Quillin, "The Negro in Cincinnati," *The Independent* (February 1910): 399–401; and Andrew E. Kersten, "Fighting for Fair Employment: The FEPC in the Midwest, 1941–1946" (Ph.D. diss., University of Cincinnati, 1997).

5. Statement of Willard J. Schilling, assistant area director of the War Manpower Commission, March 14, 1945, Cincinnati Urban League (CUL) Papers, Box 11, Cincinnati Historical Society (CHS) [hereafter, Schilling Statement]; Theodore M. Berry, "The Negro in Cincinnati Industries: A Survey Summary," *Opportunity* (December 1930): 361–63, 378; and United States Census Bureau, *Sixteenth Census of the United States*, vol. 3, pt. 4 (Washington, DC: Government Printing Office, 1943), 638–39.

6. Letter from Thurgood Marshall to William A. McClain, December 13, 1940, Microfilmed Papers of the National Association for the Advancement of Colored People (NAACP Micro), Part 13, Series A, Reel 17; memo Ernest G. Trimble to George M. Johnson, September 10, 1943, Papers of the President's Committee on Fair Employment Practice, Cincinnati Office General Files, Box 2 (Cincinnati FEPC General Files), CHS; Federal Security Agency, *Workers and the National Defense Program* (Washington, DC: Government Printing Office, 1941), 7, NAACP Micro, Part 13, Series B, Reel 11, 836–57; Office of War Information, "Negroes and the War: A Study in Baltimore and Cincinnati," Papers of President Franklin Roosevelt (FDR Papers), OF 4245 G, Box 7, Franklin D. Roosevelt Library, Hyde Park, New York: Webb Testimony, 114–16; and Kersten, "Fighting for Fair Employment."

7. Schilling Statement; Eileen Boris, "'You Wouldn't Want One of 'Em Dancing with Your Wife': Racialized Bodies on the Job in World War II," *American Quarterly* 50 (March 1998): 77–108; Robert C. Weaver, *Negro Labor: A National Problem* (New York: Harcourt, Brace, and Company, 1946), 78–81; Susan Hartmann, *The Home Front and Beyond: American Women in the 1940s* (Boston: Twayne Publishers, 1982), 77–78; and Jacque-

line Jones, *Labor of Love, Labor of Sorrow: Black Women, Work, and the Family from Slavery to the Present* (New York: Basic Books, 1985), 235–40.

8. Webb Testimony, 112–14; Schilling Statement; and War Manpower Commission, "Adequacy of Labor Supply in Important Labor Market Areas, September 1, 1943," Frances Payne Bolton Papers, Box 72, Western Historical Society Library.

9. Schilling Statement; and Webb Testimony, 112–14.

10. Memo from William T. McKnight to Will Maslow, January 4, 1945, FEPC Micro, Reel 4; and memo from Ernest G. Trimble to George M. Johnson, March 17, 1944, FEPC Micro, Reel 4.

11. Memo from Ernest Trimble to George M. Johnson, September 10, 1943, Cincinnati FEPC General Files, Box 2; and *Cincinnati Post*, March 3, 1942.

12. Memo from James M. Baker to E. L. Keenan, December 6, 1943, War Manpower Commission Records, Series 278, Box 3532, National Archives, Chicago Branch; *Cincinnati Post*, March 3, 1942, 6; *Call and Post*, November 14, 1943, 13; and *A Monthly Summary of Events and Trends in Race Relations*, January 1944, 4.

13. Letter from Harold James to Theodore Berry, March 5, 1945, Cincinnati FEPC General Files, Box 1; Verbatim Hearing Transcripts concerning Crosley Radio, Baldwin, Cambridge Tile, F. H. Lawson, Kirk and Blum Manufacturing, Schaible, Streitmann Biscuit, and Victor Electric, President's Committee on Fair Employment Practices, Records Relating to Hearings, Boxes 1 and 2 (Cincinnati FEPC Hearing Files), CHS; quote from transcript of Crosley Radio Hearing, 86; FEPC, *Final Report* (Washington: Government Printing Office, 1947), 19; *Cincinnati Enquirer*, March 15, 1945, 8; March 16, 15; March 17, 2; *Cincinnati Times-Star*, March 5, 1945, 2; March 16, 32; and *Cincinnati Post*, March 16, 1945, 24; March 17, 2.

14. Transcript of the 2 P.M. session of the March 15, 1945, FEPC Hearing in Cincinnati, Ohio, Cincinnati FEPC Hearing Files, Box 1, file 72.2, 61.

15. Ibid., 112–18.

16. Ibid., 115.

17. Merl E. Reed, *Seedtime for the Modern Civil Rights Movement: The President's Committee on Fair Employment Practice, 1941–1946* (Baton Rouge: Louisiana State University Press, 1991).

Suggested Readings

The primary sources for this essay were the papers of the President's Fair Employment Practice Committee (National Archives Record Group 228), the papers of the War Manpower Commission (RG 211), the microfilmed papers of the National Association for the Advancement of Colored People, and the Cincinnati Urban League Papers located at the Cincinnati Historical Society. Webb's story is largely contained in these archival resources. To find other ordinary women who fought for civil rights during World War II, one might also examine the pamphlets and papers of the United States Women's Bureau (RG 86) and the records of the United Auto Workers (UAW-CIO) at the Walter P. Reuther Library at Wayne State University.

The secondary literature on race, work, gender and World War II is growing rapidly. For the most current work check the following journals: *Labor History, American Quarterly,* and *Journal of American History.* Also examine Eileen Boris, "'You Wouldn't Want One of 'Em Dancing with Your Wife': Racialized Bodies on the Job in World War II," *American Quarterly* 50 (March 1998): 77–108; Andrew E. Kersten, *Race, Jobs, and the War: The FEPC in the Midwest, 1941–1946* (Urbana: University of Illinois Press, forthcoming); Jacqueline Jones, *Labor of Love, Labor of Sorrow: Black Women, Work, and the Family from Slavery to the Present* (New York: Basic Books, 1985); and Susan M. Hartmann, *The Home Front and Beyond: American Women in the 1940s* (Boston: Twayne Publishers, 1982).

15

Ethel Thomas Herold

Doing "Women's Work" in a Philippines at War

Theresa Kaminski

Ethel Thomas Herold (1896–1988) was a resourceful and resilient woman whose life illustrates the ways in which women's varied and vital contributions to community and country have been obscured by the dismissive phrase "women's work." Ethel Thomas was born on March 25, 1896, in British Hollow, Wisconsin, the youngest of five children of Clement and Elizabeth Thomas. British Hollow, a small farming village originally founded by Welsh immigrants in the southwestern part of state, was gradually subsumed by nearby Potosi. Clement, a Welsh immigrant, and Elizabeth, the daughter of mid-nineteenth-century pioneers, expected their sons and daughters to grow up to be useful citizens. According to Elizabeth, gender did not excuse idleness or helplessness. Her eldest son, Bart, first tested those beliefs in 1901 when, infused with progressive idealism, he set sail for the Philippine Islands on the USS *Thomas*. He wanted to teach English and "the principles of American democracy" to the inhabitants of a U.S. colonial possession. One of Ethel Thomas's earliest childhood memories was saying good-bye to her nineteen-year-old brother, who had to stoop down to hug and kiss his little sister. Ethel's mother cried for a whole week after Bart departed on his adventure. Although Elizabeth Thomas respected the teaching profession and wanted Bart to make his mark on the world, she remained afraid that the Philippines was an uncertain and potentially hostile environment. To Elizabeth's great relief, Bart returned from his first teaching job three years later unharmed and very enthusiastic. Young Ethel, who eagerly listened to the family readings of Bart's letters, formed a favorable, if somewhat romantic, impression of the Philippines and its people. This perception shaped her future.

Like her brother, Ethel was expected to contribute her fair share of work on the family farm. Somewhat atypical for the times,

Theresa Kaminski thanks Betsy Herold Heimke for allowing access to her mother's written materials.

Elizabeth Thomas also insisted that Ethel receive a college education and put her training to a practical use for at least five years
before marriage. Elizabeth's attitude undoubtedly stemmed from
her own life, which had been weak on formal education but strong
on the virtues of good, honest work. Elizabeth worked outside of the
home both before and during her marriage to Clement Thomas. At
the urging of his family, Clement turned over the family farm to his
son Fred around 1905 and moved Elizabeth and Ethel into a stone
house in nearby Potosi, which boasted a railway stop and was home
to the Potosi Brewing Company. Clement worked there as a mail
carrier. As much as Ethel had loved the farm, she found that she
loved this new house and life in town even more. Potosi and British
Hollow contained a combined population of about five hundred just
after the turn of the century, and although Ethel claimed that "nothing very exciting happened" there, her days were full with school,
music lessons, and farm work in the summers.[1] She excelled at
academics and gave the valedictory address at her high school graduation in 1913, choosing as her topic the very timely issue of international peace. Even as a teenager, Ethel kept a close eye on world
events; her rural Midwestern roots did not make her provincial.

Upon graduating, Ethel and her mother planned her future.
Ethel reached adulthood during the period of the "new woman,"
when increasing numbers of young, mostly middle-class women
went to college to prepare themselves for a professional career. Elizabeth Thomas thought that higher education would give Ethel self-
confidence and independence. But both mother and daughter
expected marriage to replace the career at some point. Ethel settled
on teaching, but her mother thwarted her decision to teach mathematics, because it was not a "ladylike subject." Despite the fact that
math came easily to Ethel, she compromised and agreed to teach
history and English. In the fall of 1913, Ethel traveled to Appleton,
Wisconsin, where she began her freshman year at Lawrence College,
a Methodist liberal arts institution. In addition to its academic
excellence, Lawrence provided a nurturing religious atmosphere as
well as music instruction, both of which were important to Ethel.

Ethel's transformation into a college coed made her class-
conscious for the first time in her life. She described herself as a
"bashful little country girl" whose bargain-rack and homemade
wardrobe paled next to that of the other female students, yet she did
not let any of that intimidate her. Ethel quickly learned how to
socialize with the other freshman girls who lived with her in the
Ormsby Hall Annex, enthusiastically tackled basic courses in English, history, art, and public speaking, and joined the Choral Club.
During her first few weeks at Lawrence, Ethel met a tall, dark-
haired earnest young man named Elmer Herold. Elmer was work-

ing his way through school, majoring in chemistry and physics with the intention of becoming an engineer. Much of their social life, restricted by Elmer's work schedule, revolved around activities, usually games and costume parties, sponsored by the college's YWCA and YMCA. The young couple observed the proprieties of their day; he called her "Miss Thomas" and she called him "Mr. Herold" during the first months of their courtship.

During her sophomore year, 1914–15, Ethel declared history as her major and found herself in classes with few other female students. Fortunately, her professors tended to encourage her, yet Ethel realized she had to prepare scrupulously for these classes in order to overcome general assumptions of women's intellectual inferiority. The professor of her American politics class, a course with seventy men and only two women, regularly turned to Ethel and her female colleague to hear "women's intuition" on the subject at hand. The head of the Political Science Department chose Ethel and another female student to start a woman suffrage club on campus. During the decade beginning in 1910, the woman suffrage movement gained momentum toward its final successful push for a constitutional amendment allowing women to vote. Carrie Chapman Catt, president of the National American Woman Suffrage Association, encouraged the formation of Lawrence's club and others like it on every college campus across the country, providing informational material for distribution at monthly meetings. Ethel persevered with the Suffrage Club, even though the male students ridiculed it and only about twenty-five female students joined. She wanted the club to be successful, but her interests rested with the History Club because it included men who added "spice" to the meetings. Ethel apparently did not then attach much importance to the voting rights of women. For her, the war in Europe seemed more important, even though the United States was not yet a direct participant.

Ethel's romance with Elmer Herold intensified during her junior year, but that fact troubled her. Ethel intended to abide by her mother's wishes that she teach for five years after college, so marriage in the immediate future was out of the question. With these plans, Ethel typified female college graduates of her time who tended to marry later in life or not at all. Elmer was also not ready to marry. He had borrowed money from his father to pay some of his college expenses and planned to pay off that debt as soon as possible after graduation. Stopping short of a formal engagement, Ethel and Elmer reached a "powerfully good understanding" that sustained them through the remainder of their Lawrence days.

One of Ethel's most unforgettable events that year was helping to plan for an appearance by Emmeline Pankhurst, the noted British suffragist. Pankhurst toured the United States in 1916 to whip up support for suffrage, and she agreed to give a speech in Appleton. Ethel Thomas met Pankhurst's train and sold tickets for her lecture at the Congregational Church. Ethel found Emmeline Pankhurst a "sweet little person dressed in a lovely black evening dress" whose "delightfully firm speech would have made anyone vote favorable for woman suffrage." Other Lawrence students capitulated too: Ethel recalled that Pankhurst's lecture swept away the apathy from the student body, even the fraternity members.

The headiness of Emmeline Pankhurst's visit was topped in June 1916 when Ethel and a friend were chosen by the college Suffrage Club to attend the Republican Convention in Chicago because voting rights for women had emerged as one of the main issues of the presidential campaign. Ethel marched in the pouring rain with other Republican women, each dressed in white, to show their support for woman suffrage. She then witnessed Carrie Chapman Catt's address to the convention, calling for woman suffrage, a plank that the Republicans and their candidate, Charles Evans Hughes, endorsed that year. That summer at home in Potosi was difficult for Ethel as she closely followed the war news, which seemed to get worse each day, and she joined the neighborhood women rolling Red Cross bandages and knitting socks. Ethel also followed the 1916 presidential campaign, especially the suffrage issue. A lifelong Republican, she expected a Hughes victory; she found herself living in a divided household: her father opposed female suffrage, but "to be sure Mamma did not." When Ethel substituted for her father on his mail route for two weeks, she proudly donned the straw hat she had worn during the suffrage march in Chicago. Despite her partisan sentiments, Woodrow Wilson's reelection in 1916 did not bother her, since the Democrats had also embraced suffrage, and she took comfort in the president's promise to keep the country out of war.

Nothing in her studies prepared Ethel emotionally for President Wilson's call for war in April 1917. What had begun as a peaceful final semester of college quickly spiraled into weeks of chaos and personal pain. Elmer Herold immediately applied to the officers' training camp at Fort Sheridan, Illinois, received acceptance, and reported for training in mid-May 1917; he graduated from Lawrence College in absentia. Even though Ethel understood the war intellectually, its causes and effects, the war meant that Elmer was going away and might not come back. That imminent absence prompted the young couple to make a quick decision about their future together. When Elmer visited Ethel on a weekend in early June, the two talked about what lay ahead of them. Before going away, he wanted to be sure of at least one thing—that Ethel would be there for him when he returned. Ethel recognized this as a marriage proposal and quickly said yes, disregarding her promise to her mother about working for five years after college. Elmer gave Ethel his Phi Kappa fraternity pin as a symbol of their engagement, which they agreed to keep secret for a time; after he pinned her, the two "kissed each other more that day than all the other times put together." Both assumed that Elmer would survive the war, but they decided against an immediate wartime marriage so that they would each have time to begin paying off their debts. After Elmer left Fort Sheridan in August for Camp Colt in Gettysburg, Pennsylvania, the couple did not see each other again for two years.

With her long-term future settled, Ethel now had to get through the war years. No one knew how long the fighting would go on, and Ethel wanted to make the best use of her time. During the summer of 1917 she helped her mother with Red Cross projects, helped her father plant a war garden, and pledged not to buy any new clothes, all very typical home-front support activities. For the next two years she wrote daily letters to Elmer and sent him oatmeal cookies and chocolate fudge. When summer ended, Ethel began her first job as a high school history teacher in nearby Lancaster, Wisconsin. She received a salary of $75 a month for nine months and believed herself "mighty lucky to get this good job near home and [at] a top salary for girls." She took a room in a boardinghouse populated by other Lancaster teachers, paying $28 a month for a room and the "very best of food."

The war informed Ethel's teaching: she found that her students could easily relate current events to historical ones, thereby making her job much easier than she had anticipated. When she was not teaching and not at home in Potosi on the weekends, she contributed to the war effort by serving as the head of Food Conservation for Grant County, traveling around providing women with tips on how to use rye flour and bake cakes without sugar. Ethel's talks usually ended with the singing of patriotic songs, including "Loyalty," "Keep the Home Fires Burning," and "When the Boys Come Home." Meanwhile, Elmer, commissioned as a second lieutenant and responsible for training tank recruits, continued his duties in Gettysburg. Ethel knew of his impatience to go overseas but felt relieved that he remained safely within the United States. Almost all the young men she knew from Potosi and Lancaster enlisted during America's first year at war, anxious, like Elmer, to be sent overseas to the front lines.

The summer of 1918 saw the outbreak of the Spanish influenza that killed millions of people around the world. Elmer's almost daily letters stopped for two weeks; then Ethel received a brief note from him stating that he was just recuperating from the flu, but her relief that he had survived the deadly illness was short-lived. Two weeks later she received another brief letter, postmarked New York City, which contained the veiled message Ethel had been dreading: "My Darling Ethel, My wish is coming true. All my love, Elmer." He was on his way to France. The beginning of Ethel's second year of teaching in Lancaster provided an essential diversion from her worries for Elmer's safety: although her history teaching continued to focus on the war, the process of teaching often took her mind off of Elmer. When the Armistice came on November 11, 1918, Ethel was ecstatic. The entire town of Lancaster celebrated; the school closed for the day; and people marched through the streets singing patriotic songs. The euphoria proved fleeting, as Ethel experienced a letdown when her war work ended and the flu epidemic became so serious that Lancaster closed its schools. Ethel did not receive any letters from Elmer until just before Christmas and then learned that he would not come home soon. Influenza raged through January 1919, and Potosi, like other towns across the country, virtually quarantined itself in an attempt to stop its spread. Amazingly, neither Ethel nor her parents contracted the flu, and she resumed teaching in the early spring when Lancaster high school reopened.

Elmer returned to the States in August, and he and Ethel were reunited in Potosi on August 18, 1919, two years after they had last seen each other. Ethel felt overcome by shyness when she saw Elmer in his officer's uniform, but after a few moments alone together in the front parlor of her parents' house, she realized that he had not changed. As attached as they were to each other, they again agreed that an immediate marriage was not possible. Elmer intended to get a job teaching, having given up his dream of engineering school. Through an agency in Chicago he secured a job teaching high school science in Kewanee, Illinois, and signed up for correspondence courses in engineering through the University of Chicago. Elmer then presented Ethel with a diamond ring from Tiffany's, making their engagement public. Ethel and her mother reached a compromise, reducing the five to three years of independence prior to marriage, and Elmer and Ethel planned on a spring wedding. Elmer went off to Kewanee to teach science, and Ethel went back to Lancaster for her third and final year teaching history, spending her spare time sewing items for her hope chest and trousseau. Ethel Thomas and Elmer Herold were married in the late afternoon of June 24, 1920, in her parents' home in Potosi, in front of a fireplace adorned with fresh daisies, with Ethel wearing a dress of white satin trimmed with seed pearls and silver lace.

In the fall the Herolds went to Kewanee, where Elmer resumed teaching. Ethel tried to talk him into letting her take a teaching job as well, but he refused; Elmer intended to support his wife. Ethel eschewed the behavior of the flappers, the most modern young women of the 1920s, and spent her time singing in local churches and doing some mending at the Kewanee hospital. She also joined a missionary society, volunteered for a variety of other church work, and taught herself to type so that she could help Elmer with his schoolwork. The couple spent the summer traveling, visiting both sets of parents and other family members. It was the first time that Elmer met Ethel's brother Bart, who had taught in the Philippines, and Elmer became fascinated with Bart's tales of his experiences. Elmer and Ethel immediately made their minds up to go to the Philippines to teach for two years. After completing the necessary paperwork from the Department of the Interior, they were hired as teachers by its Bureau of Education, to begin in May 1922. Elmer would earn $1,600 and Ethel $1,500. They planned to save enough money to travel to Europe on their way home at the end of their assignment, which Ethel viewed as a "great opportunity to continue the patriotic duty of helping to educate the Filipinos as well as to see the world."

The Herolds were assigned to Banguet, Abra, a remote province on the island of Luzon, containing a population of approximately thirty thousand. The buildings, Ethel noted, consisted mainly of a "great mass of old Spanish stone houses, wooden stone houses with rusty tin roofs, bamboo houses with nipa and palm roofs." Ethel and Elmer decided to share a house with another teacher rather than take the time and trouble to find one of their own, and Ethel quickly adjusted to the several servants who ran the household, enabling her to focus her attention on teaching. Elmer taught both science and English, but all Ethel's classes were English. She found the students ideal: "They listened to every word. There was no disciplining. They were there for business." In addition to the formal teaching, Ethel also taught a bit of practical farming by helping the local children grow crops to augment their diets. The teachers' focus on academics and skilled manual labor fulfilled the two main goals of the Bureau of Education, as both American and Filipino officials believed that the best way to modernize the Philippines was to teach its inhabitants English and an American middle-class work ethic. Ethel thrived in this productive environment, doing work that she loved with the man that she loved.

Her ideal world collapsed just before the second year of their teaching contract when Ethel received word from her brother Bart that their mother had unexpectedly died after a brief illness. Because she was away from home and because her mother had disapproved of the move to the Philippines, Ethel felt the loss even more keenly. She worked through her grief by busying herself with her teaching, and when school let out, Elmer planned diversionary trips for them into remote areas of Luzon. Travel was rough, accommodations simple, and food uncertain, but Ethel absorbed everything with an intellectual curiosity and came to admire the various Filipino peoples they met along the way. One of these trips brought the Herolds to the Igorote Farm School at Trinidad, to which they would later return. As their second year in Abra drew to a close, the Bureau of Education invited them to stay on another year. The young couple, anxious for their European tour, declined. Ethel also wanted to get home to see how her father was getting along, and she and Elmer planned to remain in the United States and start a family while Elmer finally finished his engineering degree. The Herolds' trip home in 1924 took about five months. They traveled through China, saw the Great Wall, then went back to Korea and Japan, where the couple experienced some hostility because of recent U.S. decisions to limit Japanese immigration, and on to India, Egypt, and finally Western Europe.

Once back in the United States, Elmer went back to teaching high school science, working in Kankakee, Illinois, to earn some money before enrolling in an engineering program. Ethel concentrated on writing a book about their experiences in the Philippines, but ultimately no publisher would bring it out. With little to do, keenly feeling the loss of her mother, and no baby on the way, Ethel began to wonder what the future held. That uncertainty did not last long. An agent from the American Book Company who had also worked as a director of education in the Philippines approached Elmer Herold about moving back to the islands to write a general science textbook appropriate for Filipino schools. Ethel eagerly assented because it meant she could resume teaching and because she firmly believed that Elmer was the proper person to write the textbook. So in 1925 the Herolds went back to northern Luzon, convinced more than ever that the Filipinos needed agricultural and manual training bolstered by English-language skills. They settled at the Igorote Farm School at Trinidad, near Baguio, the same one they had visited two years earlier. Elmer and Ethel took up their teaching duties and Ethel essentially coauthored the science textbook with Elmer. When not teaching, writing, and working on the school's farm, Ethel participated in Baguio's considerable social life, especially in bridge tournaments.

The Herolds' successes at the farm school attracted the attention of American officials and businessmen, and Elmer received other job offers, which he turned down in order to continue teaching. According to Ethel, their mission to provide practical training to the Igorotes was not yet complete. But motherhood finally interrupted Ethel's teaching career. The couple had decided to postpone children until they could afford them and used birth control to assist in family planning, but a New Year's celebration evidently disrupted their basic plan. Shortly before the birth of their first child, Clement

William (Billy), in October 1927, the Herolds moved to a house in Baguio. As they were nearing the end of their two-year teaching contract, Elmer finally accepted an offer from Herbert Heald, a veteran of the Spanish-American War, to work as a master mechanic at his lumber mill.

The Herolds lived comfortably, as did most Americans in the Philippines, because wages tended to be high and the cost of living low. The Heald lumber business boomed, securing Elmer's job, and the textbook he wrote sold well enough to pay royalties. The couple used that money to buy shares in a recently opened gold mine at Balatoc. They joined the Baguio Country Club, which was exclusively for Americans and Europeans. Their family grew again in November 1929 with the birth of Elizabeth, whom they called Betsy. Ethel summed up those years in Baguio by observing that they "were fortunate in many ways." Ethel spent the 1930s as a wife and mother, occasionally tutored students, set up a home kindergarten for Billy and then Betsy, sang at Baguio social functions, and helped found the Monday Afternoon Club. More commonly known as the Monday Club, it organized a variety of charitable endeavors and limited its membership to American and European women. Because of her genuine respect and affection for Filipinos, Ethel would not admit that this represented segregation or discrimination. Filipino women operated their own group, the Baguio Club, which Ethel joined as well. In an attempt to coordinate efforts between the two organizations, the officers of the Monday Club invited their counterparts in the Baguio Club to an annual meeting in order to map out charity strategies. Ethel's club and organizational activities expanded to include the YWCA, American Red Cross, and the Philippine Anti-Tuberculosis Board. Although Ethel knew that her family was well-off, she did not think of her activities in terms of being a "Lady Bountiful." Rather, she and Elmer "had learned that to live in a foreign country and to earn one's livelihood there, one must give something of himself to that country."

Except for a six-month vacation to the United States in 1932 and another European tour and U.S. visit in 1938, the Herolds stayed in the Philippines. Although basically untouched by the calamity of the Great Depression, the family proved not so fortunate in evading the disaster that followed closely on its heels: World War II. In 1939, Ethel observed "signs of war around" but did not express too much concern, even though the Japanese had been fighting in China for most of that decade. She noticed increasing American military activity on Luzon, heard more people talking about "if war comes," and learned in 1940 that the U.S. military ordered its dependents stateside. Ethel kept up with the European war news, listened to the accounts of the Japanese invasion of Indochina, but believed that the Japanese would not be capable of more than a blockade of the Philippines. On Monday, December 8, Pearl Harbor Day for those living on the other side of the international date line, Ethel Herold and everyone else living in the Pacific theater finally understood the magnitude of Japanese intentions in that region. After bombing Pearl Harbor, which brought the United States into the war officially, Japanese planes turned on the Philippines, and Baguio was one of the first towns bombed. Ethel acted quickly and decisively from the first. She sent Billy and Betsy to stay with some friends in the mountains, then called all the women she knew to announce the start of first aid classes the following day. With these immediate concerns settled, Ethel began packing because she assumed that she and the children would soon be evacuated to the United States. Ethel also packed a suitcase of clothes for Elmer, since she knew that he would not leave his job. Despite the bombings and blackouts, Ethel Herold and the other Allied nationals believed themselves in only temporary jeopardy.

Over the next few days, authorities rationed gasoline and food, and mail and cables stopped arriving. The last cable Ethel received informed her of her father's death, but she had no time to grieve. As she watched the increasing chaos around her, Ethel realized that help was not on the way, that women and children could not be evacuated from the Philippines, because the U.S. military did not have the capability to rescue civilians. She brought Billy and Betsy back to Baguio, endeavoring to keep the family together for whatever might come. Two days after Christmas the Japanese marched into Baguio; Ethel remembered that the town "fell silently, there was no crash, not a shot fired." When she looked out her window and saw a Heald Lumber truck drive by with a Japanese flag affixed to it, she knew that "the world was fast coming to an end." Elmer sent word from the lumber mill that Ethel and the children should remain in the house. When Elmer returned home from work at the end of the day, Ethel felt quietly optimistic that the Japanese had not shot all the Caucasian men in town. Japanese soldiers arrived at their house later that evening to inform the Herolds they had to go to Brent School for "registration" the next morning.

Registration turned out to mean internment. After gathering all the Allied nationals at Brent School, the Japanese moved them to Camp John Hay. There the Japanese crammed five hundred people into a camp that routinely lodged about sixty Filipino soldiers. They appointed Elmer Herold as liaison and insisted that all communication between themselves and the prisoners be conducted through him. The Japanese laid down a set of intricate rules and ordered the internees to police themselves. The ultimate responsibility for compliance fell to Elmer. This responsibility brought great privileges:

whereas the Japanese separated the other internees by gender and housed them in barracks, the Herolds received private living quarters. During the first few days of internment, it became clear that the Japanese did not intend to provide any kind of support for their prisoners. Elmer and some of the other men organized a Men's Committee and assigned people into work groups to build latrines, haul water, and procure and prepare food. Ethel Herold received the responsibility for coordinating the Women's Committee. Although she did not welcome this obligation, because she knew that other women would come to hate her, she believed that wartime demanded special duties.

Camp conditions were rough, causing the internees to plan and to fight for everything they needed to survive. Ethel worked more than sixteen hours each day just to help keep the camp operating. Even after living quarters had been established, regular mealtimes had been set up, and sanitation had been enforced, most internees lost weight and contracted a variety of illnesses. Ethel, like many of the other women in camp, lost twenty-five pounds during the first month of internment, and she stopped menstruating. A drastic change in diet accounted for these physical transformations, as internee meals consisted mainly of rice and vegetables, sometimes only a spoonful of the latter. Despite their desperate situation, the internees were grateful to be alive. The Japanese did not send the men off to work camps and they did not systematically rape the women. Nevertheless, the internees lost their freedom and had to cope daily with fears about what might happen.

From December 1941 until February 1945, Ethel Herold and her family remained Japanese prisoners. During that time Ethel found her typical duties as wife, mother, and community member challenged, stretched, and altered. In addition to heading the Women's Committee, Ethel also retained the presidency of the Monday Club, which continued to meet in secret for as long as possible to carry out its primary goal of charity. Even under the extreme wartime circumstances, Ethel and some of the other Baguio women recognized that some of the internees were worse off than others. The club women used the organization's money, which they managed to hide from the Japanese, to "give various people in dire need small amounts." Giving money and supplies to people who needed them constituted a joyful part of Ethel's job. Most of her duties, however, proved less pleasant, and she dreaded them. She spent much time mediating quarrels and convincing women to complete their assigned work tasks. Neither of these actions gained her many friends, and Ethel often found herself the object of snippy and hateful gossip. The hatred aimed at Ethel did not directly concern work, for she was not only a supervisor but also a tireless worker; no one in camp could reasonably charge Ethel Herold with shirking. Many women resented her because she had permission to live with her husband and children. It did not matter that the Herolds' marriage was still far from normal, since Elmer rarely spent time in the family's private room, or that his liaison duties kept him at the beck and call of the Japanese day and night. Although the private room enabled the couple to continue living under the same roof, companionship that Ethel found a necessity, she and Elmer did not engage in sexual relations. They had too much work to do, felt too tired all of the time, and once Ethel's menstrual cycle resumed, she worried about getting pregnant. Besides, she reasoned, "How can there be any sexual pleasure with every ear within 200 feet being on constant alert?" For Ethel, their private room was nothing to be jealous about, but to other women deprived of normal family formations, a private room appeared to be just short of heaven.

The war altered Ethel's wifely duties, but it enhanced and highlighted her role as mother. Billy, in his midteens, found the family's room too small and constricting and willingly moved into the men's barracks. Even though Ethel acknowledged that he was growing up, she had a hard time accepting the separation and kept close watch on his activities. Betsy remained with her parents; Ethel constantly feared that the Japanese would take the young women from camp and force them into prostitution, a fear that never materialized. In addition to worrying about her children's physical safety, Ethel worried about their future. Even during the darkest days of the war, she never really gave up hope for an Allied victory, but she realized that would take time, and she intended that Billy and Betsy spend this time productively. When the internees established a school for the children in camp, Ethel made sure that Billy and Betsy attended so that when the war ended they would not be behind in their studies. Ethel also encouraged them to shoulder their fair share of camp labor. She wanted them to learn something from the internment camp experience, not to succumb to monotony and despair.

After the Japanese moved the internees to nearby Camp Holmes in the spring of 1942, Ethel found ways to keep a positive outlook. She considered her time well spent just taking care of her husband and children as best she could, but she also needed an outlet for her private feelings. The Women's Committee planned a dangerous but inspirational project: the construction of an American flag, which Ethel considered an essential element to the Fourth of July celebration. She scrounged through the camp's clothing donations until she located enough red, white, and blue material. Members of the Women's Committee and their friends took turns secretly sewing the flag in Ethel's room. By Independence Day every woman in camp, no matter what her nationality, had contributed stitches to the flag. Throughout internment, Ethel kept the flag carefully hidden, taking it out for quick viewing at selected holidays or whenever anyone needed a special morale boost. She also participated in the camp choir; singing, one of her lifelong passions, helped her to hold on to her sanity. Every time she sang she released her hatred: "It seemed I was talking with God."

Camp life continued with few variations until December 1944. Forty-pound Red Cross comfort kits arrived at Christmas 1943, which probably saved many people from starvation. The Japanese also eventually relented and allowed families to live together if they chose. Although Ethel understood the psychological benefit to this arrangement, she feared that too many women would become pregnant, further stretching the already meager camp resources. Only two women got pregnant, though, but Ethel was right to worry about resources. By the fall of 1944 a small number of internees had died of starvation. Ethel estimated their caloric intake at 650 calories per day. Her weight dropped to ninety pounds, her brown hair turned gray, and she found that no matter how hard she tried, she could not put in a full day's work. Ironically, all this happened when the war had finally turned in the Allies' favor. Internees watched American fighters and bombers fly over Luzon, and rumors spread that General Douglas MacArthur had indeed returned. In response to the Allied advances, the Japanese shut down Camp Holmes at the end of December 1944 and moved all the internees to Old Bilibid Prison in Manila. Exactly three years after she was taken from her comfortable home in Baguio, Ethel Herold stuffed her homemade American flag into her bosom, which made the top part of her faded dress "stick out a bit pre-warish," and climbed on a rickety truck headed for Manila, about 165 miles away.[2]

The internees experienced their worst wartime conditions at Bilibid. The building had been condemned even prior to the war, but the Japanese used it first for military and then civilian prisoners. The floors and walls had holes in them, water was unavailable, flies swarmed, and bombing and gunshots reverberated through the building. Ethel knew that she and her family were starving and that only an Allied takeover could save their lives. Timing was crucial, but the Americans pulled it off: on February 3, 1945, American tanks, heading for the main civilian internment camp at Santo Tomas University, rumbled up to the gates of Bilibid Prison. Japanese soldiers took to the roof in a last-ditch effort to defend the building, but the following day they abandoned the prison to the American forces. As the Japanese soldiers departed, the internees sang a chorus of "The Star Spangled Banner"; then Ethel retrieved the hand-sewn American flag and she and a group of women hung it up for display. The former internees still lived in the middle of a war zone, but now they enjoyed the protection of the United States military and received three square meals a day and medical attention. Ethel put on more than ten pounds in the week or so following liberation. The Herolds were alive, but they had lost almost everything they owned, and the lumber mill where Elmer worked had been destroyed. In early March the family began its journey back to the United States. Billy Herold found space on a ship departing Manila on March 10. Ethel, Elmer, and Betsy followed in mid-April and arrived in San Francisco on May 9.

The Herolds spent a few months traveling, visiting friends and family, and regaining their strength. By the fall of 1945, with World War II finally over in the Pacific, Elmer became anxious to return to the Philippines. He went first, and Ethel and the children returned to Montana so that Billy and Betsy could continue their schooling. That Christmas Ethel found out that she had inherited a farm from Bertha Bonn, a neighbor in Wisconsin who had lent her money for voice lessons when she was in college. The farm would provide the Herolds with a home in the States if the situation proved too difficult in the Philippines. War and internment had not dampened her love for the islands. In the spring of 1946, Ethel left Billy and Betsy in the care of her relatives in Montana, and by June she was back in Baguio with Elmer. Their home had been burned to the ground, so they took up residence in the abandoned Heald house and settled in to help rebuild Baguio, Elmer trying to revive the lumber business and Ethel immersing herself in community work. While traveling through the United States just after their liberation, Ethel had lectured on her wartime experiences and encouraged Americans to donate supplies to the needy Filipinos who had supported the Allied war effort. When she returned to Baguio in June 1946 she unloaded duffel bags stuffed with donations. The Monday Club was in business again. Ethel continued her activities with the Red Cross as well, and she helped support both the YMCA and the YWCA.

The visit of Billy and Betsy during the summer of 1947 showed Ethel just how much she had missed her children, and their departure brought sadness. Ethel plunged deeper into her club work, and she also transcribed and typed the diary she kept throughout the war. Many of her activities mirrored those of her counterparts back in the United States, women eager to return to domestic concerns now that the war ended, but Ethel interspersed her home and community work with travel. She and Elmer returned to the United States in 1949 for a six-month visit and spent some time in the newly renovated Bonn farmhouse. After her return to the Philippines in 1950, Ethel chaired a new Hospital Advisory Board in Baguio, a position that helped her coordinate many club activities and keep her mind off the fact that Billy, now a college graduate and a married man, had been drafted for service in the Korean War. Ethel and Elmer managed a visit with him in Tokyo in 1952 as they traveled back to the States for Betsy's graduation from nursing school and her marriage to Karl Heimke, a lawyer. The celebration was a complete family affair: Billy had been discharged from the service and managed to get to Wisconsin in time for the wedding. Ethel and Elmer returned to the Philippines in November, with Billy and his family soon following. Ethel gloried in community service and in her role as grandmother. In 1956, Ethel and Elmer took a second-honeymoon trip around the world, returning to the Philippines for "one last round." Elmer was nearing retirement age, and it began to show. He spent two months hospitalized with a broken hip shortly after they came back to Baguio.

In the late spring of 1959 the Herolds began their final trip back to the United States, where they settled on the old Bonn farm outside of Potosi. Ethel found herself in great demand as a speaker at local clubs, and she charged a fee for her talks, sending proceeds to the Monday Club in Baguio. Ethel represented the Monday Club at the International General Federation of Women's Club conventions when they met in Milwaukee and Chicago. Yet during all this pleasant rural living, Ethel never forgot her prison camp experiences. Whenever she washed dishes, she thanked God for soap and hot water, basic things she had lacked in Camp Holmes.

Fifty years after he graduated in absentia so that he could serve in World War I, Lawrence College honored Elmer Herold with its Alumni Distinguished Service Award. The couple celebrated their fiftieth wedding anniversary together on June 24, 1970, in front of the same stone fireplace in Ethel's family home where they had exchanged their vows. On August 30, 1971, at the age of seventy-eight, Elmer Herold died in the couple's farmhouse. For Ethel, "life without my husband of 51 years was almost unbearable." She went to live with Betsy for a time and tried to ease her grief by writing an autobiography, which made her feel that Elmer was still with her. When her eyesight began to fail, Ethel moved into a retirement home in Phoenix, Arizona, where she died on March 30, 1988, five days after turning ninety-two. She was buried next to Elmer in the British Hollow Cemetery in Potosi, Wisconsin.

Near the end of her life, Ethel Thomas Herold reflected on her accomplishments. She and Elmer had spent most of their adult lives, about thirty-eight years, outside of the United States, yet their location only reinforced their patriotism and beliefs in what it meant to be American. Ethel believed that she had functioned as the ideal American woman: she took care of her husband and her children and she remained mindful of the needs of those less fortunate than herself. She observed that she and Elmer traveled to the

Philippines "as a patriotic duty. Even though we taught only 4 years, we aimed to be true Americans all the way. When I quit teaching, I lost my pay check, but I never ceased doing for the people. Our experience in teaching taught us to know the people and how to do for them. . . . We had attained the height of luxury and were cut down by the Japanese to the depth of despair, hunger, squalor, drudgery, fear. This was a test of everything within us." It was a test that Ethel did not fail. Wherever she saw problems, she acted to solve them, contributing all she had in the way of ideas, money, resources, and sweat.

Notes

1. Ethel Herold, "Memory Quiz," unpublished autobiography in possession of the author; all quotations from Herold, unless otherwise noted, come from this source.
2. Ethel Herold, "War Diary: December 8, 1941–May 9, 1945," 345, unpublished diary in possession of the author.

Suggested Readings

The unpublished autobiography of Ethel Herold, entitled "Memory Quiz," is in the author's possession. For information on women and farm life in the Midwest, see Katherine Jellison, *Entitled to Power: Farm Women and Technology, 1913–1963* (Chapel Hill: University of North Carolina Press, 1993). A classic study of the suffrage movement is Eleanor Flexner, *Century of Struggle: The Woman's Rights Movement in the United States* (New York: Atheneum, 1971). On World War II and the Pacific theater, see Ronald H. Spector, *Eagle against the Sun: The American War with Japan* (New York: The Free Press, 1985). Published accounts of American women's internment in the Philippines include Natalie Crouter, *Forbidden Diary: A Record of Wartime Internment, 1941–1945*, edited and with an introduction by Lynn Z. Bloom (New York: Burt Franklin and Co., 1980); Margaret Sams, *Forbidden Family: A Wartime Memoir of the Philippines, 1941–1945*, ed. Lynn Z. Bloom (Madison: University of Wisconsin Press, 1989); and Emily Van Sickle, *The Iron Gates of Santo Tomas: The Firsthand Account of an American Couple Interned by the Japanese in Manila, 1942–1945* (Chicago: Academy Chicago Publishers, 1992).

16

Betty Flanagan Bumpers
An "Ordinary Mother" Dedicated to Peace

Paula Barnes

In late September 1982, Senator Jeremiah Denton (R-AL) raged on the floor of the Senate for a period long enough to enter forty-five pages of invective into the *Congressional Record*. The object of the Senator's wrath? Betty Bumpers (b. 1925), the wife of his colleague across the aisle, Senator Dale Bumpers (D-AR). Such an attack on a spouse was highly unusual for the decorous upper house of the Congress, so what did the notorious Mrs. Bumpers do to cause this senatorial condemnation? According to Denton, who claimed to have well-documented information, Bumpers and four other unnamed congressional wives had been in league with the Soviet Union's KGB and were abetting a Communist plot designed to disrupt national security by demanding that both the USSR and the United States abandon nuclear weapons. Denton "offered facts that Peace Links [was] guided by four organizations on the advisory board either Soviet controlled or openly sympathetic with, and advocates for communist foreign policy objectives."[1] It was in part, the truth. As the founder and president of Peace Links, Betty Bumpers had indeed advocated the destruction of the two superpowers' nuclear arsenals, but not as a member of the radical Left or the Communist Party, rather, as an "ordinary mother." The red-baiting directed toward Bumpers and her antinuclear organization was typical of cold war rhetoric. At the same time, Bumpers's group linking Soviet and American mothers in an effort to prevent war echoed earlier efforts by female peace activists, such as those involved in the Women's International League for Peace and Freedom. The new twist was the cold war threat of nuclear annihilation and the postwar reemphasis on motherhood as the primary role for women.

Denton's repudiation of Bumpers and her supporters met a fierce response from other members of the Senate. Senators Paul Tsongas (D-MA) and Patrick Leahy (D-VT) both revealed that their wives had also been involved with Peace Links. Tsongas and Leahy further explained on the floor of the Senate that they had not found any reason to regard their wives subversive. Senator Gary Hart (D-CO) was far more critical of Denton. Disregarding Senate protocol, Hart openly condemned the Alabama senator, claiming that

Denton should be ashamed for raising the specter of "guilt by association," a favorite tactic of the infamous, and by then discredited, red-baiting Senator Joseph McCarthy (R-WI). Senator Dale Bumpers was also incensed and aggressively defended his wife, arguing that "if people engage in appropriate activities to show their commitment to peace—if that becomes subversive, then we can kiss everything this country stands for good-bye." In addition, Senator David Pryor (D-AR) maintained that "Betty Bumpers has had more impact than most on causes that are noble and good—and even holy—in our state and the nation."[2]

But who was Betty Bumpers, and where did she come from? Herman and Ola Flanagan named their third child and second daughter Elizabeth Callan Flanagan. Born on January 11, 1925, Betty grew up in the small farming communities of Grand Prairie and Charleston in western Arkansas. The Flanagans were fairly prosperous farmers, although they struggled to make ends meet during the Great Depression. Besides the farm, Herman also traveled as a salesman and livestock auctioneer. This situation meant that Ola was often left alone to raise her children and run the farm. Betty remembers her mother as a "large woman with powerful strength" and boundless energy. The local Methodist Church served as the cornerstone in the community. Betty Bumpers claims it defined her as "a Methodist Sunday school girl." Betty remembers it was a very simple life, steeped in traditional values and close family ties.

Betty Flanagan married her high school sweetheart, Dale Bumpers. The couple had two sons and a daughter; Dale practiced law and Betty "volunteered for everything." The Bumperses were not overt political activists at first. Nevertheless, they did get involved in the local school board election in 1954, which gave Dale Bumpers an opportunity to help implement desegregation as dictated by the 1954 Supreme Court decision *Brown v The Board of Education of Topeka, Kansas*. Some time later Dale failed in his effort to win a seat in the state legislature. So it came as a surprise to most Arkansans when Dale Bumpers announced that he was running for governor in 1970.

The unknown attorney from Charleston promised "better stewardship of present revenues" and handily defeated former governor Orval Faubus in the Democratic primary and Republican incumbent Winthrop Rockefeller in the November general election. Betty Bumpers wanted her family to have a smooth transition to the Governor's Mansion and claimed that "she was not going to sacrifice her roles as wife and mother when she became First Lady." Yet she understood the pressures of her new public position when she confessed to the *Arkansas Gazette* that her only fear was that she would be "expected to be all things to all people, and everybody will expect a different thing."[3]

That never happened. Betty Bumpers brought her own style to the Governor's Mansion and to the role of First Lady. Perhaps Arkansas was unprepared for such an open and forthright woman as the new governor's wife. Nevertheless, there were no complaints in the press. In fact, Arkansans embraced Mrs. Bumpers and enthusiastically supported her causes.

Betty Bumpers was determined that as First Lady she would use her position and available resources to help move Arkansas forward. There were many problems that demanded her attention; most were the result of generations of segregation and lack of opportunity, manifest in a grinding poverty that reached from the state's northern hills to the Mississippi Delta in the southeast corner. Bumpers found that there was a common denominator—children's health—that affected everyone. This issue had enormous consequences for quality of family life, education, and the overall productivity of each community and the state at large. It was also a familiar issue for her as a mother and as a community activist.

In the early 1970s, Arkansas children lagged behind other states in most national educational standards, in part because of poor nutrition and preventable disease. The federal government was beginning to address these conditions through various programs such as Head Start and subsidized school lunch programs, which were enjoying initial success. Yet there was a severe problem that had been ignored despite reform efforts since the turn of the century—and one that had a relatively simple remedy—immunizations against childhood diseases. By the post–World War II era, vaccines for polio, measles, mumps, rubella, tetanus, pertussis, and diphtheria were available, but fewer than 60 percent of the nation's children were receiving the immunizations. In Arkansas, the 1970 statistic was slightly below the national average, although state law required immunizations before a child entered first grade. Many parents were unaware of the law, did not have the money to immunize their children, or did not have time or transportation to go to doctors, few in number and not well distributed geographically. Lax school policies and inattention to the potential dangers of childhood diseases allowed many parents to enroll unimmunized children in school despite state law.

The medical remedy was simple, but delivery was another matter. Bumpers consulted with numerous officials in the state government, as well as health care workers and community activists. She then presented a plan to her husband that would immunize all school-age children in the state. By 1973, the Arkansas Childhood Immunization Program was under way, funded through a number of grants awarded by various agencies, not taxpayers' dollars. In order to implement the program with limited funds, Bumpers relied on volunteers to assist at every level—including the doctors. In addition, Governor Bumpers mobilized the Arkansas National Guard to ship serum, transport the First Lady and other volunteers, and directly participate in the administration of immunizations. Once coordinated, Every Child by '74 was officially launched in September 1973, on Labor Day, with Betty Bumpers as its chair.

The goal of Every Child by '74 was to immunize 90 percent of the state's five- and six-year-old children. Schools and church facilities opened as temporary clinics. The immunizations were offered free of charge in conjunction with transportation provided by the community. At the end of the Labor Day weekend, 225,000 children had been inoculated. Nonetheless, it was not until 1979 that the Every Child campaign was able to reach its goal. But the effort was viewed as a success and the Arkansas model had come to the attention of various national health organizations. Initially, the Centers for Disease Control (CDC) in Atlanta feared that such voluntary operations would hamper its own immunization program. But with the support of the assistant surgeon general and the National League for Nursing, the CDC later recognized the effectiveness of the Every Child campaign. Together these agencies and the Department of Health, Education and Welfare (HEW) asked Betty Bumpers to launch a national immunization campaign like the one in Arkansas.

The Every Child campaign went national. Typically, the states with the lowest immunization rates were in the South. Consequently, the campaign first targeted Alabama and other Deep South states. Bumpers met with the governor of the designated state to spell out the importance of childhood immunizations and demonstrate cost-effective means to inoculate children. She also asked a prominent woman in the state, usually the governor's wife, to chair a statewide immunization task force to lead volunteer doctors, nurses, and other activists in the project. The national Every Child campaign provided informational and grant-funding resources to assist each state's effort. Bumpers went on national television programs, such as NBC's *Today* show, as well as local talk shows, in order to drum up support for the program and to educate parents of the vital need to have their children immunized. The community-wide campaigns worked. Immunization goals were achieved in state after state thanks to the cooperation among political leaders, community activists, and the medical establishment. In the ensuing years, health officials recognized that children must have the series of immunizations before age two in order to ensure the elimination of childhood diseases. The Every Child campaign adjusted its emphasis to reach parents of infants through the Every Child by Two program. Bumpers expressed her commitment to the benefit of the immunization campaign, proclaiming, "One of the things our children have is a right to expect as a part of their heritage . . . a healthy future."[4] Bumpers remained committed to immunizations throughout her public career. In 1999, President Bill Clinton dedicated a National Institutes of Health AIDS immunization research facility in her name.

In the midst of launching the national immunization campaign, Betty Bumpers had moved her family to Washington when Dale Bumpers was elected to the U.S. Senate. This election also had a Cinderella quality. The two-term governor Bumpers handed a surprise defeat to the venerable senator J. William Fulbright in the 1974 Democratic primary election, and went on to overwhelm his Republican opponent that fall. Two years later, Jimmy Carter, a progressive Southern Democrat who was closely allied with Bumpers, was elected president. The president relied on the senator from Arkansas to support most of the administration's legislative objectives, and Bumpers was not reluctant to support some of Carter's most controversial goals. One of the earliest disputes involved funding the Clinch River breeder reactor, a project of the Tennessee Valley Authority under construction east of Oak Ridge, Tennessee. Although cost overruns were huge and demand for electric power had diminished, the economic issues were not Carter's main concern. The by-product of the Clinch River reactor was weapons-grade plutonium, which was used to manufacture nuclear warheads. President Carter believed that the completion of this type of nuclear reactor sent the wrong signal to the Soviet Union at a fragile moment in postdétente relations between the two superpowers. Bumpers sided with the president, claiming that the project was a "technological turkey."[5] Carter lost the fight to have the reactor project shut down, but Bumpers continued to be an outspoken opponent of the Clinch River reactor until the Congress finally eliminated funding in 1983.

The Clinch River breeder reactor debate signaled a renewed interest in antinuclear activism in the United States. The questions raised about nuclear stockpiles during the early debate became more significant after Ronald Reagan assumed office in 1981 and instructed the Pentagon to "spend what you need . . . defense is not a budget item."[6] The president seemed to be engaging in a dance of death with the "Evil Empire"—the Soviet Union. The fear of nuclear war haunted American households. President Reagan's highly charged rhetoric and increased military spending led many to believe that Armageddon was at hand—a notion that did not escape the Bumpers family.

In the summer of 1981, Betty and her daughter, Brooke, drove from Washington to Arkansas, crossing the Clinch River in east

Tennessee. That prompted Brooke to ask what would happen to her family if a serious nuclear disaster or outright nuclear war occurred. She had just completed her first year of college, and the family was now scattered around the country, so the question had many layers of importance for mother and daughter. Bumpers's immediate response was to soothe her daughter's fears by saying that the family would come home to Arkansas. "But what if Arkansas was gone and there was no home left?" Brooke responded. This was so deeply troublesome for Bumpers that she could not shake it off. For weeks she pondered why a young woman with so much ahead of her would have to be so frightened of the future.

That summer, home in Arkansas, Betty filled her time with family and friends, canning vegetables, making a quilt, and reflecting upon her daughter's fears. Betty grieved deeply over the realization that young men and women, even her own children, had little expectation for the future. She saw a whole generation that believed the world would end before they reached their prime. Why had the bomb become an overarching issue again, and what could Betty Bumpers do to help her children cope with the fear of nuclear war? In her typically pragmatic fashion, Bumpers told the *Arkansas Times*, "I couldn't sit back and wring my hands."[7]

She began to seek answers, asking myriad questions of all, from friends with children to experts on weapons and foreign policy. The general response was brutal: the Reagan administration policy of a conventional and nuclear arms buildup had revived a sense of impending destruction around the globe. Furthermore, Bumpers pessimistically concluded that there was little a homemaker and mother of three could do to change that political reality. Yet, a grassroots movement that decried nuclear weapons was spreading from Europe to the United States, and there was a hint that the dynamic could change. Betty Bumpers sensed an opportunity in the growing international antinuclear weapons sentiment.

The Nuclear Freeze Movement had its origins in Greenham Common, England, where American Pershing II midrange nuclear weapons were deployed to support the NATO strategy of a prolonged nuclear war against the Soviet Union staged in Europe. The British prime minister, Margaret Thatcher, was a strong supporter of President Reagan's nuclear policy. But women in England demanded that the weapons be removed from installations in the United Kingdom. To press the government for weapons removal, hundreds of women and children camped out at the Greenham base for extended periods of time—some for years. The Reagan-Thatcher hard-line position vis-à-vis the Soviet Union increased the outrage of the militant antinuclear activists and helped promote the goal of reversing the NATO arms deployment throughout western Europe.

In the United States, concerned New Englanders also initiated protests against the American military policy. Randall Forsberg, a former defense analyst with the Stockholm International Peace Research Institute; religious leaders such as the Reverend William Sloane Coffin, director of the National Committee for a Sane Nuclear Policy (SANE); along with other old-line pacifist organizations, joined forces with the growing Nuclear Freeze movement. They sought to get both the United States and the Soviet Union to freeze their nuclear arsenals at current levels in order to advance long-term arms-limitation talks. Bumpers viewed the freeze initiative as a reasoned approach to the problem but was uncertain whether it was a viable concept in more politically conservative Arkansas. The only way to find out was to ask Arkansans what they thought about the arms race.

But first, Bumpers hosted a coffee klatch in Washington to which she invited a number of Washington friends and associates, mostly like-minded congressional wives. It was more than a friendly get together; Bumpers sought insights from this group of well-connected, highly informed women. They considered two overarching questions: was the nuclear freeze a feasible approach to arms limitations, and could Reagan's foreign and military policies be adjusted to meet the freeze solution? Moreover, Bumpers asked them to envision the best means for women to confront such formidable issues. The women concluded that the freeze was a first step approach to eliminate the threat of nuclear war—public approval for the freeze would force the president to reassess his defense budget and Soviet policy.

They proposed a grassroots campaign to support the nuclear freeze idea. Betty Bumpers had the most experience in constituent organizing; the childhood immunization campaign would serve as a prototype to launch an educational campaign to ban nuclear weapons. Bumpers agreed to establish a model organization in Arkansas designed to bring mainstream women into the complex nuclear policy dialogue. Thus, Peace Links, an organization for women against nuclear arms, was born, not as a new entity to supersede other pacifist groups, but rather as a means to link women through established community, political, or religious organizations.

Bumpers returned home to Arkansas to assist women in Little Rock and other major towns in the state to develop chapters of Peace Links. She met with women from the immunization drives and other activist efforts, as well as Sara Murphy, a former educational specialist on Governor Bumpers's staff. The immunization program provided an established network of activists. Sara Murphy brought years of experience in political organizing, social concern, and a journalist's skill to simplify complicated issues. The two women became close friends and working partners. Bumpers was all ideas and energy. Murphy harnessed that energy, refined the ideas, and gave Peace Links a coherent message.

The Arkansas model was initially an educational resource to familiarize women with the issues. Murphy applied a technique she had used as a civil rights activist: panel discussions for communities struggling to understand the changing society.[8] Similarly, the Arkansas Peace Links organized panel discussions about the nuclear arms race, with Betty Bumpers as a leading speaker, accompanied by other well-informed community leaders. Numerous churches, women's clubs, parent-teacher organizations, and neighborhood groups sponsored panels. This was, as Bumpers often said, American democracy at its very best: small groups of individuals coming together to understand and solve a difficult and dangerous problem—in this case, to end the threat of nuclear war.

Arkansas Peace Links was an immediate success in demonstrating that mainstream women—mothers, wives, daughters, homemakers, workingwomen—could be mobilized to shift U.S. foreign policy. The supporting congressional and gubernatorial wives mobilized, too. They led the effort to expand Peace Links, and by the end of 1983, chapters had been established in twenty states. Within a year the number of state organizations doubled. The mission became clearly focused on educating the public about the mounting dangers of increased military spending and to bring political pressure on the president and Congress to reverse the upward spiral of the arms race.

Ultimately, Bumpers and the Peace Links leadership came to understand that the dialogue had to go beyond talking to one another. Critics of the freeze movement asserted that it was an enormous security risk to promote a unilateral arms reduction while the Soviet Union seemed impervious to the call for limited nuclear stockpiles. Massive antinuclear demonstrations throughout Europe and the United States had little impact on the Kremlin old guard. Consequently, for the threat of nuclear war to end, direct dialogue between the people of the United States and the Soviet Union was required to initiate a dramatic change in cold war relations. Could Peace Links promote this sort of international dialogue? Bumpers was certain that American women had much in common with Soviet women. She contended that cold war rhetoric by the state did not reflect the basic human need for a stable family and community environment. Her view was that women are the nurturers of every society and hold the same fears and hopes, which transcend politics or military aggression. If women from opposing nations were given the opportunity to develop relationships based on common maternal or nurturant goals, a mutual strength would emerge, which could be the basis for more positive international relations. Frequently, this principle was underscored by the notion that men created the nuclear arms mess, and it was, as Eleanor Roosevelt had once stipulated, "up to the women" to change things.[9] Bumpers called it a "mindshift towards peace," and Peace Links was prepared to serve as facilitator for a huge cold war mindshift.

During the 1983 summer recess, the Senate sponsored a bipartisan trip to the Soviet Union for its members and their spouses. That gave Betty Bumpers her first opportunity to travel to the Soviet Union and meet with representatives from various women's groups and professions. She discovered that although the two economic systems had provided very different environments, Soviet women were, as she had believed, very much like American women. Conditions were harsh, available housing was limited and cramped, there were few quality consumer goods, and the food supply lacked variety. Yet the Soviet women displayed what Russians call *uyutnost,* a nourishing spirit that endures all tribulations of life. Betty listened to women from Moscow and Leningrad to Tashkent speak about their needs, personal wishes, and goals for their families. The Soviets exhibited the same concerns as Americans: how to cope with jobs and family responsibilities, what would the world be like for their children, would the earth even survive? They asked if the American people hated the Soviet people. Was the cold war about personal hatred? Jointly, American and Soviet women concluded that it was not and made overtures to work together for the end of East-West tensions.

When she returned home, Bumpers, the National Peace Links board, and leaders from the Arkansas Peace Links began an exchange program to bring Soviet women to the United States to experience "everyday life" and engage in open dialogues about the arms race. Peace Links extended an invitation to Ksenia Proshurnikova, vice president of the Soviet Women's Committee, to send a delegation of fifteen women to visit the United States. The trip was nearly derailed by strains in U.S.-Soviet relations. However, in late October 1985, the first in a series of women's peace exchanges took place. After opening roundtable sessions in Washington, the delegation divided into three groups, which were sent to different parts of the country. The Soviets stayed in the homes of Peace Links members in order to experience everyday life in the United States, complete with dirty dishes, carpools, laundry, movies, pizza, and potluck suppers. The cornerstone of each exchange was the professional and educational program, which offered unique opportunities for women to explore how "the other side" worked. Both sides avoided political posturing, and the combination of the experience of daily life and professional collaboration provided the basis for the development of international friendships. This was a unique framework where women from both sides of the cold war could openly share ideas about everything from raising children to arms reduction.

The initial Peace Links exchange trip to the Soviet Union was scheduled to take place the following year, 1986. Mikhail Gorbachev had come to power and implemented perestroika to reform the economic and political systems of the USSR. The policy was accompanied by the free exchange of ideas, or glasnost. The result was a flood of social and political changes that cascaded throughout Russian society. While Peace Links and the Soviet Women's Committee were working out the agenda for the American visit, aides in the Kremlin and the White House busily arranged a summit meeting for President Reagan and Communist Party leader Gorbachev. The two men abruptly agreed in private exchanges to hold an interim summit in Reykjavik, Iceland. During the preliminary meeting, Gorbachev, in a surprise move, suggested that both sides drastically reduce their nuclear arsenals within ten years. Reagan responded by proposing that all ballistic missiles be eliminated, an extraordinary gesture in the history of nuclear arms negotiations, but such a plan would leave the United States with an advantage of nuclear-armed aircraft. Gorbachev countered that he meant *all* nuclear weapons. Historians reported that Reagan stated quickly, "That suits me just fine."[10] In the end, neither man could find a way to make the proposal official doctrine so that it would be respected in the ongoing Geneva arms control talks. The grandiose disarmament scheme was not well received by American defense officials; nonetheless, the Reagan-Gorbachev meeting was a hopeful sign for the peace movement. The "mindshift" was under way.

The U.S.-Soviet summit, and weather conditions, postponed the first Peace Links visit to Moscow until spring 1987. Bumpers, Sara Murphy, and several congressional wives met with the Soviet Women's Committee in plenary sessions before the full Peace Links delegation would arrive later that year. Armand Hammer, CEO of Occidental Petroleum and one of the few Americans to have penetrated Soviet power circles, arranged for Bumpers to meet privately with Raisa Gorbachev, wife of the Soviet leader. The two women discussed some of the most critical problems facing Soviet women. Raisa Gorbachev, a sociologist, was concerned with the impact of alcoholism on Russian families, and her determination was to have Peace Links and the Soviet Women's Committee focus on ways to solve basic family problems. They concluded that women's concerns were the building blocks to strengthen future relations between the United States and the Soviet Union. The hope for ending cold war tensions rested on an open rapport between people of the two nations, and women were the essential component to permanent cultural diplomacy.

During this visit, Peace Links and the Soviet Women's Committee created a four-part working agreement that formulated a continuing quasi-official relationship. This agreement included mutual education programs for peace, networks to empower women in the work place and at home, and a means to have women contribute to the international dialogue of nuclear arms control and foreign policy.

The first formal Peace Links visit was made up of a combination of congressional wives and grassroots activists who were professional women, journalists and lawyers, several homemakers, and one farmer. Each American was paired with a Soviet guide for the trip to Leningrad, Moscow, Georgia, Estonia, and Uzbekistan, where they were exposed to daily life in the Soviet Union. This formula of combining the everyday experience with professional development had become the hallmark of the peace exchanges. Tass, the Soviet news agency, followed the tour, reporting on the workings of the two women's groups; Tass quoted Bumpers saying that she "hadn't been able to even imagine that American and Soviet women had so many common views and problems." According to Tass, Bumpers said, "Everybody should be in the peace movement and [Peace Links] would maintain its anti-war campaign until everybody realized the mortal danger of nuclear conflict."[11]

The danger of nuclear conflict subsided with the end of the cold war, but the women's exchanges continued and flourished. Although the collapse of the Soviet Union signaled new opportunities for peace, it brought hardships for Russian citizens. Bumpers sought practical means for Peace Links to assist its many friends and others seeking help from the West. Peace Pals, a pen pal correspondence program, was initiated to generate direct communication between Russia and U.S. citizens. Peace Links placed advertisements in Russian newspapers seeking interest in the program. Bumpers expected only a handful of responses, but thousands of letters poured into the Washington office with requests for friends or partners interested in business deals or marriages; many sought educational tools, such as access to English language books or journals, and frequently individuals asked for medicines and medical equipment. Peace Links had an enormous task to translate, document authenticity, and match Russian correspondents with Americans. The result was gratifying for Bumpers and those closely involved with this project. There were a few marriages, several business ventures, but for the most part the Peace Pals program was an extension of the peace exchanges. It allowed many more individuals to establish friendships and expand the daily lines of communication between Russia and the United States.

Peace Links continued to promote cultural exchanges with its primary goal to assist Russian women in learning the skills needed to establish and support their fledgling democracy. In addition, Betty Bumpers saw the need to help women from all over the former Soviet Union; therefore, Peace Links had to expand its contacts to include women from the Islamic republics of the south as well as those in eastern Europe and the Baltic states. American women supported the new programs designed to teach entrepreneurship as well as democracy building. On the eve of the fifteenth anniversary of Peace Links, there were approximately 40,000 grassroots members as well as 150 congressional wives actively engaged in supporting the former Soviet Union in its transition to democracy and the free market economy.

Betty Bumpers recognized that the democratization of Russia has been a process of blending centuries-old cultural traditions with western political and economic forms—a process that demands patience and a thoroughly engaged dialogue between the governments of the United States and the former Soviet Union. Moreover, it requires mutual involvement between the people of these states. The nearly bloodless end of the cold war was an extraordinary achievement. Peace Links contributed to that end. But Betty Bumpers also understands that much more work is required to further develop friendships and continue peaceful relations among former enemies.

To this end, Bumpers continues to be a highly effective spokeswoman for the peace movement. Her position of political wife opened doors, but her role as an "ordinary mother" is a useful image for encouraging other women that they too can access the foreign policy establishment through nontraditional means. The various projects initiated by Peace Links gave women a voice against violence on all levels. It signaled a hopeful future for all the world's children, and to Betty Bumpers, that meant that the democratic process works.

Notes

1. Senator Denton of Alabama, Senator Leahy of Vermont, Senator Tsongas of Massachusetts, Senator Hart of Colorado, Senator Bumpers of Arkansas, Senator Pryor of Arkansas speaking for the Senate Resolution in support of National Peace Day, *Congressional Record.* 97th Cong., 2d sess., September 29, 1982, vol. 128, no. 132.

2. Ibid.

3. Quotations and personal reflections from Betty Bumpers gathered in a series of interviews conducted by Paula C. Barnes, 1989–1995, Special Collections, Mullins Library, University of Arkansas, Fayetteville; *Charleston (Ark.) Express*, June 18, 1970; Betty Fulkerson, "Future Lady Plans New Phase of Family Life," *Arkansas Gazette*, January 3, 1970, 1D.

4. Betty Bumpers speech, untitled, no date, Special Collections, University of Arkansas Mullins Library, Fayetteville.

5. Arkansas *Gazette*, September 30, 1982, 1; Bumpers repeatedly used this phrase in debates during the Carter and Reagan administrations.

6. Michael Schaller, *Reckoning with Reagan* (New York: Oxford University Press, 1992), 47.

7. Cover story and headline, *Arkansas Times*, August 1985.

8. Sara Murphy coordinated the Arkansas Panel of American Women, 1963–1972; the Panel of American Women was an organization of women from various ethnic and religious groups who sought to end discrimination through civic education; Papers of Sara Alderman Murphy, Special Collections, University of Arkansas Library.

9. Eleanor Roosevelt, *It's Up to the Women* (New York: Oxford University Press, 1992), 47.

10. Michael Beschloss and Strobe Talbott, *At the Highest Levels: The Inside Story of the Cold War* (New York: Little, Brown and Co., 1994), 8, 113.

11. The Russian Information Agency Itar-Tass, October 19, 1987, Lexis-Nexis News Service reported the English translation.

Suggested Readings

Primary sources used to write this chapter include a series of interviews conducted with Betty Bumpers between 1989 and 1997. Additional interviews of the Every Child campaign and Peace Links participants from state and local activists to national leaders were also used. Interviews of women from the former Soviet Union who participated in the exchange programs have been utilized. Assistance was provided by the National Peace Links office in Washington, DC, and Senator Dale Bumpers's offices in Washington, and Little Rock, Arkansas. A sample of secondary sources include Jean Bethke Elshtain, *Women and War* (Chicago: University of Chicago Press, 1995), in which Elshtain presents images of women and war through the ages as a means to understanding the cultural meaning of war for women. Particularly pertinent is her discussion of women and the nuclear arms race. Former Democratic congresswoman and vice presidential candidate Geraldine Ferraro explores politics from an insider's perspective in Geraldine Ferraro, *Changing History: Women, Power, and Politics* (Wakefield, RI: Moyer Bell, 1993). Betty Bumpers derived much of her understanding of the gendered concepts of war and peace from Carol Gilligan's groundbreaking *In a Different Voice: Psychological Theory and Women's Development* (Cambridge: Harvard University Press, 1982). Susan M. Hartmann's *From Margin to Mainstream: American Women in Politics since 1960* (Philadelphia: Temple University Press, 1989) is a very useful bipartisan look at women and politics in the post–World War II United States.

17

Margarita "Mago" Orona Gandara
Frontera Muralist / Artist

Miguel Juarez

Although rarely studied, the contributions of Latina women along the U.S.-Mexico border should not be underestimated. Within this history lies the shared experiences of Mexican American, Chicana, and Mexican women. Despite the similarity of ethic culture in this area, the U.S.-Mexico border separates two distinct countries: a first world power, the United States, and a third world emerging political-economic power, Mexico. On the U.S. side, there are high rates of poverty and unemployment. In contrast, in the Mexican border region a booming economy exists that contrasts with the rest of the country as well as with the communities on the U.S. side of the border. Consequently, during the late twentieth century, Latina women living along this 2,000-mile-long border have been forced to balance a unique mix of political, social, and economic factors.

The primary struggle of the Mexican American, Chicana, and Mexican women in the border region has been against well-established patriarchal structures. These include conditions within the family, where males have traditionally been seen as the head of household. Consequently, there has been a lack of financial resources for women's independence or for their higher education. Traditional religious beliefs have limited access to birth control and abortion, which has resulted in high pregnancy rates and larger families among Latina women than in the general U.S. population. In recent years the maquiladora/assembly plant industries built on the Mexican side of the border have further complicated the story. Latina females, considered passive workers by the plant owners, are the desired labor pool in these factories. Economic opportunities of this kind have altered male-female relations in some Latina families. In addition, recent union organizing efforts on both sides of the border contradict the perception that Latina women are passive. Indeed, despite gender stereotypes, Latina women have long drawn on the spirit of Las Adelitas, females who took up arms during the Mexican Revolution of 1910 to gain rights and improve conditions in the U.S.-Mexico border region.

In general, however, the contributions and independence of Latina border women have gone unrecognized. In what is considered one of the last American frontiers, Latina women along the U.S.-Mexico border have ultimately had to find a voice for themselves. One of these voices is that of the Chicana-Mexicana artist, Margarita Orona Gandara (b. February 8, 1929). "Mago" ("magician" in Spanish, a nickname for Margarita) is one of the region's cultural treasures. With dual citizenship in the United States and Mexico, Gandara is a product of the historic migration of people who move back and forth along one of the most populated regions of the U.S.-Mexico border. More specifically, she belongs to a select group of individuals who are truly border artists: persons who live and produce art in both the United States and Mexico and who have learned to live, negotiate, and navigate the "borderisms" on a daily basis.

Mago Gandara's art reflects the essence of the U.S.-Mexico border region, an area "where many different cultures 'touch' each other and the permeable, flexible, and ambiguous shifting grounds lend themselves to hybrid images. . . . By disrupting the neat separations between cultures, [border artists] create a culture mix, *una mestizada*, in their artworks." Gandara epitomizes what various writers describe as *en nepantla*, "a constant disorientation in space," which mesitzas/os experience on a daily basis when they cross back and forth over the border. In Gandara's case the personal illuminates the historic presence of Latina women and their work, which is "an exciting cultural phenomenon as real as the historical existence of the borderland itself."[1]

During the twentieth century, most Chicano/a artists have worked in obscurity. Furthermore, mural painting is an art form dominated by males. Therefore, it should not be surprising that Gandara's work has generally been overlooked in established art circles in the United States. In addition, in the early part of her artistic life, Gandara followed her husband in his career changes and relocations. In her article "Feminism and the Chicano Artist," Shifra M. Goldman argues that women artists like Mago Gandara have to "juggle the duties of a lover, wife, mother, and worker with [their] creative work" while at the same time being "sufficiently self-confident and assertive to obtain exhibition space or commissions." Primarily working in El Paso, Texas, and Ciudad Juárez, Chihuahua (cities with a combined population of about 1.5 million), Mago has struggled mostly on her own with scant funds. In her journal she notes, "As a young woman entering marriage, I knew the terrible ambition for my art would [create] stress. After all, history is full of successful male artists who made art their prime pursuit. Usually the woman was a means or a help to this end." Mago asks, "And what of the woman who has family? How can she possibly be loyal to her deep intellectual commitment of discovering beauty and the equally intense maternal protectiveness born with her children?" Her answer: "I made the decision then—that whatever my life, however mundane or trivial my function as a wife and mother seemed in our society, *that to me it would be the course of my touching, and from this prime center I would create my art.*"[2] It was not because she was catering to period art movements that Mago produced murals, but because she was compelled to make art.

Many artists strive to be included in major museum collections. Yet Mago explains that much of her art remains in the local community because she is inspired by the people she involves in her work. Although her work remains in virtual obscurity in U.S. art circles, in Mexico, in the state of Chihuahua and the city Juárez and in Colonia Libertad, the community where she resides, Mago Gandara is highly celebrated and respected. In her *colonia* she has produced fantastic murals on the walls of her studio for the people in her community to enjoy. In essence, the works and their process of creation are now a part of the history of that community—in contrast to the U.S. situation, where art is mainly relegated to objectification.

Mago's works, with their elements of movement and color and her use of mosaic technique, have increasingly become sculptural and architectural, thereby going beyond the basic definition of murals. Mago employs fragments of brightly colored glass, tile, and other materials as a painter would use paint. Works created in this medium are more durable than painted murals and better tolerate the harsh southwest desert. Her murals, enmeshed with the local ethos of the border region, are best described as a constant motion of images but architectural and machinelike. According to Chicano art historian George Vargas, Gandara's work "impacts the 'invisible ones' who are not politically or economically powerful in the border zone, the 'other' people to whom she dedicates her life's work, to educate and enlighten their communities."[3] A good example is Gandara's mosaic mural "La Niña Cosmica/The Cosmic Child," located on an exterior wall of the Douglass Elementary School's cafeteria in El Paso, Texas. Mago's decision to create the mosaic mural in that particular spot stemmed from her observation that before creating the mural, the schoolchildren walked in single file, many with their heads hanging down, to the cafeteria. After the mural was erected, the children had a reason to look up. In essence Mago gave them a reason to hold their heads high. To look at the mural as they make their way to cafeteria, the children are given the opportunity, in Mago's words, "to ponder and to dream." At the same time, the image of La Niña Cosmica in the context of the school can be seen as a guardian image for the children. The following interview, conducted in 1997 by the author, places Mago Gandara's artwork within the context of the U.S.-Mexico border region and exemplifies the role of Latina women artists in this exciting cultural area.

Mago: My history, Miguel, goes way back. I was born in 1929, so I'm a walking treasure. And, I am so tied/*ligada* with the Mexican and the United States side[s] that it has influenced my whole personal life and artistic life. My father was José Felix Gandara. He was born in Chihuahua [Mexico]. My mother was Eulalia Malvina Armendariz. She was born in Guadalajara [Mexico].[4] Her family moved to San Francisco and my grandmother educated her. But my father remained a bohemian, a photographer, a little bit of a wild man, and a lover of Mexico, to the bitter end. He never became an American citizen.

My mother and father had . . . three boys. I was not yet even thought of, but my father joined the Cristero Movement, which was a movement in Mexico, where the Villistas were hanging, torturing, mutilating revolutionaries who were defending the clerics against Pancho Villa—a kind of reverse revolution. My father gathered the wealthy of El Paso [Texas] to give him money to smuggle arms into Mexico to protect the clerics.

At that time, my mother was ready to give birth to her third son, my brother, and she was in the old Hotel Dieu. She had to have armed guards, because her life had been threatened [due] to my father's activities. My father was very Catholic and very Christian. He smuggled the arms but he got caught. He [was] thrown into prison and the *El Paso Times* headlines read: "Gandara to Be Executed in the Morning." So I suppose through money [bribes], he had a reprieve. He was released at the last minute. In other words, he wasn't hanged, but my mother told me he changed completely. He started drinking whiskey and smoking cigars, waiting to be shot. And when he came back to El Paso, the church for which he thought he was fighting excommunicated him! So he got kicked out by Mexico. President [Herbert] Hoover kicked him out and the church kicked him out. Well, he had to start all over and I learned so much.

My father went to Rome, beat, if you can imagine and he went to Saint Peter's to get back into the church and he went to the shrine of Santa Margarita. And he said, "Santa Margarita, give me a little girl and I'll call her Margarita." So, with that promise, to that shrine, and the grand St. Peter's, and the Holy Father the Pope, my father came home, made mad love to my mother and was born to them twins—Margarita Eulalia and my twin brother, Luis Ramon. So my history begins with Mexico and its Revolution and I am very aware [of] and live and understand the tension we have on this border.

MJ: Where were you educated?

Mago: I went through all the things we all go through to go to school, but destiny chose a path for me and I was to learn more out of school than in school. I got a masters [degree]. I did all the things

you were supposed to do. I obeyed. But at eight years old I contracted rheumatic fever, which meant, in those days, [that] you had to go
to bed. There was no penicillin. So at eight years old I was in bed for
one whole year. And then another year, learning to walk again
because rheumatic fever damages the heart valves. My mother,
being a pharmacist, just took exquisite care of me and I had to obey
and stay in that bed. At five years old I was already a dancer. I did
classical ballet. I [also] did Mexico and folklorico and Spanish classical [dance]. I can remember the teacher saying, "¡Miren, miren a
Margarita!/Look, look at Margarita!" And I was just [a] little thing.
I loved it. But because of the rheumatic fever, and the danger to the
heart, I could no longer dance. . . . One day, when I was eight years
old, I was sitting on the front porch. I had to take sunbaths and I
was chewing a carrot and into the top of my head came the
thought—I will be an artist! And I will teach art. That's an eight-
year-old kid! So, the education meant that I had to do my homework
at home, third, fourth grade, long division, fractions—all this stuff.
And I grew nice and fat. They called me "La Gorda/the Chubby One."
But there is the destiny, yes education. But the education was
always in my personal life.

MJ: You later studied at Otis Parson?[5]

Mago: Just for a little term. I always loved to go to school just for
a little while. I can't stand being pressed down with classrooms and
rules, which is the reason I don't teach in schools. I had gone to the
Chicago Art Institute because I had taught and had saved a thousand dollars. But I then wanted to be married because I thought I
was going to be quite a misbehaved young woman if I didn't do
something more conservative. So I said, "Well, you better get married." So I chose, with a great deal of trauma, marriage. I thought I
was going to be Miguel Angel (Michelangelo)! That's all right, that
was young ambition. But instead of being Miguel Angel, I had five
babies! So this meant that I used that environment to create my art.
My revolution wasn't a Chicano revolution, of the streets, of the bar-
rios. It was a feminine revolution, certainly Chicana, because a Mexicana woman had to stay home and take care of her kids and behave.
But I did the art all the time! I drew and sketched and did sculpture.
The house looked like an art school. These children grew up in this
incredible environment of art and today they're grown men and
women highly sensitive to beauty in the arts.

I went to California where I married. I went to the University of
Southern California and took a course in sculpture and I remember
the teacher saying, "You're very gifted, but why are you so nervous?"
Well, I had to get home to those five kids, and my husband scolding
me and I didn't have a ride; no wonder I was nervous. So I always
had this terrible tension of being a mother and a woman, which I

wanted to be, and being an artist, which I demanded to be. And it's merged now, thank God. I'm free of those scruples and those trials. I am an artist.

As a family, we traveled to Mexico, to Guadalajara, and I saw the murals of Siquieros, Orozco, and I was awed! I knew that this was my destiny. I told you I wanted to be Miguel Angel. Well, I didn't want to be Miguel Angel anymore. I wanted to be a *muralista*/muralist. So, I began. I had no money. I had very little support from my family. I bought four big panels, four by eight, my brother made them for me, and I did a big, huge male nude depicting the Epistles of Saint Paul . . . of searching the depths. I thought it was a religious piece. And when my husband took one look at it, he thought I was perverted or something; so again, the conflict. Nonetheless, that was my first mural.[6] And from there I let loose with portable panels. I did the whole "Credo," so as to solve this conflict of religion, family, and the freedom of the artist. I interpreted as best I could, the feeling of Beethoven's "La Missa Solemnis," because he's such an architect! Huge spaces. I got sponges, and man, I drew and painted and I just let loose and created this and got well, mentally. I was no longer [a] subject.

MJ: Mago, you were also a contemporary of Manuel G. Acosta when both of you were students at the College of Mines?

Mago: Oh yes. I was ahead of him because he was in the war [World War II]. Manuel was a little bit older than I was, but again, that connection with Mexico through Manuel Acosta and his great environment [was very valuable]. Ricardo Sánchez, the late poet, said of Manuel when he died, talking about us Chicanos, "You have laminated us with the beauty of ourselves." So, there's this pride in our beauty! The beauty of the whole human race, the cosmic beauty. This theme has carried me to my more recent murals—this pride of self.

MJ: At that time Urbici Soler was your teacher?

Mago: In college, at the university, at UTEP, which was the College of Mines and Engineering, yes, Soler, who did the "Cristo Rey" (a monumental sculpture atop Mt. Cristo Rey overlooking Mexico and the United States). He saw me and said, "You are a rebel!" because I wouldn't draw the way you're supposed to draw, but I conformed. I listened to him. He would say to us, "Don't breathe, you hold your breath at the awe!" It touched me. He taught us those first magnificent lines. He'd say, "You're not Picasso yet. Draw as you see it now." And I learned.

MJ: Mago, I want to talk about the major works in your career. One of them was the "Time and Sand" mural, which you created over several years, when you were an instructor at El Paso Community College.

Mago: Well, that's very exciting. An art friend said, "Hey Mago, they have a grant—[National Endowment for the Arts] Expansion Arts at the community college. They need something zany. Why don't you go apply?" So I applied, and I said, "Look, I'd like to do this mural." I think I had a sketch. And they just said, "Yeah, sure, go ahead." They didn't believe I would do it. At that time the college [El Paso Community College] was at Ft. Bliss. It was Ft. Bliss in the sand—Logan Heights with quonset huts; little wooden shacks. I said, "What is here? Sand!" At this time I was single again. I had decided that [after] twenty-five years of marriage, I had done not only my duty, but had given a great deal of love, but I wanted to be free. So I was free when I did the "Valle Verde" mural and that was my, what can you say, cum laude expression of freedom! And I designed in my mind's eye, a huge relief mural that would be created on the sand, cast in the sand, and combine technology, world technology, computerized technology with Pre-Columbian sensibility. That's been my theme from then on. It's very exciting to me, because I see in Pre-Columbian work images of our computer shapes, so there's an echo some way.

I wanted to express that human emotions are universal. Anger is universal. Love is universal. Yearning is universal. So each of these themes was created as a piece, a section, a relief, a computerized component of human emotion. And it wasn't easy because my ideas are artistic, they've not been done before. I was a woman.

I taught Chicano Art. The students used to tell me when they'd registered, "Oh, a big joke, Chicano Art, ha, ha, ha, take it," you know. And then when they got there and they saw what I was doing, they kept diaries, so I know the things they thought. I told them, say whatever you want, write it in English or Spanish; because there are a lot of Mexicanos from [Cd.] Juárez who came to our school. That's good, because there was a lot of revolution on the campus at that time. "OK," I said, "go revolt, go fight, go burn the president, go toilet paper his house, but if you're doing a mural, it's much more revolutionary than anything you see."

It took us three years and then they said, "Get that crazy lady out of here. She has college kids playing in the sand piles." I had to defend us and our idea over and over and over again, until we had a party at Manuel Acosta's house and invited the architects and the kids brought chile and frijoles, and tamales, and tacos—always our combination. David Hilles was the architect. And I said, give him plenty of wine. At that party, Hilles came over and saw what we were doing on the field. He was so thrilled and he told the president, "Do anything she says." So, we won. And in that second triumph I decided at the same time, as part of my masters, to do a project in Juárez . . . building a solar environment—a studio of solar equipment using adobe and the earth. So, in conjunction with the community college, I did both.

I walked the dusty hills. It's very difficult to be in Juárez. There's this dramatic difference. There's such beauty; raw unaffected humanity, that I love. So I began, little by little, to create from adobe and [with the help of] the workman there and my own designs, a marvelous retreat, which was an appendage to the Valle Verde project.

MJ: So you created "Cui" [pronounced Qui] at the same time?

Mago: "Cui" is the name of my studio. It's short for Cuicuilco, which is the name of an ancient round temple in Mexico which was unearthed by archeologists as a religious temple and by some destiny of the gods, I live in the *calle*/street Cuicuilco and I have a garden that's a round circle to give praise to the temple. So I call it "Cui" for short. It's easier.

MJ: You've been able to create your mosaic works on the walls of "Cui"?

Mago: Yes, the "Valle Verde" had a bit of glass mosaic, but the next step was full mosaic and I'm fascinated with the material, with the idea. It's very related to Mexican art, but for the desert Southwest, it's marvelous! It doesn't fade, and if it's done well, it doesn't get knocked by the ice, or the snow, or the wind. It's very enduring and has that faceted brilliance that takes our desert light.

MJ: Isn't mosaic more difficult? Couldn't you paint versus work in mosaic, which is very tedious and time consuming?

Mago: Yes, it's physically hard, but it's also very holy and it involves others in the project, which I love. I had [help from] the students, wonderful students, here in Valle Verde, but in Juárez I got kids that had watched me work since they were little four year olds [to make] "Milagro Tepeyac/Miracle of Tepeyac" ["The Apparition of La Virgen of Guadalupe/the Miracle at Tepeyac"]. They were grown young men and they came to me to do the project. We cut precious glass by hand, at least ten thousand pieces, thirty thousand pieces, and set them with mastic. The design is everything. Without the design there is nothing. And my power of drawing. The pieces are put on bit, by bit, by bit. It's very precious. It slows me down. It makes me patient.

MJ: You in particular have created an abstract body of work which represents icons and symbols. I think too often, in El Paso, people have had a difficult time relating to it, or [sometimes] misunderstanding your work. Why do you think people don't understand it?

Mago: At Valle Verde I had a beautiful description that should have been at the base of that mural, but I was denied the privilege of [attaching the information that would have] explained it a little bit. A little explanation goes a long way. If you take a trip to any part of the world, they have gift shops or an exhibit. They explain it. But I've done a mosaic mural at Douglass School [in El Paso, Texas] called "La Niña Comica/the Cosmic Girl," and I have yet to see a person who doesn't understand it, at least its imagery. When you've worked as many years as I have, I can create a realistic image, but it's nonetheless, a shape that is related to the abstract, but that mural, no one has trouble. "Milagro Tepeyac/Miracle of Tepeyac" [in Cui] is perfect for its environment of dusty hills and people who are involved in the religion of the miracle of the "Virgen de Guadalupe" and this is done in cosmic terms, sophisticated terms. But they understand it. And there is another one, the "Señor Sol/the Sun God" mural. It's been blocked by fences, but if one really looks at it, you can see it and a little explanation sometimes is needed, sometimes it's not. I'm always willing to give an explanation if someone wants it. But the magic is to let the viewer be impacted by the work. Why does everything need to make logical sense? Life is certainly not logical, why are we here struggling like this? It's the mystery!

MJ: Why are there not more women artists working in El Paso/Cd. Juárez—specifically muralists?

Mago: Well, I don't know. But first of all, physically it's very demanding. I . . . dig in the sand, pouring plaster, climbing up and down scaffolds. But I grew up with four brothers, so I was a tomboy. I loved, I still love, all this stuff! I don't know. We women are barely getting released. Remember what I said in the beginning, that struggle to be a Mexicana, Chicana, raise children, do what your husband needs and yet be a free person. It's not easy and *muralismo* is so big. Now, I have a lot of private work, so I have little sculptures and little paintings and little miracles that I do—*milagritos/* little miracles.

MJ: What would you like people to know about you, this particular point in history in El Paso, in this particular point in time? How do you want people to remember Mago Orona Gandara?

Mago: The most important thing is that I'm a woman that has raised a family, that has had children, and done a magnificent job and, yet, included in this raising of the family is the creation of my own art. This is where I really learned to draw. This is where I really became disciplined. I had to concentrate. I had to create. I had to go beyond myself, become bigger and this is what I'm all about.

MJ: How do you see the future of *artistas/artisa en la frontera*, on the U.S.-Mexico border?

Mago: Well, some of them have said, "I'd like to be like you." I've said, "well, go ahead." But I think I've seen more and more women artists and there's nothing wrong with combining artisanship with art and maybe we can begin to do that.

Mago Orona Gandara's monumental mosaic murals include:

"Time and Sand" (1973–1978), 50 feet high by 30 feet across, El Paso Community College, Valle Verde Campus, 919 Hunter and North Loop, El Paso, Texas.

"Señor Sol/the Sun God" (1982–1984, restored in 1992), 1,200-square-foot floor mosaic, Environmental Center, 800 S. Piedras and Paisan, El Paso, Texas.

"La Niña Cosmica/the Cosmic Child" (1992–1993), 12 feet high by 72 feet long, Douglass Elementary School, north exterior cafeteria wall, 101 S. Eucalyptus, El Paso, Texas.

"The Apparition of La Virgen of Guadalupe/the Miracle at Tepeyac" (1993–1995), approximately 10 feet high by 24 feet long, façade of Gandara's studio in Colonia Libertad in Ciudad Juárez, Chihuahua, Mexico.

"Xoichipilli, Guerrero Por el Arte/Xochipilli, Arts Warrior" (1998 to present), approximately 216 feet long, sculpture mural for the City of Ciudad Juárez, Colonia Libertad, Chihuahua, Mexico.

Notes

1. Gloria Anzaldúa, "Border Arte: Nepantla, Elguar de la Frontera," in "La Frontera/The Border, Art about the Mexico/United States Border Experience," exhibit catalog, Centro Cultural de la Raza and the Museum of Contemporary Art, San Diego, California, 107; George Vargas, *Mago Gandara: A Woman Muralist on the Border* (University of Texas at El Paso Center for InterAmerican and Border Studies, *Border Perspectives*, no. 13, August 1995): 2; Shifra M. Goldman, "The Political and Social Contexts of Chicano Art," in *Chicano Art: Resistance and Affirmation, 1965–1985*, catalog of the exhibit at Wright Art Gallery, UCLA, 1990, and in the catalog of the exhibit *Chicana Voices and Visions: A National Exhibit of Women Artists* (Venice, CA: Social and Public Art Resource Center, 1983).

2. Mago Gandara, "Artist Journal" (personal diary).

3. Vargas, "Mago Gandara," 2.

4. According to George Vargas, Gandara's father was a handsome and unschooled "bohemian" from Chihuahua, who later became a photojournalist, landscape photographer, and amateur anthropologist; he also traveled to Mexico with Erle Stanley Gardner, author of Perry Mason novels and someone who shared José Gandara's fascination for pre-Columbian history; Mago's mother studied art in San Francisco. Ibid., 27.

5. Gandara studied at the University of Southern California, University of Antioch, Chicago Art Institute, the University of Texas at El Paso, and the Chouinard Art Institute of Los Angeles (now Otis Parsons School of Design).

6. According to Vargas, in this mural, "titled 'the Search,' the expressionistic painting featured an enormous tormented male figure sitting with his head rolled back, searching the sky for answers to his spiritual questions"; when her husband saw Mago's painting, "he ordered it destroyed, but she instead turned it towards the wall so as not to offend her husband and his friends"; Vargas, *Mago Gandara*, 15.

Suggested Readings

Mago Orona Gandara's interview was conducted in 1997 in El Paso, Texas. The interview is part of the series "Frontera Artists: Mexican and Chicano Artists in El Paso." The series was developed and hosted by the author and coproduced by Gabriel Gaytan, Daniel Matta, Executive Producer, at the Center for Instructional Telecommunications (CIT) at El Paso Community College. The interview was transcribed by the author and returned to the artist for corrections and additions. George Vargas produced a monograph entitled *Mago Gandara: A Woman Muralist on the Border* (University of Texas at El Paso Center for InterAmerican and Border Studies, *Border Perspectives*, no. 13, August 1995) in preparation for a CD on Gandara's work. A separate interview with Gandara also appears in *Colors on Desert Walls: The Murals of El Paso* (El Paso: Texas Western Press, 1997).

Art historian Shifra Goldman has written on the struggles of women artists for visibility and support within Chicano and Mexican communities. In her essay "Feminism and the Chicano Artist," in "The Political and Social Contexts of Chicano Art," in the exhibit catalog *Chicano Art: Resistance and Affirmation, 1965–1985* (Wright Art Gallery, UCLA, 1990), and in the catalog of the exhibit *Chicana Voices and Visions: A National Exhibit of Women Artists* (Venice, CA: Social and Public Art Resources Center, 1983), Goldman chronicles women's efforts to challenge cultural stereotypes. Chicana author Gloria Anzaldúa, in her essay "Border Arte: Nepantla, El Lugar de la Frontera," in the catalog for the exhibit *La Frontera / The Border, Art about Mexico / United States Border Experience* (San Diego: Centro Cultural de la Rasa and the Museum of Contemporary Art, 1993), writes about artists using the border as a point of reference and reinvention.

Sociopolitical tensions have long been the subject of artists along the U.S.-Mexico border. One such group, the San Diego–based Border Arts Workshop/Taller de Arte Fronterizo (BAW/TAF), created in 1984, has had a history of creating multidisciplinary works to address border issues. BAW/TAF has produced two catalogs chronicling its work: *The Border Arts Workshop (BAW/TAF)*

1984–1989 (San Diego, CA: Border Art Workshop/Taller de Arte Fronterizo, 1988), which documents five years of interdisciplinary arts projects, and *Border Art Workshop: 1984–1991* (part of the exhibit "Destination, LA" at the Los Angeles Contemporary Exhibitions, LACE, December 20, 1991).

In 1998, the "Women of the American West: Past and Present," an Internet curriculum, made its debut. Organized by Susan Ressler, the project enables cross-disciplinary access to images, essays, and other resources on women in the arts. The site proposes to reflect the diversity of artworks and perspectives, and will expand over time. There is, in addition, documentary film based on Vera Monk and Gene Norwood's book, *The Desert Is No Lady: Southwestern Landscapes in Women's Writing and Art* (New Haven: Yale University Press, 1987).

About the Contributors

PAULA BARNES received her Ph.D. from the University of Arkansas in 1997. Having taught at the University of Memphis, Auburn University, and the University of Alabama, she is currently an independent scholar living in Memphis, Tennessee. Barnes is completing a book on Betty Bumpers entitled *Betty Bumpers' Arkansas: A View of the World from a Small Southern State.* She is also a coeditor of H-Net's H-Women, an on-line discussion network for women's history (http://www.h-net.msu.edu/~women).

ANGELA BOSWELL is assistant professor of history at Henderson State University in Arkadelphia, Arkansas. She teaches women's history as well as Southern and Early American history courses. Her other publications include articles on women and religion in antebellum Houston and on domestic violence in nineteenth-century Colorado County. She is currently finishing the manuscript of *Separate and Apart: Women's Public Lives in a Rural Southern County, 1837–73,* which is under contract.

MARGARET BREASHEARS is adjunct professor at Richland College, Dallas, Texas, where she teaches courses in American history. She earned her Ph.D. in 1999 from the University of North Texas, where her dissertation was entitled "An Analysis of Status: Women in Texas, 1860–1920 (Marital Status)." She is currently working on a full-length biography of the Osterhout women.

CAROLE STANFORD BUCY is assistant professor of history at Volunteer State Community College in Gallatin, Tennessee, where she teaches American history, African American history, and Tennessee history. She regularly conducts teacher workshops across the state on integrating women into existing curricular materials. She is the author of *Women Helping Women, the YWCA of Nashville 1898–1998* (1998) and *The Civil War Years in Tennessee* (1997). She is presently doing research on the League of Women Voters and public policy.

SUE FAWN CHUNG is associate professor of history at the University of Nevada, Las Vegas. She teaches Asian American history, Chinese history, Japanese history, and Chinese art history. Her publications include "Their Changing World: Chinese Women of the Comstock," in *Women on the Comstock: The Making of a Mining Community,* edited by Ronald James and C. Elizabeth Raymond (1997), and "Fighting for Their American Rights: A History of the Chinese American Citizens Alliance," in *Claiming America: Constructing Chinese American Identities during the Exclusion Era,* edited by K. Scott Wong and Sucheng Chan (1998).

RUTH CROCKER is associate professor of history and women's studies at Auburn University. She teaches undergraduate- and graduate-level courses in U.S. history, specializing in social and women's history. She has published articles on the Poor Law, charity, and the settlement movement and a book entitled *Social Work and Social Order: The Settlement Movement in Two Industrial Cities* (1992). She is completing a biography of philanthropist Margaret Olivia Sage.

HELEN DEESE is professor emerita at Tennessee Technological University in Cookeville. She has published *Jones Very: The Complete Poems* (1993) and various articles on the Transcendentalists. She is currently preparing a three-volume edition of the journals of Caroline Healey Dall, to be published by the Massachusetts Historical Society.

MIGUEL JUAREZ is assistant librarian in the Fine Arts/Humanities Team at the University of Arizona Library in Tucson. He is the subject specialist for art and art history. In addition to book and art reviews, Juarez has published *Colors on Desert Walls: The Murals of El Paso* (1997).

THERESA KAMINSKI is associate professor of history at the University of Wisconsin–Stevens Point, where she teaches courses on American women's history. Her book *Prisoners in Paradise: American Women in the Wartime South Pacific* is forthcoming. She is currently working on a full-length biography of Ethel Herold.

ANDREW KERSTEN is assistant professor of history at the University of Wisconsin–Green Bay. He teaches courses in U.S. economic, social, and political history. His book, *Race, Jobs, and the War: The FEPC in the Midwest, 1941–1946,* is forthcoming.

WILMA KING, Arvah E. Strickland Professor at the University of Missouri–Columbia, teaches courses in African American and American history. She is the author of *Stolen Childhood: Slave Youth in the Nineteenth-Century South* (1995) and editor of *A Northern Woman in the Plantation South* (1993). She is also coauthor with Darlene Clark Hine and Linda Reed of *"We Specialize in the Wholly Impossible": A Reader in Black Women's History* (1995). Her work-in-progress is a monograph on free African American women before emancipation in the United States.

LAURA MCCALL is professor of history and member of the Honors Faculty at Metropolitan State College of Denver. McCall teaches classes in American culture and the history of gender. Her publications include *A Shared Experience: Men, Women and the History of Gender* (1998), coedited with Donald Yacovone. Her current research focuses on gender relations in the American backcountry.

MARLA MILLER is assistant professor of history at the University of Massachusetts–Amherst, where she teaches classes in public history and Early American history. Her 1997 dissertation, completed at the University of North Carolina–Chapel Hill, "'My Daily Bread Depends Upon My Labor': Craftswomen, Community and the Marketplace in Rural New England, 1740–1820," won the Organization of American Historians' Lerner-Scott prize for outstanding work in women's history. She is currently at work on a microhistorical study of women's work and community in eighteenth-century Hadley, Massachusetts.

MICHELE NACY has been adjunct professor of history at Pacific Lutheran University, St. Ambrose University, and Pierce College. She teaches classes in women's history, military history, as well as general U.S. history survey courses. Nacy's book *Members of the Regiment: Officers' Wives on the Frontier, 1865–1890*, is forthcoming.

KATHERINE OSBURN is assistant professor of history at Tennessee Technological University in Cookeville. Her fields of specialization are Native American and environmental history. Her publications include *Southern Ute Women: Autonomy and Assimilation on the Reservation, 1887–1934* (1998), and articles in several anthologies.

PATRICIA L. PARKER is professor of English at Salem State College in Salem, Massachusetts. She teaches undergraduate- and graduate-level courses in American literature. She has published three books, including *Susanna Rowson* (1986), and a number of articles on early American fiction.

JEAN SILVER-ISENSTADT is a graduate of the University of Pennsylvania's doctoral program in the history and sociology of science. Her dissertation, now being revised for publication, is entitled "Pure Pleasure: The Shared Life and Work of Mary Gove Nichols and Thomas Low Nichols in American Health Reform." Silver-Isenstadt is currently pursuing a medical degree at the University of Maryland School of Medicine.

Index